I0199588

# THUNDER OVER NORMANDY

ALSO BY JOSEPH T. MOLYSON JR.

*Six Air Forces Over the Atlantic* (2024)

*Air Battles Before D–Day* (2025)

# THUNDER
# OVER
# NORMANDY

## HOW ALLIED AIRMEN HELPED LIBERATE FRANCE
## FROM D-DAY TO PARIS AND BEYOND

## JOSEPH T. MOLYSON JR.

STACKPOLE
BOOKS
*Essex, Connecticut*

*Dedicated to the World War II aircraft maintenance and logistics troops of the 8th, 9th, 12th, and 15th Air Forces, who kept them flying*

## STACKPOLE BOOKS

An imprint of Globe Pequot, the trade division of
The Globe Pequot Publishing Group, Inc.
64 South Main St.
Essex, CT 06426
www.GlobePequot.com

Copyright © 2026 by Joseph T. Molyson Jr.

*All rights reserved.* No part of this book may be reproduced in any form or by any electronic or mechanical means, including information storage and retrieval systems, without written permission from the publisher, except by a reviewer who may quote passages in a review.

British Library Cataloguing in Publication Information available

Library of Congress Cataloging-in-Publication Data available

ISBN 9780811777780 (cloth) | ISBN 9780811778046 (epub)

## Eleanor Roosevelt's Daily Wartime Prayer

*Dear Lord,*
*Lest I continue*
*My complacent way,*
*Help me to remember that somewhere,*
*Somehow out there*
*A man died for me today.*
*As long as there be war,*
*I then must*
*Ask and answer*
*Am I worth dying for?*

# Contents

# Maps, Illustrations, and Tables

## MAPS

## ILLUSTRATIONS

## TABLES

# Preface

This is my third book on the aviation contribution to Operation OVERLORD, the invasion of northwestern France on June 6, 1944. The first book, *Six Air Forces Over the Atlantic*, covered the airpower contribution to victory in the Battle of the Atlantic campaign. Without this achievement, Britain might today be a province of Nazi Germany. For context, it also covered the early war period and the development of the six air forces described.

The second book, *Air Battles Before D-Day*, focused on preparations for the invasion of France. This included the strategic bombing of Germany to reduce its industrial capability, especially in regard to aircraft production. The advent of effective long-range American escort fighters, in the form of P-51 Mustangs, enabled the reduction of the German fighter pilot force at a rate greater than their capability to replace trained aircrew.

This third book, *Thunder Over Normandy*, focuses on the landing itself and the subsequent push inland, the liberation of Paris, and the crossing of the Seine River. For participants in World War II, the events were life experiences, not phases to be described leading to some preordained conclusion. To ensure that *Thunder Over Normandy* is complete in its own right, the reader may note some duplication from the earlier books.

Joe Molyson
Lilburn, Georgia
March 2025

# Introduction

*If England wins the war, France will be restored in her dignity and her greatness.*
—Winston Churchill to French Prime Minister Paul Reynaud,
just prior to French capitulation to Germany, June 13, 1940[1]

Operation OVERLORD was the largest amphibious operation in history. It began early on June 5, 1944, when the first of 255 minesweepers left their ports to sweep ahead of the naval assault. They were symbolically led by Polish navy-in-exile destroyer *Slazak*, because the 1939 German invasion of Poland led to the British and French declaration of war against Germany. It ended on August 31, 1944, as the Allied armies approached the borders of Belgium, Luxembourg, and Germany.

The entire enterprise of liberating northwestern France was termed OVER-LORD. The initial phases, when naval considerations were dominant, received the separate codename NEPTUNE. This component of OVERLORD concluded on June 30, 1944, when the Lodgement area was considered firmly established.

June 5 was selected for predicted favorable moonlight and tidal conditions. It was the 1,739th day of the war and the 1,444th day of the German occupation of France. The weather in the Channel did not cooperate, and the fleet was called back. Some leading elements reached the midpoint of the journey to the invasion beaches but were not detected.

The weather cleared enough to allow the Allied fleet of some 6,000 to 7,000 vessels to again attempt the journey on June 6, a date forever remembered as "D-Day." Over 3 million men from a dozen or more countries would fight in Normandy for the next eleven weeks until a massive breakout from the so-called Lodgement area was accomplished. In this campaign, some 367,000 men from both sides would be killed or wounded, more than 10 percent of the combatants. A third of these casualties would be Americans.[2]

By June 1944, the Allies enjoyed air superiority over the English Channel and France and air parity over Germany. Allied aircraft made operations near the occupied coast hazardous for German Navy vessels, especially U-boats. Operation POINTBLANK, strategic attacks to cripple German industry and, in particular, the *Jagdwaffe* (German fighter force) had succeeded. The Allies came ashore in strength and liberated Paris by August. Even introduction of new *Luftwaffe* weapons such as the V-1 cruise missiles and jet fighters failed to seriously threaten the invasion.

By the time Allied troops landed, the Germans had been subjected to a year of intensive attacks on their aircraft, installations, and factories. The order was simple: Destroy the *Luftwaffe* wherever it could be found. By D-Day, the Allies had reduced German airpower in all of France to about a thousand combat aircraft, including approximately 175 fighters. The American and British forces smothered the invasion area, lines of communications, and German airfields with thousands of aircraft, including almost 3,500 fighters. Even the vaunted *Jagdwaffe* (the German fighter force) could not beat 20-to-1 odds.

I have chosen to end the detailed narrative on August 31, 1944. The Allies had arrived at the borders of Belgium and Germany, and most of France was free. From this day, the Allied war effort refocused from the liberation of France to the liberation of Belgium, Holland, and Germany.

## Airplanes

Aviation is a people-centered enterprise. An airplane cannot plan, dream, or conceptualize; neither do aircraft exhibit courage, overcome fear, bleed, or die. They respond only to human input, whether that input is positive or negative to the airplane's mission. An aircraft that is flown with respect for its capabilities responds respectfully. An airplane that is sufficiently disrespected will kill you. Human input begins when the aircraft is conceived and designed and continues as the airplane is operated, maintained, scrapped, wrecked, or shot down. An aircraft's ability to respond indicates if it is mission-capable or broken.

## People

To the layman, the various terms for those involved in aviation can be confusing. The term "pilot" is reserved for those who are trained to fly airplanes. "Aircrew" refers to all members of an airplane's crew, both pilots and those with other jobs in the aircraft. The crew members are also sometimes called "aviators." Some common wartime jobs in various aircraft include pilots, bombardiers/bomb aimers, navigators, gunners, radar and radio operators, flight engineers, crew chiefs, and others.

"Operators" include both aircrew and those who directly support them, including air intelligence, control tower and command post people, communicators, flight surgeons, etc. "Maintainers" are the maintenance personnel who work directly or indirectly on the aircraft, including those who load it with munitions and cargo. "Logistics personnel" are the people who provide the supplies and equipment to keep the aircraft and its crew operational. All are essential to keeping airpower efficient and effective.

## SERVICES

The United States, Great Britain, and Nazi Germany all possessed three kinds of combat branches: air, military, and naval. "Air" primarily fights with aircraft, "military" with ground forces, and "naval" with ships. The term "military" can refer to air and ground forces collectively as opposed to naval forces. It is also sometimes used to refer to all three combat branches collectively, depending on the author. "Joint" refers to two or more combat branches fighting together, while "combined" refers to the forces of two or more countries fighting together.

The US combat branches in World War II included the United States Army Air Force (USAAF), the United States Army (US Army), and the United States Navy (USN). For Britain, the branches were the Royal Air Force (RAF), British Army and Royal Navy (RN). For Nazi Germany, the designations were *Luftwaffe* for air forces, *Heer* for the German Army and *Kriegsmarine* for the German Navy. They were collectively termed the *Wehrmacht*. I italicize the German service names throughout the book for clarity.

## NATIONALITY

In referring to some British military functions, the term "Imperial" was formerly used but was intermittently replaced by "Commonwealth" from 1931. In World War II, long-serving politicians and military members still referred to the "British Empire," already in transition by 1939. In this book, units composed of British, Canadian, and other members of the British Commonwealth provided to the Allied forces by the United Kingdom are termed Commonwealth or British. Units composed of American troops and provided by the United States are termed American or US units. Free French and Free Polish units are identified as such.

I use the term "German" in reference to those forces subordinate to Adolf Hitler, whether or not they considered themselves National Socialists (Nazis). The *Waffen SS (Schutzstaffel)*, the armed SS, was effectively the Nazi Party's private army and considered the most elite of ground units. They did, however, fight under the direction of the local *Wehrmacht* commander.

The "group," approximately thirty-six to forty-eight fighter aircraft or eighteen to twenty-four bomber aircraft, was the basic air fighting organization for the American and European air forces. Each American group consisted of three or four flying squadrons plus supporting personnel and units, most often flying from a single base. In the *Luftwaffe*, the equivalent organizational level was termed a "*Gruppe*"; in the Royal Air Force it was termed a "wing."

American groups were normally assigned to "wings" of identical or similar aircraft for ease of command, control, and logistics. Each American wing typically consisted of three or four groups plus supporting personnel and units. In the *Luftwaffe*, the equivalent organizational level was termed a "*Geschwader*"; in the Royal Air Force it was termed a "group." The reverse terminology of groups and wings between the American and British air forces was resolved mainly by long years of close integration and cooperation.

I use the term "Britain" to refer to the United Kingdom (Northern Ireland, Scotland, England, and Wales). What we call "Normandy" in regard to OVERLORD actually is Lower Normandy, the area between the Cotentin Peninsula and the River Seine estuary. Normandy also includes a large coastal area east of the Seine, from the Seine estuary to the Pas-de-Calais, called Upper Normandy. In terms of invasion coast topography, the two Normandys were relatively distinct from one another. (See map 4.1.)

The area of the Baie de la Seine where Allied shipping waited to be unloaded was termed the "anchorage." The "beachhead" in Normandy was the initial area once all five amphibious assault beaches and the two airborne assault areas were connected by land during the first week of operations. After that time, the Allied-occupied area was termed the "Lodgement." Attacks out of the lodgement were termed "breakouts." [*Author's note:* The spelling "lodgement" was used in most Allied documents of the time, although in 1944 vintage American documents, the spelling "lodgment" is sometimes seen. I prefer the former.]

## QUOTES AND STATISTICS

The reader should understand that statistics and other numbers quoted in this book are at best approximations of reality. Much historical information was lost in confusion, combat, and retreat. The author has endeavored to make them as accurate as possible by cross-validation from reliable sources when available.

There are numerous quotes in the texts, all attributed. The author's clarifications, if any, are in parentheses.

# CHAPTER ONE

# Air Plans for OVERLORD

*The real importance of the air war consisted of the fact that it opened a second front long before the invasion of Europe. That front was the skies over Germany . . . from the accounts I have read, no one has yet seen that this was the greatest lost battle on the German side.*

—ALBERT SPEER IN *SPANDAU, THE SECRET DIARIES*[1]

At the ARCADIA Conference in December 1941, General Marshall convinced both Roosevelt and Churchill that a Combined Chiefs of Staff (CCS) should be formed to manage the military part of the war. It was composed of the American Joint Chiefs of Staff (JCS) based in Washington and the British Chiefs of Staff Committee (COS) based in London. The CCS was thus composed of the most senior air, ground, and naval members of the American and British militaries.

Roosevelt and Churchill were senior to this organization, and it was required that they approve both objectives and plans originating at the CCS. At the national level, the JCS and COS were both "joint"; that is, they were composed of officers from all three services. The CCS was "combined," consisting of officers from more than one country.

By agreement with Churchill and consultation with the CCS, Roosevelt appointed General Dwight D. "Ike" Eisenhower as the Supreme Commander, Allied Expeditionary Force (SCAEF) in December 1943. His command center in Britain would be the Supreme Headquarters, Allied Expeditionary Force (SHAEF).

Ike's most senior airman was RAF Air Marshal Sir Arthur Tedder, who functioned as Deputy Supreme Commander as well as director of all OVERLORD air operations. Eisenhower confirmed his role to the CCS on March 17, 1944: "The Supreme Commander has announced his intention of designating his Deputy, Air Chief Marshal Tedder, to supervise all air operations under the control of OVERLORD."[2]

On March 25, 1944, Ike called a meeting of his senior airmen to set priorities and responsibilities for airpower in support of Operation OVERLORD, the invasion and subsequent liberation of France. Each man present or represented was allowed to give his opinions on these priorities.

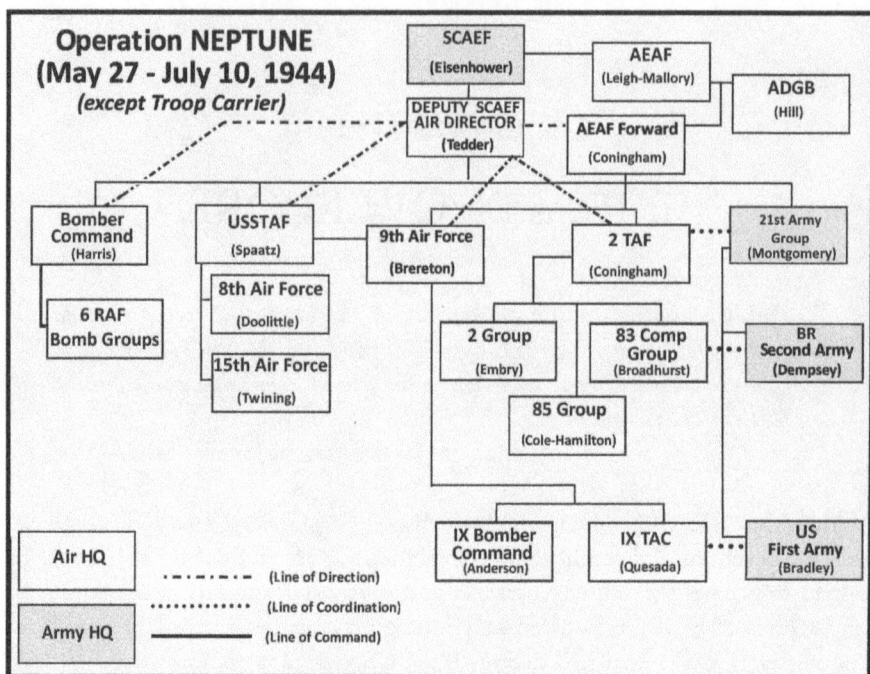

Figure 1.1. Air command relationships for the NEPTUNE phase of OVERLORD, excluding troop carrier matters, which were controlled by the AEAF under Leigh-Mallory. (See appendix 1.)

## TEDDER

It was time to clarify once and for all how Eisenhower would control the airpower for OVERLORD. Eisenhower decided to turn over all management of OVERLORD airpower to Tedder. Tedder was to provide "direction" to five primary air commanders: Harris, Spaatz, Leigh-Mallory, Brereton, and Coningham. Tedder's directions overruled any conflicting normal chain of command orders. Ike explained Tedder's authority at the March 25 meeting as air director in no uncertain terms. This was necessary, for it was a meeting of strong-willed, determined men.

Air Marshal Arthur Harris commanded the RAF Bomber Command. American Lieutenant General Carl Spaatz commanded the United States Strategic Air Forces in Europe (USSTAF). Harris and Spaatz collectively "owned" all Allied four-engine heavy bombers attacking the German homeland.

Tedder and Spaatz were already trusted colleagues and veterans of the Mediterranean fighting brought north by Ike. To this point in the war, Spaatz and

Harris had fought under the general direction of the Combined Chiefs of Staff. Harris bombarded Germany using nighttime area bombardment of cities. Spaatz bombarded Germany using precision daylight attacks on its industry and resources. When the four-engine heavy bombers of USSTAF and Bomber Command were not required, it was made clear that Tedder would release them back to the general direction of the CCS.

Lieutenant General Lewis Brereton commanded the US Ninth Air Force (9th AF). His immediate commander was Spaatz because Spaatz was the most senior American airman in Europe. For OVERLORD, however, 9AF was to provide the IX Bomber Command of medium and light level bombers for the invasion, and the IX Tactical Air Command (IX TAC) was to support the US First Army with fighters and fighter-bombers. IX TAC and First Army coordinated air support directly between the two headquarters.

Air Marshal Sir Arthur Coningham commanded the RAF Second Tactical Air Force (2TAF). In the Mediterranean, Tedder and Coningham had worked out the tactics for air support of ground armies, now intended doctrine for both the British and Americans. Tedder brought Coningham north to apply this doctrine to OVERLORD operations. Coningham looked to Tedder for operational guidance, not Leigh-Mallory.

2TAF supported the invasion with three RAF Groups. 2 Group provided medium and light level bombers for the overall invasion; 83 (Composite) Group supported the British Second Army with fighters and fighter-bombers; and 85 Group provided air defense to 2TAF installations. 83 (Composite) Group and British Second Army coordinated air support directly between the two headquarters.

Air Marshal Trafford Leigh-Mallory was appointed by Churchill to command the Allied Expeditionary Air Force (AEAF). Eisenhower had wanted Tedder to hold this assignment but was overruled by the Prime Minister, who made Tedder Ike's deputy instead. This led Eisenhower to designate Tedder as the overall director of OVERLORD air operations, not Leigh-Mallory.

Leigh-Mallory's defensively-oriented RAF Fighter Command was reorganized in November of 1943 into what would become the AEAF. The original intention was that he would be the senior air commander for the invasion; however, the appointment of Tedder to that role reduced his span of control. Therefore, although Leigh-Mallory "commanded" the AEAF components, Tedder often circumvented Leigh-Mallory by providing "direction" directly to various AEAF headquarters.

The air defense flying units of RAF Fighter Command, primarily operating Spitfires at the time, were responsible for maintaining air superiority over England and the Channel. These became a component of the AEAF called the Air Defense of Great Britain (ADGB). Leigh-Mallory's prowess in air defense was reflected in ADGB's accomplishments defending the OVERLORD ports of embarkation before D-Day and the city of London during the German V-1 flying bombing offensive during the summer of 1944.

By March 1944 and Ike's meeting with his senior airmen, two air campaigns were being conducted from British bases, Operation POINTBLANK and the Transportation Plan. Both campaigns were in preparation for OVERLORD. Over 15,000 Allied aircraft in Britain were executing myriad missions. Opinions on their employment were as varied as their intended use, from strategic bombardment of Germany to air-sea rescue of downed Allied (and sometimes German) aircrew. It was the intention of the CCS and Eisenhower to use as many of these aircraft as necessary for the success of OVERLORD.

Both Air Marshall Harris and General Spaatz were World War I veterans who had shot down enemy planes. They had watched from above as trench warfare in French territory had consumed much of a British, French, and German generation of young men. In World War II, they hoped to avoid a ground invasion of France by defeating Germany solely by strategic bombing day and night. OVERLORD ended those hopes.

CHAPTER TWO

# The Oil Plan

On March 31, 1944, having lost the debate on the use of his heavy bombers, General Spaatz sent another memorandum to General Eisenhower. He suggested that continued bombing of the German Air Force (GAF) facilities and rail targets should continue, but that additional attacks against oil production and petroleum transportation targets be added. Spaatz wrote: "The effect from the oil attack, while offering a less definite impact in time, is certain to be more far-reaching. It will lead directly to sure disaster for Germany. The rail attack can lead to harassment only."[1]

Unlike Spaatz's earlier arguments, this time it changed Eisenhower's mind. Eisenhower agreed that the heavy bombers could be released from direct OVERLORD support whenever the weather was more favorable over Germany or when heavy bomber support was unnecessary. Eisenhower directed Spaatz to continue Operation POINTBLANK against German aviation and related industries, with the understanding that his bombers would hit OVERLORD targets as a priority when directed by Tedder.[2]

The B-17 and B-24 heavy bombers flown by Spaatz's United States Strategic Air Forces were not designed to bomb on or near the front line; instead they were intended for long-distance attacks against enemy industry. USSTAF included the 8th AF, based in Britain, and the 15th AF, based in Italy. Their radii of action allowed all heavy bomber targets in Europe to be attacked even as the long-range escort fighters continued to destroy the German day fighter force. The Allies also had thousands of light and medium bombers as well as fighter-bombers to attack rail and other important German targets in France and Belgium while the heavy bombers were hitting the German heartland.

## THE GERMAN OIL INDUSTRY

Germany had little domestic oil production; therefore, it depended on imported supplies. Ploesti, Rumania,[3] was the Reich's major source of natural petroleum. In the southern Soviet Union, Hitler's plans to capture the Baku oil complex of the Caucasus failed and the Red Army pushed the German Army back toward its own borders. In addition, the Russians threatened the Ploesti petroleum complex.

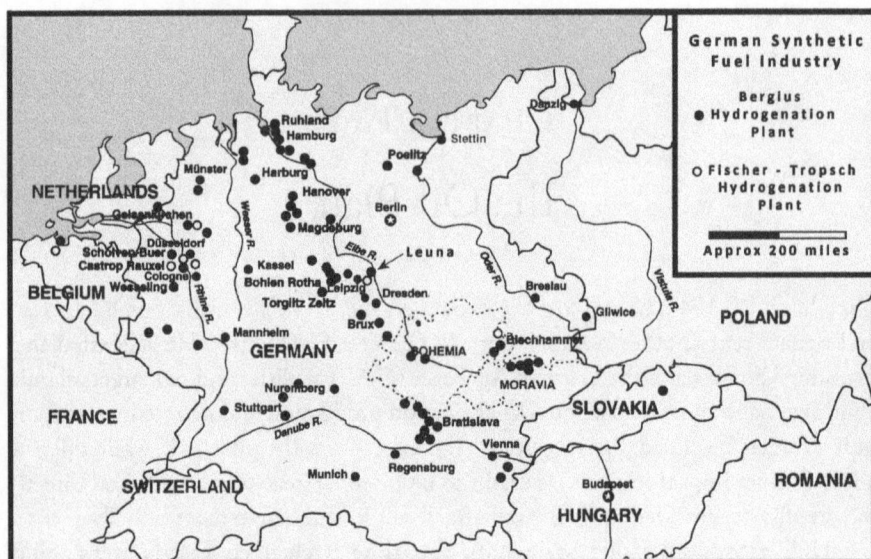

Map 2.1. German Synthetic Oil Industry MOLYSON AFTER DAVIS[4]

World War I demonstrated Germany's vulnerability to oil starvation. Germany depended on synthetic fuel plants able to convert coal to critical products, including aviation fuel and diesel for German Army vehicles. By World War II, using abundant coal reserves located in Germany, synthetic fuel promised a blockade-proof energy source for the German war machine and the domestic economy. Airpower overcame that promise.

The primary synthetic process used by the Germans to turn coal into various liquid fuels was the Bergius hydrogenation process (BHP). In this method, hydrogen gas under high temperature and pressure was used to "cook" the coal, turning it from solid to liquid. A second process, the Fischer-Tropsch (FT) process, used hydrogen gas under high temperature and pressure to "cook" carbon monoxide gas rather than coal into liquid fuel. Both kinds of plants covered many acres, and the layout of the works was distinctive from the air. The BHP and FT plants were exactly the kind of targets the B-17 and B-24 were designed to destroy.

With Eisenhower's limited permission in response to Spaatz's memorandum, in April 1944 Allied attack on German oil production intensified. On April 5 Spaatz targeted a rail center near Ploesti, but his Fifteenth Air Force airmen "accidentally" dropped 588 tons of bombs on the adjacent Astra refinery complex. He sent the Fifteenth back again on April 15 and April 26 to get that pesky rail yard, but somehow both missions hit the refineries again! Although the "critical" rail yards were only lightly touched, the German oil imports from the area declined some 44 percent, from 186,000 tons in March to 104,000 tons in April.[5] The rail yards simply had much less oil to transport.

In addition to the Ploesti attacks, refineries in the Vienna area were hit. Synthetic fuel production facilities at Leuna, Brûx, Böhlen, Zeitz, and Lûtzendorf were all attacked and heavily damaged. The attacks continued into May, forcing more German fighters to abandon front-line duty and return to defend the Reich. The Reich itself had become the front line. Even as Germany increased its fighter production by dispersing aircraft assembly facilities, the fuel to train new pilots and utilize new aircraft dwindled away. The horse remained the prime mover of much of the German Army artillery.[6]

On May 12, 1944, Albert Speer, who directed German war production for Hitler, decided that the technological war was lost. Over 900 American heavy bombers had attacked several synthetic fuel plants in Germany. The blow was repeated on May 28–29, and the refinery complex at Ploesti was hit yet again. The result of these attacks was the loss of half of Germany's fuel production capacity. Added to the hemorrhage of experienced fighter pilots, it was a compound catastrophe for the *Luftwaffe*.[7]

## Table 2.1. Effect of Attacks on Leuna Plant, Only One of Germany's Several Synthetic Oil Plants

| Date | Bomber Force | Effect |
|------|--------------|--------|
| 12 May | 224 B-17s | Production halted for repair |
| 28 May | 63 B-24 | Repairs and production interrupted |
| June 3 | — | Reduced production resumes |
| June 6 | — | D-Day in Normandy |
| June 30 | — | Production restored to 75 percent of April levels |
| July 7 | 51 B-17 | Production halted; repairs continued |
| July 18 | — | Production restored to 51 percent of April levels |
| July 20 | 155 B-17 | Production halted; repairs continued |
| July 25 | — | Production restored to 35 percent of April levels |
| July 28 | 652 B-17 | Production nil, extensive damage |
| July 29 | 569 B-17 | Production nil, additional extensive damage |
| August 24 | 185 B-17 | Production nil, additional extensive damage |

*Source*: Alfred Price, *The Last Year of the Luftwaffe* (Gaithersburg, MD: Wrens Park Publishing, 2001), 95.

## Table 2.2. Approximate German Aviation Gasoline Production and Consumption, April–September 1944

| Month | Tons of Aviation Gasoline Produced | Percent Decline in Production Since April 1944 | Tons of Aviation Gasoline Consumed |
|---|---|---|---|
| April 1944 | 180,000 | — | 165,000 |
| May 1944 | 160,000 | –11.2 | 200,000 |
| June 1944 | 50,000 | –72.3 | 185,000 |
| July 1944 | 35,000 | –80.6 | 135,000 |
| August 1944 | 15,000 | –91.7 | 115,000 |
| September 1944 | 5,000 | –97.2 | 60,000 |

Note that production began to decline in May even as consumption increased. From June, consumption far exceeded new production.

Source: W.A. Jacobs, "Operation OVERLORD." In Case Studies in the Achievement of Air Superiority, edited by Benjamin Franklin Cooling (Washington, DC: Center for Air Force History, US Air Force, 1991), 297.

Destruction of the synthetic fuel industry thus became the primary Allied strategic air objective by July 1944. Flak defenses around oil refineries were increased dramatically but failed to protect the facilities adequately. It was not only flak that was diverted to oil facility defense. Skilled engineers and slave laborers were reassigned from other vital industries. Deadly Me 163 rocket interceptors were deployed near the oil center at Leipzig. Like flak, they were lethal against the American daylight bombers but could not stop their attacks. The American daylight bombers and escort fighters were too brave, too many, and too effective to be turned away.[8] By August, German bomber units were withdrawn from France and many deactivated to conserve fuel for fighters.

# CHAPTER THREE

# Mistletoe in March

While the Allies planned and argued to ensure the success of OVERLORD, the Germans continued to develop weaponry designed to stop it. Operation TORCH, the invasion of North Africa in November 1942, demonstrated that the Allies had the forces and determination to conduct amphibious invasions of Axis territory. German weapons researchers could not ignore the Allied fleets in action off the occupied coasts of Western Europe. Allied naval forces included heavily armored warships as well as thin-skinned escort vessels and troop transports.

The *Luftwaffe* developed and deployed two types of air-to-surface anti-ship guided missiles in 1943. Both were carried into combat on specially modified He 111 medium bombers. The Hs 293 was a radio-controlled glider weapon designed to destroy merchant vessels and light warships. The Fritz X radio-controlled rocket weapon was designed to penetrate the armor of cruisers and battleships. Both were successfully used in the Mediterranean against free Italian, American, and British vessels.

Figure 3.1. Bf 109 and Ju 88 *Mistel* composite aircraft. Note the "elephant trunk."
AIR FORCE HISTORICAL RESEARCH AGENCY KARLSRUHE COLLECTION

A third weapon was also developed, designed to be used against Allied vessels and onshore concrete structures. The *Mistel* (Mistletoe) was a German weapon intended to employ war-weary pilotless Ju 88 medium bombers as anti-ship missiles. Junkers Aircraft Test Engineer Siegfried Holzbaur had first proposed the *Mistel* concept in 1940, but it would be mid-1943 before design and testing went forward.[1] The worn-out bomber had the front crew compartment removed and a huge warhead installed in its place.

## THE THIESSOW INCIDENT

The modified aircraft was appropriately called the *Grossbombe* (large bomb). Extending forward from the aircraft's nose was the *Elefantenrüssel* (elephant trunk). This was a long probe, tipped by instantaneous crush fuses, to ignite the explosive in the main portion of the copper-lined shaped-charge warhead. This allowed a huge jet of molten metal to form properly and melt its way through armor or concrete.

A fighter-type control aircraft would be mated to the top of the *Grossbombe*, and its pilot would fly the composite aircraft to the target area. When the intended victim was spotted, the pilot entered a 15-degree dive about three-quarters of a mile from the desired impact point. Once he was sure the bomb was correctly aligned, he activated the explosive joints holding the two aircraft together and climbed away. The Ju 88 was stable enough to hold the dive until impact.[2]

Figure 3.2. Captured Fw 190 and Ju 88 *Mistel* S2 training aircraft being examined by US Army troops. Note that the *Elefantenrüssel* has not been fitted to the Ju 88, which still has a cockpit so that the training aircraft can be flown back to base.
USAAF PHOTO 72492A, NATIONAL ARCHIVES

The weapon was a flying bomb without radio guidance. Unlike the Fritz X or Hs 293 anti-ship guided missiles, it could not be jammed by Allied countermeasures. The initial *Mistel* design used a Bf 109 as the control aircraft, but this was later replaced by an Fw 190. The Fw 190 was equipped with the same type of engine.

The first test flight of a *Mistel* with a live *Grossbombe* was attempted in February 1944. Holzbaur took off from Peenemünde Test Center bound for the island of Møn, in the Danish archipelago some 65 nautical miles northwest. By this time, the *Luftwaffe* was losing some twenty-seven aircraft for each Allied ship sunk by air attack and had already completed tests on the Hs 293 and Fritz X. At the eastern tip of the island was Møns Klint, a 300-foot chalk cliff that would function as target. The *Mistel* was on course above the German island of Rügen when something went wrong, possibly a break in the electrical control cable between the two aircraft.

Unable to regain control, Holzbaur separated the *Grossbombe* from his fighter and climbed away. The Ju 88 continued downward, impacting near the tiny German village of Thiessow. The good people of Thiessow were lucky that day; the *Grossbombe* could have leveled their tiny town. Instead, the spectacular explosion of 1,800 kilograms (3,960 pounds) was relatively harmless. *Oberleutnant* Diploma Engineer Horst-Dieter Lux reported after rushing to the scene:

> *The village is in uproar. Windows are broken and houses have lost their roofs but the devastation is only of secondary importance. The 800 inhabitants are hurrying to the scene of the accident and the secret is in danger of being revealed. The situation is rescued! A lorry bringing first aid personnel and coffins rushes to the scene of the crash, where there is nothing to see but an enormous crater. People attempt to recover what is believed to be the four-man crew of the bomb-laden aircraft, or so it seems. Secrecy is preserved and nobody realises that an unmanned aircraft with a very large bomb has crashed and a crucial test has failed.*[3]

The empty coffins of the imaginary dead aircrew were later buried with full military honors. The secret was preserved, but the test failure delayed *Mistel* development for crucial weeks. The failed flight test, however, allowed for additional testing of the weapon's complex fuse and warhead systems.

## MISTLETOE IN MARCH

March 14, 1944, was sunny but cool at Toulon, the main French naval base in the Mediterranean just to the east of Marseille. Toulon was not far from the struggling Allied forces at Anzio, still fighting desperately to hold onto their beachhead on the approaches to Rome. Tied up in the harbor were two retired French battleships,

Figure 3.3. Toulon harbor—site of the *Mistel* test, March 14, 1944 AIR FORCE HISTORICAL RESEARCH AGENCY KARLSRUHE COLLECTION

*Condorcet* and *Ocean*. Too old for active service, they had been mostly ignored by the occupying Germans until requisitioned the previous fall for some type of mysterious weapons test. Mistaken for more modern warships, they had been attacked without effect by American bombers on March 7.

Suddenly, there was an ear-splitting explosion aboard *Ocean*, much larger than one might expect from a simple aircraft bomb. The old French battleship, misidentified in many histories as the (nonexistent) *Oran*, had been selected as a test target for a *Grossbombe* warhead. The engineers wanted to ensure the efficacy of the 4-ton armor-piercing explosive. The test showed the warhead design worked.

The warhead had been installed on the old ship in front of the forward turrets. Delivering the attack using a *Mistel* would have prematurely revealed its existence. *Ocean*'s 300mm turret armor had been augmented by another 100mm of German armor.[4] On detonation, a jet of molten copper was propelled by the hollow charge blast and passed through the first turret with the additional armor. It passed through a second turret and then into the ship's armored superstructure, an equivalent penetration of over 6 feet of hardened steel. The impact sprayed secondary shrapnel into the neighboring *Condorcet*.[5]

Figure 3.4. *Mistel* warhead explosion on target French Courbet-class battleship *Ocean*
AIR FORCE HISTORICAL RESEARCH AGENCY KARLSRUHE COLLECTION

Figure 3.5. Damage to number 2 turret of the *Ocean* from *Mistel* warhead AIR FORCE HISTORICAL RESEARCH AGENCY KARLSRUHE COLLECTION

The *Grossbombe* test was repeated against simulated bunkers at a test site in East Prussia. Like the Toulon test, the warhead performed flawlessly. Engineers found they could pierce 18 meters (almost 40 feet) of reinforced concrete. The warhead was ready to go.[6] It was May 25 before Holzbaur repeated his mock attack against Møns Klint; this time the flying bomb made it to the attack area but missed the canvas target on the cliff by 75 yards.

Lack of accuracy would continue to plague the *Mistel* because, unlike the German anti-ship missiles, it had no terminal guidance system.[7] Production and training were slow, and it would be late June before the first *Mistel* attacks were attempted against the Allied fleet off Normandy at Courseulles-sur-Mer. These attacks failed to significantly affect the invasion fleet.

# CHAPTER FOUR

# Arena

From the beginning of its involvement in the war, the US Army pushed for an invasion across the English Channel into northwestern France. General George C. Marshall, Army Chief of Staff and America's senior soldier, had several reasons for desiring such an operation. A buildup of American forces in Britain, Operation BOLERO, provided the closest assault assembly point from the US East Coast ports. This allowed minimum exposure of embarked American units and supplies aboard merchant ships to the U-boat threat in the Atlantic.

Britain could provide numerous airfields to base American airpower. This airpower could engage German industrial strength with daylight strategic bombing of its homeland and deplete German forces in the Low Countries and France with attacks by shorter-ranged light and medium bombers and fighter aircraft. American bombing operations from Britain against German forces in Western Europe began on July 4, 1942, when six American and six RAF Boston light bombers attacked *Luftwaffe* airfields in the Netherlands.[1]

The Americans belonged to the 15th Bombardment Squadron, Eighth AF, and the RAF to No. 226 Squadron. Such an operation also promised to threaten the German position in Western Europe, diverting some of their forces currently (1942) from the Eastern Front and reducing the pressure on America's beleaguered Soviet ally. Finally, landing on the French Channel coast could provide good access to Germany itself by attacking to the east once a beachhead had been secured.

In 1943 COSSAC (Chief of Staff Supreme Allied Commander) was established as the planning headquarters for the intended invasion of France. Lieutenant General Frederick Morgan, Royal Army, was selected as its leader, and around him he gathered a select British and American staff of officers and enlisted men with varied but relevant areas of expertise. COSSAC's job was to identify the most feasible location to return an Allied army to Northwestern Europe.

By July 30, 1943, Morgan's staff produced a "Digest of Operation OVERLORD," which was distributed to a limited number of national leaders and senior officers. The Digest identified either the Pas-de-Calais or Normandy areas of France as the most feasible landing sites. Both had significant advantages and disadvantages, including but not limited to proximity to Germany, state of German defenses, available harbors and beaches, and other factors.

The Digest set the goal for OVERLORD:

> *The object of Operation "Overlord" is to mount and carry out an operation, with forces and equipment established in the United Kingdom, and with target date the 1st May 1944, to secure a lodgement on the Continent from which further offensive operations can be developed. The Lodgement area must contain sufficient port facilities to maintain a force of some twenty-six to thirty divisions and enable that force to be augmented by follow-up shipments from the United States or elsewhere of additional divisions and supporting units at the rate of three to five divisions per month.*

After approval, COSSAC continued to gather additional information to ensure success of the operation. As early as 1942, in conjunction with the American invasion plan called SLEDGEHAMMER, Allied planners determined that attacking northwestern France from Britain would require improvement of important Channel ports such as Falmouth, Plymouth, and Southampton. In addition, some London docks would have to be used. Maritime operations in these ports had been curtailed after Dunkirk due to the *Luftwaffe* threat from French bases. Therefore, the approaches to each port would have to be cleared and kept clear of German mines. The facilities would have to be refurbished and the German air threat reduced. All these things were accomplished, but long after SLEDGEHAMMER had been tabled.[2]

Early in the planning process, the feasibility of landing on the north coast of the Brittany Peninsula was considered. There were acceptable beaches between Avranches and Brest, but tidal conditions were often unfavorable. The Germans had occupied the British-controlled Channel Islands in the Golfe de Saint-Malo in 1940; there were extensive coastal artillery and antiaircraft batteries located there. Brittany was rejected and the planners looked farther east, from Cherbourg to the French-Belgian border.

Among the other factors considered was the necessity to avoid the heaviest concentration of Nazi defenses located in the Pas-de-Calais. Hitler considered the Pas-de-Calais the most suitable coast for invasion and where he ordered the most formidable of beach defenses for the *Atlantik Wall* to be constructed.[3] The Channel coast of the Haute-Normandie, or Upper Normandy, east of the Seine had frequent chalk cliffs that mirror those of Dover and restricted the points at which an invading army could land.[4] The heavily defended ports of Le Havre and Dieppe were located

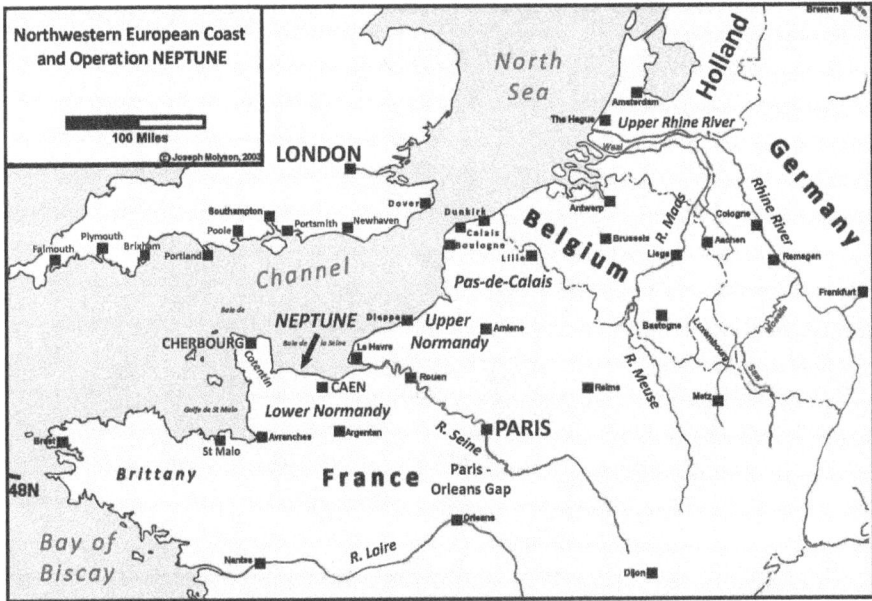

Map 4.1. Northwestern European Coast and Operation NEPTUNE MOLYSON

here, making this area as unsuitable as the Pas-de-Calais for the assault. Certainly no one wanted to revisit Dieppe, where an "experimental" landing in 1942 to seize a French port intact failed, leading to more than 3,000 casualties.

This left the area west of the Seine, termed the Basse-Normandie, or Lower Normandy, as the best alternative. Its coast offered acceptable beaches, although some were backed by cliffs, rapidly rising ground, or swampy areas. In many if not most military histories, the term "Normandy" actually refers to the Lower Normandy region. Therefore, it was Lower Normandy that was selected as the best fit for the concept of operations envisioned in the Digest, specifically landing on the beaches between Cherbourg in the west and Caen in the east.

For the invaders, the Normandy Campaign would be fought in Lower Normandy and the subsequent pursuit of the German Army to the borders of Belgium, Luxembourg, and Germany would be fought mainly across Upper Normandy and the Pas-de-Calais.

## HISTORY AND TERRAIN

Normandy is at the west end of the North German Plain. The Plain has relatively flat terrain with few obstacles. It stretches east across France, Germany, and Poland and into Russia as far as the Urals. This terrain is regularly interrupted, however, by

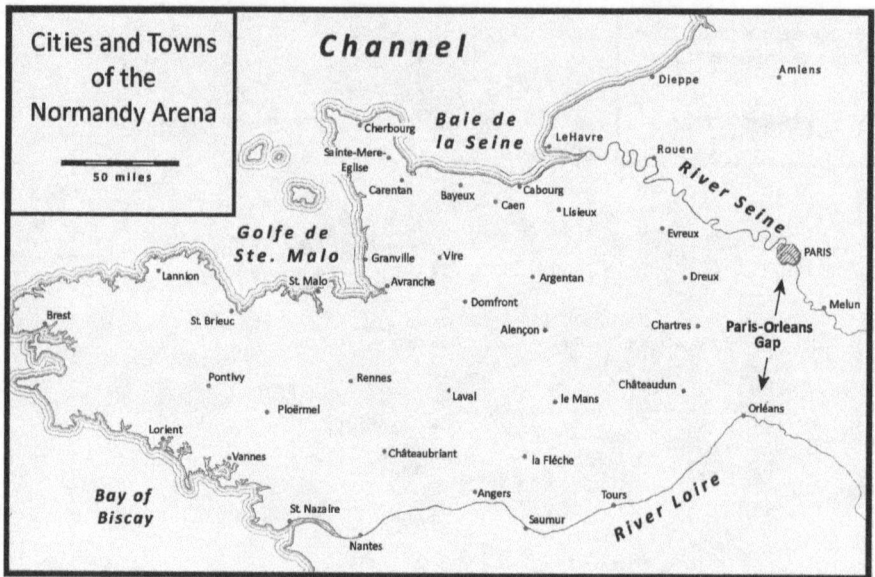

Map 4.2. Cities and Towns of the Lower Normandy Arena MOLYSON AFTER HARRISON[5]

major rivers and their valleys, such as the Seine, Meuse, and Rhine. This ensures that these waterways and their bridges are major planning factors in attack and defense.[6]

Normandy is an ancient land occupied since the Stone Age by a succession of invaders. The Romans came in AD 98 and were replaced by the Franks in the fifth century. The Vikings raided and later settled here in the tenth century, swearing loyalty to the French king in exchange for the land. The name Normandy is a derivation of "Northman," or "Norman." Caen served as capital of western Normandy in those days.[7] In AD 1066, the Duke of Normandy, William the Bastard (later William the Conqueror), embarked his army just east of Caen and overcame England to become King William II.

Lower Normandy was conquered again in 1346 and 1417 by William's Anglo-Norman descendants from England.[8] The Norman city of Rouen, on the River Seine north of Paris, was the site where Jeanne d'Arc was martyred by the English and pro-English French on May 30, 1431.[9] The Germans and British were allied against Napoleon in the first decades of the nineteenth century, but the battles were fought mainly outside France. The Germans invaded in 1870 after France declared war on them, occupying Paris and parts of Normandy. They came again in 1914, but did not reach the River Seine. In 1940 Hitler's army overran Normandy as well as much of the rest of France. In 1942, in reaction to Allied landings in North

Africa, they completed the occupation of France. The people of Normandy were used to invasions, not so much to liberation from outsiders.

## THE BATTLEFIELD

The arena in which Operation OVERLORD and the Normandy Campaign would be fought is bounded by the Seine and Loire Rivers. This includes Lower Normandy as well as adjacent lands in the Brittany Peninsula and territory north of the valley of the Loire. The terrain in northwestern France slopes toward the sea, with the Seine emptying into the English Channel and the Loire into the Bay of Biscay.[10] The lower Seine meanders slowly northward from Paris to the coast at Le Havre, providing a good visual aircraft navigation feature in clear weather. This section of the Seine runs about 86 miles by boat, but direct line of flight from Paris to the sea is less than 50 miles.[11]

The only entry into the Normandy-Brittany area not blocked by a major river was through the Paris-Orleans Gap, where the two major rivers were close but did not merge. The significance of the boundary rivers was that they required sturdy bridges that were not easily replaced if they were badly damaged or destroyed. This was especially critical for railroad transportation.

France is as far north as Wisconsin but is more benign in temperature. Western Europe's climate is moderated by the Gulf Stream, with enough warm days and

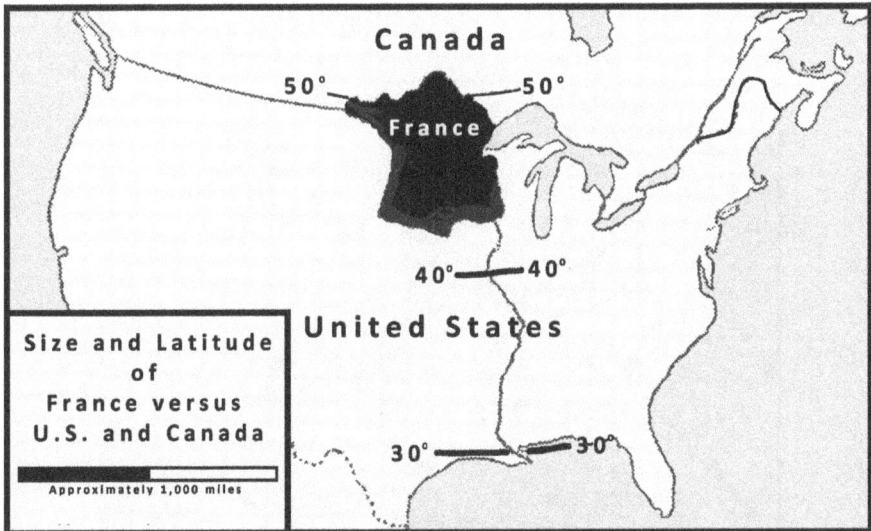

Map 4.3. Size and Latitude of France Compared to the United States and Canada
MOLYSON AFTER DAVIS[12]

sufficient moisture to sustain intensive agriculture over the millennia.[13] In early June there were sixteen daylight hours, which favored Allied air operations but reduced rest time for Allied ground troops.[14] Fortunately, the short nights limited the ability of the Germans to conduct movement without a constant air threat. Offshore, sea conditions for the invasion fleet were best in May and June.

Tidal conditions also favored the Normandy coastline, neither too extreme like Brittany nor too little like the Pas-de-Calais. The beaches are relatively narrow and, except for the Cotentin Peninsula, are bordered by uplands up to 300 feet in elevation.[15] The coastal plain along the shore of the Baie de la Seine is well watered; around Carentan, in the estuary of the River Vire, is marshy and perilous. The River Vire separated Utah Beach to the west from Omaha Beach to its east. Many of the American paratroopers dropped on the Cotentin Peninsula were victims of the German flooding of the lowlands. British airborne troops encountered similar problems when they landed east of Caen.

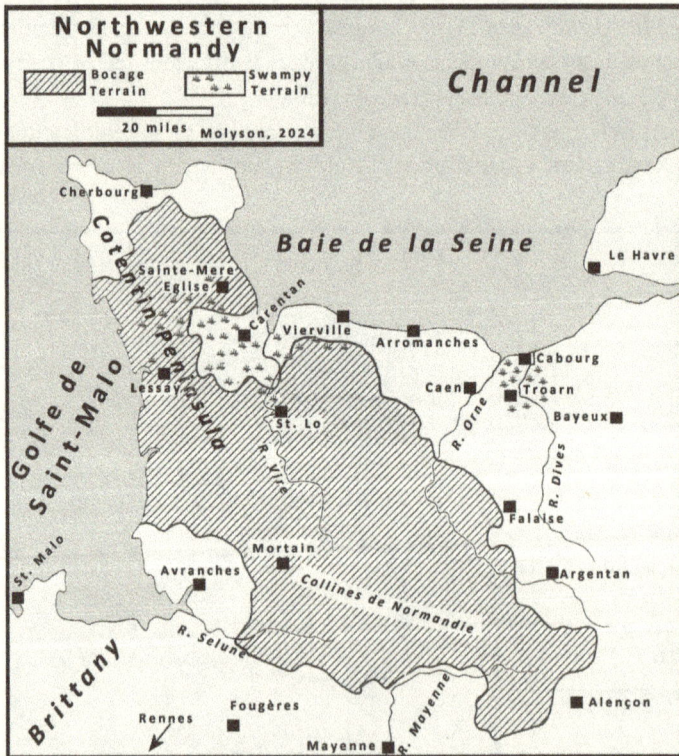

Map 4.4. Northwestern Normandy Terrain MOLYSON AFTER BLUMENSON AND FORD[16]

## BOCAGE

The most significant terrain feature in the Cotentin Peninsula and Lower Normandy is perhaps the *bocage*, or hedgerow country. The hedgerows were boundary walls of stones or banks of earth to mark the fields they encircled. After thousands of years of agriculture, these could grow to 10 feet or more in height, topped by trees, shrubs, and brush. Roads and paths established between the hedgerows were winding and narrow, channelizing road traffic. Tanks and other heavy tracked vehicles climbing over the debris exposed their poorly armored bottoms to infantry anti-tank weapons. The soft soil of the bocage could also have made tracks left by heavy German vehicles easier to spot from the air, but these vehicles moved mainly at night, and traces of their passage were carefully removed.[17]

Field Marshal Sir Alan Brooke, who was familiar with the bocage country, had mixed thoughts about the projected rates of advance from the beachhead. Brooke was Chief of the Imperial General Staff (CIGS) and the most senior soldier in the British Army. He also chaired the British Chiefs of Staff (COS) Committee. Brooke thought Normandy's hedgerow country would be of great defensive value for the German infantry withdrawing from the coast.

Brooke considered OVERLORD "a good plan but too optimistic as to rate of advance to be expected." The hedgerows would also limit the effects of air support

Figure 4.1. Bocage on the Cotentin Peninsula USAAF VIA WIKIPEDIA COMMONS

because of the cover they provided. He had a high opinion of German skills in establishing defensive positions and infiltration, and he thought those skills would be expertly applied in this close country. Morgan disagreed, and thought the invaders might be the ones who would benefit most from infiltration tactics. In the event, Brooke's opinion of the effects of the hedgerow country proved more accurate.[18]

Although the troops training for NEPTUNE were extensively exercised before the invasion, they practiced in flat wasteland terrain in Britain and were not ready for close combat in France's bocage.[19] The amphibious practice beach at Slapton Sands had no cliff top to assail and was more similar to Sword Beach at the east end of the beachhead than Omaha Beach on the western side.[20] There were no "easy" beaches, but Omaha was the most challenging of the five Allied amphibious-assault beaches. Just beyond the narrow beach were steep cliffs, and beyond those was the bocage country.

Hitler declared the defenses along the Channel coast a portion of his *Atlantik Wall*. Allied planners studied these defenses in great detail, but some failed to appreciate the ideal defensive terrain the bocage offered the German Army as the Allies pushed inland. The planners thought the bocage was hard to defend and that Allied troops could quickly infiltrate inland. Instead, it was the Germans who mastered infiltration and delayed the Allied advance by weeks.[21] Much of the bocage country between Saint-Lô and Argentan, called Collines de Normandy (the Hills of Normandy) by the French, was hilly. Like the bocage, the hilly terrain greatly favored the defenders.

One of the primary objectives of the invasion was to push south of Caen on the first and second days, seizing the relatively flat, open terrain south to Falaise.[22]

Figure 4.2. Omaha Beach at Vierville, showing narrow beaches and bocage US ARMY MILITARY HISTORY INSTITUTE PHOTO, AFTER ZALOGA[23]

Here there was little bocage; the ground was perfect for building air landing grounds (ALGs) to bring forward fighter and fighter-bomber aircraft from Britain.[24] Morgan and others were particularly vexed by the short range of the Spitfire, and ALGs would help extend their reach.

It was obvious that either longer-ranged fighters were needed or airfields would have to be captured early in the OVERLORD operation.[25] The Germans countered the attempt to seize Caen and the ground to its south by deploying armor and anti-tank guns, particularly the much-feared 88mm flak/anti-tank gun. For weeks after D-Day, hundreds of British and Canadian armored vehicles were slaughtered on this open ground.

Located between the Channel coast and Paris, Normandy was well-served by railroads. Railroads, not motor vehicles, were the most utilized means of intercity movement, major and minor roads providing a secondary transportation network. The German Army preferred to move by rail rather than road when possible; their armored vehicles were prone to mechanical issues on long road marches.

Military supplies were also bulky, and the German Army was always short of trucks. Moving by rail from Germany or other parts of Europe means crossing either the Seine or the Loire River over established bridges. This, in combination with necessary marshaling and maintenance yards, made railroads, and thus the German Army, vulnerable to air attack.

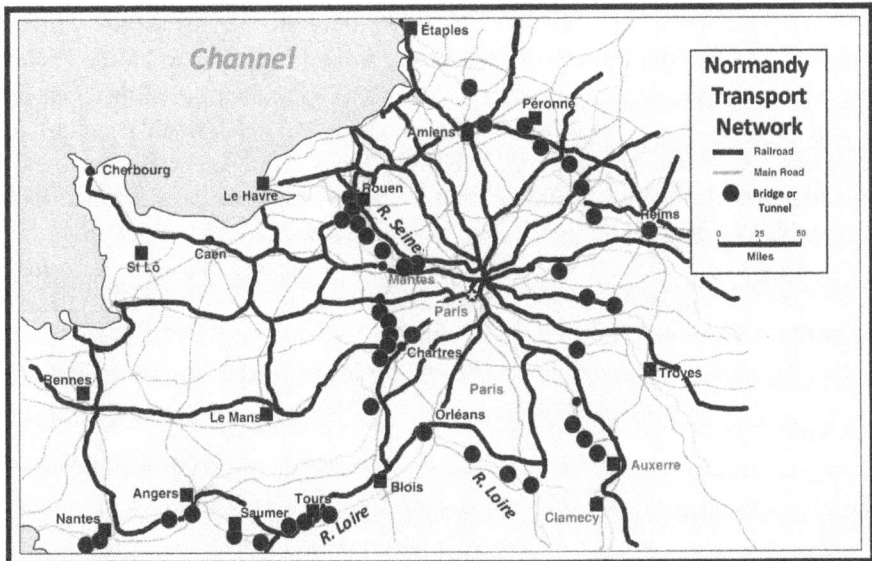

Map 4.5. Normandy Transport Network MOLYSON AFTER DAVIS[26]

## CHAPTER FIVE

# Best Laid Plans

COSSAC's original OVERLORD assault plan called for landing three amphibious infantry divisions between Vierville and Lion-sur-Mer on the Normandy coast in the Baie de la Seine (see map 5.1). COSSAC's plan was based on available resources, not necessarily all the resources General Morgan thought were required to land in France and establish a secure lodgement there. The number of airborne brigades[1] and amphibious assault divisions was insufficient to effectively pierce the *Atlantik Wall*. There were additional units available; that was not the problem.

The limiting factor was the means of troop and supply delivery. Also, there was no major port in the intended landing area to bring in supplies and reinforcements. General Morgan made this clear to anyone who would listen. The only adequate factor was the location of the landing, within Allied fighter range of Britain. At least these aircraft could fend off the *Luftwaffe* and delay the inevitable German Army counterattack.

The ground plan was relatively simple. As three amphibious assault infantry divisions engaged the *Atlantik Wall* defenses, airborne brigades would be landed inland to secure the flanks of the attack. The total airborne force on the flanks would be about one division. Two-thirds of a British airborne division would be landed in the Caen area to seize the vital road hub there. The British infantry division landed on the eastern flank of the beachhead near Lion-sur-Mer would press south as soon as possible to relieve the airborne forces holding Caen.

An American airborne brigade would also be landed to block the main road from the Cotentin Peninsula near Isigny. It would be relieved by the US infantry division landing near Vierville. Even with the expected small unit operations of British commandos and the French Resistance in the area, it was a smaller force than landed in the Sicily invasion of July 1943 against a weaker enemy farther from Germany.

## IMPROVING THE PLAN

It was important to get the four-division airborne and amphibious force quickly into the fight and resupplied with beans and bullets once they were in France. The

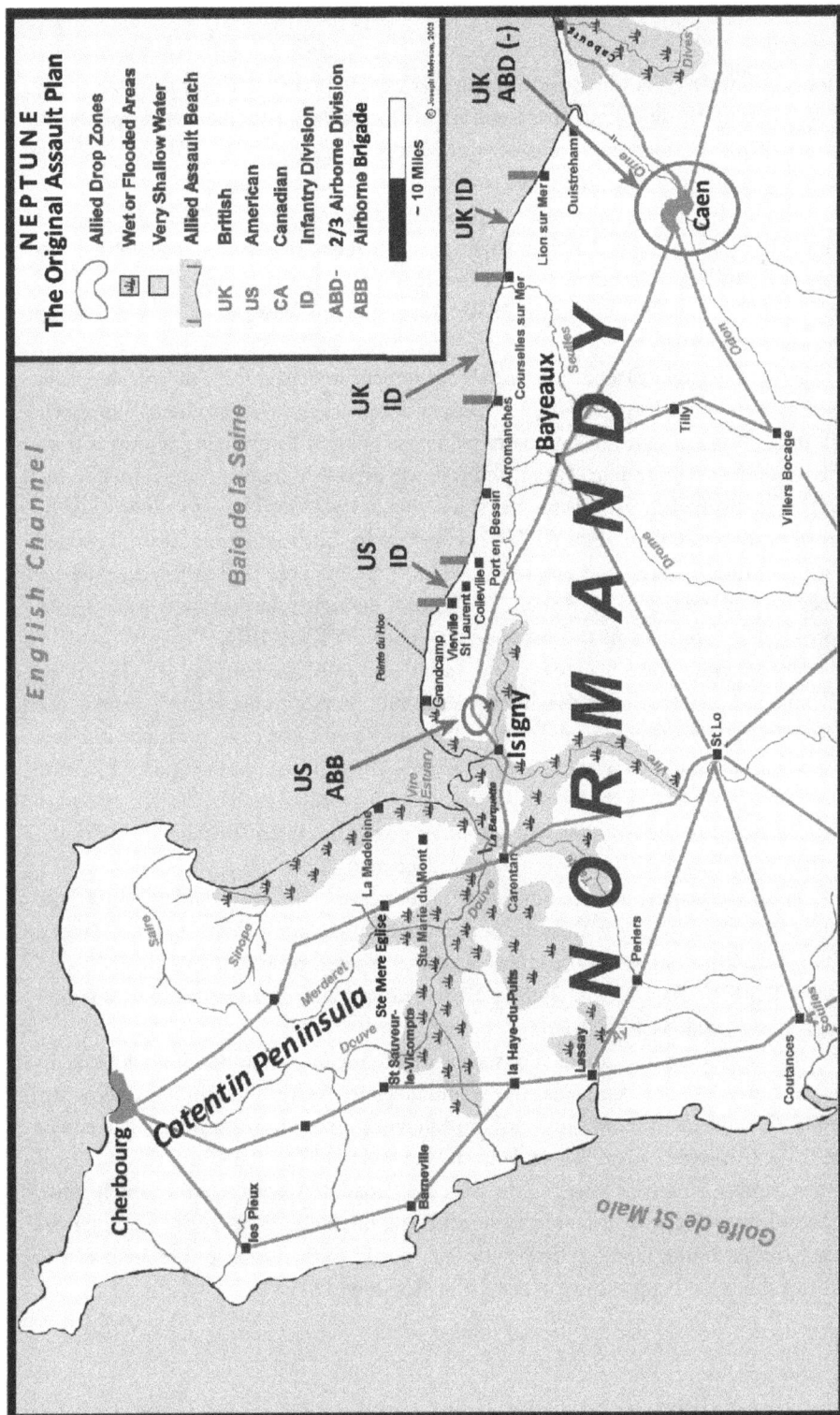

Map 5.1. COSSAC's Original OVERLORD Assault Plan MOLYSON AFTER HARRISON AND BRADLEY[2]

limited number of landing craft and troop carrier planes determined how many soldiers could be delivered. There was no lift available for the necessary follow-on two-division reinforcement and continued logistics support, except for surviving vessels and aircraft on round-trips to Britain from the beachhead.

The lowly landing craft and troop carrier airplanes became the throttles on the whole enterprise. General Omar Bradley, commander of American ground forces for OVERLORD, considered the lack of landing craft the principal reason Hitler was unable to invade England in 1940.[3] Now Bradley, Morgan, and the rest faced the same problem.

After Generals Eisenhower and Montgomery reviewed the original plan, they were able to help Morgan find the resources necessary for a larger attack. The short-fall in landing craft and troop carrier planes was closed by diverting resources from the Mediterranean, Indian Ocean, and training establishments in the United States. D-Day in Normandy was postponed from May 1, 1944, until June to allow for additional production. Operation ANVIL, a landing in southern France, was postponed until two months after the proposed D-Day. Landing craft and airlift reserved for ANVIL was redirected to Britain. In the end, enough transportation was begged, borrowed, or stolen to allow for the expansion of OVERLORD.

The separate assembly areas of the various amphibious divisions and their ports of embarkation were due to the differences in supply systems between the Americans and British. The systems were incompatible and could not cross with one another. American units and supplies arrived in Britain through the western port of Bristol. The Americans would thus land on the western assault beaches. British resources were clustered in the London area and other points in eastern Britain. Therefore the British would land on the eastern beaches (see map 5.3).

With the acquisition of additional assault vessels and troop carrier aircraft, the final plan called for eight airborne and amphibious infantry divisions to be landed on D-Day. This was twice the strength of the original proposal. This first phase of Operation OVERLORD, including overwhelming air and naval assaults, was formally designated NEPTUNE.

The amphibious assault area was expanded to include Utah Beach on the eastern shore of the Cotentin Peninsula. This would facilitate the early capture of Cherbourg. It was thought this port was essential to follow-on operations from the Lodgement area. The American 82nd would land on the west side of the Cotentin to cut off German reinforcements traveling the west coast road. In late May, Allied intelligence reported large German infantry reinforcements on the west coast of the Cotentin. The 82nd Airborne Division drop zone was moved to the center of the peninsula to protect the inland approaches of the 101st Airborne Division.

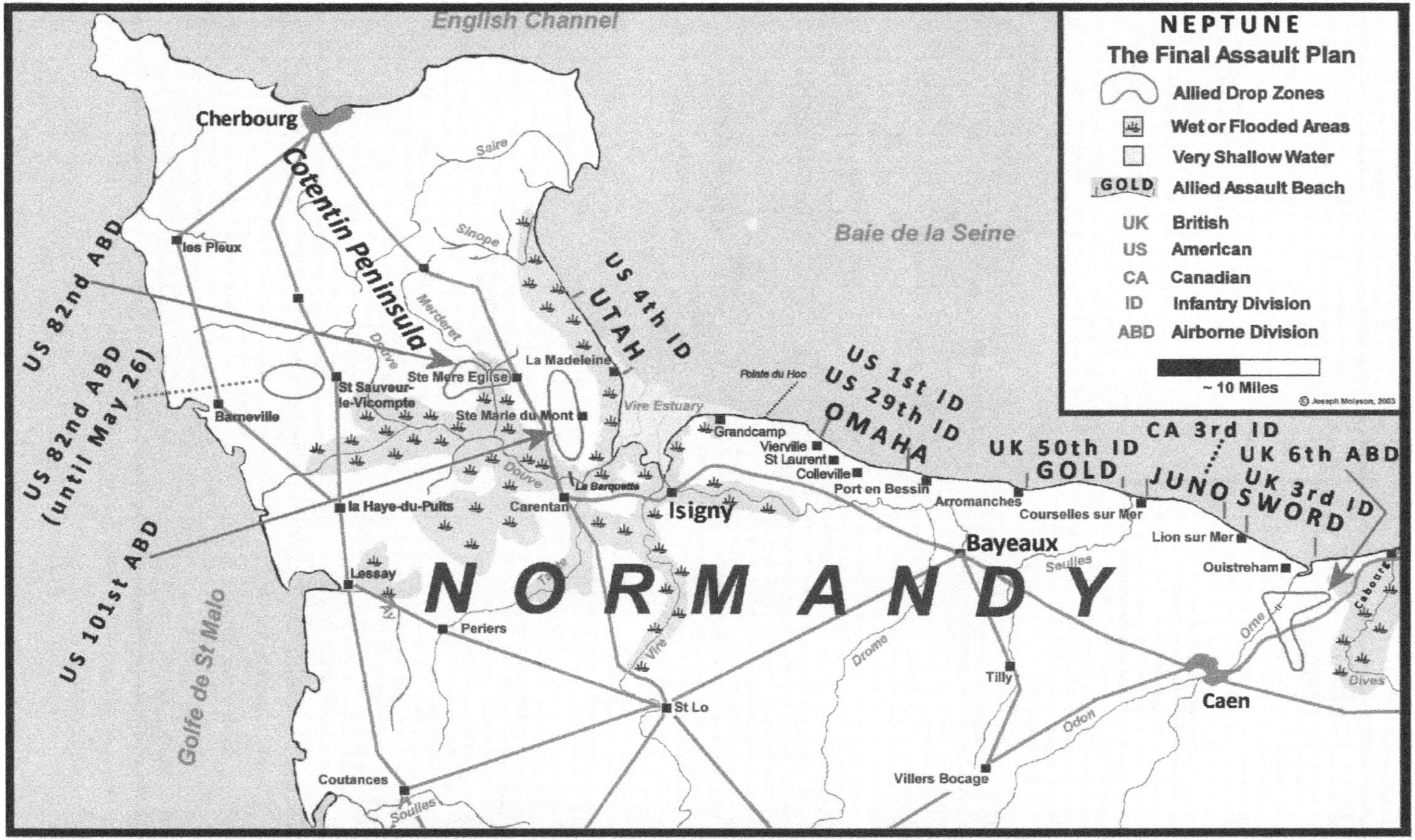

Map 5.2. NEPTUNE—The Final Assault Plan. Note that after the Germans reinforced the Cotentin Peninsula in April and May, the 82nd Airborne Division drop zone was moved closer to Utah Beach on May 31. MOLYSON AFTER HARRISON AND BRADLEY[4]

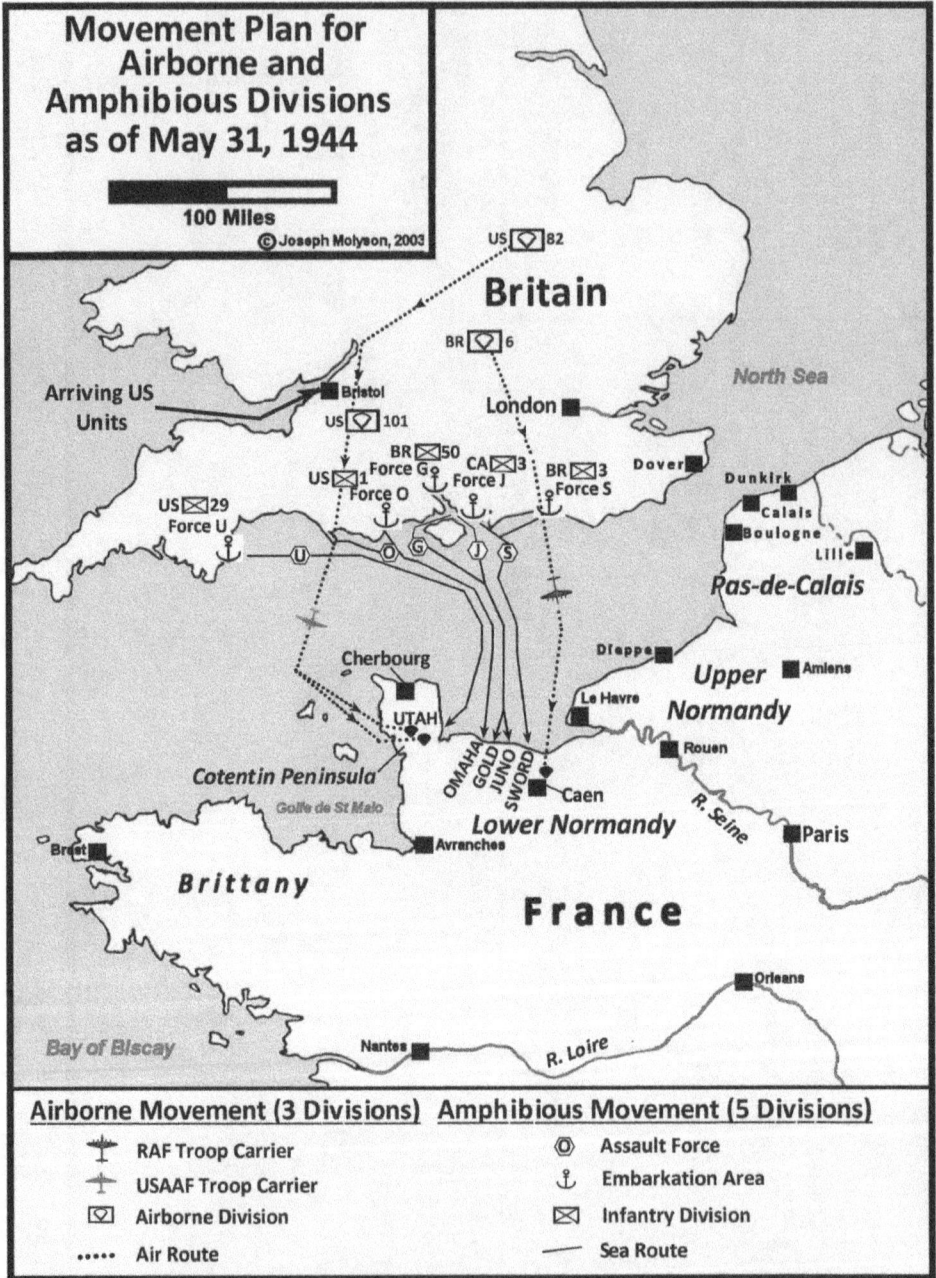

**Movement Plan for Airborne and Amphibious Divisions as of May 31, 1944**

100 Miles

© Joseph Molyson, 2003

US 82

Britain

BR 6

Arriving US Units

Bristol

London

US 101

BR 50 Force G

CA 3 Force J

BR 3 Force S

Dover

US 1 Force O

Dunkirk

Calais

Boulogne

Lille

US 29 Force U

Pas-de-Calais

U O G J S

Cherbourg

Dieppe

Upper Normandy

Amiens

Le Havre

UTAH

Rouen

Cotentin Peninsula

Golfe de St Malo

OMAHA GOLD JUNO SWORD

Caen

R. Seine

Lower Normandy

Brest

Avranches

Paris

Brittany

France

Orleans

Bay of Biscay

Nantes

R. Loire

**Airborne Movement (3 Divisions)**    **Amphibious Movement (5 Divisions)**

RAF Troop Carrier      Assault Force

USAAF Troop Carrier      Embarkation Area

Airborne Division      Infantry Division

····· Air Route      —— Sea Route

Map 5.3. Planned Movement of Assault and Airborne Divisions for NEPTUNE

MOLYSON AFTER MORISON[5]

The 101st Airborne Division would land in the eastern Cotentin to seize the exits from Utah Beach. The US 4th Infantry Division would land at Utah, push through the captured exits and drive inland to overrun the Cotentin, join with the American airborne divisions, and eventually seize Cherbourg.

Looking eastward from Utah, the other American beach was Omaha. A composite landing force from the US 1st and 29th Infantry Divisions would land there, facing the most powerful German fixed defenses to be overcome in NEPTUNE. To the east of Omaha was Gold Beach, where the British 50th Infantry Division would land. Farther east, the Canadian 3rd Infantry Division would land at Juno Beach and the British 3rd Infantry Division would land at Sword.

It was hoped that Commonwealth forces from Juno and Sword Beaches would quickly drive south and seize Bayeux and Caen. The British 6th Airborne Division would secure the eastern flank, landing northeast of (but not in) Caen. Once the Allied forces had overcome the *Atlantik Wall* defenses and moved inland, the area would transition from beachhead to Lodgement area. The plan called for Allied forces to reach the Loire River by D+35, July 11, 1944.

## INLAND

In February 1944, Montgomery's 21st Army Group headquarters issued a forecast of its operations after the landing had been accomplished. Once the immediate bridgehead was secure, it was planned to develop air landing grounds (ALGs) south of Caen and bring forward fighters and fighter-bombers to operate from them. Even before the ALGs were built, all ground forces would be amply supported by the US 9th AF and the RAF 2TAF flying from British bases.

Follow-on ground reinforcement units would swell the size of the assault force, which would continually drive the German Army away from the beaches and out of Lower Normandy. Artillery reinforcements and air support aircraft were particularly critical, since the battlelines would be pushed well beyond the range of naval gunfire support.

The initial ground forces for the landing were all part of the 21st Army Group and consisted of the American divisions assigned to the US First Army and the Canadian and British divisions assigned to the British Second Army. It was hoped that by approximately D+25 (July 1), the American 12th Army Group, consisting of the US First and Third Armies, would be formed to move west into Brittany and south toward the Loire.

The 21st Army Group would be expanded to include the British Second Army as well as the Canadian First Army. The British units would attack east out of the Lodgement area, pushing across the Seine north of Paris with their left flank on

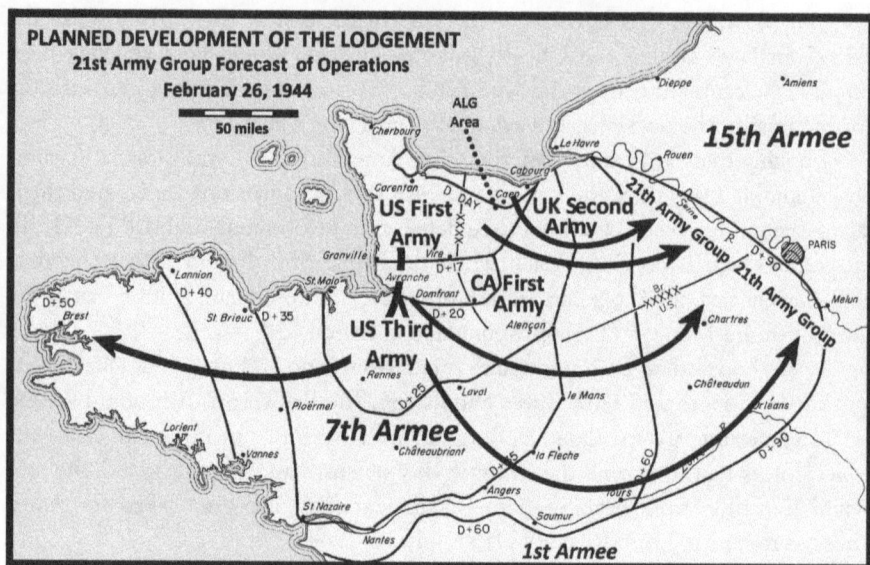

PLANNED DEVELOPMENT OF THE LODGEMENT
21st Army Group Forecast of Operations
February 26, 1944

Map 5.4. Planned Development of the Lodgement Area HARRISON MAP III[6]

the Channel coast. They would continue the attack toward Belgium. After seizing Brittany, the Americans would also turn east with their right flank on the Loire. They would cross the Seine south of Paris and, like the British, attack toward the German border.[7] There would be no direct liberation of Paris in the hopes that damage to the city could be avoided.

At D+50 (July 26), the entire Brittany Peninsula would be overrun and the fortress ports of Brest, Lorient, and St. Nazaire cut off and under siege. This would also threaten the U-boats based in these harbors and the remaining German coastal forces of the *Küstenstreitkräfte* (German Navy coastal forces) in the west of France.

By D+60 (August 5), it was planned that the Loire River valley would be occupied, cutting off the German *1st Armée* to the south. By D+90 (September 4), Paris and Rouen would still be under German occupation but might be liberated or bypassed by Allied attacks in September. The remnants of the *7th Armée* would have been pushed out of Lower Normandy or destroyed, but the formidable *15th Armée* would still be defending Upper Normandy and the Pas-de-Calais to the east of the River Seine. At least, that was the plan.

# CHAPTER SIX

# Festung Europa

Operation OVERLORD, the invasion of northwestern France, began on June 6, 1944, 1,445 days after the Third French Republic surrendered to Nazi Germany. France is an isthmus, the only European country to have coastlines on the North Sea, the English Channel, and the Mediterranean. Over 50 percent of France's borders are coastline, and when the Allies became resurgent in 1942, the Germans were faced with a coastal defense problem.

There were three area commands defending France. *OB West (Oberbefehlshaber West* / Commander-in-Chief West) directly controlled German ground troops,

Map 6.1. Europe 1939 Borders MOLYSON AFTER USMA-HD

including *Waffen SS* and *Luftwaffe* formations operating with the regular army.[1] *Luftflotte 3* (Air Fleet 3) was responsible for the air defense of France, Holland, and Belgium, including both offensive and defensive *Luftwaffe* aircraft as well as the radars and antiaircraft guns of the subordinate *III.Flakkorps*.

*MGK West (Marinegruppenkommando West / Naval Group West)* controlled *Kriegsmarine* forces covering the southern North Sea, the Channel, and the Bay of Biscay. This included both vessels and their crews, port garrisons, some coastal gun emplacements, and a few coastal aviation aircraft. An independent submarine commander, *BdU (Befehlshaber der U-Boote/*U-Boat Commander-in-Chief), controlled the U-boats based in the Bay of Biscay.

*OB West* did not control *Luftflotte 3*, *MGK West*, or *BdU*. Requests for air or naval assistance were made through liaison officers, not by orders. Hitler's military headquarters, *Oberkommando Wehrmacht*, often interfered with the coordination system, making it less efficient. Many of the critical German armored divisions were kept under Hitler's direct control, which on D-Day made them slower to respond to the Allied landing.

The Germans had about sixty divisions in France, Belgium, and Holland to oppose an Allied invasion force of about thirty-nine divisions. This represented only about 20 percent of the German ground strength distributed throughout Europe.[2] Some German divisions were "static" with very limited mobility, manning coastal defenses ranging from concrete bunkers to dirt trenches. Even the regular infantry divisions were short of transportation.

Only the panzer (tank) and panzer grenadier (armored infantry) divisions were truly mobile, but the long daylight hours and Allied aircraft limited their movement. Some of the mobile divisions were below authorized strength, rebuilding from combat operations in North Africa, Italy, and the Eastern Front.

The OVERLORD Allied units were fresher and generously supplied. They enjoyed air supremacy overhead, naval bombardment support on the coast, and better artillery inland. The German units had more combat veterans with better tanks and infantry small arms. Over large areas of Normandy, the Germans also enjoyed excellent cover in the bocage.[3]

## HEER

The *Heer* (German Army) in France was the primary defensive force in France, supported to some degree by *Luftflotte 3* and *MGK West*. The primary focus of pre-invasion Allied air operations was to block the railroads supporting German ground troops. By June of 1944, *OB West* was *Generalfeldmarschall* Gerd von Rundstedt. His territory was divided into three combat commands. In the north the Netherlands was occupied by the *LVXXXVIII Korps* under General Hans-Wolfgang Reinhard, who also commanded the occupation and coastal defense troops in Holland. The swampy terrain made Holland a natural fortress of its own.

Belgium and northwestern France from the Belgium border to Brittany was the province of *Heeresgruppe B* (Army Group B), commanded by the legendary *Generalfeldmarschall* Erwin Rommel. In the 1940 invasion of France, Rommel had led a panzer division from the German border to the Channel coast, helping split the Allied armies in two. He later took skillful command of the *Afrika Korps*, earning the nickname "The Desert Fox" by both friend and foe. Hitler evacuated him back to Germany in March 1943 before his North African forces were crushed between Montgomery in the east and Eisenhower from the west.

After convalescent leave, in July Rommel was assigned to command an army group in Greece. The following day, however, Mussolini fell from power in Italy as Germany's Axis partner faltered. Rommel was immediately transferred to command another army group in the north of Italy. He later helped disarm Italian troops after Italy surrendered to the Allies.

In November Rommel was reassigned as General Inspector of the Western Defenses. He inspected the *Atlantik Wall* and the troops behind it and was dismayed at the lack of fortifications along the coastline. By January he asked for and was made commander of *Heeresgruppe* (Army Group) B. It was Rommel's troops who would meet his old enemies Eisenhower and Montgomery in Lower Normandy in June 1944.

Within the Army Group B area of responsibility were two field armies: the *15th Armée* in Upper Normandy and the Pas-de-Calais and the *7th Armée* in Lower Normandy. In addition, the powerful *Panzergruppe West* (PzG West) was located in the Army Group B area as the *OB West* reserve but could not be employed by Rundstedt or Rommel without the express permission of Hitler. This fact alone may have saved OVERLORD in the first hours of the invasion.

In the south of France was Army Group G, consisting again of two field armies. The *1st Armée* guarded the Bay of Biscay coastline south from the River Loire to the Spanish border; the *19th Armée* guarded the French Mediterranean coast and secured the Italian border. Army Group G was considerably weaker in tanks and troops than Army Group B, consistent with the perceived threat of invasion from Britain across the Channel.

After five years of war, German troops were still dependable defenders of the Reich. Bad decisions by the leaders, however, would reduce their capability to fatal levels.

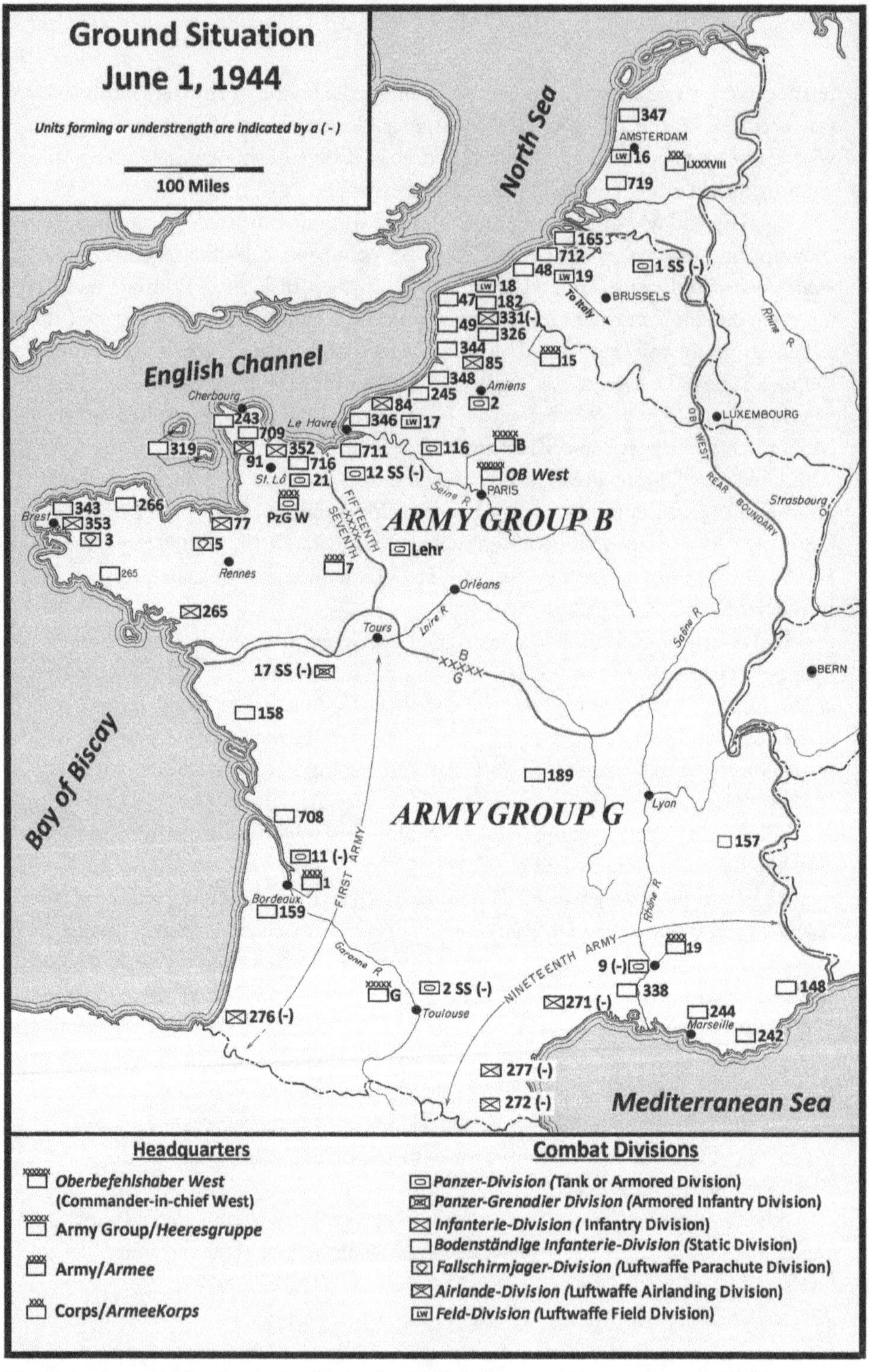

Map 6.2. Ground Situation in the Netherlands, Belgium, and France, June 1, 1944
MOLYSON AFTER HARRISON[4]

CHAPTER SEVEN

# Improving the Odds

*Of all the terrors we faced, however, none seemed more menacing than the threat*
*of German air. For our army, huddled on a narrow beachhead, could be severely*
*mauled should the Luftwaffe break through in strength. And a naval force con-*
*centrated offshore would offer Goering a tempting target for all-out air attack.*[1]
—LIEUTENANT GENERAL OMAR BRADLEY,
COMMENTS ON THE 1943 INVASION OF SICILY

Hitler's forces in France had five potential advantages in late 1943. These and other considerations had established COSSAC's prior conditions for OVERLORD. First and foremost, the World War II German Army had never been beaten in France. Second, the *Luftwaffe* was still a potent threat in the skies over France. Third, once ashore, the Allied army as well as the fleet would be for a while weakened by the rigors of the landing and vulnerable to air attack. Fourth, the Germans occupied all the high-capacity ports in the Pas-de-Calais, Normandy, and Brittany and were prepared to defend and, as necessary, incapacitate them. Fifth, the defenders would be able to move in reinforcements from other theaters via the excellent rail system serving Western Europe.[2]

## DECEPTIONS AND DIVERSIONS

To counter the strong German Army in France, Allied deceptions convinced Hitler that the anticipated Allied invasion would come in the Pas-de-Calais, not Normandy. This was reinforced by the distribution of air attacks. For every pre-invasion air attack into Normandy, two attacks were accomplished in the Pas-de-Calais. As a result, strong German forces in the Pas-de-Calais were frozen in place for the first critical weeks of the invasion.

The Allies also encouraged the Soviets to increase the pressure on the Eastern Front. By November 1943, Allied intelligence estimated that two-thirds of the German Army field divisions were fighting on the Eastern Front, and more were headed there. German troops were transferred from Italy, the Balkans, Norway, Germany, and (most importantly to the OVERLORD planners) France.[3]

During the first half of 1944, relentless Soviet attacks bled the German Army. Northwestern Europe was a quiet area and battered combat formations from the east were rotated into France. Rebuilt units were returned to the fighting in the east. Soviet successes also consumed huge quantities of German war materials, depleting the German units in France.

On May 31, just before D-Day, the fortress of Sevastopol fell to Soviet forces as the Germans evacuated Crimea. The southern part of the Eastern Front was beginning to collapse, the German Army having occupied more territory than they could defend from the advancing Red Army. Rome was in danger of imminent liberation by the beginning of June. This alone distracted some German attention from the Channel beaches.[4]

## Decimation of the *Luftwaffe*

To help fend off the threat of German air attacks against the beachhead during the first seventy-two hours of the landing, the Allies attained air superiority in France by crippling the *Luftwaffe* in northwestern Europe. This effort, codenamed POINTBLANK, was already in progress by escorted bombing daylight attacks into Germany. Intensified attacks were also made against German aviation facilities in France and Belgium, both command and control as well as airfields and aircraft maintenance facilities. Reduction of the German Air Force was the top priority of the OVERLORD Digest. Paragraph 34 clearly summarized the supreme importance of POINTBLANK to OVERLORD:

> *Above all, it is essential that there should be an over-all reduction in the German fighter force between now and the time of the surface assault. From now onwards every practical method of achieving this end must be employed. This condition,* above all others (emphasis added), *will dictate the date by which the amphibious assault can be launched.*[5]

## Derailing the German Army

German dependence on the railroads to move people and materiel was a characteristic of European civil society. Personal motor vehicles were the exception rather than the rule. Prewar Germany averaged 37.5 people per motor vehicle as compared to the United States, with only 4.4 people per vehicle. Britain, with 32 people per vehicle in 1939, benefited from rapidly increased wartime truck production and the generous supply of American trucks and jeeps. Conversely, the Germans struggled with a chronic shortage of trucks even after capturing large numbers of vehicles in their conquest of bordering countries.

According to the invasion planners, there could be no more than twelve German panzer (tank) and panzer grenadier (armored infantry) divisions in the intended operational area west of the Seine and north of the Loire.[6] These were fast-moving ground units, designed to attack the Allied lines and penetrate deep into rear areas. This determination was calculated based on the anticipated delivery of Allied divisions from Britain to the beachhead. More than twelve German divisions would overwhelm the defenders and push them back into the sea.

German infantry divisions were much less capable in what was hoped to be a fast-moving, mobile fight. Their main form of transportation was the human foot, with some units being supplied with bicycles. Their artillery was horse-drawn. In April the Allies intensified the blocking of the rail and road system leading into the operational area.[7] Sufficient interdiction was applied so that no more than three fast-moving additional panzer (tank) or panzer grenadier divisions could enter the operational area within two months of landing.

The first effort to interdict the German logistics network was attacks on railroad marshaling yards and trains. Railroads provided numerous targets throughout France. There was a relatively dense network of railroads even west of Paris, away from the industrial French north. Locomotives and other rolling stock were also plentiful.[8] These attacks began in France in April 1944 and continued as long as German forces occupied the country. Although the Germans were the target, the so-called "Transportation Plan" caused numerous French civilian casualties as well. The Germans conducted an effective repair and replacement effort and simply took what they needed from the French to augment their reserves.

A second method of interdiction, first developed far to the south in the Italian Campaign, augmented the Transportation Plan by attacking vulnerable bridges crossing major rivers. There were three potential lines of interdiction between

## Table 7.1. Number of People per Motor Vehicle, 1939

| Country | Population (millions) | Vehicles (millions) | Persons per Motor Vehicle |
|---|---|---|---|
| Britain | 48 | 1.5 | 32.0 |
| France | 42 | 1.8 | 23.3 |
| Germany | 75 | 2.0 | 37.5 |
| Italy | 39 | 0.3 | 130.0 |
| United States | 132 | 30.0 | 4.4 |

Source: James F Dunnigan and Albert A. Nofi. *Dirty Little Secrets of World War II* (New York: William Morrow and Company, 1994), 27.

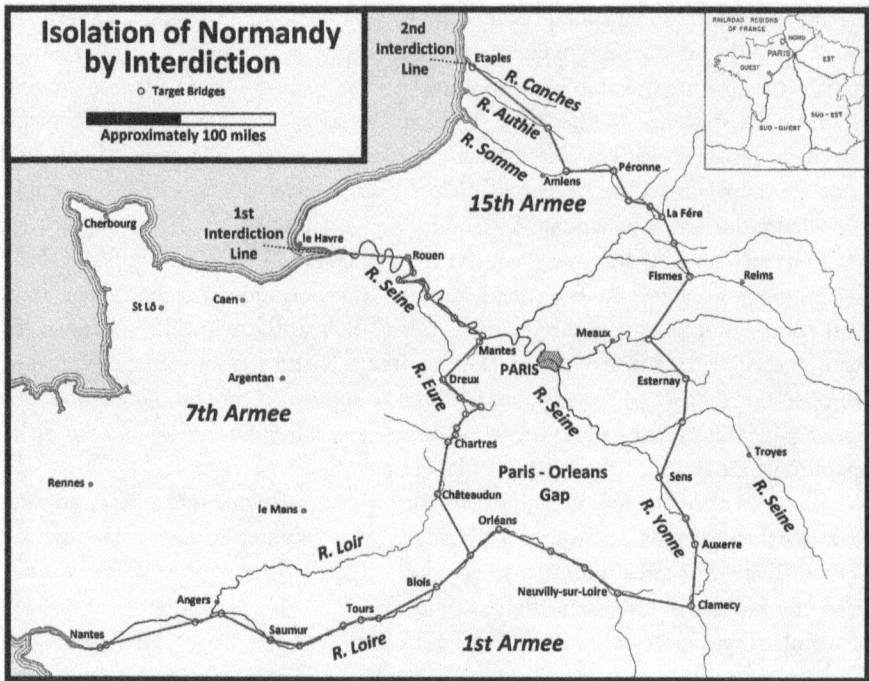

Map 7.1. Isolation of Normandy by Interdiction of Bridges MOLYSON AFTER HARRISON[9]

German forces in the homeland and the *7th Armée* in Normandy. The *7th Armée* defended the coastline of Lower Normandy, including the area chosen for the assault (see map 7.1)

The first line of bridge interdiction followed the River Seine from its estuary near Le Havre to Mantes, northwest of Paris. The line was drawn southwest from Mantes and connected to a tributary of the Seine, the River Eure, at Dreux and then south to Chartres. The line then connected to Châteaudun, on the small River Loir, a tributary of the major River Loire. Finally, it connected to the Loire west of Orleans.

The second line of interdiction began at Étaples on the French coast, continuing southwest to Amiens and then to La Fère. It then continued south, crossing the Seine west of Troyes and meeting the River Yonne at Sens. It continued along the Yonne to Clamecy.

A third line of interdiction was the River Meuse, originating in northeastern France running north into Belgium and the Netherlands as the River Maas (see map 7.2). It formed a natural barrier between the industrialized areas of Germany and those of northern France, Belgium, and the Netherlands. The critical bridges here were harder to attack due to heavier German air defenses closer to the homeland.

Figure 7.1. Bombs from an Allied level bomber hit a rail bridge. NATIONAL ARCHIVES

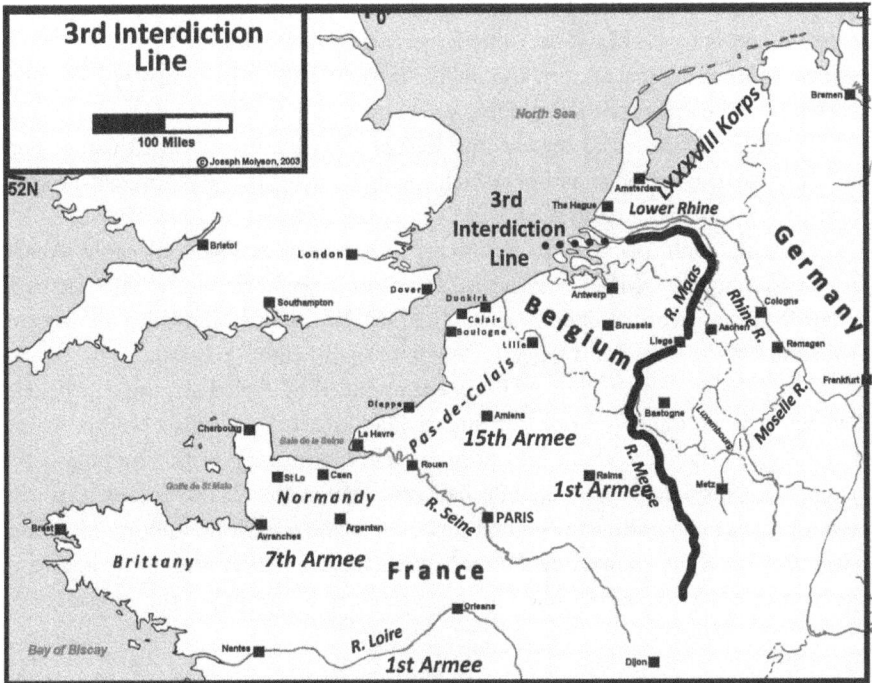

Map 7.2. Third Line of Interdiction MOLYSON

The first line of interdiction isolated the *7th Armée* from rapid reinforcement from either the *15th Armée* or the German homeland. The second line of interdiction isolated the *15th Armée* from either the *7th Armée* in Lower Normandy or the *LXXXVIII Korps* in the Netherlands. After D-Day, a fourth line of interdiction was established along the Loire. This action was delayed to continue the deception that the Pas-de-Calais was the intended target area. This isolated the *7th Armée* from the *1st Armée* to the south and forced it to withdraw toward the east. The attacks, from April until June, against German units and infrastructure in France cost some 12,000 Allied airmen and about 2,000 aircraft.[10] This was more than the approximately 10,000 Allied casualties during the first day of the actual invasion.

## ARTIFICIAL HARBORS

World War I's landing at Gallipoli (April 1915) to seize the Bosporus Strait at Constantinople demonstrated the importance of supply and reinforcement to assault troops. It was the first major opposed amphibious assault of modern times. The Gallipoli peninsula lacked an adequate port, and it is doubtful the landing force could have seized it even if the port had existed. The campaign, which lasted eight months, failed, and the troops were withdrawn after sustaining a quarter of a million casualties. This was a lesson not lost on the British First Lord of the Admiralty—at that time, Winston Churchill.

After the fall of France in 1940, the Germans held all the ports on the French coast. The disastrous Allied 1942 landing at Dieppe taught that a direct sea assault against Cherbourg, Le Havre, or other large, fortified ports on the French coast was suicidal. Without a major port, the ability to supply the Allied armies over open beaches must be accomplished. Therefore, an alternative to the existing ports needed to be developed. This led to the eventual design and construction in Britain of prefabricated floating artificial harbors which could be moved to the Normandy beaches within a few days of the initial landing.

Churchill commissioned the Admiralty's Department of Miscellaneous Weapons Development (DMWD) to begin design of a prefabricated, mobile artificial harbor for use adjacent to open beaches. The DMWD, whose innovative minds were nicknamed "Wheezers and Dodgers," took on the job with a passion.

It was the secure working environment provided by Allied airpower in Britain that allowed thousands of military and civilian workers to build these immense structures and then tow them into position at the beginning of the landing. Once in place in Normandy, these mobile harbors enabled the Allies to land over the assault beaches and complete the first phase of the attack. More importantly, using the artificial harbors allowed the Allies to avoid another costly attempt to seize and refurbish an occupied harbor like Dieppe at the very beginning of the invasion.[11]

Figure 7.2. Whale Pier, Mulberry B Arromanches, June 1944 NAVAL HERITAGE AND HISTORY COMMAND

# CHAPTER EIGHT

# The Outer Rampart

*German troops along the coast often shot down carrier pigeons used by the Resistance to carry messages back to London. The weapon most used was a low-tech shotgun wielded by a German sportsman turned soldier.*[1]

In May 1944 *Festung Europa* was a scarred but formidable presence on the world stage. Around it the Nazis had arrayed a series of concentric defenses. The innermost "rampart" was the so-called *Atlantik Wall*, the sum total of all German defenses from the Pyrenees to Holland. Another segment, less developed, extended into Scandinavia.

Manning the wall was the *Wehrmacht*, the joint German military whose supreme commander was Adolph Hitler. The *Wehrmacht* included German ground, air, and naval forces. While the German Army was undefeated in France, the *Luftwaffe* and *Kriegsmarine* were both now overmatched by the corresponding Allied forces.[2]

The middle rampart was the sea. It formed a moat of sorts, at least where and when it was defended by German air and naval forces. This rampart had been pushed back from the East Coast of the United States to the Atlantic coastal waters of France. The surviving U-boats were joined by a formidable German coastal navy of small combatants, mine warfare, and patrol vessels. Extensive defensive minefields were also in place.

The outermost German defense line was real but intangible, consisting of Allied and neutral countries' perceptions and misperceptions about German military power and Hitler's ability to wield it. The outermost defense was a tribute to Joseph Goebbels more than Hitler. As propaganda minister for the Nazi Party he had, since the early 1930s, constructed a wall of misinformation. It was made from false promises, half-truths, and outright lies. Occasionally the prowess of the *Wehrmacht* and the blunders of opponents were added. From behind these defenses, *der Führer* looked out and continued to categorize his neighbors as timid friends, potential victims, or dangerous enemies.

The German people themselves were in Goebbels's thrall: "Nothing is easier than leading the people on a leash. I just hold up a dazzling campaign poster and they jump right through it."[3] The belief of *das Volk* (the people) in their Nazi leaders was declining, tempered by round-the-clock bombing, food shortages, lost relatives, and the shrinking perimeter of German-controlled territory. The belief in their country and the righteous nature of their fellow Germans, however, remained strong. In neutral and Allied capitals, most estimates about German production and manpower greatly exceeded the facts. The very fear of what Germany had done and was capable of doing limited the Allied approach to attacking this citadel of hate.

Like any fight, there were natural adversaries in the battle for the "outermost rampart." Diplomatic personnel on both sides attempted to penetrate enemy propaganda and spread their own. Counterintelligence forces tracked, trapped, and captured enemy espionage agents. Fighter aircraft treated enemy reconnaissance planes as a priority target. Photographic interpreters (PIs) learned to penetrate the best efforts of enemy camoufleurs, personnel who developed and applied the camouflage hiding critical installations.

Signals intelligence personnel attempted to intercept and exploit the information sent by enemy communications personnel in encrypted (coded) messages. Cryptographers, experts in codes and ciphers, on each side attempted to protect information by scrambling messages while enemy cryptographers attempted to unscramble them. Even weather personnel tried to pinpoint where enemy forces might be observing and reporting key weather patterns.

In the year of remarkable transition from May 1943 to May 1944, no greater "defense of the Reich" myth would fall than that of Nazi invincibility. The Allies collected thousands of radio intercepts, photographs, and espionage reports to build the intelligence weapon to pierce the German outer rampart of information and disinformation. At the same time, the Allies strengthened their own information defense, denying German collection attempts against them. Once the *Wehrmacht* was well understood, it could be defeated by masterful deception.

## Chapter Nine

# Postcards

While the Germans maintained a capability to collect battlefield, or *tactical*, intelligence until late 1944, their ability to collect strategic intelligence was severely limited by active and passive Allied efforts. Although long-range reconnaissance squadrons (*Fernaufklärungstaffeln*) were part of each German air fleet, increasing Allied air superiority severely limited their effort.

Long-range *strategic* air reconnaissance over Britain had greatly declined since 1940, and German aircraft were prevented by the RAF from overflying areas where the invasion forces were assembling. Occasional access was allowed to noncritical areas or those in which decoy facilities and units had been established. The southwestern part of Britain became an information desert for the Germans.

It was a basic characteristic of the Nazi regime to maintain centralized power by keeping various parts of the government and military forces in brutal competition. This was especially true of the civilian and military functions that collected intelligence. The Germans employed all of the various methods to collect information that the Allies used, but the threads of information were seldom collected together and dispassionately scrutinized. A regime built on lies and competition could hardly be comfortable with the routine sharing of information among rivals. This detracted from German capability to validate one form of intelligence with data from other sources.

The Germans therefore had limited capability to do intelligence *fusion*, the process by which information from many sources is combined to yield the best possible insight into a particular situation. When properly accomplished, fusion provides a mastery of information not available to the casual or cloistered observer. In OVERLORD, the Allies used multisource information to yield a timely and accurate picture of what would occur in the invasion area.

Conversely, German intelligence agencies most often worked in isolation from one another. German military intelligence, the *Abwehr*, collected information from its overseas agents, diplomats, and military and naval sources. It was distrusted by its chief rival, the *Sicherheitdienst* (SD). The SD was the intelligence organization of the SS and the Nazi Party. In fact, by 1944 the SD was routinely reviewing and editing *Abwehr* information before it was provided to Hitler and his high command headquarters, OKW.

While the Germans were able to collect and effectively use the relatively simple tactical data required to support a land force in a single battle, they never mastered the kind of interservice and international cooperation that was the hallmark of Allied intelligence. This made them vulnerable to *deception*, the intentional manipulation of information to alter the perceptions of an adversary.

The belligerents were locked in a fight for information superiority every bit as critical as air superiority. It was the Allies' overall prowess in collecting and exploiting all kinds of information that made OVERLORD possible, especially in regard to establishing air superiority. The British were especially adept in this fight, and the Americans emulated them quickly. Operational intelligence on the environment, allies, and enemies enabled Eisenhower's troops to break into Fortress Europe on D-Day.

## OPERATIONAL INTELLIGENCE

Efficient and continuous collection of basic meteorological and topographic knowledge was necessary to properly plan OVERLORD. It was this effort that led COSSAC (Chief of Staff, Supreme Allied Commander) to select Normandy as the assault area. Similar collection of information about the enemy caused the Allies to increase the OVERLORD force from three to five infantry divisions supported by three airborne divisions. Allied collection methods were eclectic and included espionage and other human intelligence, signals intelligence, aerial photography, and lots and lots of postcards. The first question to solve was obviously where to land:

> *There was a mass of information on winds, tides, coastal defences, enemy troops, and airfields all along the 3,500 miles of coast from Norway to Spain. As a result of an official request broadcast by the BBC, the public sent in over 10 million holiday photographs and postcards, providing topographical details from which a specialist team at Oxford University drew up maps of astonishing accuracy.*[1]

Of course, much of the coastline analyzed was topographically not suitable to land troops. Troops were best landed in ports, but capturing ports from the Germans was not practical. Beaches were the best alternatives, preferably within range of Allied air cover. It was important to have ports relatively close to the landing so that they could be subsequently captured from their land side. In the end, only the Pas-de-Calais and Lower Normandy provided the best beaches.

Information was used *defensively* in an attempt to distort the German perception of Allied capabilities and intentions. While collecting and exploiting myriad accurate and timely intelligence, the Allies were able to deny the Nazis the same sorts of information. This was information the Germans needed and didn't get for the successful defense of Europe. Propaganda, various subterfuges, selective destruction of *Luftwaffe* reconnaissance aircraft, effective communications and physical security, and other means were used to confound and confuse the defender.

The various German functionaries that collected and hoarded intelligence made the Allies' job easier than it would have been had they faced a more collegial enemy. Only when deception was impractical did the Allies physically destroy Nazi information and communications resources. For example, the Germans amassed great repositories of police dossiers on Dutch Resistance fighters. There was no way to easily discredit these records. Therefore, the central German records center housing some of these dossiers in The Hague was bombed and destroyed.[2]

CHAPTER TEN

# FORTITUDE

*In wartime, truth is so precious that she should always be attended by a body-guard of lies.*

—WINSTON CHURCHILL

At EUREKA, the 1943 Tehran conference of Stalin, Churchill, and Roosevelt, Churchill promised Stalin that a "bodyguard of lies" would protect the invasion of France, the long-promised second front in Western Europe. By January 1944, the Combined Chiefs of Staff (CCS)[1] had approved a massive overall deception strategy against Germany called Plan BODYGUARD.

Two major Allied landings were planned against France for the summer of 1944: Operations OVERLORD and ANVIL. OVERLORD would be mounted over the beaches of Normandy between Cherbourg and Le Harve. ANVIL's forces would land in southern France and advance up the Rhône valley. Using simultaneous landings, the Allies hoped to catch the German Army in France in a huge pincer, while preventing forces in the north or south from reinforcing one another. A CCS report noted:

> *The German General Staff will this winter be considering the strategic disposition of their forces to meet offensive operations by the United Nations in 1944. Though they will be forced to maintain the bulk of their forces on the Russian front, they already suspect that large-scale Anglo-American operations will be undertaken in Western Europe sometime in 1944. It is, however, doubtful whether they have at present sufficient information regarding the timing and scope of this threat to justify any immediate changes in their strategic dispositions. At a later stage, however, preparations for OVERLORD and lesser degree for ANVIL will be on such a scale and of such a type that the enemy cannot fail to appreciate our intention to carry out a cross-channel operation and an amphibious operation in the Western Mediterranean.*[2]

Strategic surprise, where the Germans might be completely unaware that an invasion of Europe was coming, was unattainable. The Allies accepted the fact that they could still hope for tactical surprise. They therefore trumped the tactical intelligence expertise of the Germans with an overall superiority in operational deception. Successful tactical surprise would mean that Rommel would not have his major ground formations properly deployed to meet the invasion in Normandy. The Joint Intelligence Subcommittee (JIC) of the Joint Planning Staff (JPS) in London evaluated the chances for a surprise invasion:

> *It will be impossible for the Allies in the OVERLORD area to obtain strategic surprise. Germany will be aware of the build-up in the United Kingdom and, however efficient the security and deceptive measures employed by the Allies, she must expect that the main attack will, because of the need of adequate air cover, be made against the coastline facing the English Channel. The most that the Allies can hope for is tactical surprise, by keeping the enemy in doubt up to the last moment as to the exact date of the operation, the points of landing, and the methods of assault. There is, perhaps, more chance of strategic surprise for ANVIL since the Germans will not be certain that the main objective of the build-up in the Western Mediterranean is the South of France and not the Gulf of Genoa.*[3]

## ULTRA

The ability to deceive the Germans was greatly aided by their ability to read encrypted German communications on a regular basis, the so-called ULTRA intelligence. This allowed Allied leaders to evaluate the effectiveness of their own deception efforts, and to detect similar efforts by their enemies. When Hitler colluded with Stalin to overrun Poland, he was already planning for a further attack into the Soviet Union. Temporarily sharing the spoils of war was a masterful German deception.

In 1941, when Churchill provided Stalin a warning about the German invasion of Russia based on ULTRA intercepts, Stalin refused to believe it because the information was too painful to bear. For him it was simply "unbelievable." Millions of Russians paid the price of Stalin's misperception of the Germans.

In 1943–1944, the Allies knew of the Germans' own misperceptions about the imminent invasion of France, as expressed in their message traffic. Therefore, the Allies crafted a story that Hitler and his generals *wanted* to believe.[4] The activity that implemented the OVERLORD deception program was called Operation FORTITUDE. Separate plans called Operation ZEPPELIN and DIADEM covered ANVIL, the subsequent invasion of the Mediterranean French coast (see appendix 2).

FORTITUDE NORTH was designed to convince the Germans that a major diversionary Allied attack was to be made against Norway prior to the main landings in the Pas-de-Calais.

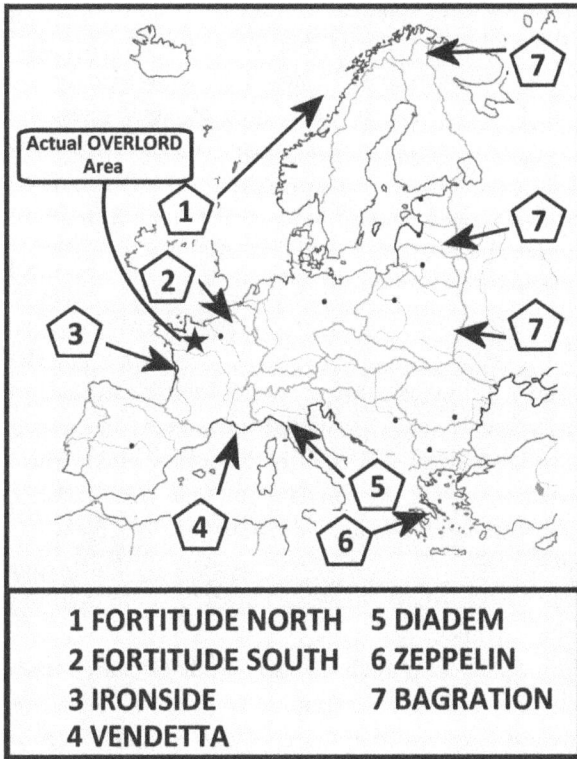

Map 10.1. Selected Deception Operations in Support of OVERLORD MOLYSON[5]

At the Tehran conference, Stalin agreed to assist the Allies by cooperating in FORTITUDE NORTH. This would keep the Germans pinned down in Norway and Finland. They were also ready to conduct a massive but diversionary attack during the OVERLORD operation to keep the Germans pinned down in Russia.[6]

FORTITUDE NORTH's diversionary efforts were based on a fictitious "British Fourth Army," with headquarters (supposedly) in Scotland. Since German reconnaissance aircraft no longer visited this area thanks to the RAF, it was sufficient to provide appropriate radio traffic to simulate the regular communications of such a large mass of troops. By various means it was made known that this army required ski equipment and training, as well as instructors proficient in rock climbing. Since Scotland lay just opposite Norway, this kind of intercepted and uncorroborated traffic convinced the Germans that Norway was at risk. No large German formations were withdrawn from Norway until long after OVERLORD had commenced.[7]

FORTITUDE SOUTH aimed to convince the Germans that the major landing in France would occur across the Strait of Dover into the Pas-de-Calais. Southeast England was the most likely base for the associated assault force. Since the Germans grossly overestimated the number of Allied divisions in England, it was easy for them to envision major diversionary attacks prior to the "real" invasion.

Because of the proximity of German forces in the Pas-de-Calais to southeast England, a more elaborate deception had to be created in the south of England. This included the services of Lieutenant General George Patton, still in the doghouse for slapping two GIs in Sicily. Patton, the Allied general most respected by the *Wehrmacht*, moved into temporary lodging to "command" FUSAG, the fictitious First United States Army Group.

Elaborate and continuous business radio communications were fabricated. MPs chatted by unsecure radio about the movements of various road convoys that did not exist. Hundreds of inflated rubber decoy tanks, trucks, cannon, and other equipment blossomed in the simulated buildup area. FUSAG made mission requests and published and disseminated commendations for work accomplished. Dummy tent cities were set up. German agents, all under control of British counterintelligence, fed corroborating data on FUSAG to their unwitting former masters across the Channel.

The Allied air forces supported FORTITUDE in many ways, including how they executed the pre-invasion interdiction campaign. At least twice as many air attacks were mounted against the Pas-de-Calais beaches than were attempted around Normandy. Between May 24 and June 6, the US 9th AF dropped eighteen of the twenty-four bridges between Paris and Rouen on the Seine River. This cut almost all rapid land movement between the *7th Armée* in Normandy and *15th Armée* in the Pas-de-Calais.

The Germans misread this distribution of the air attacks as intended to isolate the *15th Armée* rather than the *7th*. This was logical—the Allies' main attack was supposed to hit the Pas-de-Calais. Once the actual landings began, all the bridges over the Loire River to the south of Normandy were also dropped to complete isolation of the *7th Armée*.[8] This failed to tip off the Germans, who perceived it as part of the "diversionary" landing.[9]

Before the actual landings, OVERLORD's real 12th and 21st Army Groups were assembling on the south coast of England. The FORTITUDE SOUTH plan assumed that if any German agent or aircraft got a peek at this real invasion force, they would assume it was for the "diversionary" landing in Normandy. The few German reconnaissance planes that got through Allied air defense were rewarded with tantalizing peeks at Patton's rubber FUSAG; however, they were never allowed to approach the real assembly area.[10] It was the rumbling sound of more than 6,500 vessels passing close by the Cotentin Peninsula before dawn on the morning of June 6 that gave the Germans the first warning about the actual invasion fleet to be taken seriously.[11]

The *OB West* "Estimate of Allied Intentions" for June 5 (the day before OVER-LORD) clearly indicates that the deception worked as intended:

> *The systematic and distinct increase of air attacks indicates that the enemy has reached a high degree of readiness. The probable invasion front still remains the sector from the Scheldt [in Holland] to Normandy . . . and it is not impossible that the north front of Brittany might be included . . . [but] it is still not clear where the enemy will invade within this total area. Concentrated air attacks on the coast defenses between Dunkirk and Dieppe may mean that the main Allied invasion effort will be made there . . . [but] imminence of invasion is not recognizable.*[12]

Even after the landings began, Hitler still considered Patton's FUSAG the main threat. The *Führer* still looked upon Normandy as a diversionary effort, as had been intended when executing the FORTITUDE SOUTH deception. The bogus information collected by the *Abwehr* was uncorrected by accurate reconnaissance or espionage, and the perception was built and maintained that the "real" invasion would be in the Pas-de-Calais.

FORTITUDE was so successful that a German intelligence map dated July 3, 1944, still showed Patton's FUSAG waiting in England ready to invade the Pas-de-Calais.[13] This was almost a month after the actual landings in Normandy. It was as long as two months before Hitler and his military realized that they had been so thoroughly duped. Perhaps it was the appearance of Patton breaking out of Normandy at the head of the real US Third Army that finally turned on the lights at OKW.

During the actual event, a lack of sufficient landing craft prevented the near-simultaneous assault against northern and southern France the Allies desired. OVERLORD was executed in June 1944 and ANVIL, renamed DRA-GOON, in August. Yet the very threat of a second landing in Norway, somewhere in the Mediterranean, and in the Pas-de-Calais kept major German formations out of the Normandy fighting.

## Table 10.1. Estimated Number of German Divisions Distributed around Occupied Europe, June 1944

| Theater/Front | Associated Plan | Divisions | Percentage |
| --- | --- | --- | --- |
| Eastern Front | BAGRATION | 179 | 59.3 |
| Southeast Europe/Balkans | ZEPPELIN | 26 | 8.6 |
| Italy | DIADEM | 22 | 7.3 |
| Norway and Scandinavia | FORTITUDE NORTH | 16 | 5.3 |
| France | FORTITUDE SOUTH | 59 | 19.5 |
| Total | — | 302 | 100.0 |

Source: Anthony Cave Brown, *Bodyguard of Lies* (New York: HarperCollins, 1975), 437.

German Army deployments distributed between the various fronts also did not significantly change. Hitler decided that no part of his empire's periphery could be weakened to increase defenses of the Western Front. Less than 20 percent of Hitler's regular army and *SS* divisions were in France, one-third the number of divisions on the Eastern Front.[14] This fact alone justified both FORTITUDE and ZEPPELIN.

CHAPTER ELEVEN

# The Information War

Dawn had not yet touched the skies as the first warplanes crossed the Channel coast into Normandy on D-Day. Hundreds of planes were on the move, unchallenged by the blinded and deceived *Luftwaffe*. Some crews, well trained for this night, navigated using radio waves in various devices while others relied on dead reckoning of position. Some dropped bombs or paratroopers; others released gliders. Among the vanguard of this aerial armada were aircraft carrying warning leaflets for coastal residents from the Cotentin Peninsula to Holland. It was the latest in a series of missions that had begun long before.

The RAF had begun operations over Germany in 1939, with an emphasis on Ministry of Information (MoI) leaflet dropping. These were codenamed NICKEL missions. The PWE (Political Warfare Executive), an offshoot of the (British) Special Operations Executive (SOE), was established in August 1941. Its job was to undermine the social fabric of Germany's armed forces. Once PWE was established, they helped MoI produce the NICKEL leaflets.[1]

After the entry of the United States into the war, propaganda elements of the US Army were sent to London and eventually joined forces with PWE to form the Psychological Warfare Division (PWD) of Eisenhower's SHAEF headquarters. MoI and the US Office of War Information (OWI), as well as the US Office of Strategic Services (OSS), also assisted. Propaganda broadcasts as well as leaflets were produced. A principal aim of all this activity was to demoralize German civilians and accentuate the philosophical chasm between the *Wehrmacht* (the regular German military) and the Nazi Party.

By March 1942, RAF Bomber Command curtailed the NICKEL missions in order to pursue other priorities. By May 1943, the opportunity to deliver propaganda into Occupied Europe was seized by the US Eighth Air Force. Commander Major General Ira Eaker directed his three bombardment wings to initiate leaflet operations. Development work was accomplished to determine how to distribute leaflets from American heavy bombers. Soon, the barometrically fused Monroe leaflet bomb had been devised and tactics for its use developed. It was decided to drop leaflets as part of all normal bombing missions.

Figure 11.1. Monroe bombs contained 80,000 leaflets. US ARMY AIR FORCE

The first American mission with leaflets was flown into Germany on July 28, 1943. The Americans accepted the fact that "leaflets are weapons of attack."[2] Soon it was decided that this was one task too many for the hard-pressed regular bomb groups. In September 1943, the 422nd Bomb Squadron and its B-17s were assigned to continue the campaign by night. The 422nd was dropping over 45,000 pounds of leaflets and newsletters monthly over Germany, Belgium, and France by December 1943. That month 20 million leaflets were dropped on Northern Europe. By April 1944, that figure had risen to more than 67 million. It was later estimated that over three-quarters of all German prisoners taken in France from D-Day on had carried or otherwise used Allied surrender leaflets. The ability to change perceptions has a value all its own.

Most Allied efforts were toward *white propaganda*, what the Americans called a "Strategy of Truth."[3] USAAF aircraft periodically dropped up to 750,000 copies of *Nachrichten für die Truppe* (*Newsletter for the Troops*) on German troop concentrations identified by Allied ground commanders.[4] This newsletter included not only military news but also the (mostly bad) news from the home front. By this time the German situation was bad enough for the unvarnished truth to be a useful weapon for the Allies. Surrender leaflets were of course mostly white propaganda; in truth German

Figure 11.2. Safe Conduct Pass, also called a "surrender leaflet"
AIR FORCE HISTORICAL RESEARCH AGENCY KARLSRUHE COLLECTION

POWs were generally as well treated as advertised. German POWs often continued to receive the *Nachrichten für die Truppe* once they reached their prison camps and often used the leaflets to settle bets, testament to their perceived reliability.[5]

The Allies seldom used *black propaganda* (intentionally lying to the target audience) after 1942 because there was no need. Relatively open societies are ill-equipped to keep such lies secret for very long. The Nazis were masters of black propaganda, using bluffs to intimidate their adversaries long after the military power to make good on their threats had dissipated.

The weaknesses of the *Atlantik Wall* were glossed over by German propaganda, which became so blatant that Rommel refused to be photographed inspecting defenses. He knew that little of the 1,300 miles of coast in his charge was protected with the huge coastal guns like those shown near Calais in German propaganda films. In the end, the German claims fooled no one but themselves.[6]

The Allies did occasionally shade their white propaganda into gray to achieve one or more deception objectives. Gray propaganda slanted the truth or told only a partial story. The radio show *Soldatensender Calais angeschlossen der Deutsche Kürzwellensender Atlantik* (soldiers' Calais broadcast in association with the German Atlantic shortwave broadcasting station) never claimed to be a German broadcast or identified itself as an Allied product, it simply avoided the issue. *Nachrichten für die Truppe* also was unattributed but written in such a way as to seem an official German Army product.

## SIGNALS INTELLIGENCE

Allied efforts at perfecting signals intelligence (SIGINT) paid big dividends. During periods when German codes were broken, coded messages provided a bonanza of information. By the eve of World War II, Polish intelligence had exploited the German code machine, termed "Enigma," and some German codes. They had been reading some Enigma traffic since 1932. The French broke in by 1938.[7] When Warsaw fell to the Germans in 1939, Polish expertise was passed on to the British.

Work by the French crossed the Channel to England when Paris fell in 1940. The Brits were already making some advances in reading encrypted German messages, but the Polish and French gifts were a windfall. Remarkably, the Germans failed to detect that two of their conquered enemies had already beaten their "impregnable system." A center to continue the work was established at Bletchley Park in Buckinghamshire. ULTRA was the code name for intelligence information derived from exploitation of Enigma and other Axis signals.

In regard to OVERLORD, Allied SIGINT enabled senior Allied leaders to gauge the effects of their deception efforts and to observe the evolution of German plans for the defense of Occupied France. Among the many duties of the French Resistance was the interruption of enemy telecommunications and actions to sow confusion in the enemy rear area, especially in support of the invasion itself.[8]

As destruction of the landlines associated with German military operations escalated, the Germans placed increased emphasis on radio communications.[9] The Japanese representative to Berlin added to the intelligence bonanza by using a borrowed Enigma to report his observations of the European War back to Japan.

In Spring 1944 ULTRA revealed the locations of reserve airfields built to receive German Air Force reinforcements responding to an Allied invasion of France. These fields were selectively and intensely attacked beginning May 11, 1944. This disrupted efforts to prepare the fields to receive *Luftwaffe* reinforcements. As a result, the armada of carefully husbanded *Luftwaffe* fighters was quickly decimated when they moved to France from Germany in response to D-Day.

Allied fighters tipped off by ULTRA intercepts ambushed some German squadrons. Other squadrons became lost while trying to find emergency alternates, and ground personnel were often unable to find the survivors they were supposed to support. The rebuilding of the German Air Force combat power in the west, greatly depleted in the series of Allied campaigns beginning in August 1943, was fatally delayed by this action.[10]

ULTRA also revealed the plans of Admiral Karl Dönitz for use of U-boats to attack the invasion fleet. All but two of the thirty-five or so U-boats deployed for this mission were prevented from entering the English Channel before June 18. The few that ran the gauntlet of Allied aircraft and ships after that date arrived too late for any significant defense.

Although ULTRA revealed some operational information on German torpedo boat operations, such communications were rarely able to provide timely warning of attack. Instead, US Army Air Force medium and heavy bombers dealt with these threats by demolishing their coastal bases. More successful was Allied SIGINT efforts to detect German surface ships moving north from the Bay of Biscay. ULTRA provided their route and time of departure, resulting in three destroyers and one large torpedo boat sunk.

The Germans used signals intelligence to good effect at the tactical level. They were especially good at intercepting Allied field communications, where radio messages were seldom encrypted. Since there was roughly one radio for every two soldiers in the invading armies, the German "take" from such work was enormous.[11] The Americans and Brits loved to talk on their many short-ranged radios, providing a running commentary of operations to their German adversaries.

Tactical communications intercepts were, however, of little value in defending the *Atlantik Wall*. What was needed was good strategic signals intelligence validated by aerial photography and espionage, as well as the trust of senior leadership. No German air reconnaissance over the south and southeast of England was permitted from mid-May.[12] None of this was available to the German SIGINT troops monitoring the Allies across the Channel. While the Germans listened to American sergeants chat about home by radio, the Americans and British listened to German generals discuss the defense of the homeland by wire.

## CHAPTER TWELVE

# Wounded Hearts

The message *"Les sanglots longs des violons de l'automne"* (The long sobs of autumn violins) was broadcast by the BBC on June 1, 1944, as part of the program *"Les Français parlent aux Français"* (The French speak to the French). This precise code phrase was intended for Philippe de Vomécourt's "Ventriloquist" resistance network, based in Sologne (south of Orléans). It alerted Resistance fighters to prepare to sabotage communication routes in their sector, on orders and within seven days of the message being sent.

The second part of the message, *"Blessant mon Coeur d'une langueur monotone,"*[1] was broadcast on the same radio station on June 5, 1944, at 2115 Paris time, simultaneously with several dozen other codes. This message, still intended for the Ventriloquist network, meant that sabotage operations in Sologne had to be carried out within forty-eight hours.[2]

German military intelligence did manage to piece together some of the code phrases then being transmitted by the BBC to the French Resistance. The information was distributed to military intelligence listening posts along the coast, such as that of *Oberstleutnant* Helmuth Meyer, chief of intelligence for the *15th Armée* in the Pas-de-Calais. Among his other duties was the operation of a thirty-man tactical signals intelligence station. These men listened, recorded, and analyzed the flood of radio traffic emanating from various sources. This included the BBC news and entertainment broadcasts as well as the fake traffic being transmitted as part of FORTITUDE.

Meyer had been briefed by Admiral Canaris, chief of the *Abwehr*, about certain phrases that would be transmitted to the Resistance just prior to the invasion. Apparently, Canaris's agents or some lucky German interrogator had learned of these phrases and their meaning. Both Canaris and Meyer had good reason to respect the capabilities of the Resistance; it was a well-organized force of several hundred thousand men and women. The Resistance was supported by Allied aircraft based in southern England that delivered Allied agents and tons of supplies throughout France.

Thanks to the effort of the SS and the *Abwehr*, the average life expectancy of these people was only about six months. Still, they constituted an Allied ground force-in-being already in France. The critical message to the Resistance would be

Figure 12.1. RAF Lysander short takeoff and landing (STOL) aircraft helped transport agents to and from their operating areas in France. NATIONAL ARCHIVES

in two parts, each a line in French poet Paul Verlaine's "*Chanson d'Automne*" (Song of Autumn). "*Les sanglots longs des violins de l'automne*" informed the Resistance of invasion within two weeks. "*Blessant mon Coeur d'une langueur monotone*" warned of an invasion within twenty-four hours.[3]

Late on 3 June, Meyer's men intercepted the signal "URGENT PRESS ASSOCIATED NYK FLASH EISENHOWER HQ ANNOUNCES ALLIED LANDING IN FRANCE." It was the start of a sleepless night of phone calls. Meyer assumed it was simple Allied harassment of his operation. Actually, a radio communications clerk had accidentally transmitted a message created for practice only.

Only an hour after the false AP message had been received, however, another message was intercepted: "*Les sanglots longs des violins de l'automne*." The *15th Armée* went on alert. By dawn on the 4th, it was obvious that no landings were occurring on the French coast. Unknown to Meyer, the invasion fleet had been turned around due to worsening weather. Three Allied airborne divisions ready to pounce were also held back on their bases.

The invasion warning was flashed from *15th Armée* to the Armed Forces High Command, *Oberkommando Wehrmacht* (OKW). This was Hitler's personal headquarters as supreme commander of German forces. It was also telephoned to both von Rundstedt's *OB West* and Rommel's *Heersgruppe B* headquarters. It was here that the system broke down and would do so again during the following night when the invasion actually began.

*Generalfeldmarschall* Jodl at OKW did not call an alert for German forces in the West. He had apparently been somewhat desensitized by the series of Allied deceptions associated with FORTITUDE. He assumed von Rundstedt at *OB West* would do that if necessary, but von Rundstedt was also desensitized and was worried that too many alerts had already been issued.

The warning message from *15th Armée* in the Pas-de-Calais never made it to its neighbor *7th Armée* in Normandy. That was the job of Rommel at *Heersgruppe B*, in charge of both field armies. Rommel, still at his headquarters at La Roche-Guyon on 4 June, apparently discounted the message either because of the worsening weather or his own misperceptions based on the elaborate deception campaign. Therefore, no action was taken on one of the most critical pieces of signals intelligence intercepted in World War II. The German war machine continued its long and fitful slumber along the *Atlantik Wall*.

On June 5, 1944, the eve of D-Day, German Supreme Headquarters had no idea that the decisive event of the war was upon them. For twenty-four hours, more than 6,000 ships were again on the move across the Channel toward Normandy, but there was no air or naval reconnaissance to spot them. In view of the weather and tides, Rommel, von Rundstedt, and Hitler had no idea that a landing in the immediate future was even possible.

The principle military staff officer at Hitler's headquarters (OKW), General Warlimont, later commented on the lack of accurate intelligence reaching his headquarters:

> We did not even know that for some days now there had been wireless silence in the concentration area in southern England—the normal indication of an imminent attack, though admittedly frequently used for deception purposes. Equally we did not know that as early as January 1944 Admiral Canaris had discovered the text of a (two-part) radio message to be transmitted from England shortly before the start of the invasion as a standby signal to the French Resistance. . . . On the afternoon of 5 June the Intelligence Service informed Jodl that during the night of 4 June the second of these two sentences had been heard by the Security Section of Fifteenth Army. But no action was taken (at OKW).[4]

On the night of 5 June, Meyer's team intercepted *"Blessant mon Coeur d'une langueur monotone"* again. The invasion had a false start, and the second sentence had been transmitted on two consecutive nights—the 4th (when the fleet had to turn around because of weather) and again on the 5th. Meyer was confused because the message was only supposed to be sent once. Nevertheless, he excitedly interrupted a card game hosted by the commander of *15th Armée* , General von Salmuth. Salmuth listened calmly then ordered Meyer to place *15th Armée* on higher alert. Then he returned to his cards.

Again, no message was flashed to *7th Armée*, whose commanders were in Rennes preparing to play a *Kriegspiel* (wargame).[5] In any case, their communications had been cut by the Resistance. The unlikely scenario the wargamers intended to simulate would actually begin in just three hours, when 18,000 paratroopers would descend on Normandy. Shortly after that, the first landing craft would beach.

Then the *7th Armée* would begin to die.

# Chapter Thirteen

# Blinded

On May 10, 1944, the Allies began the sustained physical destruction of German coastal radar along the *Atlantik Wall*. As a result of some 2,000 fighter-bomber sorties[1] by D-Day, less than one in five radars were still operational (sixteen of ninety-two). These sixteen radars survived to be jammed or deceived on D-Day, spared because they would be part of the deception effort.[2]

On the night of May 30–31, the RAF completed the anti-radar bombing campaign on German coastal surveillance. The radars and control centers in the Cherbourg area were subject to a raid by ninety-five RAF bombers, which devastated the early-warning capability in the area.[3]

To add to German confusion as the invasion commenced, the Allies mounted a massive electronic deception targeting the surviving radars in the Pas-de-Calais.[4] Reports from the few operational radars were ignored because there was no way to corroborate reports from multiple radar sites. Before dawn on D-Day, another Allied deception played out.

Figure 13.1. The RAF Typhoon fighter-bomber was instrumental in attacks against German coastal radars. AIR FORCE HISTORICAL RESEARCH AGENCY KARLSRUHE COLLECTION

## German Radar Sites Early May 1944

☐ Air Defense Radar

⬤ Naval Defense Radar

⬠ Air/Naval Defense Radars

**100 Miles**

© Joseph Molyson, 2003

Bristol

London

Southampton

Nor

0°

40 41 42
39
38 33
37 34 Lille
36
35 32 31
29 30
7 8 9 10 23 24 25 26 27 28 21 20
11 22 Amiens
Cherbourg 19
6 Baie de la Seine Le Havre 18
5 12 14 17
4 13 16 Rouen
Golfe de St Malo St Lo Caen 15

Faiaise

3

1 2 Avranches Argentan Paris

Brest

Seine

48N

France

Orleans

Bay of Biscay Nantes

Loire

0°

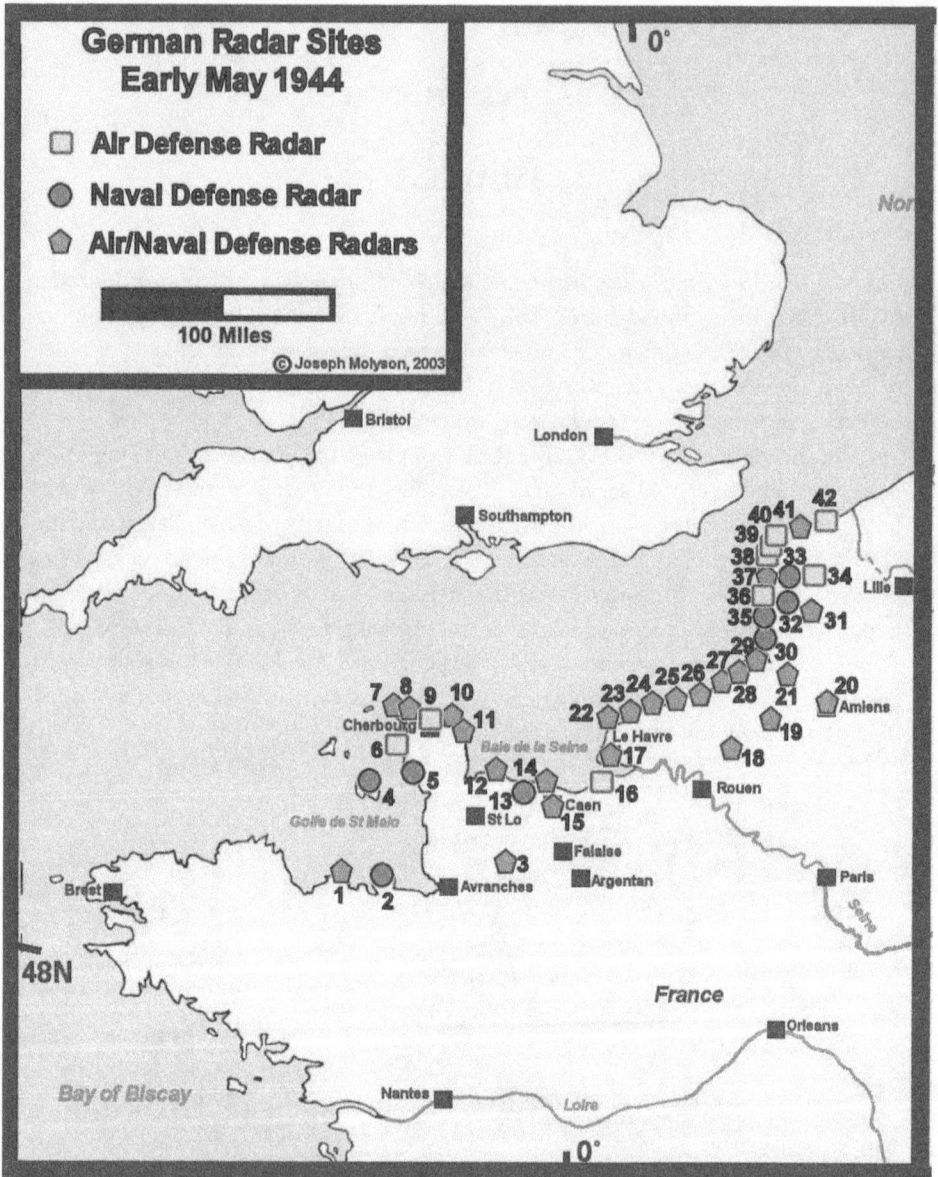

Map 13.1. German Radar Installations in the Invasion Area, May 1944. The Germans were heavily dependent on radar surveillance to protect French airspace. Only 20 percent of the sites survived the anti-radar campaign (see appendix 3). MOLYSON AFTER MAN[5]

Before dawn on D-Day, heading toward Pas-de-Calais came an ingenious electronic deception that created two ghost fleets in the Channel. Operation GLIMMER mimicked an invasion force aimed at Le Havre and Operation TAXABLE an invasion force aimed at Boulogne. Twenty-four motor launches, each towing 29-foot-high reflector balloons, mimicked the radar images of 10,000-ton assault transports.

Above the ghost fleet, carefully trained RAF bomber crews flew precise patterns dropping WINDOW, strips of aluminum foil. The WINDOW partially flooded radar screens, appearing as a massive fleet of aircraft over the fake ship images. Those few radar stations still operating reported an assault by massive air and sea forces was underway. This diverted available *Luftwaffe* interceptors away from the areas through which the actual attack would occur.[6]

The total WINDOW field dropped by the aircraft produced a reflection some 15 miles wide for each "fleet." Other aircraft flew along the English coast, operating MANDREL radar-jamming transmitters from nonoptimal locations. This allowed the Germans to "see" through the jamming and detect the ghost fleets. The surviving radar station at Caen in Normandy detected the real fleet approaching Lower Normandy, but the report was mixed into the Pas-de-Calais reports and was never properly addressed.

In Operation TITANIC, four RAF bomber squadrons dropped hundreds of miniature dummy paratroopers in the Normandy and Pas-de-Calais areas.[7] These added yet another element to the overall confused situation.

To the east of the ghost invasion, two squadrons of RAF Lancasters carrying *Airborne Cigar (ABC)* equipment flew up and down the River Somme. They jammed *Luftwaffe* night fighter control frequencies, electronically attacking and disrupting the *Himmelbett* night fighter control system. The German night fighter force was rendered ineffective. It was morning before the Germans could dispatch reconnaissance planes and boats to seek out the phantom invasion fleet, which by that time had vanished.

Navigation using radar and other electromagnetic devices had flourished during the war years. Beginning in 1940, the Germans had demonstrated primitive night bombing capability using a radio device call *Knickebein*.[8] By D-Day, the aircraft of RAF 218 and 617 squadrons used a British navigation system called Gee to perform the exact navigation required for Operations TAXABLE and GLIMMER.[9]

While TAXABLE and GLIMMER displayed fictitious fleets to the Germans, a path of radar-reflecting buoys in the Channel guided many Allied aircraft and ships to their targets.

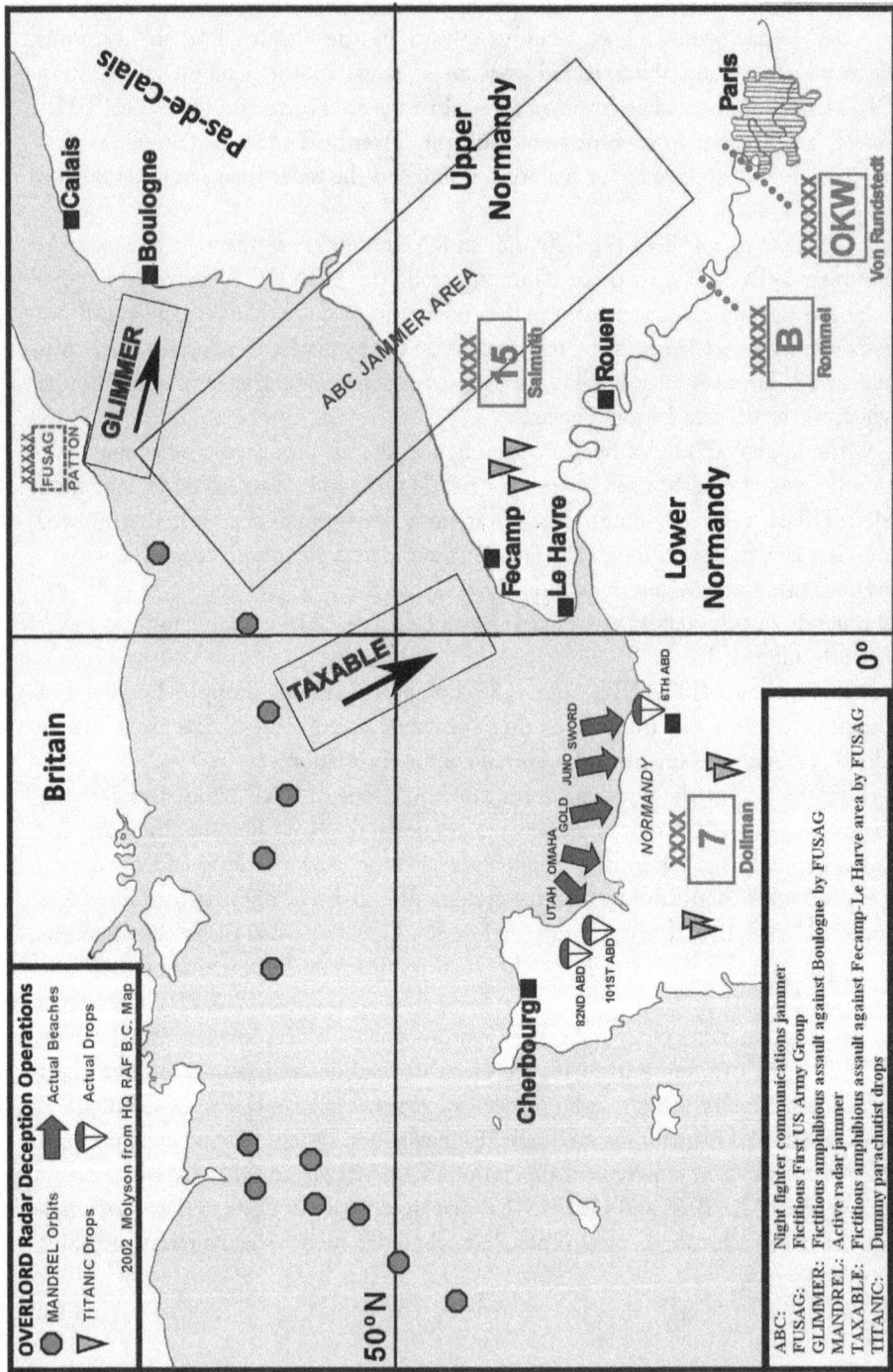

**OVERLORD Radar Deception Operations**

MANDREL Orbits — Actual Beaches
TITANIC Drops — Actual Drops

2002 Molyson from HQ RAF B.C. Map

Britain

50°N

Cherbourg

82ND ABD
101ST ABD

UTAH OMAHA GOLD JUNO SWORD

6TH ABD

NORMANDY

XXXX
7
Dollman

Lower Normandy

0°

TAXABLE

Fecamp
Le Havre

XXXX
15
Salmuth

Rouen

ABC JAMMER AREA

Upper Normandy

Calais
Boulogne

Pas-de-Calais

GLIMMER

XXXXX
FUSAG
PATTON

Paris

XXXXXX
OKW
Von Rundstedt

XXXXX
B
Rommel

ABC: Night fighter communications jammer
FUSAG: Fictitious First US Army Group
GLIMMER: Fictitious amphibious assault against Boulogne by FUSAG
MANDREL: Active radar jammer
TAXABLE: Fictitious amphibious assault against Fecamp-Le Harve area by FUSAG
TITANIC: Dummy parachutist drops

Map 13.2. OVERLORD Electronic Deception Operations AIR FORCE HISTORICAL RESEARCH AGENCY KARLSRUHE COLLECTION AND MAPS

The Allies enjoyed the same degree of information superiority as air superiority over western France—total dominance. The tactical orientation of the German intelligence effort was overshadowed by Allied operational intelligence and deception. Signals and other intelligence allowed German air and naval forces to be destroyed piecemeal as they approached the Normandy area. As for land forces, a massive Nazi effort would be applied at the wrong part of the coast and maintained for weeks after D-Day.

# CHAPTER FOURTEEN

# Storms

The scene is famous, a "must do" for any movie or book about Eisenhower and the Allied invasion of Europe. After years of preparation, a coastal area of northwestern France has become the focus of war and the fulcrum of the twentieth century. Ike's Supreme Headquarters Allied Expeditionary Force (SHAEF) first dispatched the invasion fleet on June 4, 1944, only to recall it in the face of unacceptable air, sea, and landing conditions. A storm was lashing the Channel and southern England.

The dominant weather over the Channel came from the west, spawned over the North Atlantic and influenced by air from the Arctic as well as tropical air from the Gulf Stream. Rainfall made France fertile, and winds made the Channel treacherous at times. It was necessary to gather daily weather information from across the North Atlantic Basin, including meteorological observations from the Canadian Maritimes, Greenland, Iceland, the free Norwegian island of Spitsbergen north of the Arctic Circle, and the western British Isles.

Reports were also received from Allied convoys and naval patrols. Four-engine strategic bombers, never designed for such work, flew specified routes, climbing and descending to various altitudes. This was especially hard on the engines of the "met" aircraft, and some were lost with their crews in the deeps of the North Atlantic.

On June 5, weather officer RAF Group Captain James Stagg provided his forecast to Ike's senior staff at Southwick House. Meteorology was the province of airmen because aircraft were especially vulnerable to weather conditions. Stagg solemnly predicted a temporary hiatus from the stormy conditions clearly audible outside headquarters. A decision to send out the fleet a second night must now be made, and that decision was Eisenhower's to make. More than 150,000 Allied lives were at stake.

Weather observations had to be interpreted by professionals like Stagg. Meteorology was and is both an art and a science—misapprehensions are common. Stagg told the assembled SHAEF leaders that there would *probably* be a pause in the storm. It was a prognostication, not a promise. Ike's principal commanders had mixed opinions but no consensus. Now a synergy between Stagg's scientific art and Ike's artful leadership occurred. Eisenhower glanced out the window and then sim-

# Table 14.1. Environmental Requirements for OVERLORD

| Factor | Planned Requirement | Actual Conditions |
| --- | --- | --- |
| **Winds** | No more than 10–15 knots blowing over beach from north to clear smoke; no more than 12 knots onshore and 18 knots offshore to maintain landing craft stability | Exceeded 17 knots |
| **Swell** | Light to moderate (4–8 feet) | 3–4 feet, rougher in some portions of the achorage |
| **Visibility** | 3–5 miles | Mixed; complicated by smoke and dust from air and naval bombardment of the beach defenses |
| **Cloud Cover** | Less than 60 percent coverage, with none below 3,000 feet for bombing | Mostly cloudy |
| **Low Cloud** | None below 1,000 feet for air support; absent for airborne drop | Intermittent low cloud and/or ground fog |
| **Moonlight** | Late moonrise for airborne attack | Achieved. Moon at highest point just after 1:00 a.m. |
| **Low Tide** | Needed to expose beach obstacles; one at dawn and one later in the day for second landing wave | Assault began at low tide as anticipated, enabling many vessels to avoid obstacles underwater at high tide. High tide came in more quickly than expected, increasing casualties caused by underwater obstacles. A strong offshore wind narrowed the eastern assault beaches, which delayed clearing them. |

*Source*: Neville G. Brown, "Weather," in *The D-Day Encyclopedia*, eds. David G. Chandler and James Lawton Collins (New York: Simon and Schuster, 1994), 587–89; Sir Max Hastings, *Overlord: D-Day and the Battle for Normandy* (New York: Simon & Schuster), Kindle edition, 166.

ply said, "I am quite positive we must give the order. I don't like it, but there it is. I don't see how we can do anything else."[1] Generals and admirals rushed from the room—the show was on.

Across the Channel, the Germans looked at the low scudding clouds and the waves breaking hard against the anti-landing obstacles along the beaches. The Allies had rolled up most of the Axis weather observation stations north and west of England, the spawning ground of northwestern France's coastal weather. Lack of this data crippled the forecast of Stagg's German counterpart, *Luftwaffe* Colonel Professor Walter Stöbe. Now he worked mainly from local observations and the occasional clandestine U-boat report. Stöbe's information was insufficient to spot the potential temporary good weather period to come, and he predicted bad weather to continue unabated for several days.

This faulty forecast was briefed on June 5 to the staff of *Generalfeldmarschall* Gert von Rundstedt at *OB West* (*Oberbewfehlshaber West*) in Paris. Von Rundstedt was Ike's counterpart and commander of all German forces in France and the Low Countries. The forecast was also sent to the *Luftwaffe* and *Kriegsmarine* headquarters and to *Generalfeldmarschall* Erwin Rommel's *Heersgruppe B* headquarters at La Roche-Guyon, halfway between Paris and the Normandy coast. Under von Rundstedt's tenuous guidance, Rommel commanded the *Atlantik Wall* from Brittany to Holland with the *7th Armée* in Brittany and Lower Normandy, the *15th Armée* across the Seine in the Upper Normandy and Pas-de-Calais area, and the *LXXXVIII Armeekorps* in Holland.

The June storm ruined Rommel's rose garden, but there was a certain misery in the weather that promised a holiday from the invasion threat. The Channel was so rough that *Luftwaffe* and *Kriegsmarine* patrols were canceled. The vicious S-boats, the fangs of the coastal *Kriegsmarine* that so long troubled Allied naval operations in the Channel were kept in port. These canceled patrols would not spot the vanguard of the approaching Allied armada, the Allied minesweeper force that reduced a major obstacle to the landing.

During periods of bad weather in France, it was normal for the RAF Bomber Command and US Eighth Air Force to resume bombing strategic targets in Germany. When visibility over France allowed, German railroad, airfield, V-1 missile facilities, and other infrastructure targets were attacked. At least a hundred fighters of *Jagdgeschwader 26* (Fighter Wing 26) were withdrawn from *Luftwaffe* forward bases to counter anticipated daylight *Viermot* (Allied four-engine bomber) attacks on Germany. Lately, when the weather was bad in France the *Viermot* attacks intensified.

The *7th Armée* seized the bad-weather opportunity to schedule its senior commanders for a *Kriegspiel* (wargame) at Rennes for 6 June. Rennes is almost 100 miles by road from the Normandy beaches. The wargame scenario was a hypothetical Allied invasion of Normandy, with the landings preceded by a massive paratroop assault on the Cotentin Peninsula. Many of the generals, ignoring orders to the contrary, departed their headquarters on the afternoon of 5 June for an evening of cognac and old comrades. They would be absent from their command posts the next day, D-Day. After the French Resistance executed Plan Green during the night of 5 June, all telecommunications from Rennes and the other headquarters were cut.

Rommel left for a quick motor trip home for his wife's birthday, gray size 5½ suede shoes handmade in Paris on the seat next to him. Frau Rommel's birthday was June 6, and she had priority over any wargame for the Desert Fox. Later, Rommel planned to meet with the *Führer* to continue his quiet duel with von Rundstedt for Hitler's ear.[2]

It was Rommel who named the pivotal first twenty-four-hour period of the assault *Die langsamer Tag* (the longest day), and he missed it. Before he could return from Germany, the invasion had begun and the Allies were ashore. Eisenhower, with the impetus of history and a good weather report, simply called it "D-Day."

To delay again, Ike would have had to wait for the next proper conjunction of moonlight and tides. D-Day would have been rescheduled for 19 June—coincident with the worst Channel storm in fifty years. It was a storm that would have grounded Allied airpower, smashed the landing craft, and blown the paratroopers out to sea.

It was that close.

## CHAPTER FIFTEEN

# Unfinished Business

In May 1943, the Allies achieved a major victory in the North Atlantic. Forty-one U-boats were sunk, causing the Germans to withdraw their surviving submarines from the area. Allied shipping losses declined to an acceptable level in June, although they rose again in July 1943 during the invasion of Sicily (Operation HUSKY). In September 1942, 102 ships had been lost to U-boats. A year later, in September 1943, losses declined to eleven ships for the month even as convoys grew, bringing larger and more frequent Operation BOLERO forces into England.[1]

Antisubmarine efforts provided BOLERO, the force buildup from North America into England in preparation for D-Day, with an open "highway" along which hundreds of thousands of troops traveled. By May 1944, Allied antisubmarine air and naval forces had gutted the German *Ubootwaffe* (submarine force); 807 of the 1,150 U-boats launched had been sunk, and 85 percent of the crews were dead, POWs, or missing.[2] Allied shipping losses on the BOLERO routes declined from fifty-seven in May 1943 to five in May 1944.[3]

The U-boats based in France were controlled by *Befehlshaber der U-Boote* (Commanding Admiral Submarines), abbreviated *BdU*. In January 1943, *Grossadmiral* Karl Dönitz replaced Erich Raeder as *Oberbefehlshaber der Kriegsmarine*, commander in chief of the German Navy. He retained personal control of the German U-boat force through its headquarters, *Befehlshaber der Unterseeboote (BdU)*.

All operational orders for German submarines came directly from Dönitz via *BdU* radio communications. This included the submarines based at the French ports of Brest, Lorient, St. Nazaire, La Pallice/La Rochelle, and Bordeaux. All had hardened concrete pens that so far had defied Allied bombing. The submarines represented the most significant naval threat to the D-Day landing.

RAF Coastal Command, in conjunction with Royal Navy escort warships, had established domination of the seas between the United Kingdom and France and the waters of the eastern North Atlantic. Coastal Command antisubmarine patrols constantly covered the Bay of Biscay, along whose coast the German bases were located.

By March 1944, ULTRA message decryption and photoreconnaissance indicated that the *Kriegsmarine* was building up its Biscay submarine force with new

Figure 15.1. Liberty ships—favorite victims of U-boats US COAST GUARD

construction and diverting submarines from their normal patrols. A similar massing of U-boats in southern Norway was designated *Gruppe Mitte* (Middle Group), while the Biscay boats were designated *Gruppe Landwirt* (Group Farmer).[4]

Just before D-Day, twenty antisubmarine warfare (ASW) aircraft, including Sunderlands, Wellingtons, Liberators, and Halifaxes, established day and night Operation CORK patrols between Ireland and Brittany. The objective of the CORK patrols was to limit the number of U-boats anywhere in the English Channel, reducing the submarine risk to the huge Allied armada destined for Normandy. Both *Gruppe Mitte* and *Landwirt* had the range to enter the Channel from the west. The eastern Channel had been closed to U-boats by minefields since 1940.

Allied aircraft and other forces were able to stop all U-boats not equipped with a snorkel, a device that allowed a U-boat to run its diesel engines underwater. Since non-snorkel boats would need to run on the surface to recharge their batteries, they could be detected in daytime by visual sightings and at night by ASV (air-to-surface vessel) radar.

Some twenty-two such U-boats were caught on the surface and seven attacked. Two subs were sunk and four more so heavily damaged that they withdrew to their bases in western France. On the night of June 7, the day after the initial landings, a Liberator of Coastal Command's 224 Squadron sunk U-373 and U-629 within fifteen minutes.[5] Other forces dealt with the few snorkel-equipped boats that did

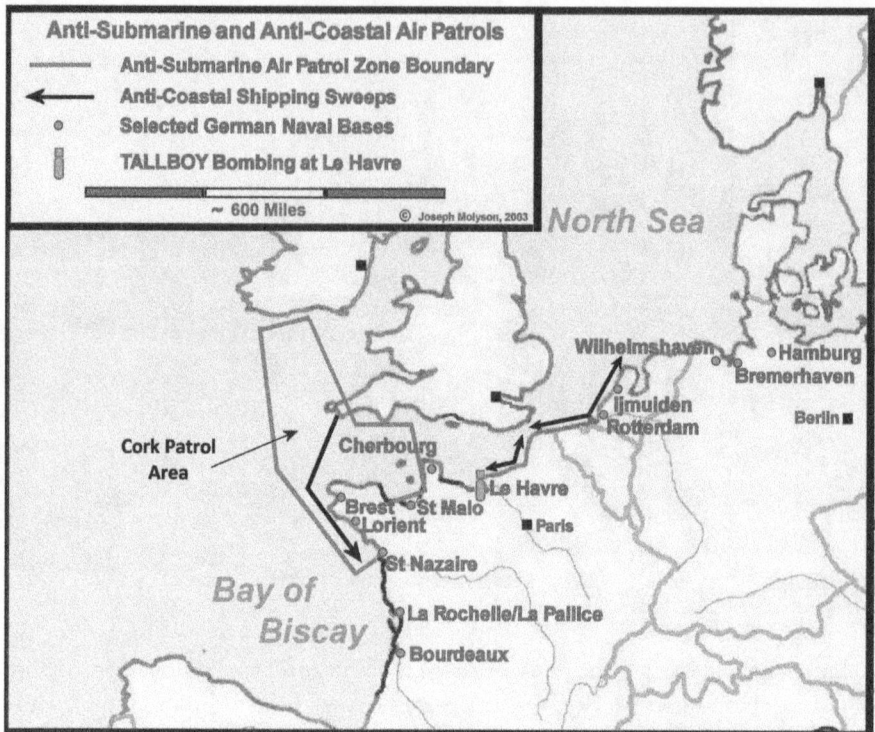

Map 15.1. Antisubmarine and Anti-Coastal Patrols during NEPTUNE–OVERLORD
MOLYSON[6]

penetrate the screen.[7] During June, Allied forces in the Channel sunk U-767, U-971, U-1191, U-269, and U-988.[8]

## THE HEAVIES

Complementing the war against the U-boats was another against the *Kriegsmarine* surface navy. By March 1944, Allied ULTRA message decryption, naval patrols, and air reconnaissance monitored the activity of the remnants of the German heavy warship force. These were armored ships larger than destroyers, mounting batteries of heavy guns. They were designed to raid Allied commerce far out at sea, and until the end of 1941 they were a significant threat to the Atlantic sea lanes.

Based at Brest on the tip of the Brittany Peninsula, they had easy access to the open sea. As the *Luftwaffe* in France was significantly reduced to provide airpower on the Eastern Front and the Mediterranean, the air defense of the port was in the hands of a thousand or more flak guns. Despite the defenses, brave RAF aircrews repeatedly damaged the big ships with bombs and torpedoes. By February 1942, battlecruisers *Scharnhorst* and *Gneisenau* and heavy cruiser *Prinz Eugen* were forced to withdraw to Germany. *Scharnhorst* hit an air-delivered mine, which delayed its availability until summer.

*Gneisenau* also hit an air-delivered mine and, like *Scharnhorst*, went into repair on return to Germany. Before the ship could be readied for sea, it was hit and permanently disabled during an RAF bombing raid. *Scharnhorst* did not make it to Norway until March 1943, joining the battleship *Tirpitz* and pocket battleship *Lützow*.

All the big German ships based in northern Norway had the mission of threatening Allied convoys traveling to the Soviet Union via the Arctic Ocean. By November 1943, only *Scharnhorst* and *Tirpitz* remained. Most of the other surviving big ships had returned to Germany for repairs, for training, or to provide naval gunfire support in the Baltic. In December 1943, after attempting an operation in the Arctic, *Scharnhorst* was sunk.

Only *Tirpitz*, one of the most powerful battleships in the world, remained in its snug harbor at Alta Fjord in far northern Norway. The battleship had been repeatedly but not fatally damaged by air attacks. In September 1943, however, *Tirpitz* was crippled by British midget submarines. Repairs took months, and by April 1944 she was ready for high-speed trials. On April 3, the Royal Navy struck first. A major airstrike by forty Barracuda carrier-based dive bombers was launched from two fleet and four escort carriers.

Figure 15.2. Fairey Barracuda carrier-based divebomber NATIONAL ARCHIVES

One RN aircraft was lost to flak, but the bombs severely damaged the ship's superstructure and killed over one hundred crewmen. Among the more than 300 men wounded was its captain, *Kapitän zur See* Hans Meyer. Two of the main gun turrets were lightly damaged, and both Ar 196 spotter floatplanes were obliterated. Other hits penetrated the hull, causing more serious damage. A near miss disabled the starboard engine, and firefighters contaminated the boiler feedwater with salt water pumped from the fjord. By D-Day the ship was repaired, but it was doubtful she would sail south toward overwhelming Allied air and naval strength. Carefully watched, *Tirpitz* remained in her Alta Fjord lair—removed as a threat to D-Day.[9]

# Chapter Sixteen

# The Slapton Sands Disaster

The US 4th Infantry Division as an organization was a veteran of World War I, but its men were green and its leadership untested. After years of Stateside training, the 4th traveled from the United States to Britain over waters relatively free of U-boats, thanks to the previous efforts of Allied air and sea forces. It arrived safely in Bristol in January 1944. Like the other US ground forces, it was moved to an assembly area near the southwest coast of Britain to prepare for the invasion.

Unlike the Allied divisions arriving from the Mediterranean, the unit arriving from the United States had seen no combat in WWII. D-Day would be the most ambitious amphibious assault in history, and the fate of Western Europe rested upon its success. The British secretly established a practice invasion area at Slapton Sands

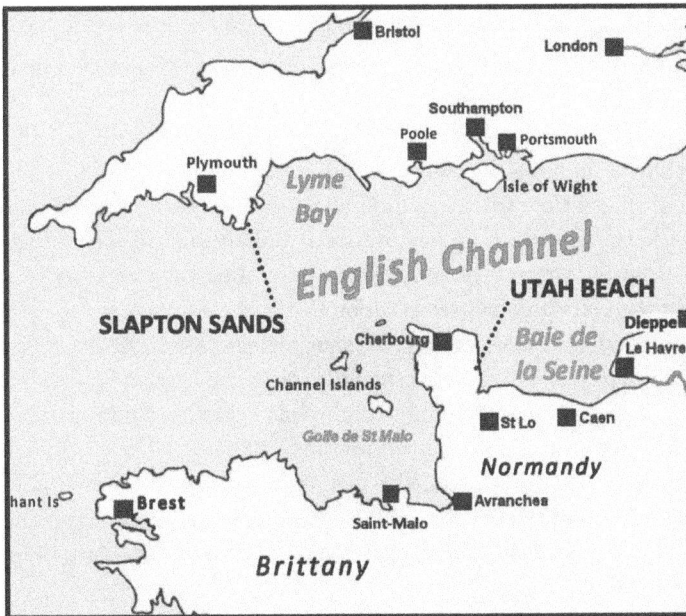

Map 16.1. Bristol, Lyme Bay, and Cherbourg MOLYSON

in Lyme Bay, close to the ports from which the five Allied seaborne assault divisions would embark for France. Over 3,000 locals were evacuated from the security zone. The troops were to be trained to load aboard their landing ships and assault practice beaches that were as close to a match of the Normandy beaches as possible. Live ammunition for both troops and ships was ordered.

## EXERCISE TIGER

Exercise TIGER was a series of practice landings for the 4th Infantry Division, whose assembly area in Devon was close to its intended embarkation ports of Plymouth and Brixton. The selected beach for TIGER was Slapton Sands, and it was here the 4th Infantry Division would train for the assault on Utah Beach, on the eastern coast of the Cotentin Peninsula in western Normandy. Throughout the winter and early spring, American soldiers and sailors learned the craft of amphibious landings against an entrenched enemy. The enemy, however, would not wait until D-Day to strike the Americans.

Beginning on April 22, marshaling and combat loading were practiced. Combat loading involved placing the troops aboard in the reverse order that they would leave the ship during the actual attack. Men were fully armed and their weapons locked and loaded. Vehicles carried full fuel tanks and were waterproofed so they could drive through relatively shallow water onto the beach. By the morning of April 27, the tank landing ships (LSTs) were carrying the main elements of the 4th Infantry Division from Portland and Brixton, cruising around Lyme Bay to simulate a voyage across the Channel.

Overhead, RAF day and night fighters supervised by radar bored endless tunnels in the sky, continuing the vigil that had begun in 1939. They must both protect the men and ships below from *Luftwaffe* attack and, if possible, perform reconnaissance. A picket of destroyers and patrol boats covered the wide entry to Lyme Bay, hoping to deter or intercept German naval forces. This all worked well in daytime, but at night the German Navy's coastal forces had the advantage.

Off Cherbourg, nearest of the German S-boat (*Schnellboot*) bases, a second patrol line monitored any German attempt to leave the base and cross the Channel toward Britain. S-boats were armed with torpedoes, fast, and hard to hit with gunfire. They were small and unlit, almost invisible to the eye. The rocky French coast made them hard to spot on radar. The British called the same craft "E-boats," for "enemy boats." A uniquely capable craft, the Germans had packed half the torpedo firepower of a U-boat into a craft that could attain over 40 knots (46 miles per hour) in open water.

Figure 16.1. *S-111* was captured by British forces in 1941. NATIONAL ARCHIVES

Somehow, between April 25 and April 27, one or more furtive German reconnaissance planes spotted one of these practice convoys on Lyme Bay. German signals intelligence, listening to chatter on GI radios and ship-to-ship transmissions, confirmed something was up. Adding to the possible information leak, there was a so-called "friendly fire" incident when some ships late for the practice assault forced the admiral in charge to delay the landing. Unfortunately, some of the first assault wave didn't get the word and were hit by Allied naval gunfire on the beach. The limited information available after the war did not include the number of casualties, although postwar writers speculated numbers in the hundreds.[1] In any case, the exercise had to continue because the time until the invasion was short.

On April 27–28, in darkness, the eight LSTs of convoy T-4 carried the combat engineers and other special troops of the US 4th Infantry Division toward their practice assault. This force was moving east along the Channel coast toward Lyme Bay, on whose western side Slapton Sands lay. Leading T-4 in a single-file formation was corvette HMS *Azalea*. The route was designed to simulate the time it would take to reach Utah Beach on D-Day (see map 16.2). A second escort, destroyer HMS *Scimitar*, had been accidentally rammed by an American landing craft earlier that day and remained in port under repair. No one thought to replace her.[2]

The news of the convoy was flashed by a German patrol aircraft or a signal monitoring unit to the German Naval Command West headquarters in Paris, which in turn alerted its S-boat force at Cherbourg, France. Apparently guided by

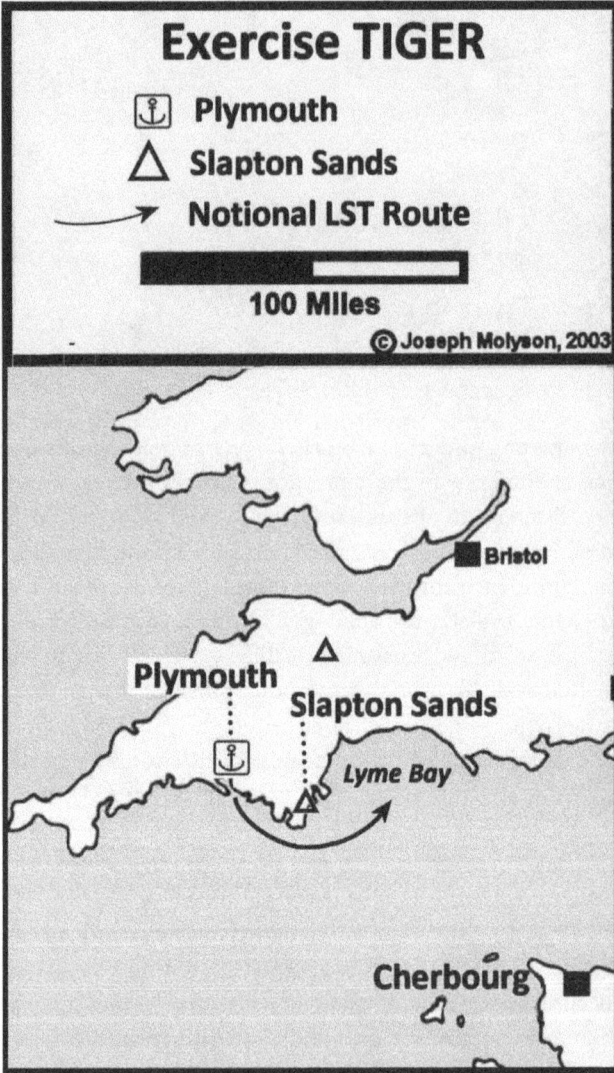

**Exercise TIGER**

⚓ Plymouth

△ Slapton Sands

➤ Notional LST Route

100 Miles

© Joseph Molyson, 2003

Bristol

△

Plymouth

Slapton Sands

⚓

Lyme Bay

Cherbourg

Map 16.2. Exercise TIGER MOLYSON

Figure 16.2. LSTs on Omaha Beach, a favorite target of the S-boats US ARMY MILITARY HISTORY CENTER

German intelligence, having avoided the British motor torpedo boats off Cherbourg, nine S-boats approached the convoy against the background of the dark French coast to the south. How far they got into the bay is uncertain, and their exact route is unknown.[3]

Single escort *Azalea* was overmatched by the approaching craft. The first German torpedo, fired from *S-130* hit LST 507. More impacts followed. At the end of the engagement, the S-boats escape unscathed while two American LSTs were sinking and a third was crippled with its stern blown off. Some of the S-boats apparently strafed the LSTs with their antiaircraft guns, adding to the carnage. Water temperature was 42°F and daylight was hours away. Almost 750 men were killed, either floating lifeless in the water or trapped in the sunken ships. Many more were wounded and either in the water or on the surviving ships.[4]

Ten American officers holding BIGOT clearances, indicating that they had been briefed on the plans for the actual invasion, were lost in the Channel. An intensive search of the temporary morgues and water found all ten bodies, ensuring that none of the men were in enemy hands.[5] SHAEF chose not to publicize the disaster; radio discipline was reinforced. The day and night patrols against the S-boats were intensified, and mines were laid to threaten the boats as they left their ports.

The 4th Infantry Division would land at Utah Beach on D-Day and suffer fewer casualties than it had in Exercise TIGER. Fortunately, potentially bad weather in the Channel canceled the S-boat patrols from Cherbourg and Le Havre on the eve of D-Day.

CHAPTER SEVENTEEN

# Defending the Coast

Prior to, on, and after D-Day, RAF Coastal Command scoured the French coastline from the Loire Estuary to Holland. These patrols deterred but did not eliminate German coastal operations, and small German warships remained a problem for months after the landing. The moving targets of Coastal Command, the German surface forces, were controlled by *MGK West*.

Early in the war, Allied escort vessels (destroyers, frigates, sloops, and corvettes) were desperately needed to protect vital convoys crossing the Atlantic. To replace them in home waters, the Royal Navy built motor torpedo boats (MTBs) and motor gunboats (MGBs) to counter German coastal warships. The MTB and MGB vessels were collectively called Royal Navy "light forces." These small warships provided a night force to supplement RAF Coastal Command.

## BATTLE IN THE NARROW SEAS

The Royal Air Force (RAF) and Royal Navy (RN) began fighting German coastal forces soon after the German occupation of France in the summer of 1940. At first it was the potential German invasion of Britain that caused RAF Bomber Command to attack small *Kriegsmarine* warships and barges in French ports along the Pas-de-Calais. After German failure in the Battle of Britain, both sides settled in for a long war in the Narrow Seas between Britain and continental Europe. Along the Channel coast, concrete shelters were built for the S-boats and other small warships of the *Kriegsmarine* coastal forces.[1]

The RAF supported the RN as it attempted to control the Channel, sometimes at great cost. The RAF Coastal and Bomber Commands dominated the daytime hours over the Channel. RAF aircrew assigned to Coastal Command fighting in daylight were just as likely to be lost as their brethren in Bomber Command fighting at night over Germany. By February 1942, air attacks in Brittany and in the Channel had driven all German warships larger than destroyers into northern Norway and Germany. British coastal batteries were a threat to all German vessels passing through the Strait of Dover.

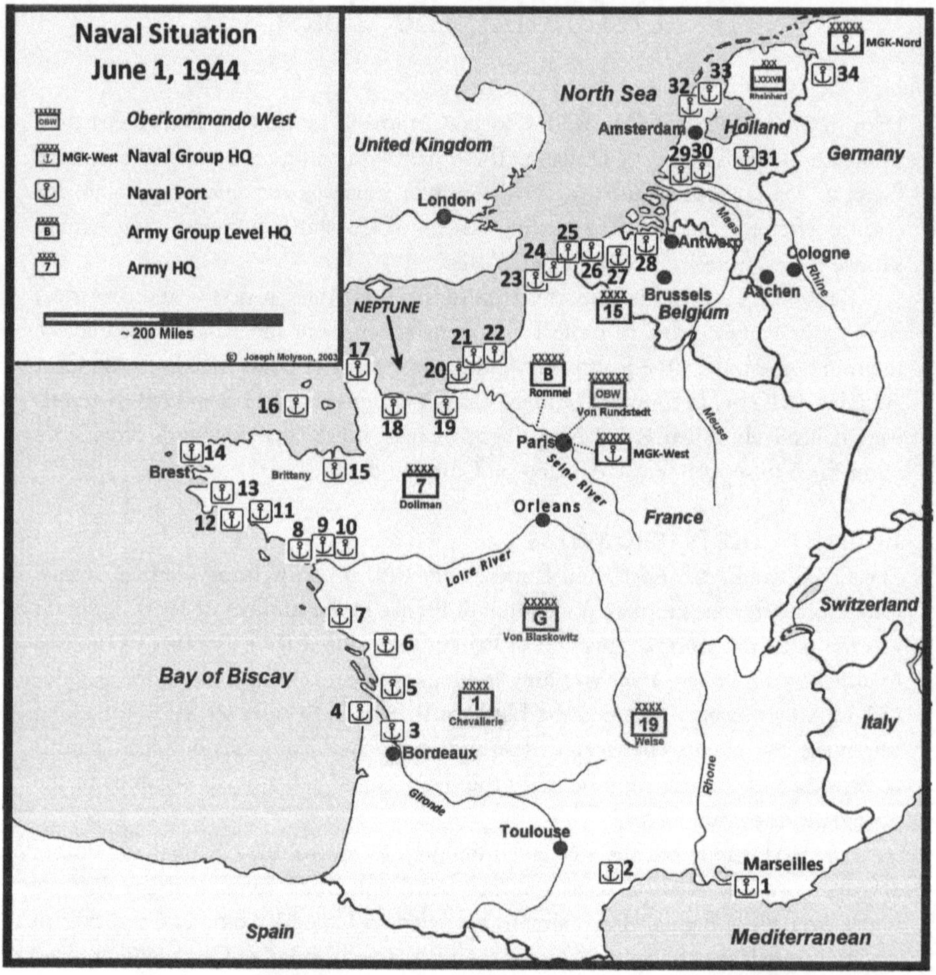

Map 17.1. Naval Situation in France, May–June 1944. (See facing page for key to *Kriegsmarine* port numbers.) MOLYSON AFTER TARRANT[2]

| Number on Map 17.1 | Port |
|---|---|
| None | Bordeaux (city is labeled) |
| None | Paris (city is labeled) |
| 1 | Marseille, France |
| 2 | Languedoc (Sete/Port-Vendres), France |
| 3 | Pauillac, France |
| 4 | Gironde (Pointe de Grave), France |
| 5 | Royan, France |
| 6 | La Rochelle / La Pallice, France |
| 7 | Les Sables-d'Olonne, France |
| 8 | Saint-Nazaire, France |
| 9 | Paimboeuf, France |
| 10 | Nantes-Couëron, France |
| 11 | Lorient, France |
| 12 | Concarneau, France |
| 13 | Bénodet, France |
| 14 | Brest, France |
| 15 | Saint-Malo, France |
| 16 | Channel Islands |
| 17 | Cherbourg, France |
| 18 | Isigny-sur-Mer / Port-en-Bessin, France |
| 19 | Ouistreham, France |
| 20 | Le Havre, France, and nearby Honfleur |
| 21 | Fécamp, France |
| 22 | Dieppe, France |
| 23 | Boulogne-sur-Mer, France |
| 24 | Calais, France |
| 25 | Dunkirk, France |
| 26 | Ostend, Belgium |
| 27 | Brugge, Belgium |
| 28 | Terneuzen, Netherlands |
| 29 | Vlaardingen, Netherlands |
| 30 | Rotterdam, Netherlands |
| 31 | Utrecht-Oudenrijn, Netherlands |
| 32 | IJmuiden, Netherlands |
| 33 | Den Helder, Netherlands |
| 34 | Bremerhaven, Germany (controlled by *MGK Nord*) |

By March 1943, the entire RAF effort had sunk only 107 German coastal vessels by strafing, rockets, or bombing. This cost 648 RAF aircraft, or about 4.2 RAF aircraft per ship sunk. In contrast, RAF air-dropped mines accounted for 369 vessels, with 329 mine-laying aircraft lost. Airdropping mines by RAF aircraft was code-named "Gardening," and the air-dropped mines themselves were termed "Vegetables."[3] This worked out to about 1.1 aircraft per vessel sunk, or roughly about one-quarter of the losses of direct attacks.

Even after the advent of specialized RAF "strike wings" in April 1943, mines were the best way to sink *Kriegsmarine* coastal forces.[4] Because of the extensive use of British mines emplaced by both aircraft and surface vessels, the *Kriegsmarine* was forced to expand and maintain an extensive minesweeping force. This detracted from its other coastal missions, including laying its own mines.[5] The Germans also laid aircraft- and ship-delivered mines, so minesweeping became a major RN mission in the coastal seas. As the war went on, improvements and modification of fuses produced mines that could be detonated by contact, pressure, or sound.

German coastal operations were generally conducted at night to reduce the threat from RAF Coastal Command aircraft. RN light forces followed the *Kriegsmarine* into the darkness. Most German vessels were generously equipped with light and medium antiaircraft guns because it was impossible to restrict all operations to hours of darkness. Besides light 20mm guns mounted in pairs or fours, the Germans embarked 75-, 88-, and 105-millimeter *flak* weapons.[6] These were effective against both RAF aircraft and RN vessels.

Like the campaign against the U-boats, Coastal Command's anti-coastal operations increased in intensity as NEPTUNE approached, joined by available American aircraft bombing *Kriegsmarine* harbors and support facilities in France, Belgium, and Holland. The RAF provided the primary air threat to the Channel and Biscay coasts and German units operating offshore. The French Mediterranean coast was covered by Allied air forces operating from Corsica, Italy, and North Africa.

## NAVAL GROUP WEST

Admiral Theodor Krancke at *MGK West* had three main missions. He was responsible for defending the U-boat bases from air and naval attack and for providing surface escorts for the submarines entering and leaving the often-beleaguered ports. Krancke's forces also had to maintain and protect German coastal convoys. Finally, he had to defend the coasts of France, Belgium, and the Netherlands from Allied landings. For these purposes, he had various surface vessels and coastal defense guns. After D-Day, he was also assigned a midget submarine force.

Figure 17.1. American B-26s hit the *Kriegsmarine* base at IJmuiden, Netherlands, March 26, 1944. AIR FORCE HISTORICAL RESEARCH AGENCY

Under *MGK West* were three regional commanders: *Admiral Kanalküste*, who controlled the Channel coast of France, Belgium, and the Netherlands; *Admiral Atlantikküste*, who controlled the Channel Islands and the Brittany coast from St. Malo south to the Spanish border; and *Admiral französischen Südküste*, who controlled the French Mediterranean coast. In these three regions, *MGK West* had no fewer than thirty-three port facilities of various sizes. Each regional commander controlled these ports and other shore installations, but operational orders for *Kriegsmarine* coast defense batteries and surface naval vessels were issued directly from *MGK West*.

## ONSHORE DEFENSES
The German Navy provided significant numbers of antiaircraft guns to defend its critical facilities, especially ports. The German Navy also operated a series of coastal defense radars, which were heavily attacked before D-Day. Enough of these installations were allowed to survive so that the Allied deception operations on D-Day could be detected.[7]

Naval guns were installed on the coast by the *Kriegsmarine* to provide direct fire on targets offshore. This required the construction of large concrete protective structures. Some navy installations had revolving armored turrets for the guns. The army installed their batteries under heavy camouflage behind the coast for less-accurate indirect fire on the beaches.

The German Navy had difficulties in providing enough coastal artillery to meet Hitler's requirements for the *Atlantik Wall.* The army supplied supplementary guns, but much of their ordnance was obsolete and their crews were not as proficient at hitting ships as navy crews. Army gun positions did not have as much protection as their naval counterparts. A 210 cm (8.3-inch) naval gun position at St. Marcouf, behind Utah Beach, survived bombardment to sink destroyer USS *Corry* on D-Day. It was eventually overrun by US ground troops.[8]

## FLOTILLAS AND VESSELS

In both the German and Royal navies, small warships were commissioned in groups known as *flotillas* (German *Flotille*). Like combat aircraft in squadrons and groups, the vessels in a flotilla were similar in design and capability and fought collectively. Flotilla leaders also evolved tactics to avoid "friendly fire" between flotilla members in the confusion of a battle. A flotilla was normally based at a single port.

*MGK West* operated attack flotillas of destroyers (*Zerstörer*), torpedo boats (*Torpedoboote* or *T-boote*), and fast boats (*Schnellboote* or *S-boote*). All three were heavily armed with torpedoes and antiaircraft cannon. The *Zerstörer* and *Torpedoboote* also were both armed with 4-inch or larger naval cannon. The torpedo boats appeared similar to small destroyers or British corvettes. They were significantly slower than the S-boats but more seaworthy. Yet it was the small but powerful S-boats that struck the American LSTs so disastrously in Lyme Bay. The *S-boote* was similar in size and appearance to the American PT boat.

The German *Zerstörer* and *Torpedoboote* based on the Biscay coast often threatened Allied antisubmarine groups entering the bay. They and other German coastal forces escorted German blockade runners returning from overseas supply missions. The French Mediterranean region operated only small minesweepers and submarine chasers. Their mission was to keep Marseille and the smaller French ports open.

*MGK West* also operated defensive or "security" vessels. These included a variety of minesweepers to keep the ports clear. They were also used to lay offensive minefields in enemy waters and defensive minefields to protect coastlines. Types of minesweepers included the heavy minesweepers (*Speerbrecher,* or *Sp-boote*); the medium minesweepers (*Minensuchboot,* or *M-boots*); and the smaller motor minesweepers (*Räumboot,* or *R-boote*).

The *Kriegsmarine* mined the English Channel using aircraft and various coastal warships. Minelaying by day was hazardous because of RAF Coastal Command, which attacked the minelayers continuously. A plan to rapidly lay *Blitzsperren* (lightning barrier) on warning of invasion provided little deterrence to the invaders. Some minefields in this program were laid, but not opposite the actual invasion beaches. The first Allied ships to approach Normandy were minesweepers, which cleared mine-free lanes as necessary.[9]

Various trawlers and other craft used for patrol were called outpost boats (*Vorpostenboote*, or *Vp-boote*). Appropriately armed submarine chasers (*Unterseebootjäger*, or *Uj-boote*) were found at some ports. The Germans also armed self-propelled barges with conventional land artillery, called artillery carriers (*Artillerieträger*, or *AT-boote*) or artillery ferries (*Artilleriefährprahm*, or *AT-boote*). Heavily armed with flak guns, all were used to escort German convoys moving along the coast.

Flotillas were assigned to the various ports and coasts based on need and operating environment. The Bay of Biscay, an extension of the North Atlantic, demanded more seaworthy craft than the Channel or Mediterranean coasts. The vessels assigned to the Channel coast, in close proximity to the strike wings of Coastal Command, had more antiaircraft guns per vessel weight than the other coasts.

# CHAPTER EIGHTEEN

# Water's Edge

Channel weather prevented the relatively small craft of the German coastal forces from patrolling in the early days of June 1944. They missed both Eisenhower's false start of June 4 and the invasion fleet on June 5–6. Very early on June 6, German coastal radar stations began to report electronic jamming in the Channel to Naval Group West. The German Army reported paratroopers landing at several points in Normandy. These warnings were in turn flashed to German naval bases all along the coast from Brest to Holland. *Vizeadmiral* Krancke at *MGK West* sent out the message "Mass landing in the Seine Estuary" at 03:00[1] (see map 17.1). Meanwhile, the Allied armada settled into its anchorage and unloading zone off the assault beaches. The anchorage, and the convoy routes from Britain's south coast running through a route convergence area called the "Spout," would become a magnet for German *Schnellboote* in the days ahead. (see map 18.1).

Before the Allied dawn bombardment began, *9.S-bootsflotille* (Ninth Fast Boat Flotilla) sent S-boats from Cherbourg east into the Baie de la Seine. They spotted the approaching fleet and fired a long-range torpedo salvo before returning to harbor to reload. German coastal batteries on the French coast came under fire at dawn. The *5.S-bootsflotille* emerged from Cherbourg in early daylight and were driven back by Allied fighter-bombers.[2] Fire from the German gunboats of the *6.Artillerieträger-Flotille* in Port-en-Bessin was quickly silenced by Allied warships. The port was captured the next day by Royal Marines, with air support from three squadrons of RAF Typhoon fighter-bombers.[3]

## THE TORPEDO BOATS

At Le Havre, shortly before 05:00 on June 6, *Korvettenkapitän* Heinrich Hoffman led three T-boats of the *5.T-bootsflotille* out of the harbor before dawn. Accompanying them were an unknown number of *Vorpostenboote* patrol boats of *15.Vp-Flotille*. Heading west, they encountered the smoke screen being laid by RAF Boston bombers to protect the invasion fleet from German coastal batteries.

Three *Kriegsmarine* ships, the *T28*, *Jaguar*, and *Möwe*, penetrated the screen and encountered the largest naval armada ever assembled. They saw the battleships,

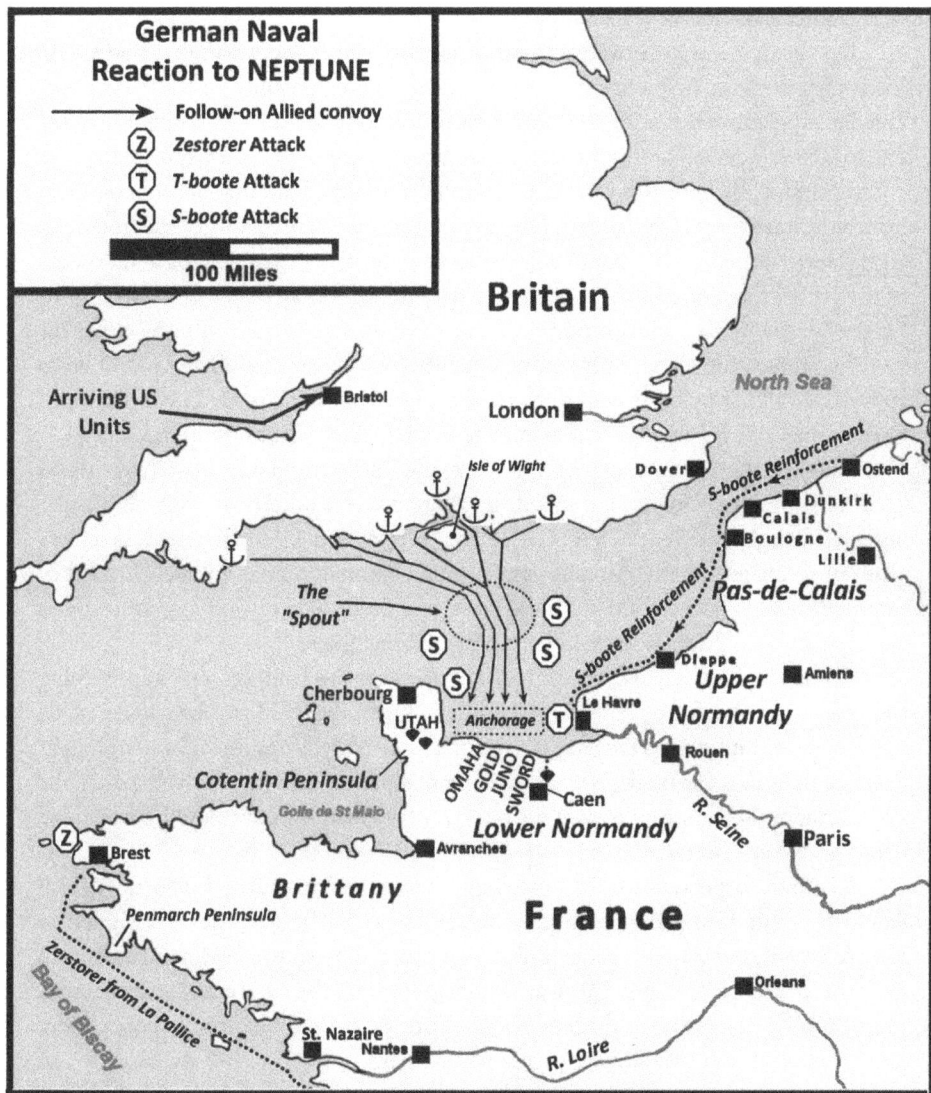

**German Naval Reaction to NEPTUNE**

→ Follow-on Allied convoy
Ⓩ Zestorer Attack
Ⓣ T-boote Attack
Ⓢ S-boote Attack

100 Miles

Britain

North Sea

Arriving US Units

Bristol

London

Isle of Wight

Dover

S-boote Reinforcement

Ostend

Dunkirk

Calais

Boulogne

Lille

The "Spout"

S-boote Reinforcement

Pas-de-Calais

Dieppe

Amiens

Upper Normandy

Cherbourg

UTAH

Anchorage

Le Havre

Rouen

Cotentin Peninsula

Golfe de St Malo

OMAHA
GOLD
JUNO
SWORD

Caen

R. Seine

Paris

Lower Normandy

Ⓩ Brest

Avranches

Brittany

France

Penmarch Peninsula

Zerstorer from La Pallice

Orleans

Bay of Biscay

St. Nazaire

Nantes

R. Loire

Map 18.1. German Immediate Naval Surface Force Reaction to NEPTUNE MOLYSON

cruisers, and destroyers screening the amphibious landings on Sword Beach further west. It was a David-versus-Goliath scenario. Some might say it was an "impossible situation"; others, a "target-rich environment." Courage is a matter of attitude, opportunity a matter of perception.

The weather was fully overcast, with winds to 7 knots and waves up to 6 feet. At 0531, torpedo boat *T28* was strafed by an Allied fighter, possibly an RAF Typhoon. This lightly damaged one of her loaded torpedo tubes but not the torpedo inside.[4] The low clouds probably saved the German warships from other aircraft attacks.

Battleship *Warspite* was some 7,000 yards away and beginning its firing on German positions ashore. Undeterred, Hoffman ordered an immediate attack, unloading an eighteen-torpedo salvo from his three torpedo boats. The battleships and cruisers of the Allied force turned their secondary batteries on them, saving the bigger guns for the beach. As they ran for home, one of the patrol boats (*V1509*) was either hit by Allied return fire or ran over a mine at 0548. It began sinking. Other patrol boats approached the crippled vessel to rescue the crew. Hoffman's torpedo boats temporarily turned toward the Allied warships to draw fire away from the rescue effort.

By 0610, the rescue was partially successful, but other patrol boats were damaged and some crewmen were killed or wounded. A rescue float with eight men observed clinging to it was left. On return to harbor, a German rescue boat was sent out to retrieve them. Aircraft continued to harass Hoffman's vessels until they returned to Le Havre by 0648. There were two dead on the surviving vessels and twelve wounded. Twenty-six men were reported missing.[5]

Hoffman's near suicidal attack had no effect on the landing craft approaching the beach, but the Royal Navy bombardment force off Le Havre had losses. One torpedo passed near the *Warspite*. *Warspite* had been hit during the 1943 landing at Salerno, Italy, by a German *Fritz X* anti-ship missile, requiring extensive repairs. She still carried unhealed scars of that encounter. A torpedo hit now would have ended her World War II service.[6]

A second torpedo narrowly missed another battleship, HMS *Ramilles*. A third would have hit HMS *Largs*, the flagship of Force S (the naval force assigned to Sword Beach), but an emergency full-astern order allowed the German torpedo to pass just in front of the bow. This was fortunate for both the crew and the invasion. A fourth torpedo hit the free Norwegian destroyer *Svenner*, exploding its boiler room and breaking it into two sinking pieces.

There were thirty-four dead, but the remainder of the crew was rescued. A second destroyer, HMS *Virago*, would have been hit, but the torpedo ran out of fuel just before it impacted. With over 650 warships available, these losses were insignificant except to those sailors who suffered them. None of the amphibious transport ships or landing craft were hit.

The tiny German force returned to Le Havre. The other major Allied naval losses on D-Day (two destroyers and one LST) were from German coastal batteries and sea mines.[7] Like the *Luftwaffe*, the *Kriegsmarine* had been smothered by numerical superiority. The S-boats and other coastal forces hunkered down in their well-defended harbors and pens and continued to harass but not seriously impede the Allied fleet.

## BISCAY REACTION

In addition to Cherbourg and Le Havre, *Vizeadmiral* Krancke's invasion alert was passed to the *Admiral Atlantikküste* and thus to the Biscay bases. Three destroyers of *8. Zerstörer-Flotille* were ordered from the La Pallice anchorage to regroup at the port of Brest, from which it could sortie into the Channel in search of Allied transports. Its commander was *Kapitän zur Zee* Theodore von Bechtolsheim. These were the largest surviving German warships west of the Netherlands.

Unfortunately for von Bechtolsheim, the orders were intercepted by Allied code breakers and passed to RAF Coastal Command. A later decryption revealed their exact destination and time of arrival. At 20:30 hours on D-Day, 40 miles southwest of St. Nazaire, the German ships were pounced on by thirty-one RAF Beaufighters and Mosquitos (No. 404, 248, and 144 Squadrons). The flyers killed three German sailors and wounded twenty-one. The ships' superstructures were riddled with holes. The attack was repeated just off Penmarch Peninsula south of Brest.

During the night, the German ships reached the safety of Brest harbor and its heavy antiaircraft defenses. Necessary repairs and replenishment of antiaircraft ammunition began immediately, and von Bechtolsheim's force was reinforced by torpedo boat *T24* from *4. Tbootsflotille*, already at Brest. All this delayed the German counterattack. Their orders were to hit the Allied follow-on convoys supporting the landings.

The four German ships left Brest and moved toward the Channel in the pre-dawn of June 9. They were intercepted by eight Royal Navy destroyers. Two German destroyers were sunk and the other vessels turned back in a furious night naval battle. This was termed "The Battle of Ushant," after the nearby French island.[8] After dawn, twenty-four Beaufighters (No. 144 and 404 Squadrons) bombed the wreck of destroyer *Z32*, which had run aground to avoid sinking. The planes ensured that the vessel would not be salvaged. The Allied invasion force was not affected.

### *SCHNELLBOOTE*

The S-boats did not successfully attack any ships during daylight hours on D-Day. Strong air and naval patrols prevented their approach on either flank of the invasion. The S-boats remained in their bombproof concrete shelters at Cherbourg and Boulogne. The *Kommandant Schnellboote* sent out orders for night attacks on the evening of June 6. British code breakers quickly deciphered the messages and forwarded them to Allied naval commanders.

S-boat operations from Cherbourg were concentrated to the west and south of the Isle of Wight, which approximately bisects the English Channel. S-boat operations from Boulogne concentrated to the east of the island. This meant the primary threat to the western flank of the Allied invasion fleet was from Cherbourg, with two S-boat flotillas, and on the eastern flank, with a single S-boat flotilla at Boulogne (see map 17.1).[9]

*5. S-bootsflotille* from Cherbourg was ordered to attack the western flank of the invasion off the American beaches. On approach in the early hours of June 7, one of the twelve attacking boats hit a mine and sank. Despite Allied surface forces, the surviving eleven managed to fire three torpedo salvoes into the Allied landing vessels offshore, sinking two LCTs (small tank landing craft). On withdrawal, another S-boat was destroyed by a mine.[10]

*4. S-bootsflotille* from Boulogne was ordered to screen the Pas-de-Calais coast to prevent additional Allied landings and, if possible, attack the eastern flank of the convoy routes. Later that night they approached the "Spout," where the convoy routes from Britain to Normandy converged. The S-boats tried unsuccessfully to attack destroyer HMS *Hambleton* with torpedoes but were driven off with radar-directed gunfire in the darkness. Further east, the Ostend S-boats (*2. S-bootsflotille*) reconnoitered the Belgian coast, while the boats from IJmuiden (*8. S-bootsflotille*) patrolled the Dutch coast without sighting targets.

On June 8, *4. S-bootsflotille* moved from Boulogne to Le Havre, while the *2. S-bootsflotille* moved from Ostend to Boulogne. On June 9, LST 314 and LST 376 were sunk by S-boats south of the Isle of Wight. On June 10 Cherbourg S-boats sank British transports SS *Dungrange* and SS *Brackenfield* in mid-Channel en route to Juno Beach. On June 11 frigate HMS *Halsted* lost its bow to an S-boat off Cherbourg. On the nights of 11–14 June, German S-boats dropped "oyster mines" in the Baie de la Seine.[11, 12]

On June 12, three *5. T-bootsflotille* vessels (*T28*, *Falke*, and *Jaguar*) sparred with Norwegian destroyer *Stord* and British destroyer *Scorpion* on the eastern edge of the anchorage, but neither side scored significant hits. This was the last surface action by the Le Havre-based torpedo boats. The German vessels and many of their crewmen had only forty-eight hours to live.

Also on June 12, the two Cherbourg flotillas evacuated their threatened base and moved to Le Havre. There were now three S-boat flotillas at Le Havre. On June 13, S-boats attacked shipping off Utah Beach, badly damaging destroyer USS *Nelson*.

All these attacks were at night to avoid Allied aircraft. This fact prompted naval commander Admiral Ramsey to cancel night convoys south of the Isle of Wight into the anchorage. He also requested a heavy bomber raid to eliminate the threat of S-boats from Le Havre so close to his convoy routes and anchorage.[13]

## OPERATION ASTONIA

On the night of June 8, 1944, RAF 617 Squadron tested a new bomb in combat. This squadron had previously employed a unique bouncing bomb to breach two dams in Germany in 1943. The bouncing bombs and these new "Tallboy" bombs were the work of engineer Barnes Wallis, a brilliant English weapons designer. The 12,000-pound Tallboy was one of the largest conventional bombs used in World War II and would later be used to destroy the German battleship *Tirpitz* in its Norwegian lair. Only the modified RAF "Lancaster Special" bomber could deliver it. Their target this night was no battleship, however, but a key railroad tunnel crossing of the Loire at Saumur, France.

Flying Lancaster Specials, 617 Squadron dropped nineteen Tallboys on the tunnel and its approaches. The tunnel roof collapsed, blocking the rail line for the rest of the war. "This was 'interdiction' indeed—and part of a significant transition of Bomber Command from massed area to precision bombing."[14] With the Tallboy bomb, the RAF had a weapon that could crack the concrete pens sheltering the German Navy from Bordeaux to Bremen.

By mid-June, the S-boats in Cherbourg were threatened by Allied advances on the ground and evacuated to Le Havre, joining the significant German naval force

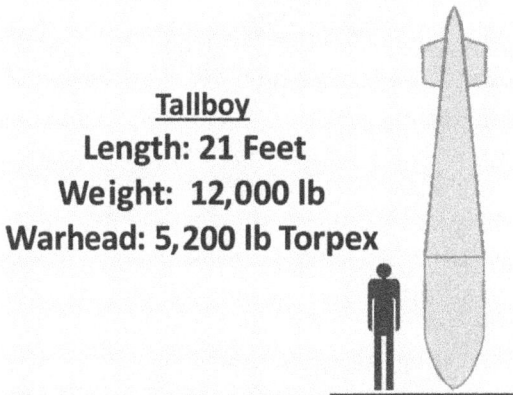

**Tallboy**
**Length: 21 Feet**
**Weight:  12,000 lb**
**Warhead: 5,200 lb Torpex**

Figure 18.1. Tallboy MOLYSON

Figure 18.2. Tallboy bomb being dropped by a Lancaster Special LIBRARY OF CONGRESS

already there. Le Havre was now the most powerful outpost of the *Kriegsmarine* on the Channel, and the closest to the OVERLORD beachhead. June 13 was a bad-weather day, and all the S-boats stayed in port. They could not use their speed advantage in heavy seas, and slowing down was death in the Allied-controlled Channel. ULTRA intercepted the orders to remain at Le Havre. The Allies had the intelligence they needed to strike effectively.

At 1245 on June 14, Flight Lieutenant P. J. Kelley took off from RAF Benson to confirm that the German Navy was still at Le Havre. Previous flights had been aborted because of the weather, but this time the RAF was not to be frustrated. Kelley flew over Le Havre at 30,000 feet. The Spitfire XI was designed for one job, taking pictures from high altitude; passing over Le Havre, Kelley's Spitfire did just that.

The Germans far below responded with a heavy flak barrage, but somehow Kelley made it through. He set course for home. The film was quickly processed, and the RAF photo interpreters (PIs) began their work. It was a simple task; the German ships were spotted around the crowded harbor confident that their heavy AAA defenses would deter an Allied attack in daylight.

The PIs could make out four of the destroyer-like T-boats, at least five S-boats, and numerous R-boats (patrol-minelayer craft), as well as large numbers of smaller craft. The alert went out immediately to RAF Bomber Command, which was on standby to hit Le Havre. It was important to hit the target before nightfall because the German vessels would depart for their deadly patrols under cover of darkness.

Shortly before dusk on June 14, the RAF began its work. Twenty-two 617 Squadron Lancaster Specials and their Tallboys hit Le Havre, followed by several hundred other more conventional Lancasters carrying 500-, 1,000-, and 4,000-pound demolition bombs. The harbor was turned into a cauldron as the Tallboys and other bombs cascaded down on the hapless Germans below. The Tallboys demolished the concrete S-boat pen, collapsing the roof.

Near misses fell into the water, sending a tidal wave to sweep out any craft that might have escaped the collapse within. The wave also added to the general destruction of other vessels in the harbor. Casualties among *Kriegsmarine* personnel were extremely high. Three T-boats, ten S-boats, fifteen R-boats, several patrol and defense vessels, and fifteen other small craft were sunk. The mission was a great success. Unfortunately, some bombs also hit the town, exploding the German naval munitions stores there. Le Havre was heavily damaged and over 700 civilians killed.[15]

At dusk the next night, the RAF hit Boulogne harbor. Twenty-five R-boats and other small craft were sunk and ten damaged. Although several replacement S-boats were subsequently shipped to Le Havre by rail, the German surface vessel threat to the beachhead was much diminished. Even later German strikes by miniature submarines were considered only nuisances and were countered by a close blockade of Le Havre harbor.[16]

## MIDGET SUBMARINES

The *Kriegsmarine* deployed two kinds of craft in their *Kleinkampfverband* (small battle unit) to the Normandy Coast at the Port of Honfleur and Favrol Woods northeast of Ouistreham. These included the *Neger* midget submarine and the *Linsen* explosive speedboats. The midget subs attacked with the vessel awash, not submerged. With sufficient light, the defending ship and its escorts could see the approaching danger. This made casualties high in the few attacks actually made by the subs.

The *Linsens* attacked in groups of three speedboats—two piloted warhead-equipped boats crammed with explosives and one control vessel. Prior to impact, the pilot of each warhead boat would set the radio control for remote operation and dive into the water. The control boat would then attempt to complete the attack and pick up the other pilots. The Germans were showing signs of desperation in their defense of the coast.

The *Linsens* arrived first on June 21 with ten control boats and twenty-four warhead boats. Four nights later, as they prepared for their first operation, one of the pilots accidentally detonated a *Linsen* warhead, which killed him and destroyed two nearby control boats and an R-boat. The operation continued with the *Linsens* being towed by R-boats. The water was rough that night off Normandy, and all but six of the speedboats were swamped. After two additional failed attacks, the unit commander suspended operations.

Mindful of the British miniature submarine attack that had damaged the *Tirpitz* the previous September, the Allied naval forces wanted to ensure that the German small boats and midget submarines did not reach the vulnerable landing ships in the anchorage. Additional air and sea patrols were used to intercept these slow but deadly vessels before they could do harm.

Forty of the *Neger* midget submarines arrived on June 28 and set up shop. On July 5, twenty-six were launched into the rough waters of the Baie de la Seine. Mechanical failures, poor navigation, and alert defenders were encountered; only nine midget submarines survived. No Allied ships were damaged.

On July 7 a *Neger* badly damaged the old Polish cruiser *Dragon*. It was a constructive loss and was added to the breakwater offshore. The sub pilot was taken prisoner. A second ship, minesweeper HMS *Pylades*, was also sunk by a *Neger* torpedo. The waters were relatively quiet that night, and the *Negers*, which were awash and not submerged, were easy to spot. This operation involved twenty-one midget subs, all of which were sunk by British gunboats and RAF 26 Squadron Seafires.

On the night of July 20, destroyer HMS *Isis* was sunk off Sword Beach by a *Neger* midget submarine in a combined attack.[17] The *Linsens* sunk one landing craft at a cost of twenty-two *Linsen* craft. A new midget submarine, the *Marder*, was delivered during this time. It was an improved *Neger*, with dive tanks to allow it to submerge after its attack. On the night of August 3, fifty-eight midget submarines and thirty-two *Linsen* explosive speedboats attacked the NEPTUNE anchorage. The midget subs sank the frigate HMS *Quorn* and minesweeper HMS *Gairsay* at a cost of forty-one of their own.[18]

The Operational Record Book of No. 132 Squadron recorded the events of August 3, when its Spitfires were sent on early-morning patrol against the tiny warships operating from Le Harve:

> *Quite a considerable amount of excitement added spice to the first series of low patrols flown by 132 Squadron from 0634. The spice (was) no less than the presence of German midget submarines and human torpedoes attempting to attack our shipping in the sea from the Orne Estuary. On this first patrol 132 made attacks on 11 of the midget subs and claim them destroyed. Further patrols yielded a further bag of five more midget subs. No human torpedoes were seen but some of our smaller vessels were seen unloading depth charges in the area and on the 1126*

*patrol flown by 453 (Squadron) no more of these Hun nuisances were reported, but the Navy was seen liberally sprinkling the infested area with depth charges.*[19]

## ENDGAME

The Royal Navy's Operation KENETIC began on August 1 as the US Army approached the Brittany ports that had been declared fortresses. This operation culminated on August 23, when Allied warships destroyed a German convoy off the Biscay coast. KINETIC, along with Coastal Command patrols during the day, isolated German naval forces on the Biscay coast.[20]

The *Kreigsmarine* removed its surviving coastal forces from the Lower Normandy coast on August 23, reinforcing their flotillas farther east. The last operational U-boats left the Biscay ports toward the end of August, returning via the North Atlantic to Norway.[21]Allied armies completed the liberation of the French Channel coast by the end of August.

Total Allied losses on D-Day were six warships: three destroyers, one minesweeper, and two motor torpedo boats. By the end of June, when NEPTUNE ended in victory, the Allied naval cost was twenty-four warships and thirty-five transports. At least one-quarter were sunk by mines, every countries' most effective ship killer in the Channel.[22]

## CHAPTER NINETEEN

# Airborne

In the spring of 1944, a Free Czech officer, Captain F. O. Miksche, published his book *Paratroops* in England. Among his many insightful ideas was a plan for a three-division paratroop assault into Normandy followed by an amphibious attack very near the planned Utah Beach. A map detailing the drop zones was included. This made the Allied generals very nervous; they were sure the Germans would see the book as well, which they did. Nothing was done to pull the book from shelves because that would have highlighted its accuracy. History does not record if Captain Miksche was encouraged to delay his writing career until after the war, but it seems likely.[1]

Having witnessed costly but successful Allied airborne operations in the Mediterranean, *Generalfeldmarschall* Erwin Rommel prepared for such an assault somewhere along the French coast. This could be part of the main Allied invasion or a diversion. The Allies amassed large numbers of airborne troops, troop carrier aircraft, and gliders in Britain.

In Britain, Eisenhower was given every available asset he demanded. How different things were across the Channel, where Rommel prepared to receive Eisenhower's attack. Meddling from Hitler and the political generals back in Germany was rampant. Rommel had to fight for men and materiel constantly. Still, Rommel persevered and even thrived on adversity. First, he studied the beach defenses from Calais to Brittany. He designed and ordered the placement of more than half a million steel obstacles on the beaches of the *Atlantik Wall* to protect it from amphibious attack.

Supplementing the steel obstacles were wooden poles with Teller anti-tank mines on top that were capable of destroying a landing craft. In addition, Rommel increased the number of land mines on or near the beaches to some 5 million. He put as much artillery as he could gather in emplacements firing down on likely invasion beaches. Once Allied aircraft began the Transportation Plan and bridge attack campaign in March, resources for such construction became even more scarce. Still, the work continued into June.

Even as Rommel strengthened his beach defenses, he looked at the hinterlands behind the coastline. The Allies had used airborne forces while fighting in North Africa, invading Sicily, and also at Salerno in mainland Italy. This Allied capability was not lost on the Desert Fox. Behind the beaches, Rommel's laborers implanted thousands of wooden stakes the size of telephone poles called *Rommelsspargel* (Rommel's asparagus). *Rommelsspargel* were 6 feet high aboveground and 1 foot thick. The density specified by Rommel was 3,000 per square mile.[2] Rommel wrote:

> *Hence the important thing is to ensure that all territory which might conceiv-*
> *ably be used for landing airborne troops is treated in such a manner that enemy*
> *aircraft and gliders will break up while landing, and the enemy as a result suffer*
> *severe losses in men and materiel in addition to those caused by the quick opening*
> *of our defensive fire.*[3]

Every open field within 8 miles of the coast was to have these poles emplaced. Trip wires connected many of these posts to detonate the mines or shells that were to be placed on top.[4] Labor, stocks of wooden poles, and the supply of mines and shells were, however, limited. Only a few days before the invasion, Rommel had arranged the release of a million captured shells for his obstacles. Fortunately, there was no time to install them. The *Rommelsspargel* installations were insufficient to stop the airborne assault.

Figure 19.1. *Rommelsspargel* installations were insufficient to stop the airborne assault. US ARMY MILITARY HISTORY INSTITUTE

## DEFENDING THE COTENTIN

Using his intuition and perhaps hearing of the Miksche book, Hitler sensed the vulnerability of the Cotentin Peninsula to an airborne invasion. The Cotentin was Germany's left flank in the Normandy defenses. Hitler sent the crack *91st Luftlande* (Air Landing) Division, the *6th Fallschirm* (Parachute) Regiment and an independent panzer battalion to bolster defenses in the spring. No one doubted the prowess of German airborne troops as tough defending infantry, even though massive losses of German Ju 52 transport aircraft in previous operations limited their offensive potential.

All these German units were well equipped with numerous light and medium flak guns, a partial offset for the depleted *Luftwaffe* fighter force. Their orders were specifically to defend against airborne assaults. Allied intelligence soon detected the beefed-up defenses using aerial reconnaissance, French Resistance reports, ULTRA intercepts, and other means. As information was received, it was given immediately to the senior leadership at SHAEF and the higher ranking field commanders.[5] Cotentin would be a fight between attacking and defending airborne troops.

Figure 19.2. German 2cm light flak. The *Luftwaffe's* light flak was to prove deadly in the airborne assault on Normandy. AIR FORCE HISTORICAL RESEARCH AGENCY KARLSRUHE COLLECTION

As D-Day approached, several factors determined the timing for NEPTUNE, the assault phase of Operation OVERLORD. The original May 1 date was postponed to early June to allow for the collection of sufficient landing craft and troop carrier planes. This also allowed Allied bombing to complete the isolation of the *7th Armée* sector under the Transportation Plan and subsequent bridge attacks.

The exact date for D-Day was determined using meteorological data. The weather had to be clear enough to allow the use of the substantial Allied air fleet to support the attack. A late-rising moon was needed to allow the airborne troop carrier force to navigate to the designated paratrooper drop zones (DZs). The perfect days, assuming adequate weather, were June 5 and 6. The next possible day was June 19, but there would be no moonlight for the airborne troops.[6]

The Germans were aware of the meteorological factors involved with selecting an invasion date, including weather impacts on airborne operations. Average rainy days with extensive cloud cover in June were eleven for Cherbourg and nine for Caen.[7] So for at least a third of the month, it would be difficult for the Allies to use their airborne forces to advantage.

Despite *Luftwaffe* efforts at conservation, Operation POINTBLANK had left the Germans with only about 160 single- and twin-engine fighters in France. The single-engine fighters were in *Jagdgeschwader 2* and *Jagdgeschwader 26* (JG 2 and JG 26). The aircraft of JG 2 were based on two airfields north of Paris. JG 26, now headquartered at Lille, was spread over eastern France and the Mediterranean coast. This allowed JG 26 to assist in the air defense of the German homeland. Rommel was not optimistic that they would be able to operate effectively in the face of Allied air supremacy.

To the west of Normandy were the long-range Ju 88Cs *Zerstörer* twin-engine day fighters that threatened Allied antisubmarine aircraft in the Bay of Biscay. These *Luftwaffe* aircraft were not trained to fight at night and in poor weather. None would attack the Allied troop carriers approaching under cover of darkness on June 6.

By the time of the invasion, bombardment of German airfields within 100 miles of Caen limited their capability to support even the limited number of single-engine German fighters remaining. German meteorologists predicted a period of bad weather for early June, and it seemed no invasion was likely. Of greater significance to the Allied troop carrier force was that there were no night fighters at all based within 150 miles of the drop zones.[8]

A final German misstep helped seal the eventual fate of the German defenders of the Cotentin Peninsula. The *7th Armée*, under the command of which the defenders in the Cotentin operated, ordered its senior commanders to its headquarters at Rennes for an invasion *Kriegspiel* (wargame). General Marcks, who commanded the

*LXXXIV Korps* defending the Cotentin Peninsula, would play Eisenhower. His plan was to begin the theoretical Allied invasion with an airborne attack, an attack that was indeed occurring even as he prepared to depart for Rennes.

*Oberstleutnant* Friedrich Freiherr von der Heydte, who commanded the tough paratroops of the 6th *Fallschirm* Regiment in the Cotentin, later noted his surprise at the decision to call away the senior commanders from their posts:

> *Although the authorities were frequently at odds in their estimates as to where and how the Allied invasion would take place, it was nevertheless apparent that since the middle of May commanders and troops were agreed in assuming that an invasion was to be expected during the first ten days of June. Consequently, the lower headquarters were astonished when all division commanders, and one regimental commander from each division, the corps artillery commanders and the commanders of the corps headquarters reserves were ordered to report to Rennes on 6 June 1944 at 0830 in order to spend the entire day in an army group map exercise. . . . The majority of officers, who had been ordered to report, left for Rennes on the evening of 5 June and spent the night there.*[9]

CHAPTER TWENTY

# Getting There

After completing large-scale American airborne operations in the Mediterranean, the Army Air Force began concentrating most of its troop carrier units in England. The units, flying C-47 and look-alike C-53 aircraft,[1] were assigned to the IX Troop Carrier Command, part of the US 9th AF. From the end of 1943 until D-Day and after, the American troop carrier aviators and the paratroopers they transported went into an intensive training regimen:

> *The troop carrier training program prior to NEPTUNE was unequaled at any other time during the war. Gen. Paul Williams, who took over IX Troop Carrier Command near the end of February, brought along many experienced staff members from Mediterranean operations. Much attention was given to night formation flying, practice jumps, and glider tows with live airborne troops. Troopers were assigned, when possible, to practice with the troop carrier units with whom they would fly into Normandy.[2]*

New pilots and aircraft arrived in England to augment the veteran forces brought up from the MTO (Mediterranean Theater of Operations). There is an unfortunate myth among some historians that somehow these men were poorly trained for their job. In fact, they were at least as well prepared as their compatriots in the fighter and bomber units. By this time, the Mediterranean veterans were very experienced; most had performed one or more combat paratrooper and glider drops. Airfields and navigation aids, especially in North Africa, were primitive at best. Yet the men had prevailed and learned their craft, sometimes under fire from "friendly" as well as enemy forces.

## BUILDING UP

New crews arriving from the States were also well prepared, benefiting from an increased supply of C-47s in the I Troop Carrier Command training establishment. Like bomber and fighter crews, these men benefited from the operational and replacement training unit (OTU/RTU) organization the Army Air Force had bor-

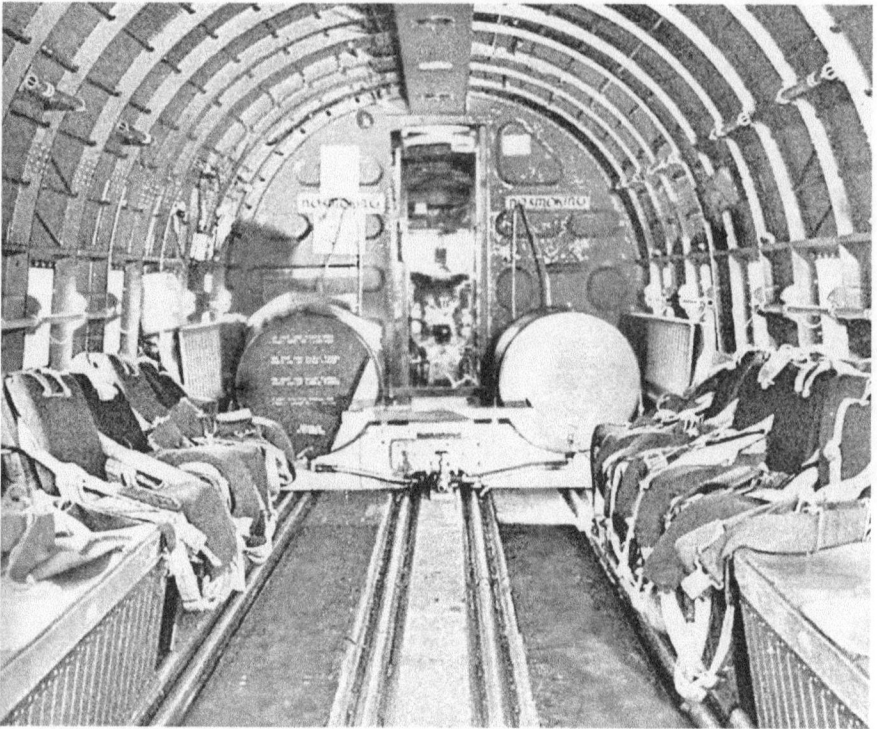

Figure 20.1. Fuselage tanks extended the range of the C-47 for trans-Atlantic flights.
US AIR FORCE

rowed from the RAF. They were ready when called upon to take their aircraft across the Atlantic and into the war.[3]

Pilot Gerald "Bud" Berry was one of these newly trained pilots, with about 250 hours of flying time. He picked up a brand-new C-47 at Fort Wayne, Indiana, for delivery to England. His crew was also green, except for the experienced Air Transport Command navigator along for the trip. The only cargo was the crew's luggage and four 100-gallon fuel tanks in the cargo compartment added for range. The twenty-two-day trip began with a flight to Macon, Georgia, and subsequently to West Palm Beach, Florida. From there Berry flew to Borinquen Field, Puerto Rico, and then to Atkinson Field in British Guiana. From Atkinson Field the next leg was to Belém, Brazil. On this leg, Berry was cautioned to stay along the coast; there were headhunters reported inland.

The next leg was from Belém to Natal, Brazil—the last stop before leaving South America. They flew across the Atlantic to lonely Ascension Island, where the runway stretched the width of the island, cresting in the middle. From there Berry and his crew went to Roberts Field in Liberia, where they were delayed by weather somewhere on the route ahead of them. From Roberts Field, Berry then flew to Dakar in French West Africa, then to Marrakech in French Morocco. At Marrakech, Berry's plane was delayed again for weather.

When he finally got the word to go, Berry and his crew reported for their final briefing. The briefer told them:

> *"You're getting off a bit late and you are going to be crossing the Bay of Biscay during the daylight hours. The Germans fly out the fighters, the Me 110s, to shepherd submarines into the pens along the coast there in France. So we're sending you out to the 13th meridian instead of the 12th meridian."*[4] *Well that meant a much longer flight up. But then they said the day before a B-24 had been shot down over the Bay of Biscay. So we were happy to go on and fly the 13th!*

The flight to England from Africa was twelve hours and twenty minutes. Fortunately they had sufficient fuel to fly up into Scotland, because England was "socked in." No one was landing there unless they were out of fuel. After several more adventures they arrived at Bottesford airfield, headquarters of the 50th TCW (Troop Carrier Wing). Berry was subsequently assigned to the 439th TCG (Troop Carrier Group) at Balderton and eventually to RAF Upottery in southwest England. He recalled:

> *When I came down out of the airplane, a major was standing there. He came up to me and he said, "Lieutenant, what kind of an airplane is this?" I said, "It's a good airplane, sir." He said, "How are the engines?" I said, "They run very smooth, no problems." He asked, "How about the stability?" I said, "Very stable aircraft."*

Berry didn't know why the major was asking these questions, but the next day he found out:

> *That airplane was equipped with a glider pickup mechanism, and he* [the major] *was an expert in glider pickup. So he was interested in that airplane. Two or three days later I checked into Operations and I was scheduled to fly. I went out to the flight line and I was flying copilot for the major who was commanding the 91st Squadron. He had taken the airplane over that I had flown across, and that's why he was interested.*[5]

Figure 20.2. The C-47 could carry a stick of twenty-one parachutists, although in combat the normal load was sixteen to eighteen. NATIONAL ARCHIVES

Berry and other new guys became copilots for the experienced troop carrier pilots, many if not most of whom had combat experience. The addition of new aircraft like Berry's was necessary to expand the troop carrier fleet to match the increased size of the anticipated airborne assault on D-Day.

## PATHFINDERS

A major lesson of the 1943 airborne assault on Sicily, at the beginning of Operation HUSKY, had been the difficulty of finding assigned parachute drop zones at night. On March 1, 1944, IX Troop Carrier Command, part of the US 9th AF, established a Pathfinder School in Britain to train troop carrier aircrews in precision delivery of pathfinder paratroopers. Commandant of the school and subsequently the commander of the provisional 1st Pathfinder Group, 1st PFG (P), was Lieutenant Colonel Joel Crouch, a no-nonsense officer and ex-airline pilot who insisted that his airmen attain the highest level of proficiency. The hand-picked pilots and navigators received extensive training in pinpoint navigation at night and in weather.

The term "pathfinders" referred both to the airmen of the 1st Pathfinder Group (Provisional) and the pathfinder troops they carried into combat.

An officer with one of the pathfinder teams later recalled how each team was organized and equipped:

*The regimental pathfinder team was divided into three battalion teams, each composed of eighteen men. About eight of these men were to provide security for the rest of the team who were designated to set up the navigational aids used to assist the (follow-on) aircraft in locating the DZ. Our special equipment consisted of a "Holophane Light" obtained from the British and modified by providing triangular metal legs and a Eureka unit which communicated with a Rebecca unit in the (follow-on) aircraft. For daylight operations we carried smoke grenades and panels.*[6]

The US 82nd and 101st Airborne Divisions were assigned to conduct the intended airborne assault against the Cotentin Peninsula at the beginning of Operation NEPTUNE. Each consisted of three paratroop infantry regiments (PIRs) and one glider infantry regiment (GIR) plus supporting specialist units. Each regiment had three parachute infantry or glider infantry battalions. Each battalion had its own Battalion Pathfinder Team. All pathfinders, even those in glider regiments, were dropped by parachute from troop carrier aircraft. Each team's job was to locate and mark the parachute drop zone (DZ) or glider landing zone (LZ) assigned to its parent battalion.

## EUREKA

A huge night airdrop operation was planned, and finding the airborne drop zones was both difficult and critical. Each Battalion Pathfinder Team carried two 30-pound electronic beacons called *Eurekas*. The Eurekas emitted a signal corresponding to the drop or landing zone assigned to the parachute or glider battalion the team supported. The leading aircraft carrying the main force of paratroopers were equipped with *Rebecca* receivers for the Eureka beacon signals. In theory this allowed each battalion to be placed near its intended zone and target.

Unfortunately, due to the marginal weather conditions on D-Day, many of these pathfinders were themselves dropped off-target. German light flak also played a role in degrading the accuracy of the pathfinder drop. To ensure guidance to the correct drop zone, the Rebecca would only receive the signal for the Eureka it was supposed to home in on. The Rebecca detection range of the Eureka beacons was 30 miles at 1,500 feet, but the troop carriers were flying lower than 1,000 feet.[7]

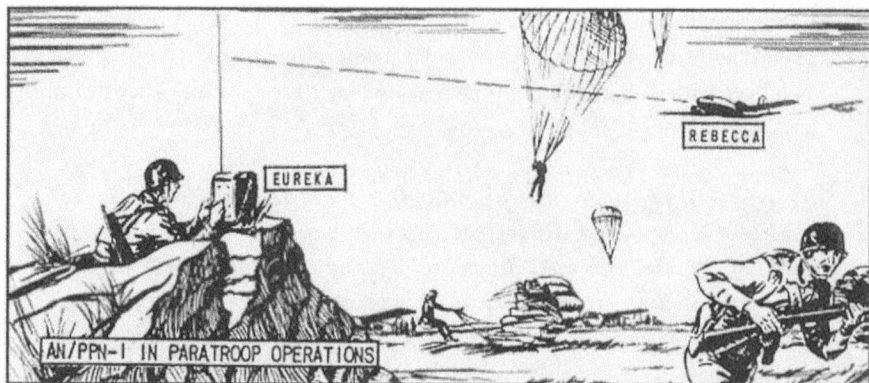

Figure 20.3. Eureka–Rebecca system US NAVY[8]

The lead aircraft navigators learned to operate the Rebecca sets as well as the available British *Gee* electronic navigation systems while honing the navigational skills they had already mastered.[9] Unlike the British aircraft assigned to airborne operations, the Americans had few Gee navigation sets. The Gee systems, like the Rebeccas, were mostly installed in formation lead aircraft.

The crews also became well acquainted with the ground pathfinder teams they would carry. One ground pathfinder team leader recalled:

> *Colonel Crouch insisted on his pilots making at least one jump with us (he made about nine, I think) and since this was verbotten [sic] for the Air Force, many sprained ankles went on the books as having occurred jumping from a two-and-a-half ton truck.*[10]

As training intensified in May, the C-47s and gliders were made as technically ready as possible. Engines were changed as required, aircraft rerigged if the controls were sloppy, and radios were tuned. Even small problems were addressed aggressively. As an example, the crew relief tube in the C-47 was located under the pilot's seat. A crewman other than the pilot would have to exchange places and sit down in the pilot seat to use the funnel while the copilot flew the plane.

The resulting urine passed down a rubber tube to the plane's exterior. The crew chiefs fixed the problem by drilling a hole in the bulkhead behind the pilot, disconnecting the funnel, and rerouting the rubber tube back to the passenger compartment. It allowed for this convenience to be used without disturbing the pilot.[11]

On May 26 intelligence was received that the German *91st Luftlande* Division[12] had taken up positions on the Cotentin. Located in the center of the peninsula, its job was "to repel possible Allied airborne operations."[13] The unit was highly rated, and it sent Bradley and the American airborne generals into a new evaluation of their plan.

It was decided to move the US 82nd Airborne Division to drop zones nearer the village of Sainte-Mère-Église. The village and key bridges across the Merderet River would now be captured by the 82nd. This strengthened the American position greatly, allowing the 101st Airborne to concentrate on seizing the beach exits from Utah.[14] Without the beach exits in American hands, the amphibious troops could be trapped on the beach (see map 6.2).

CHAPTER TWENTY-ONE

# The Eve of Battle

It may be strange to some that the battles of paratroopers and glider troops would be examined in detail in a book about the contribution of airmen to victory in Europe. Parachute and glider infantry are part of airpower in that airplanes bring and sustain them in battle. In the *Wehrmacht*, the parachute and glider warriors were part of the *Luftwaffe*, commanded by *Luftwaffe* officers. On the Allied side, parachute and glider infantry were under the command of the local ground commander once they were delivered by air. By May 1944, both the British and American air forces had each amassed a fleet of troop carrier and glider tug aircraft.

On June 3, 1944, the order was given to paint white-and-black invasion marking on all the planes. The huge air fleet consumed just about all the black and white paint in the United Kingdom. A total of five alternating white and black stripes, each 2 feet wide, would be painted on each wing and around the rear of the fuselage. D-Day should have been June 5, but weather forced Eisenhower into a twenty-four-hour delay.

With the troops on edge, accidents happened. Major General Maxwell Taylor, commander of the 101st Airborne Division (ABD), walked with a slight limp. He had torn a ligament playing squash the previous afternoon, but nothing was going to keep him from jumping in with his division.[1] At the 440th Troop Carrier Group base at Exeter, the cancellation was met with increased tension. The jump wasn't off, just postponed.

Some of the men went to a movie in a hanger next to where they were billeted. As luck would have it, it was a war movie. At a point in the movie where bombs were being dropped, a fire extinguisher fell off the hanger wall and begin hissing as it lost its filling. The Germans were still conducting occasional harassment bombing at night, and in the tense atmosphere anything seemed possible. The hissing extinguisher sounded like a bomb about to blow, and there was a scramble for the door. In the crush, two troopers broke their legs and many others were less seriously injured. It was a hell of a way to begin a war.[2]

On the evening of June 5, Eisenhower visited the troop carrier bases, talking with and encouraging the men. It was still daylight, even at 2200 local, because of

Figure 21.1. The paratroopers were heavily overloaded with equipment intended to sustain them in isolated combat. AIR FORCE HISTORICAL RESEARCH AGENCY

British double daylight time. Ike was now the loneliest man among all the airmen, soldiers, and sailors in England. His decision, and his alone, to "go" changed the lives of them all. His message to the paratroopers was simple: "Full victory—nothing else."

Then it was time for each trooper to don his equipment and move to the troop carrier aircraft again. Once all the equipment was on, a trooper weighed between 250 and 300 pounds. This included the bulky leg bags recently supplied by the British, crammed with up to 80 pounds of equipment. They literally needed to be pushed and pulled into the waiting aircraft. The gentle urging of "get your ass up here" was heard from the aircrew and other paratroopers as each man struggled up the boarding ladder. It would take forty minutes or more to load a stick of eighteen paratroopers into each plane.[3] 82nd Airborne Division trooper Otis Sampson recalled:

*By the time I had on all my equipment I had quite a load: Grenades, Tommy gun, ammunition, length of rope, field glasses, compass, and a first aid kit. A backpack with various articles such as a raincoat, change of underwear, shelter half, mess kit and toilet articles. In a concealed zipper pocket in our jump suit near our throat we all carried a switch blade knife. Some of the troopers carried a trench knife, the brass knuckles over the hand grip could be seen sticking out of the top of a trooper's boots.*

*Each carried an entrenching tool, pick, shovel, or hatchet. On our left shoulder was a packet containing morphine, to help ease the pain if wounded. Some of us carried an escape kit. Food rations were stored away in one or more of the many pockets. I replaced most of my food rations for extra Tommy gun ammunition. There were many more various articles that seem to find their place.*

*In combat I always carried a 38 Colt revolver; on the jump it was handy under my reserve chute, but as soon as I landed it was moved to my right hip where it always stayed. This side weapon gave me added assurance. A sheathed knife hung from a webbed belt next to a canteen of water. When I came to get in the plane I appreciated the help that was given me, thankful it would not be a long trip.*[4]

With the paratroopers so loaded down, the danger from accidental discharge of weapons was very real. At the 315th TCG base at Spanhoe, one of the last troopers to board tossed his M-1 rifle on the floor of his aircraft as he began to laboriously crawl up the steps. The loaded rifle discharged, hitting a Gammon anti-tank grenade in the leg pocket of one of the troopers near the front. The exploding grenade set off several white phosphorous grenades.

This was deep inside a fully fueled C-47 loaded with heavily armed paratroopers and weapons. Three troopers died; fifteen other troopers and the radio operator of the aircraft were badly injured.[5] Colonel Ekman, who commanded the 505th PIR (Parachute Infantry Regiment) reported on the loss of this C-47 and its stick before the unit had even left the runway:

*Regimental Headquarters and the 1st Bn. got in the planes, and just about five or six minutes prior to taking off a huge explosion occurred. Someone had set off a Gammon Grenade which in turn set off all the ammunition. I was initiated into combat that way. I saw a lot of dead bodies lying around after the explosion.*[6]

Figure 21.2. Cramped interior of a C-47 NATIONAL ARCHIVES

The flyers were also overloaded with gear. Bud Berry, now a copilot and relatively junior officer, recalled:

*We got the briefing late in the evening. Got out to the airplanes and we had no armor plate on C-47s, we had no self-sealing tanks on the 47 like a lot of other airplanes, so we were required to wear mostly GI-type combat stuff. We had the tin hat, the tin helmet that we wore. We had a Mae West on. We had a flak suit on which had a vest with a little thing down on the front and a back piece that all came together when you drew up straps.*

*Then we had a parachute harness over that, and the parachute that was the pilot's and copilot's were hanging on the bulkhead immediately behind their seats. We did not wear the parachutes during the mission. If you had trouble you reached back and got the chute and hooked it on. (The cargo hatch at the left rear of the fuselage) was the best exit. There was a hatch up above the (pilots') compartment where, if you had to, you could crawl out.[7]*

If the aircrew and troops were loaded with equipment, they were also loaded with serious intent to get on with the job. As he boarded his aircraft for the jump into Normandy, one paratrooper of the 101st called out a challenge that would be taken up by all the Americans that night: "Look out Hitler, here we come!"[8]

## Chapter Twenty-Two

# The Approach

The two-division American airdrop into the Cotentin Peninsula of Normandy was the largest air assault yet attempted in World War II Europe. At approximately 2145 on June 5, twenty C-47s[1] from the 1st Pathfinder Group (Provisional) (1st PFG (P)) began taking off from RAF North Withim in the English Midlands in seven serials at five-minute intervals.[2] A "serial" was defined as a group of aircraft with a common mission and drop zone (DZ). This was the first of several operations that would ensure the airborne units could accomplish their missions and defend the territory they seized.

The first six serials of the 1st PFG (P) each consisted of three C-47s in Vee formation, for a total of eighteen aircraft. Aboard each plane was one battalion pathfinder team. The teams in each three-ship serial were assigned to mark the same paratrooper drop zone, providing triple redundancy. The seventh serial was of two C-47s, each carrying a battalion pathfinder team to mark the glider landing zones to be operated the next morning.[3]

The serials flew south one behind the other and from one ground navigation point to the next with code names Atlanta, Burbank, Cleveland, Dallas, and finally Elko. Airspeed was 140 knots (about 161 mph) and altitude of 1,000 feet, course south-southwest. This put them below the horizon of the surviving German radar stations on the coast of France. Southwest of Elko and near Portland Bill on the Channel coast, the troop carriers flew out over the water.

Their designated corridor was well to the west of the huge invasion fleet. The route into Normandy took the troop carrier aircraft to the west of the Cotentin and then across the peninsula. The planes were well marked with special invasion stripes on the wings and fuselage, but no one expected these markings to be visible at night. The 1943 Sicily invasion encounter with US Navy "friendly fire," which cost the Allies twenty-three troop carrier aircraft and eighty-three dead, was fresh in everyone's mind. Many of these men, both aircrew and paratroopers, had flown on that mission.

At navigation point Gallup they descended to 500 feet, airspeed maintained at 140 knots, still flying south-southwest. Following the ship-based beacons, they

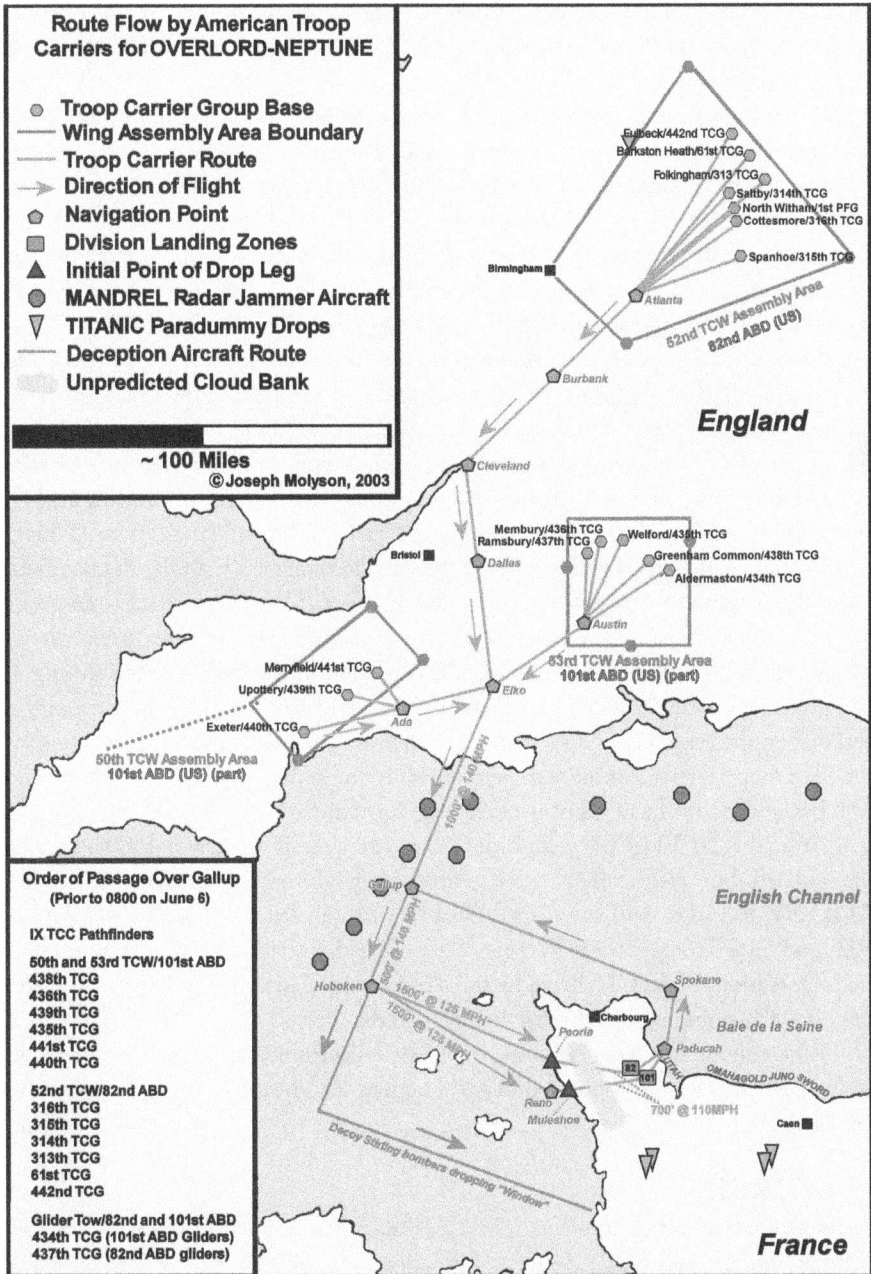

**Route Flow by American Troop Carriers for OVERLORD-NEPTUNE**

- ⬡ Troop Carrier Group Base
- ⸻ Wing Assembly Area Boundary
- ⸺ Troop Carrier Route
- ⟶ Direction of Flight
- ⬠ Navigation Point
- ▣ Division Landing Zones
- ▲ Initial Point of Drop Leg
- ● MANDREL Radar Jammer Aircraft
- ▽ TITANIC Paradummy Drops
- ⸺ Deception Aircraft Route
- Unpredicted Cloud Bank

**~ 100 Miles**
© Joseph Molyson, 2003

**Order of Passage Over Gallup**
(Prior to 0800 on June 6)

IX TCC Pathfinders

50th and 53rd TCW/101st ABD
438th TCG
436th TCG
439th TCG
435th TCG
441st TCG
440th TCG

52nd TCW/82nd ABD
316th TCG
315th TCG
314th TCG
313th TCG
61st TCG
442nd TCG

Glider Tow/82nd and 101st ABD
434th TCG (101st ABD Gliders)
437th TCG (82nd ABD gliders)

Map 22.1. Routes Flown by American Troop Carrier Aircraft on D-Day MOLYSON[4]

arrived at point Hoboken, where they turned eastward toward the Cotentin Peninsula, climbing to 1,500 feet and slowing to 125 knots (about 144 mph). The climb helped bleed airspeed.

After the pathfinder force took off, the main body of the airborne force was launched. The first of over 800 main-force C-47s began taking off at 22:15 carrying over 6,000 paratroopers of the 101st Airborne Division (ABD). As the C-47s climbed, they formed up in three-aircraft "Vees." The Vee elements then combined into nine-aircraft "Vee of Vees" flights. A typical troop carrier group, including its spare aircraft, could generate nine of these nine-ship Vee of Vees formations. A similar procedure and course was flown by the C-47s delivering the 82nd ABD.

Each troop carrier group divided its aircraft into two serials. Each serial was led by a senior pilot of the group or squadron and had specially trained navigators on board. Once a serial assembled, it joined the other serial from its parent group. All of this forming and maneuvering went on within the wing's assembly area over Britain, at night and with only minimal formation lighting. Remarkably, not one American aircraft was lost to midair collision during the entire airborne operation on D-Day.

Finally, each formed group entered the corridor assigned them by the planners, following it to reach Navigation Point Elko. It was at Elko that correct timing was most important, because this was the point where the C-47s of three troop carrier wings had to blend together, over 800 aircraft flying in the dark and converging at one point. The Americans had been training in night formation flying for months, and during the assembly and movement to the French coast it paid off. The pilots of the IX Troop Carrier Command were arguably the only airmen in the world who could assemble and fly at night in such large formations.[5]

After the 1st PFG (P) pathfinders, the first aircraft to arrive at Elko carried the untried but well-trained 101st Airborne Division. Codenamed Operation ALBANY, the 101st had been lifted from the coastal airfields by 433 C-47s of the 50th and 53rd Troop Carrier Wings.[6] Next came the veteran 82nd Airborne Division, Operation BOSTON, lifted by the 52nd Troop Carrier Wing from airfields to the east of Birmingham in the English Midlands.

When all aircraft were airborne, the 821 C-47s formed a dagger nine airplanes wide and 250 miles long pointed at the German *7th Armée* units on the Cotentin Peninsula.

## MANDREL

Flanking the Airborne's route were MANDREL radar-jamming aircraft. With low altitude and the jamming, the huge formation was invisible to the few surviving German air surveillance radars. During the last two weeks of May, Allied air forces attacked enemy radar sites along the occupied Channel coast. By the first week of June, the strikes had destroyed over 80 percent of German coastal radar capability.[7]

In advance of the pathfinders, RAF Stirling bombers had flown the route and continued southwest at Nav Point Hoboken. Eventually they turned southeast and dropped "Window" to further confuse the Germans. Window, or chaff, consisted of strips of aluminum foil cut to the wavelength of German search radars. It produced an opaque cloud on radar screens.

Another deception tool used was Operation TITANIC, the drop of dummy "parachutists" far south of the actual drop zones.[8] When they landed, these dummy parachutists ignited pyrotechnics simulating weapons firing. It added to the confusion of their sudden appearance. On the Cotentin Peninsula and the rest of Normandy, French Resistance fighters were cutting phone wires. Between the jamming, Window, dummies, and dead telephones, no German headquarters was able to discern exactly what was happening on the Cotentin Peninsula.

So far, the weather guys had gotten it right. The night was very dark but clear. The moon would rise by the time the main body of aircraft reached their drop zones. Fortunately the navigation beacons on vessels placed along the route of flight were easily visible. Each serial passed Nav Point Gallup six minutes after the one preceding it.[9] It would take five hours for all the C-47s to pass over Gallup.

At Hoboken, all lights on the planes were turned off except for tiny blue formation lights on top of the wings and fuselage. These formed a dim cross visible only from behind and above, the trailing positions of the wingmen in each Vee. These were set to half power by rheostat.[10] The faint glow of the shielded engine exhausts provided two additional dim light sources. It was no mean feat of airmanship to maintain such a formation at night, even in good visibility it required a continuous effort by the pilots to keep in position.

## THE CLOUD

Beginning with the pathfinder planes, the great column split at Nav Point Hoboken. The 101st ABD aircraft proceeded to Nav Point Reno and then crossed the coast at Nav Point Muleshoe. The aircraft destined for the 82nd ABD drop zones flew from Nav Point Hoboken and crossed the coast at Nav Point Peoria. By the time they reached the coast, the troop carrier aircraft were at 1,500 feet and had slowed to 125 mph. Flak from the Channel Islands was noted by most serials, but the route had been planned to keep the C-47s out of range.

The pathfinder aircraft were the first to travel the well-marked 5-mile-wide corridor from England into Normandy. The weather over the ocean and coastline was clear and all the navigational beacons were visible. Just after crossing the coast, the pathfinder crews spotted rising ground fog and cloud forming over the western part of the Cotentin. This would affect the following formations, including some of the later pathfinder aircraft.

Unfortunately, the NEPTUNE planners had failed to establish a weather contingency procedure. There had been no "weather bird" sent ahead of the troop carrier aircraft. By this time in the war, a weather reconnaissance aircraft preceded American and British bombing missions, but NEPTUNE had no such arrangement.

Perhaps the excellent weather for the EAGLE rehearsal exercise the previous month had instilled a measure of complacency among the air planning staffs at the AEAF and US 9th AF. For whatever reason, there was no preestablished code word for adverse weather in the drop area. The devil was in the details.

Navigating to the correct point on the Cotentin Peninsula in the dark was the first of a series of near-miracles required for the system to work as planned. Clear weather would clearly have been an advantage to the pathfinder aircraft crews, as would the absence of German flak. Instead, in addition to encountering the cloud, the first arriving aircraft also ignited a spirited flak defense.

Some aircraft separated from their formations in the cloud, a standard no-visibility weather procedure. These aircraft had neither Gee nor Rebecca sets for navigation. The ground below the cloud was invisible from the air; therefore, navigators were forced to "guestimate" their location once they crossed the coast. There were no GPS satellites in 1944; with no visibility, dead reckoning became the primary means of navigation.

A total of twenty pathfinder C-47s left England, but only nineteen delivered their teams to the Cotentin. German flak became intense as the pathfinder aircraft entered the airspace over the Cotentin. One plane, carrying a 101st ABD pathfinder team for Drop Zone C, was forced to ditch in the Channel with battle damage. Before ditching, the navigator–radar operator was able to pick out a nearby ship using radar on the plane.[11] They went into the water near the vessel. The crew and pathfinders were rescued. This may have been the pathfinder team incorrectly reported in some sources as "dropped in the Channel."

# CHAPTER TWENTY-THREE

# Over the Cotentin

When an aircraft crossed the coast there was about eight minutes to the planned DZ and twelve minutes before the aircraft would reach the opposite coast. Many jump-masters had their men stand and hook up at this point, anticipating the red light that would come on in just a few minutes. As expected, no German night fighters inter-cepted the airborne force. Total day and night air superiority over Normandy made the environment permissive enough to allow almost a thousand slow, unarmored troop carrier aircraft to approach in close formation.[1] (See map 6.2 for approximate desired routes and drop zones.)

Leading the 821-aircraft column, in the lead airplane of the 1st PFG (P), were Lieutenant Colonel Joel Crouch and copilot Captain Vito Pedone. Behind them in the airplane was the "stick," eighteen fully loaded pathfinders led by Captain Frank Lillyman of the 101st ABD. Captain Lillyman, the first American paratrooper to land on the Cotentin, was jumpmaster. Each paratrooper weighed between 250 and 300 pounds with his equipment. Later suggestions that the Gooney Birds dropped their sticks at 200 knots are counterfactual; the C-47 could not reach such speeds with such a load, certainly not in low-level flight.

Colonel Crouch maintained radio silence as instructed and proceeded with his mission. Pedone turned on the red light at the calculated drop-minus-four-minute point. The training and intensive preparation were evident as Crouch flew unerringly to the drop zone. Pedone and Lillyman joked about the title "the first American in Normandy," since copilot Pedone was in the cockpit, 18 feet forward of Lillyman in back of the plane. Over the DZ, the green light was illuminated and the battalion pathfinder team led by Lillyman jumped from Crouch's plane. By this time the plane had descended to about 700 feet and was flying intentionally nose-high at about 110 mph.

This was tricky; it was fairly close to stall speed, and the attitude of the air-craft had to be a bit nose-high so that the paratroopers could exit properly. The heavily overloaded men walked "downhill" from their seats to the exit. Lillyman touched French soil at 00:15 on June 6. About the same time, British pathfinders were landing far to the east. Suddenly, the Germans no longer had the best army in France.

Having accomplished his mission, Crouch descended to 100 feet, accelerated to 150 mph, and crossed the coast into the Baie de la Seine. He then turned north at Nav Point Paducah, northwestern at Nav Point Spokane, and northeast at Nav Point Gallup. Flying back toward Elko, the aircraft still heading toward Normandy in the corridor were visible to the west.[2]

The other pathfinder pilots and navigators achieved much the same success despite the deteriorating weather. Various combinations of fixes by the SCR 717 aircraft radar, dead reckoning, visual identification of the DZ, and British Gee navigation receivers were used to navigate to the correct DZs.[3] Gee was accurate to within 400 to 600 yards, still a long walk in the dark with the German Army on the prowl. Most of the pathfinder teams were dropped on or near their assigned DZs. "Though only two serials achieved the degree prescribed in the directives, all teams were put near enough to their zones to perform their missions in spite of cloudy weather."[4]

Once they landed, the pathfinders marked their DZ with the Holophane lights and the Eureka beacons. The Rebecca receivers in the follow-on troop carrier aircraft were set to receive the Eureka signal only from the DZ to which the troops they carried were assigned. At each DZ, the Holophane lights were arranged in a Tee. The stem of the Tee was four lights; the crossbar was formed by three lights.

The Eureka beacon was placed at the bottom of the Tee. The direction of flight for the follow-on troop carrier aircraft was up the stem of the Tee. Each copilot was supposed to give the green light to the paratroopers in the back of his plane when he arrived over the crossbar. The beacons would be turned on thirty minutes prior to the scheduled arrival of the assigned aircraft over the DZ.

Each Eureka was automatically coded with the code letter designating the DZ. It could also be keyed manually.[5] Michael Chester, also an 82nd ABD pathfinder, assessed his stick's delivery:

*Actually, I would say that as far as the 505th PIR Pathfinders were concerned the execution of our mission went as planned and was routine and uneventful. By that I mean we took off on schedule, followed the air route we were supposed to follow, were delivered into the exact DZ on which we were supposed to land, reorganized in less than ten minutes (minus only one man), set up our lights and Radar equipment and then assisted in reorganization as much as we could. At no time during the initial landing do I recall our being shot at by small arms or any other enemy action that interfered with us in accomplishing our mission—except perhaps intermittent artillery fire which, I guess, everyone was receiving.*[6]

The pathfinders, whether they marked the exact DZ or not, performed a great service in that they allowed the troops to be dropped in larger concentrations than would have been otherwise possible. When asked, "Do you think your lighted T was a great factor in your getting to your destination?" battalion commander Lieutenant Colonel Vandervoort (2nd Battalion 505th PIR, 82nd ABD) replied:

*It meant a great deal to us. I saw planes coming in from various directions, from 40 degrees to 90 degrees off course. They came in close to the T and dropped their personnel. I think some planes from the 101st circled and dropped their people there.*[7]

The troop carrier groups carrying the two airborne divisions followed the pathfinder aircraft into Cotentin airspace. The cloud bank had not been predicted, but there it was. As time went on it rose up to perhaps 2,000 feet. It was extensive enough to cover the approach routes of both the 82nd and 101st. Vision was sometimes totally obscured; adjacent planes were hidden in a blur of dark gray. General Gavin, commander of the 82nd ABD, later related that by the time he arrived over the Cotentin, the cloud was so dense that he could not see the wing tips of his plane.[8]

Colonel Ekman, who had seen the accident with the Gammon grenade before takeoff, reported that by the time his aircraft arrived over the Cotentin, the rising cloud began 3 miles west of Saint-Sauveur-le-Vicomte and did not dissipate until the Merderet River was reached.[9] Sustained northwestern winds were blowing over the eastern Cotentin at 25 to 30 miles per hour, dissipating the cloud bank.[10] So the planes emerged from the clouds as they approached the DZs. Waiting for them were numerous German light- and medium-flak guns. The Allied air forces had been pounding the German Army in Normandy for ten weeks; therefore, the Germans had beefed up their already formidable air defenses.

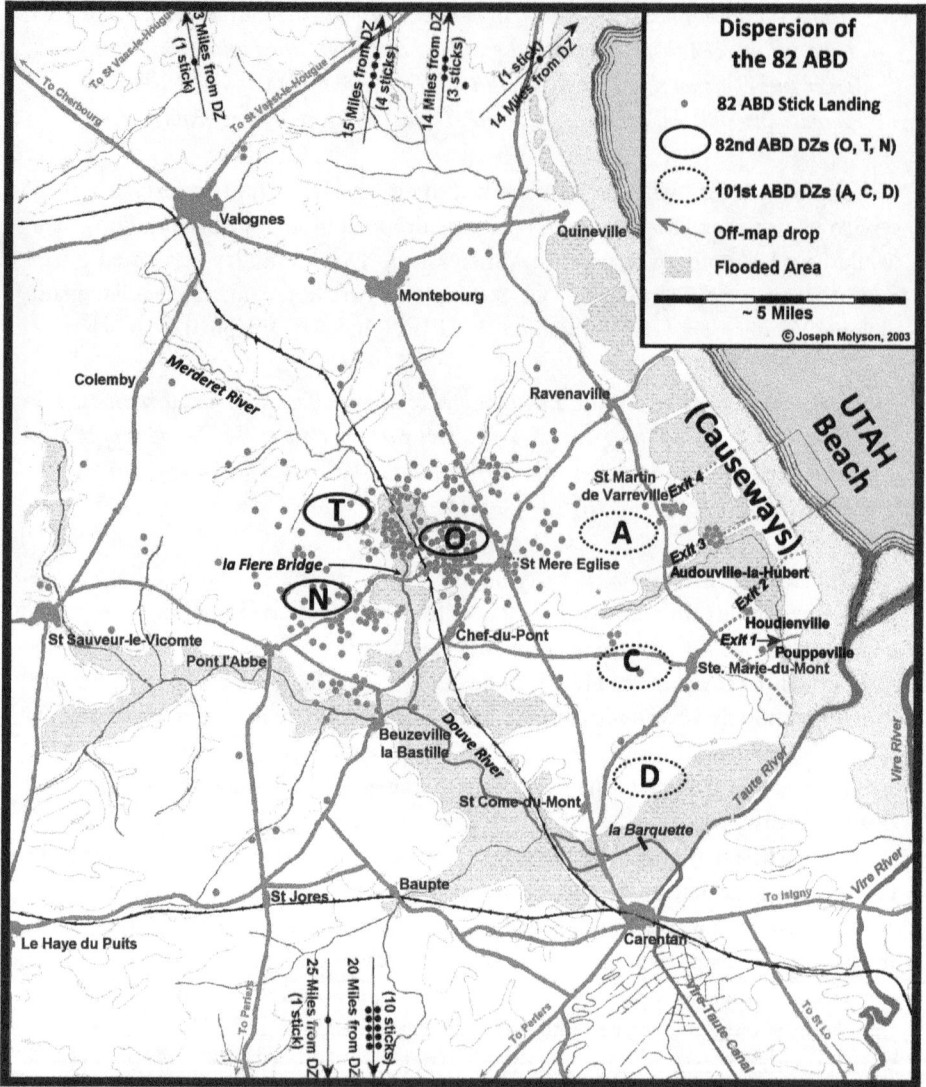

Map 23.1. Dispersion of the 82nd Airborne Division "Sticks" in Operation BOSTON. Each stick was eighteen to twenty-one paratroopers. A similar pattern was experienced by the 101st Airborne Division closer to Utah Beach. MOLYSON[11]

**First Serial, 439th Troop Carrier Group from Upottery Airfield carrying elements of the 506th Parachute Infantry Regiment, 101st Airborne Division**
{Pilot and Stick Number}

Col C.H. Young  1 (includes 506th PIR Commander Col Sink)

Praetor  3    R.A. Barrere  2

G.C. Giles  7

E.A. Nachowitz  4

Kanau  9    R.B. Overfield  8

D.L. Reidy  6    C.D. (?)  5

W.V. Morrisey  10

Armstrong  12    T.F. Corrigan  11

Larsen  16

R.E. Bacon  13

Opheim  18    Slagle  17

W.C. Bailey  15    M. Drozda  14

J.A. Beck  19

G.M. Rubald  21    Roy H. Lanz  20

J.W. Cratty  25

R.H. Rothman  22

R.J. Leonard  27    Wm. K. Ramser  26

J.B. Forshay  24    Unknown  23

W.W. Martindale  28

R.W. Hussey  30    J.D. Stites  29

J.N. Corgill  34

B.E. Deck  31

R.F. Ingram  36    J.T. Hurley  35

R.J. Hall  33    M. Sargent  32
Downed, Stick Lost

H.T. Anderson  38

V. Ruby  39    A.R. Anderson  38

H.Q. Kennedy  43

D.W. Banky  40

T.R. Connor  45    M.F. Stripling  44    Several aircraft also damaged with wounded crew and troopers aboard    A.E. Strey  42    Unknown  41

© Joseph Molyson, 2003

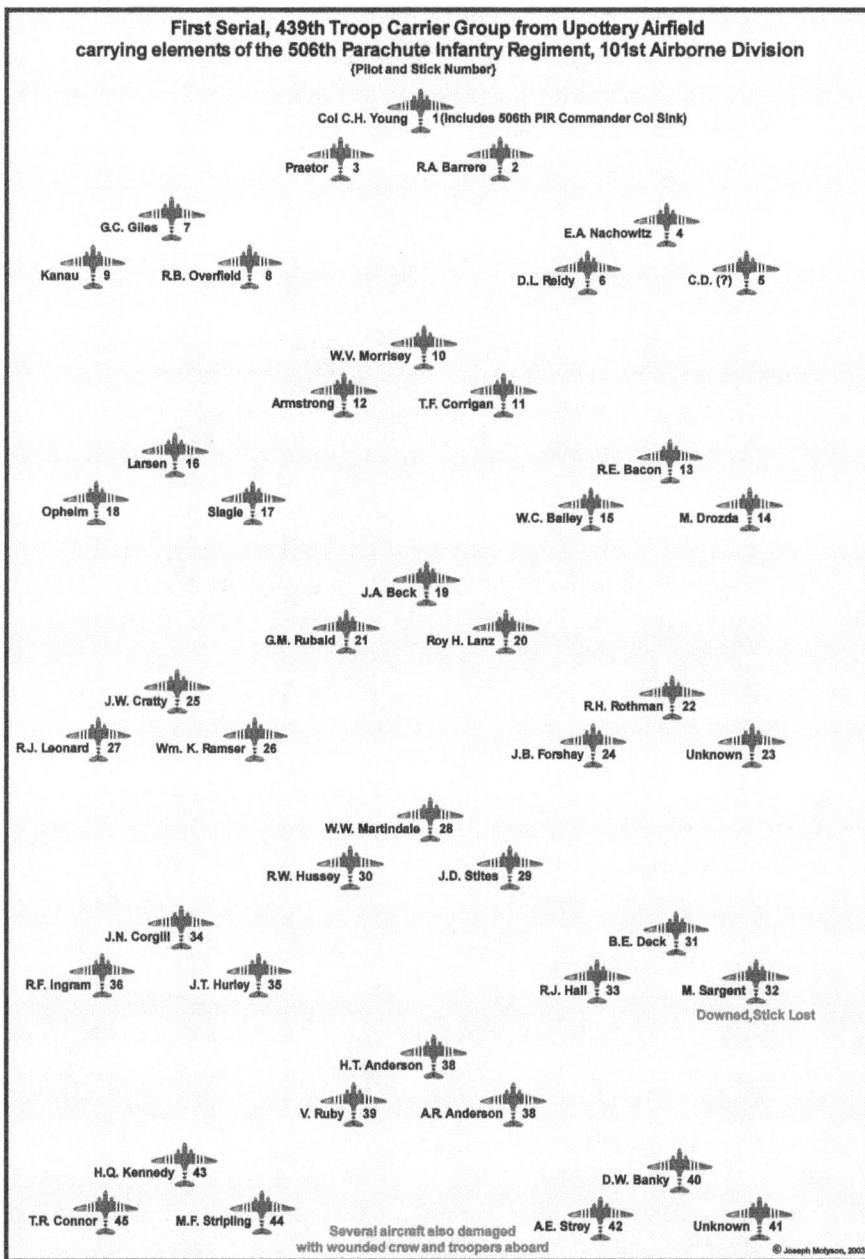

Figure 23.1. First serial 439th Troop Carrier Group MOLYSON, COURTESY OF GERALD C. "BUD" BERRY[12]

# FLAK

Copilot Bud Berry's 439th Troop Carrier Group carried the 506th PIR, whose story was told in Stephen Ambrose's *Band of Brothers*. He recalls the flak that claimed the lives of almost forty 506th Parachute Infantry Regiment paratroopers and the crews who flew them:

> *Just before Ste. Mère Église there is a railroad track. The track was just to the west of Route 13. Now, on that railroad track just south of the center of Ste. Mère Église, there were some flak cars and that area was a real hotspot for anti-aircraft activity. . . . I was flying in position 64. (Stick) 58, which was just to the right in the element in front of us as well as the man on our left wing (Stick 66) were shot down at that point. You can relate it to that anti-aircraft battalion or whatever it was on that railroad track.*[13]

Lieutenant Marvin Muir's aircraft, carrying Stick 58, crashed just to the southwest of Sainte-Mère-Église. Muir received a posthumous Distinguished Service Cross for keeping his burning C-47 airborne long enough for his stick to jump. The aircraft on Berry's wing, carrying Stick 66, crashed just to the northeast of Sainte-Mère-Église at a little town called Beuzeville-au-Plain. The pilot, Harold A. Capelluto, slept in the bed next to Berry in the barracks. Capelluto, his crew, and paratroopers perished. Berry commented on the damage to his own aircraft:

> *We had only one 0.30 caliber bullet hole in the wing of the airplane, so we were lucky. You never know in those things, so you have to take the wing off to check for damage. Sure enough that 0.30 caliber bullet had taken half of the strands of the aileron control cable. How lucky can you get!*[14]

## FINDING THE DROP ZONES

In the Rebecca-equipped planes following the pathfinder aircraft, the navigator standing between the pilots in the cockpit watched a cathode ray tube that displayed a white bar on a distance indicator in the center of the screen. Only formation leaders had Rebecca sets to receive the Eureka beacon signals from the ground pathfinder teams, a ratio of about one in forty airplanes.[15]

When the Rebecca set and the airplane it was mounted in was flying toward the Eureka beacon on its drop zone, the white bar was centered on the distance line. When the plane deviated away from the beacon, the bar would move out of position. The navigator would then talk the pilot back on course.[16] While he was doing this, the navigator also continued to navigate by dead reckoning (navigation by tracking

**Second Serial, 439th Troop Carrier Group from Upottery Airfield
carrying elements of the 506th Parachute Infantry Regiment, 101st Airborne Division**
(Pilot and Stick Number)

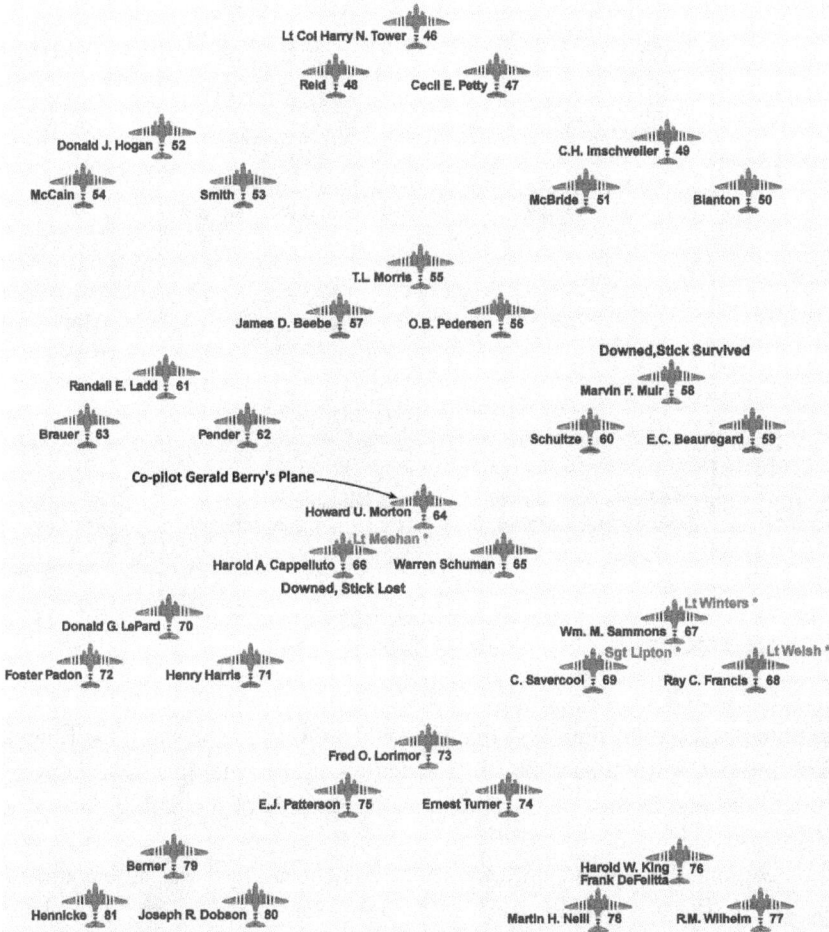

Lt Col Harry N. Tower ┊ 46

Reid ┊ 48    Cecil E. Petty ┊ 47

Donald J. Hogan ┊ 52    C.H. Imschweiler ┊ 49

McCain ┊ 54    Smith ┊ 53    McBride ┊ 51    Blanton ┊ 50

T.L. Morris ┊ 55

James D. Beebe ┊ 57    O.B. Pedersen ┊ 56

Downed, Stick Survived

Randall E. Ladd ┊ 61    Marvin F. Muir ┊ 58

Brauer ┊ 63    Pender ┊ 62    Schultze ┊ 60    E.C. Beauregard ┊ 59

Co-pilot Gerald Berry's Plane ⟶

Howard U. Morton ┊ 64

Lt Meehan *

Harold A. Cappelluto ┊ 66    Warren Schuman ┊ 65

Downed, Stick Lost

Donald G. LePard ┊ 70    Lt Winters *

Wm. M. Sammons ┊ 67

Foster Padon ┊ 72    Henry Harris ┊ 71    Sgt Lipton *    Lt Welsh *

C. Savercool ┊ 69    Ray C. Francis ┊ 68

Fred O. Lorimor ┊ 73

E.J. Patterson ┊ 75    Ernest Turner ┊ 74

Berner ┊ 79    Harold W. King ┊ 76
Frank DeFelitta

Hennicke ┊ 81    Joseph R. Dobson ┊ 80    Martin H. Nelli ┊ 78    R.M. Wilhelm ┊ 77

Several aircraft also damaged
with wounded crew and troopers aboard

**\* Characters In book *Band of Brothers***

© Joseph Molyson, 2003

Figure 23.2. Second serial 439th Troop Carrier Group showing some *Band of Brothers*
historical characters MOLYSON, COURTESY OF GERALD C. "BUD" BERRY[17]

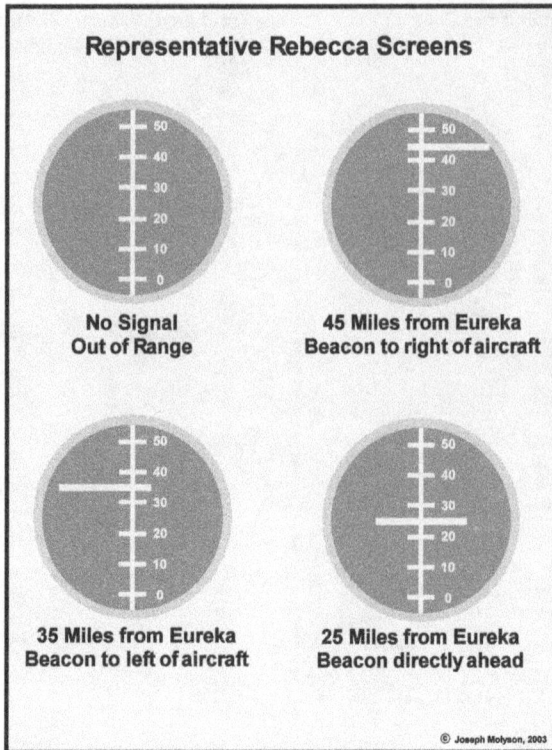

Figure 23.3. Representative Rebecca screens
MOLYSON AFTER DEAR[18]

elapsed time on a certain course) so that he would know where he was if the Eureka was knocked out. It was a busy job. The Eureka sets allowed multiple sticks of paratroopers to descend in the same area. This made assembly of the ad hoc American battle groups easier.

Looking out the window once the cloud was encountered was all but useless for navigation. This accounts for much of the dispersion shown on map 23.1. After emerging from the cloud, if your aircraft was not Rebecca-equipped, the pilot had to use dead reckoning. If lucky he could spot landmarks in the pale moonlight to find his way or see the dim Holophane lights put out by the pathfinders. Throughout all of this, the Germans were throwing all the flak they could at the aircraft flying overhead.

Experiences on approaching the drop zones varied. Pilot Ben Kendig, leading the 44th Troop Carrier Squadron, 316th Troop Carrier Group, remembered the clouds as starting soon after he crossed the coast. As a formation leader, he had a navigator and Rebecca equipment on board. Although Kendig could see the details along the coastline, he remembers seeing the clouds immediately after the coast.

*My first reaction, which was kind of screwy, they (the clouds) seemed to be almost in rows and I thought, "God, the Germans are gassing." Then I said, "Why would they do that?" We wore gas masks and impregnated clothing, tin helmets, flak suits, so we were conscious of gas. Then I said, "No, no, it can't be gas." I knew it wasn't, but that was the first reaction I had.*

*I soon picked up the Rebecca-Eureka. That started coming in. At this point I didn't know what to do. I knew if we went down into the clouds, the formation would break up and things would get scattered all over. So, I decided that the best thing to do was stay on top of the clouds and hope it breaks up. And sure enough about 5 miles from the drop zone it broke up. I chopped my throttles and down we went. . . . We got down fairly good and we slowed down fairly well, and I thought we had a pretty good drop cause I could see the lights from the pathfinders and I thought we hit the target right on.*

*Compared with Sicily (the flak) was nothing. I knew there was some shooting and I could see some flak, but nothing seemed to come all that close to us. I would guess we were at about 120 mph and 700 feet, but the rest of the squadron I'm sure was stacked up a little higher (normal formation procedure). My opinion of the whole thing is if the cloud cover hadn't been there we would had a lot of perfect jumps.*[19]

For the formations that entered the cloud, near misses with other aircraft were common. It was standard procedure to break out of the formation if visibility with neighboring aircraft was lost. There were no midair collisions that night, although many near misses occurred as the planes dispersed. Paratrooper Lieutenant Colonel Krause (commanding 3rd Battalion, 505th PIR, 82 ABD) remembered:

*The trip was very uneventful on the way over. As we crossed the coast of France I talked to my pilot on the interphone, and said, "It looks like a good deal." I looked back and saw my ships behind me. Just about that time we hit the soup (fog or cloud), and we started to see fires on the ground, a little ack-ack and we had some fighters come in on us and fire at us.* [Author's note: No German fighters were in the area; this was probably ground fire.] *An element of three ships was directly under us and not more than thirty feet below. One came up from under and passed miraculously between my ship and the left wing ship. I*

Figure 23.4. Paracrate. These were mounted on bomb shackles under suitably equipped C-47s and were dropped just before the first paratrooper in the aircraft jumped.
AMC MUSEUM, DOVER AIR FORCE BASE, DELAWARE

*would say that in the next three minutes I came as close to being crashed in the air as I ever hope to.*

*We tried to keep our formation, but ships constantly over ran each other. The pilot called for evasive action and we split up.* [Author's note: Colonel Krause was in back of the plane, not in the cockpit. No radio communication was allowed; evasive action under these conditions was normal operating procedure.] *Some went high, some went lower, others right and left. This split our formation and we were well spread. Just about two or three minutes before drop time we saw this green T. It was a Godsend and I felt that I found the Holy Grail. I would say I dropped from 2,000 feet. It was the longest ride I had in over fifty jumps, and while descending, four ships passed under me and I really sweated that out. Just as I landed, a mine bundle hit about 80 yards from me without a parachute and exploded.*[20]

In a 1959 letter to General Gavin (who was helping Cornelius Ryan collect remembrances for his book *The Longest Day*), Gavin's former aide Hugo Olson recounted the encounter with "The Cloud":

*When we left England, the night was bright and clear and we could see the air train for a long distance back. All the planes were in a tight formation and we came in over the Normandy Peninsula* [Author's note: actually the Cotentin Peninsula] *in good shape. I was either right behind you or third man in the stick. As we came in over the Peninsula about three miles, we went into a cloud bank and you could literally see the planes scattering to avoid collision. I will never forget the sensation when we came out of the clouds and found ourselves all alone.*

*Just before we jumped, I saw some of the other planes coming out of the clouds but they were at least one-half or three-quarters of a mile away and were flying on diverging courses. It was just as clear on the land side of the cloud bank as on the sea side, and I suppose if we had had another ten miles to fly, the planes would have resumed their formation somewhat, but as it was, we could not have been more scattered if we had tried. We jumped all alone and as we were floating down, I could hear a lot of shooting going on. In the position I was in, I thought I was the only target they had.*[21]

It was the cloud, not the lack of training or the flak, which caused many of the serials to disperse as they arrived over the Cotentin. Without warning, each serial leader had to decide whether to climb over the cloud bank or penetrate it. The ones who flew over had to dive quickly once they emerged in clear air to descend to the appropriate drop altitude of 700 feet. At least they remained in intact formations with their Rebecca-equipped leaders. The planes that penetrated the cloud lost contact with the other aircraft in their Vee if the formation broke up. Once he emerged from the cloud mass, a pilot had only two to four minutes to find the DZ before his plane crossed the east coast of the Cotentin Peninsula. General Gavin later recounted, "When it was almost time for the green light we emerged from the clouds. There were no ships (C-47s) in sight."[22]

Historian S. L. A. Marshall recounted: "Those planes which had moved too far out, in some cases made three or four passes at the drop zone before the green light was flashed."[23] When a pilot could not find the appropriate DZ for his stick, he was required to find another DZ and drop it there. If a plane crossed the coast with its stick still aboard, the pilot had to execute a right 180-degree turn and drop on DZ "D" near Carentan. This meant searching for a drop zone while under fire and entering an area where hundreds of other unlighted C-47s were likely to pass. No one was to bring unwounded paratroopers back to England, under pain of court martial.[24] Courts martial also awaited men who refused to jump:

*They told us to keep radio silence and they also said that we were to drop them no matter what. If they wouldn't jump, turn around and do it again. They also said*

Figure 23.5. C-47 dropping a door bundle. These were pushed out the door just prior to the first paratrooper to jump. Sometimes they jammed in the door and the pilot had to circle for another drop. US ARMY MILITARY HISTORY INSTITUTE

*that if they don't jump the second or third time over the drop zone, and I don't think that anybody would want to do that, the crew chief should go back and place the paratrooper under arrest. I always had a laugh. You could see the paratrooper sitting back there with all this armament, hand grenades, rifles and knives, and everything, and who the hell is going to go back there and tell him he's arrested?*[25]

Fortunately, very few paratroopers failed to jump on their night of nights.

CHAPTER TWENTY-FOUR

# Shot Up and Shot Down

Some paratroopers later complained that they were dropped too low or too fast. For the pilots emerging from the clouds or descending to drop altitude after overflying the cloud mass, attaining the proper drop parameters was a paramount consideration. Some pilots reduced the power generated by their engines while increasing the RPM of the propellers. The props functioned as a speed brake.

For the men in the back, the resulting roar sounded like their C-47 was increasing rather than decreasing speed. Of course they had neither airspeed nor altitude instruments available in the cargo cabin. Unfortunately, the laws of aerodynamics remained in effect, and it would have been near impossible for all the heavily loaded aircraft to attain the perfect 110 mph airspeed at 700 feet. For example, an aircraft that crossed over the cloud would have increased speed as it descended to the drop altitude. In any case, holding the slightly tail-high attitude required for jumping at 110 mph with an overloaded C-47 required climb power on the engines, generating a tremendous prop blast clearly heard through the cargo door.[1]

Those pilots still in formation also had to adjust to speed changes made by the aircraft in front. Pilot Roger Airgood recalled his flight leader slowing to 110 mph very quickly, forcing the pilots of aircraft on each wing to cut power and pull up the noses of their aircraft to avoid running over the leader. The overloaded C-47s lost speed very quickly, falling behind the leader. The pilots of the trailing aircraft then had to add power to resume formation. When the green light was flashed from the lead plane, the trailing pilots had accelerated back to about 105 mph, but the engines of their aircraft were generating a tremendous prop blast—into which the troopers jumped. This too would have given the sensation of dropping much faster than the actual speed.[2]

The overloaded troops were also dropping heavier than ever before attempted. With equipment, some of them weighed 275–300 pounds. As they jumped into the darkness with no ground reference, they would have experienced much more deceleration than on a training run with a normal load. They would also have descended into the darkness faster, giving the sensation of a low drop. Since the planned drop was from 500 to 700 feet, the aircraft could not have been significantly lower for such heavily loaded men to have survived the experience. Gusts of 20–30 mph were

Figure 24.1. Hedgerow country west of Sainte-Mère-Église HATLEM COLLECTION, US ARMY MILITARY HISTORY INSTITUTE[3]

blowing, adding to the number of landing injuries. It is likely that some paratroopers were fatally carried into the swamps by these gusts.

The problems weren't over when the troopers hit the ground, either. The terrain was segmented in the so-called hedgerow country, called "bocage" by the French. Much of the Cotentin and the rest of Normandy was bocage country. The small fields were separated by rows of trees, brush, and soil up to 10 feet high. The Germans used the terrain well, digging into the excellent cover. A paratrooper didn't have to land very far off the DZ to be separated from the rest of his unit. A single stick might be distributed over several fields. The extensive flooding also claimed its share of lives and contributed to the separation of individual jumpers.

In the first serial of the 314th TCG was the aircraft of Captain Charles Cartwright. Cartwright was flying the Number 7 position, leading the left Vee of the first nine-ship squadron of the serial. Aboard was a stick of combat engineers under jumpmaster Captain Smith (not his real name). Like many other paratroopers on D-Day, it was Smith's first combat jump.

Like so many other flights that night, the approach to the Cotentin went smoothly. On reaching Nav Point Peoria, the overcast tops were at 1,500 feet as the formation entered the cloud. For the next few minutes the formation flew blind and dispersed somewhat, breaking out of the overcast in very loose formation just before the DZ at between 600 and 900 feet. With clear air came the flak, rated as "moderate" by the crew. Heavier flak was noted north and south of their particular course.

Cartwright's plane was a lead aircraft of its Vee and had a Rebecca set but wasn't receiving an adequate signal. The navigator believed the Germans were jamming the Eureka beacon signal for Drop Zone N. Fortunately the navigator was able to use the Gee system to determine the drop location. Such jamming was never confirmed.

When the serial's lead ship began dropping its stick, Cartwright called for copilot Alma Eagleby to hit the green jump light. Paratrooper Smith, in the back of the plane, thought they were too low and told the crew chief to tell the pilot (through the intercom) that they couldn't jump. The intercom was inoperative, so the crew chief went to the front of the plane and told navigator Second Lieutenant Edward Osborne what was happening in the back of the plane.

Pilot Cartwright had no choice but to return to the DZ for a second run, climbing a bit as he did so. By this time, Smith himself had come forward to the cockpit to confer. As they approached the DZ for the second time, two rounds of medium flak (probably 37mm) hit the plane, with shrapnel wounding one of the troopers. Cartwright told Smith, "Get the hell out; everyone except your stick has jumped!" Again Smith refused to jump with his men, honestly still thinking they were too low. Both engines began to burn from flak damage.

Cartwright made another turn, forcing his now-crippled plane back toward the DZ for a third time. Navigator Osbourne told Smith that the plane was going to force land; it was now or never to jump. At that point, Smith led his men out the door and into the ground battle. He would later be killed heroically in action. The plane suddenly went quiet as both burning engines quit. Cartwright turned again, hoping to glide as far as the ocean to ditch. It was too far, so he continued his deadstick turn until he was heading southwest toward the flooded area of the Douve River south of the DZ.

Still on fire, Cartwright clipped the top of a hedgerow as he belly-landed the C-47 in an empty field. The wounded paratrooper and the crew exited the burning plane and made their way to cover at the edge of the field. The wounded paratrooper was given morphine, and the pilot returned to the burning airplane to recover the first-aid kit. The crew eventually made it back to their unit, but not before being mistakenly shot at by other paratroopers, resulting in navigator Osbourne being wounded.[4]

In another incident, Sergeant Raymond Crouch and Private Leonard "Sam" Goodgal of Company I, 3rd Battalion, 506th PIR, were aboard a 440th TCG C-47 based at Exeter. As they approached their jump point over Drop Zone D, flak burst within their formation. For a few seconds the pilot lost control of the aircraft, which plummeted toward the earth and eternity. As they pulled out, the right engine was burning.

Having missed the DZ, the pilot began a turn for another run. The battle damage was clearly fatal to the aircraft, however, and the crew illuminated the green "jump" light. Paratroopers Crouch and Goodgal had to crawl "uphill" to the door, fighting the G-forces inside the doomed plane. Crouch was using a leg cargo bag, which could weigh 80 pounds or more. Like so many of the British-designed bags, it separated as the heavily laden trooper hit the slipstream from the plane. Still, Crouch had a good chute.

He could hear German fire coming up at him as he descended into the water just off Pointe du Hoc, a major promontory between Utah and the next American beach at Omaha. Crouch hit the water. Fortunately, it was only waist-deep or he might have drowned. Goodgal hit further out. His parachute had a quick-release buckle or he might have ended on the bottom of the Baie de la Seine.

The men joined and waded ashore just to the east of the promontory. There they had a balcony seat for massive RAF bombing, shelling by the battleship *Texas* and bombing by B-26 Marauders that preceded a Ranger attack on Pointe du Hoc. They joined that attack and then remained with the Rangers three more days before the linkup between the Utah and Omaha forces. When they rejoined their unit, no one was interested in their story. Company I had also had a tough fight.[5]

## CHARLIE'S STORY

Technical Sergeant Charlie Bortzfield, a crew chief with the 100th Troop Carrier Squadron, 441st Troop Carrier Group from Merryfield had a stick of the 101st Airborne Division on board. Charlie had spent his first night in England in jail. It was so crowded at St. Mawgan, where his plane had landed, that arriving crewmembers were being billeted in the guardhouse, where beds were available. That was March 29, 1944, and since then Charlie and his unit had been training hard for OVER-LORD. Now Charlie and many of the other men in the 441st TCG were on their first combat mission.

*I was standing opposite the jump door. My job was to have a headset on to be in contact with the copilot. The signal light system on the aircraft signaled the paratroopers when to hook up and when to jump. Red was to hook up and green was to go, jump. If that system were shot out I would have to yell to the paratroopers when to hook up and when to jump. Fortunately all the lights came on when they were supposed to.*

*I was hit pretty quickly after we crossed the coast. The formation was so darn long we had probably woken up the German gunners by that time. I don't think the flak was too hairy; I only saw a couple of strings of tracer coming up and a*

Figure 24.2. Charlie Bortzfield's crew in 1944: LT Richard H. Worl, pilot from Skidmore, Mississippi; LT James A. Steward, copilot from Corpus Christi, Texas; SGT Thomas P. Small, radio operator from Many, Louisiana; and S/SGT Charles Bortzfield, crew chief from Lynbrook, New York COURTESY CHARLES BORTZFIELD

Figure 24.3. Charlie Bortzfield and comrades in 2003: Donald M. Stonestrom (navigator); Clifford D. Kantz (pilot); James P. Whalen (pilot); Charlie Bortzfield (crew chief); Richard D. Mudrow (pilot and operations officer); Jean G. Crawford (pilot) MOLYSON COLLECTION[6]

*couple of searchlights. I was hit by shrapnel.* [Author's note: Four paratroopers in Charlie's plane were also hit at this time.]

*I don't know what kind of injuries they had, but they were still able to get up and hook up and jump out. One of them yelled to me, "I'm hit, how about you?" I said, "Yeah, I think so." I was down on one knee. They all jumped out, every one of them. I was told later there were a bunch of holes in some of the seats and some of them had puddles of blood in them. Yet every one of those boys jumped out.*

*I worked my way back up to the forward section. I didn't attempt to take in the static lines, which was my job. I figured if I went over there I might go out the door. I didn't feel any pain, but I knew something wasn't right. So I worked my way to the navigator's compartment, which is opposite the radio operator, and told him, "You gotta go back and pull the static lines." He was just a little guy, blind in one eye. He went back and then came back and told me, "Charlie, I can't pull them in!" So I yelled up to the copilot and sent him back to give him a hand. The two of them pulled the lines in and then came back.*

*In the meantime the pilot's yelling for the copilot to come back to help fly the plane. So he got back, got it settled. They shut the left engine down because it was running very rough. Shortly after that there was a smell of gasoline in the cabin, which is not normal. I know it was hit by flak or something. I don't know if the carburetor was hit, but a fuel line must have been leaking somewhere. Then the pilot came back with a vial of morphine. He wanted to give me a shot. I said, "No way! We might have to jump out of this thing and I don't want to be all doped up." I wanted to know what I was doing, but I didn't really know what I was doing, because they told me later my parachute was full of holes. So it wouldn't have been a good idea to jump anyway!*

*We got close to England and our pilot wanted to try to make our home base, which was way inland. There was a discussion and the copilot won out. "We can't go that way," he said. "We've got a wounded man in back, we gotta get down as soon as we can!" They had different codes for landing at different fields, so I guess the radio operator got us clearance to go into a coastal base we could find.*

*We were coming in to land and the copilot yells back to me, "Put the gear down. We got no hydraulic pressure left."* [Author's note: The crew chief could lower the wheels manually with a wobble pump, but this required a lot of effort.]

*I asked him, "Do we have a green light?"* [Author's note: This indicated the wheels were already down and locked.]

*"Oh yeah," he said.*

*"Land it!" I said.*

*So anyway, we got the gear down but we didn't have any brakes or flaps then, the (hydraulic) pressure was gone. I sat there, saying to myself, "I hope we still got tires, I hope we still got tires!" The wheels were right underneath the engines where the flak came up. Why they weren't flat I don't know, but he made a beautiful landing. As we rolled down the runway the good engine stopped. We were out of gas!*[7]

They took Charlie off the plane and got him to a field hospital where he was operated on. The doctors, seeing a wounded man come in and all news about D-Day blacked out, were asking, "What's going on?" Charlie didn't say much about what happened, and even in 2003 the words didn't come too easily when I interviewed him. Charlie was in the hospital for about three months. His right leg had a compound partial fracture, the bone shattered. Shrapnel was found in one finger. Two other pieces of shrapnel had gone through his arm without hitting bone. He still carried some shrapnel in his shoulder when I interviewed him fifty-nine years later.

Many of the downed C-47s had burned after being hit, probably resulting from the lack of self-sealing fuel tanks. It only took a spark or a tracer round to turn a damaged C-47 into a torch. Copilot Roger Airgood's plane, part of the 436th TCG at Membury, was hit by a single machine gun round near Sainte-Mère-Église. There was soon a strong smell of gasoline in the aircraft. Landing at Membury, pilot Len Hayes turned off at the first hard stand and evacuated his crew:

*When Hayes and I alighted, Norb Milczewski, Hoytt Rose, and Tom Anderson were already standing about 100 ft away in the grass. Gasoline was running out of the tail and the moisture drain holes along the trailing edge of the wing. Later it was found that a 0.30 caliber slug had punctured the tank and lodged in the float. The hole in the tank was the only hit we had.*[8]

Eight hundred twenty-one troop carrier C-47s were dispatched and 805 dropped their sticks, for a mission completion rate of 98 percent. Twenty-one aircraft were lost the first night, or just less than 3 percent. Almost 200 C-47s were damaged, or 24 percent. Even with dispersion, some 40 percent of the troopers were dropped within 1 mile of their DZ, and 80 percent within 5 miles.[9]

The early capture of Sainte-Mère-Église was because of an exceptionally good drop of the 505th Parachute Infantry Regiment (PIR), 82nd Airborne Division, northwest of the town. In this case the pathfinders had marked the drop zone clearly, and the troop carrier pilots maneuvered to drop the troops exactly as planned. The capture of this town gave the 82nd control of the road net behind Utah Beach. All across the eastern Cotentin, the paratroopers had landed and were moving toward their major objectives.

## CHAPTER TWENTY-FIVE

# Gliders

One hundred and four CG-4A WACO gliders (fifty-two for each airborne division) arrived at 04:04 on June 6 carrying jeeps, heavy weapons, and gun crews on Missions CHICAGO for the 101st ABD and DETROIT for the 82nd ABD. CHICAGO landed on Landing Zone (LZ) E. DETROIT landed on LZ W, 5 miles northwest. Although scheduled for a dawn landing, the attack was rescheduled to 04:00 to take advantage of the darkness. This was to avoid the extensive flak encountered by the troop carrier aircraft.

This was the first American nighttime glider assault in history, and almost all the aircraft were damaged in the landing. Forty to 50 percent of the gliders landed within 2 miles of the intended landing zone in a storm of German fire. Weather, darkness, incomplete intelligence on the glider landing zones (LZs), misplacement of some markers, and German flak contributed to the reduced number of gliders arriving on target.[1] Two C-47 tugs were lost as well as one glider downed before reaching the LZ. Many more crashed on arrival; *Rommelsspargel* and other anti-glider devices took their toll. The suggestion made before the mission to use the hedgerows to cushion the landings was ill advised; many hedgerows concealed stone fences and hundred-year-old trees.

Brigadier General Don F. Pratt, assistant division commander for the 101st ABD, was killed when his glider crash-landed during this phase. Pratt's glider carried a jeep with heavy command radios. Someone had bolted extra armor under the general's seat, just enough to kill him. It was too much, and the glider landed very heavy and was smashed. Both Pratt and the copilot, Lieutenant John M. Butler, died. Pratt's aide, Lieutenant John L. May, and the pilot, Lieutenant Colonel Mike Murphy, survived.[2]

Even with the problems and off-LZ crash landings, much of the equipment and most of the men survived and added to the firepower of the paratroopers. The gliders carried in 57mm anti-tank guns and jeeps that might have been critical if the Germans had unleashed a concentrated tank attack. As it was, the jeeps gave small groups of paratroopers the mobility they needed. There was no mass tank attack, but the guns were used for a variety of tasks.

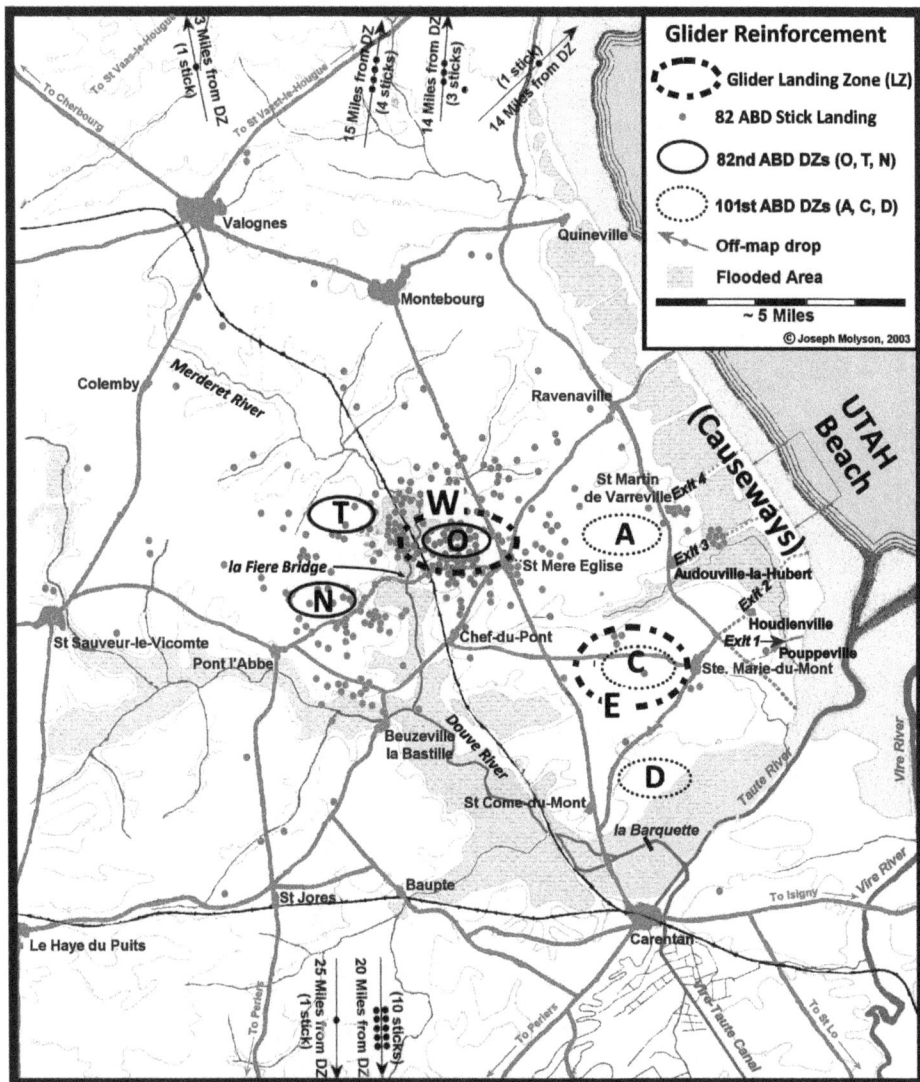

Map 25.1. Landing Zones E and W MOLYSON

Figure 25.1. Gliders in the bocage, June 7 US ARMY MILITARY HISTORY INSTITUTE

At 06:30, less than two hours after the gliders arrived, the amphibious landings began. By that time, the causeway exits off Utah Beach were either captured by the parachutists or in the process of being cleared. The major goal of opening the door for the seaborne invaders had been accomplished. Airborne troops also killed or captured many of the German defenders retreating from Utah and silenced a heavy artillery battery firing on the beach. Shortly after dawn, troops of the 82nd ABD ambushed and killed the commanding general of the *91st Luftlande* Division (General Falley), returning from the wargame at Rennes.[3]

The dawn mission was the last troop carrier movement through Nav Point Hoboken across the west coast of the Cotentin. Subsequent missions would fly to Gallup and then turn east for Spokane and Paducah. On the course outbound from the DZ/LZ, the C-47s flew on a parallel course just south of the inbound course. Beginning at dusk on D-Day, more heavy weapons, command and communications equipment, and medical equipment was brought in by thirty-six CG-4A and 172 Horsa gliders flying the new route in Mission ELMIRA.

The heavy payload of 6,900 pounds made the British-built Horsa the glider of choice for heavy equipment. Losses were much worse than the dawn landings; the Horsa gliders were much larger than the CG-4As and unsuitable for the area into

Figure 25.2. A Horsa pierces a hedgerow and comes to rest in a Normandy road.
NATIONAL ARCHIVES

which they were sent.[4] The Horsas in American service were planned to be used only for daylight deliveries; their landing speed was too high for night arrivals. Exigencies of war, however, prevailed.

At dawn on D+1 (June 7), another wave of gliders and C-47 door bundle resupply was also conducted, designated FREEPORT. It started with a collision between two C-47s as they taxied to the runway at a blacked-out British airfield. It was the first troop carrier collision of the NEPTUNE operation and resulted in the death of pilot 1st Lieutenant Calvin Heinlein. To add to this misfortune, many of the bundles landed in enemy territory. The drop had been preplanned, and the areas actually controlled by US troops did not conform to the plan.[5]

On the way to the drop zone, bombs dropped from a friendly aircraft flying above the troop carrier formation apparently hit a 440th TCG C-47 piloted by 1st Lieutenant John Goodwin. The plane, based at Exeter, had picked up cargo at the base at Welford and was enroute to Drop Zone E. The right side of the cabin was blown out, badly injuring the navigator. The crew chief, radio operator, and a soldier in the back of the plane preparing for the drop were killed. The burning plane ditched in the Channel. The observant crew of an American PT boat rescued the three survivors immediately.[6]

If things were confusing for the Americans landed by parachute or glider, the Germans below were even more perplexed. The dispersion of two airborne divisions, for whatever reason, caused them to cover much more territory than originally planned. This greatly fragmented the German defense as the attackers isolated German units and cut them off from their headquarters. The lack of an aggressive German response allowed the outnumbered and outgunned Americans to win the night battle and hold on until reinforced by the seaborne echelon and glider infantry. The Germans were no match for the airborne attackers, who were able to seize and

Figure 25.3. Ditched C-47, victim of a "friendly fire" incident US AIR FORCE PHOTO

hold most of their major objectives in a timely manner. In particular, the exits from Utah Beach were opened and kept open.[7]

A Ninth Air Force historian put the cost of the successful airborne assault in perspective:

*The American airborne force would suffer 2,500 casualties on D-Day, including well over a thousand dead.[8] Total troop carrier losses for June 5–7 were 41 C-47/C-53 missing or known destroyed, and 449 damaged. 13,215 paratroops, along with 223 small artillery pieces and over 8,000 tons of bundled equipment and supplies, were dropped. The gliders delivered an additional 4,047 troops, 110 medium artillery pieces, 281 jeeps, and over 2,000 tons of equipment and supplies.[9]*

Figure 25.4. C-47s with gliders in tow formations were flown in a column four aircraft wide. Gliders shown were WACOs. US ARMY MILITARY HISTORY INSTITUTE

In his final report on his division's role in NEPTUNE, Major General Matthew Ridgway summarized from his perspective as 82nd Airborne Division commander the performance of the IX Troop Carrier Command:

*The dispersion of gliders, of paratroops, and of supplies dropped by chute, while representing a tremendous improvement over similar phases of the SICILIAN Operation, was still greater than what we may reasonably expect with continued intensive training. Out of 6,300 sent by parachute* [Author's note: in the 82nd ABD]*, there are still 1,200 officers and men missing (as of July 25, 1944) as a result of widely dispersed drop patterns. Some of this dispersion was no doubt due to individual pilot failures, but like failures occur, and probably in equal numbers, among other ground and air forces. In no event should the failure of the few obscure the success of the many, whose gallantry, determination and skill comprised the vital contribution of the IX TROOP CARRIER COMMAND to the accomplishment of our joint mission.*[10]

The airborne attack made possible the relatively light casualties among the troops of the 4th Infantry Division landed by sea on Utah Beach, so it can be said that the cost in men and planes was acceptable to the generals who had designed and ordered the attacks.

After the August invasion of southern France, the Americans and British would conduct no more night airborne operations in World War II. Later airborne attacks in Holland and across the Rhine would be dropped by day. The slow, vulnerable C-47s never got their armor or self-sealing tanks, even though the flak was better aimed in daytime. The motto of one unit, the 316th Troop Carrier Group, applied to all of the IX Troop Carrier Command: *Valor without Arms*.

# CHAPTER TWENTY-SIX

# The Paras

*Do not be daunted if chaos reigns; it undoubtedly will.*
—BRIGADIER JAMES HILL, COMMANDER OF
THE 3RD PARACHUTE BRIGADE[1]

As the Americans were beginning their airborne assault on the Cotentin to secure the western edge of the invasion area, the British 6th Airborne Division (6th ABD) was arriving on the eastern flank. British airborne troops were nicknamed "Paras," short, of course, for parachutists. The Germans in the North Africa battles had named them the "Red Devils" because of their maroon berets, fighting prowess, and

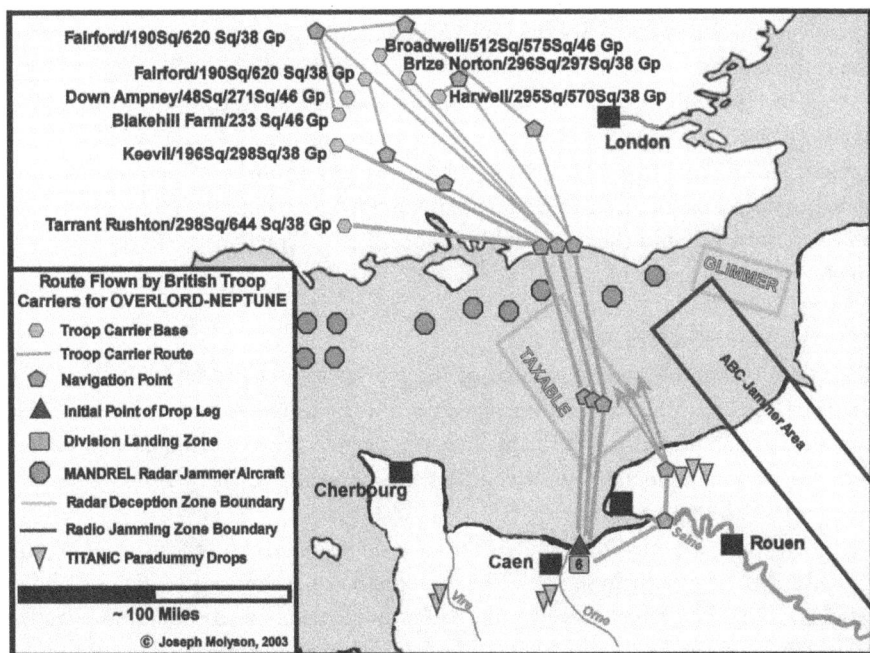

Map 26.1. Routes Flown by British Troop Carriers MOLYSON AFTER WARREN[2]

tenacity. Bad weather adversely affected the British drops just as it had the American operation. Storms and turbulence were encountered over the Channel.

A few of the overloaded Horsa gliders broke their towropes, to be swallowed by the dark Channel waters and lost forever with their occupants. The Brits made do with hemp towropes rather than the stronger nylon ropes of their more fortunate American counterparts.[3] The German antiaircraft fire was as bad along the coast near Caen as it was against the Americans over the Cotentin. Horsa glider pilots Bill Shannon and Taffy Howe approached with troops and equipment of the British 6th ABD.

Through the cloud patches, Bill made out a darker line ahead. The approach to the French coast brought the dangers of flak. As shells started to burst around them, there was a blinding flash from port. The glare temporarily dazzled the pilots as a neighboring glider exploded. Apparently, a trailer of anti-tank mines aboard the other Horsa had received a direct flak hit. The remains of the glider, its two pilots, seven troops, jeep, trailer, and a motorcycle tumbled toward the dark sea below. For them, D-Day was over.

Bill and Taffy exchanged a quick glance of mourning as their Halifax tow aircraft began a series of evasive turns. The unpowered glider was unable to match the turns of the ex-bomber, and the hemp towrope parted at an altitude of just 1,400 feet. The rope snapped back into the upper canopy, damaging it. Now they were on their own and had to reach dry land and, hopefully, the target landing zone. They had about three minutes of gravity-powered flying time remaining.

At intervals, Bill called out the altimeter readings to Taffy, both pilots having hands on the controls just in case. They didn't make the beach, forced by battle damage and the laws of physics to ditch in shallow water just offshore. German machine guns began to rake the shattered glider, killing Taffy. Ditching the glider in shallow water allowed Bill and the other soldiers aboard to escape the wreckage. They had no choice but to surrender.[4]

## 6TH AIRBORNE DIVISION

The 6th Airborne Division consisted of three brigades: the 3rd and 5th Parachute Brigades and the 6th Air Landing Brigade. The British were very keen on glider assaults, more so than the Americans. The Americans tended to bring in their gliders with the heavy equipment in the second echelon of an attack. This was the American plan for the D-Day air assault.

The British also used their gliders for coup de main attacks—those involving the sudden arrival of overwhelming numbers of troops on an enemy target, such as a bridge or fortification. The target was overrun before its garrison could mount an effective defense. Gliders allowed the attackers to achieve instant concentration of troops, unlike parachute troops, which often took extended periods of time to assemble.

The benefit of the sudden arrival of a large armed force at a specific target enabled them to overwhelm the local defense. Targets such as bridges could be captured and exploited or thoroughly destroyed, depending on the situation. Troops arriving for training as pilots in the Glider Pilot Regiment received a warm welcome and immediate orientation into the force they had volunteered to join. The glider pilots had to be both expert flyers and capable infantry, able to use a variety of weapons, including those of the enemy. This required dedication and personal discipline of the highest order.[5]

As part of their infantry training, glider pilots were sometimes dressed in German uniforms and engaged in mock combat with the Paras. To provide experience in urban combat, some of this training occurred in bombed-out sections of London. Glider pilot Bill Shannon, who was taken prisoner after his D-Day crash, remembered becoming separated from his unit while involved with urban warfare training in a ruined neighborhood in London.

Playing the part of an enemy soldier in the exercise, he was dressed in a German uniform and was carrying a Schmeisser submachine gun. He was accidentally left behind at the end of the day. Alone, he had to walk back to his barracks across town in the British capital. Fortunately, the English were accustomed to a variety of foreign uniforms. Shannon later said: "Not one person challenged me, the whole way. In fact I lost count of the number of times I was saluted![6]

By D-Day, the RAF would have two groups of troop carrier and glider tug aircraft available for NEPTUNE: 460 powered aircraft, 1,050 Horsa gliders (29 troops or 3 tons of cargo each), and 70 Hamilcar gliders (40 troops or 8 tons of cargo each). It was this force that would carry the British 6th Airborne Division into Normandy.[7]

Number 38 Group RAF was a mixed force of Albemarle, Stirling, and Halifax aircraft—all ex-bombers modified for airborne operations. The Albemarle was

Figure 26.1. Albemarle ex-bomber, used as a troop carrier and glider tug in Number 38 Group RAF AIR FORCE HISTORICAL RESEARCH AGENCY

underpowered as a bomber, more so as a troop carrier and glider tug. Still, a number of them were available after the RAF rejected it as a medium bomber. The Stirling squadrons had been transferred from active service with Bomber Command due to performance problems at higher altitude. Two Halifax squadrons had also come from Bomber Command as it standardized on the Lancaster. Number 46 Group RAF flew the C-47, called the *Dakota* in British service.

## Eastern Flank Airborne Targets

Key targets for the British coup de main gliders on D-Day included two key bridges over the Caen Canal at Bénouville and the Orne River near Ranville, designated Operation DEADSTICK. Six Halifax bombers would tow Horsas to this target. The landing zones (LZs) for the bridge assaults were designated "X" and "Y." These bridges were vital for any German counterattack from the east against Sword Beach. More importantly, their capture would allow British armored forces from Sword to move out of the invasion area to the south and east and flank German units around Caen. So the bridges had to be both seized and held.

Another glider target was the Merville Battery, whose guns were capable of putting heavy fire on the British amphibious beaches, or so it was thought. Three gliders towed by Halifax tugs were assigned to this operation. The LZ for this assault was the battery itself. 3rd Parachute Brigade troops dropped in the nearby DZ V would coordinate their attack on the Merville guns with the glider coup de main.

The coup de main attacks would occur even as the rest of the 3rd and 5th Parachute Brigades were being dropped as the first wave of Operation TONGA. The initial objective for the two parachute brigades was the destruction of five bridges on the Dives River and its tributary, the Divette. These target bridges (near Varaville, Robehomme, Bures, and Troarn) would not be seized by coup de main. Instead the parachutists would land to the west of the targets in Drop Zones K, N, and V and move to the bridges via foot or jeep.

With additional gliders, these bridges too might have been attacked by glider troops, but there was a RAF-wide shortage of glider tow aircraft.[8] After driving off the German defenders, each bridge over the Dives was to be destroyed. The Germans had flooded the Dives River valley to deter such an attack. Now, the flooding would actually magnify the effect of British troops dropping the bridges.

If all the objectives were met, the lightly armed airborne troops could defend the east flank of the invasion area. Sufficient ground would be held east of the Orne to ensure that the vital bridges at Bénouville and Ranville were kept in Allied hands. Destruction of the Merville Battery would assist in the rapid landing of the seaborne troops, who would silence other heavy batteries around Ouistreham. After the par-

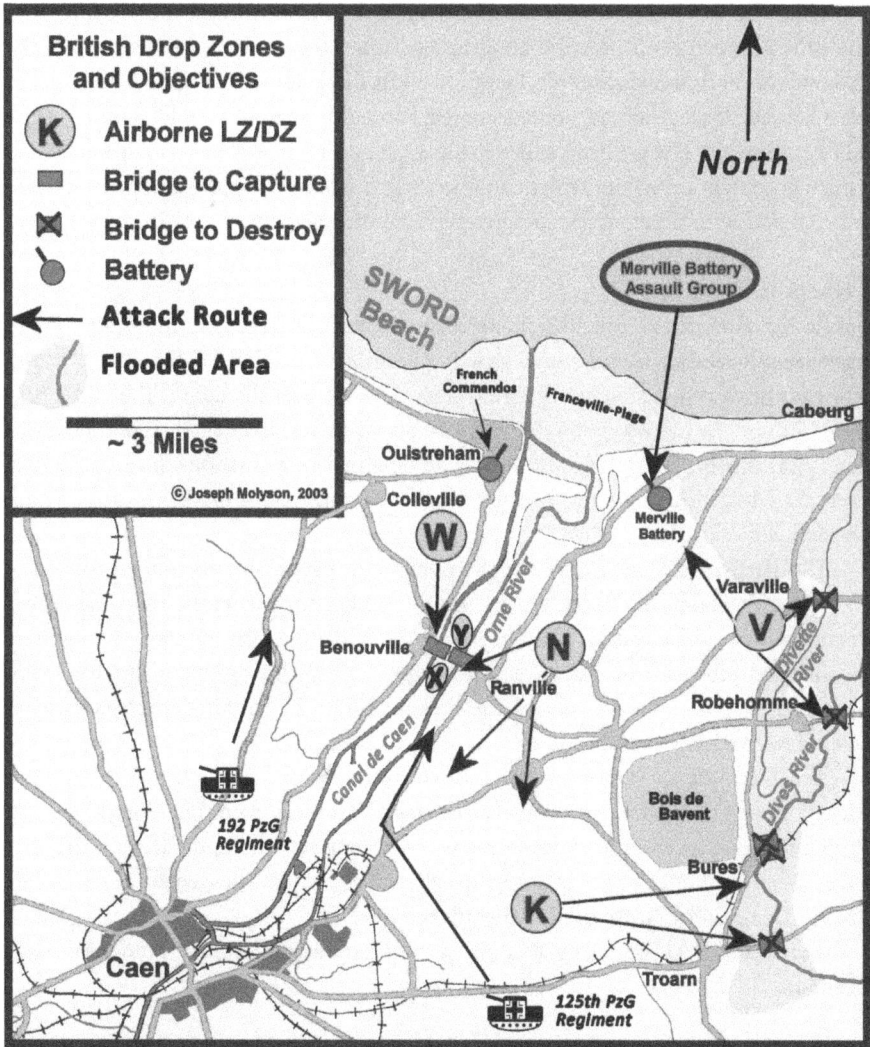

**British Drop Zones
and Objectives**

(K) **Airborne LZ/DZ**

■ **Bridge to Capture**

✗ **Bridge to Destroy**

● **Battery**

← **Attack Route**

**Flooded Area**

**~ 3 Miles**

© Joseph Molyson, 2003

Map 26.2. British Drop Zones and Their Objectives MOLYSON AFTER BARBER[9]

achutists had secured the main LZs, the remainder of the 6th Air Landing Brigade, the glider portion of the 6th Airborne Division, would arrive with heavy equipment and more troops. These men would also be put to work defending the eastern flank of the landing.

With the bridges over the Caen Canal and Orne River in 6th Airborne Division hands, destruction of the Dives bridges would create a third impassable waterway, impeding the westward movement of the German Army toward the landing area. The Dives River system was the boundary between the *7th* and *15th Armées*. If the elaborate deception measures of Operation FORTITUDE failed and Hitler ordered the *15th Armée* to attack the invasion area, it would have to completely bypass the area between the Caen Canal and the Dives. All in all it was just as audacious and critical an operation as the American assault and would allow the seaborne echelon to be landed with much-reduced opposition by the enemy.[10]

## Chaos Reigns

Unlike the Americans, the British airborne did not fly large aircraft formations in night assaults. Instead, their force flew in the more typical RAF "bomber stream," with each crew responsible for bringing their airplane over the target. The glider tugs of 38 Group flew in loose pairs (two tugs and two gliders) in twenty-second intervals along the course. The Dakotas of 46 Group flew in Vee formations at thirty-second intervals. Most British aircraft had Gee radio navigation sets, unlike the Americans, who had very few.[11]

The British had been flying night bomber missions since 1940, and half the troop carrier/glider tug force consisted of bomber-type aircraft, so the bomber stream tactics were well practiced. Over the Channel, the aircraft and gliders encountered storms, turbulence, and towrope issues. The surviving aircraft made landfall near Caen, having crossed the area where an electronic deception mission called TAXABLE was underway.

The RAF troop carrier aircraft also benefited from the anti-radar bombing leading up to D-Day and the MANDREL radar jammers operating along the coast. Surviving German coastal defense radar could not see the approaching airborne force. Despite all of this, like other Allied aircraft, German flak greeted them as they arrived over eastern Normandy. A few planes were hit.

The heavy RAF bombing was also a problem, as glider pilot Andy Andrews recalled:

> *We flew at about 1,200 feet and the trip to the English coast was uneventful. . . . While still a few miles off shore we could see a number of familiar landfalls and all was well. It was at this juncture that Bomber Command entered the picture. Quite suddenly the coast ahead erupted in the bursting of bombs and the flashes from A.A. batteries just as suddenly, it seemed, the coastline disappeared as we flew into a cloud of smoke and debris.*[12]

The first RAF troop carrier aircraft to cross the coast were six Albemarle bombers carrying the 22nd Independent Parachute Company, the Pathfinders for the British 6th Airborne Division. They left Harwell at 23:00 on June 5.[13] Winds drove some aircraft off course, and some pathfinders were not delivered to their assigned LZ/DZ locations. Once they left the aircraft, winds tended to blow the parachutists further east than planned. Winds also affected the main body of troops when they arrived.

The result was poorly marked DZs and the drowning of some troops in the floodwaters of the Dives River. Fortunately, enough Eureka beacons and Holophane-lighted Tees were established to allow adequate numbers of paratroopers to land and assemble. Following the Pathfinders over the Channel came the main body of paratroopers. At least one fell out of the belly hatch of his Albemarle by accident and was lost in the Channel.[14]

Some 30 percent of the force was dropped on the correct DZ; another 35 percent were landed within 2 miles. Waiting for the attacking gliders and paratroopers were the same kinds of flooded fields and anti-landing poles the Americans would encounter in the west.[15] Although German flak exacted a toll on the arriving Brits, as in the Cotentin, German confusion reigned and their actions failed to dislodge the Red Devils.[16]

## Chapter Twenty-Seven

# DEADSTICK

The idea for the attacks on the bridges at Bénouville and Ranville came from Major General Richard "Windy" Gale, commander of the British 6th Airborne Division. Gale's division wore the Pegasus emblem on their sleeve and a maroon beret on their heads, both the symbols of the Paras. He determined the capture of the bridges, Operation DEADSTICK, to be a primary objective of the initial assault. Without them his division area would be split by the twin waterways of the Caen Canal and Orne River.[1]

If the Paras failed to capture both bridges, the eastern flank of the invasion was in jeopardy. Capture of one of the pair was not enough; the Caen Canal and Orne River ran parallel for much of their course. Loss or destruction of either bridge could isolate part of the 6th Airborne Division from Sword Beach. Since from Sword the British were to send relief columns to reinforce and relieve the airborne troops, it was important that the entire route from the ocean to the eastern edge of the 6th Airborne Division bridgehead at the Dives River be held.

The assault force consisted of the four platoons of Company D of the Oxford-shire and Buckinghamshire (Ox and Bucks) Light Infantry reinforced by two platoons from Company B and thirty sappers (combat engineers) from the 249th (Airborne) Field Company, Royal Engineers. Each of the platoons and a share of the sappers would ride in a Horsa glider towed by a Halifax tug.[2] Company D was part of the Air Landing Brigade of the 6th Airborne Division.[3]

Three would land on LZ X, immediately adjacent to the Caen Canal bridge at Bénouville. D Company commander Major John Howard would lead this group. The other three gliders, assigned to LZ Y, would assault the nearby Orne River bridge near Ranville, less than half a mile east. This group was led by Captain Brian Priday, the company's second in command.

The group took off from Tarrant Rushton airfield at 22:56 on June 5. After crossing the Channel, the Halifaxes released the gliders at 6,000 feet near Cabourg on the Normandy coast at 00:07 on D-Day.[4] This would allow the Horsas to silently approach the targets. German flak on the coast greeted the force. The gliders dived to 1,000 feet as the Germans continued to fire on the bombers droning

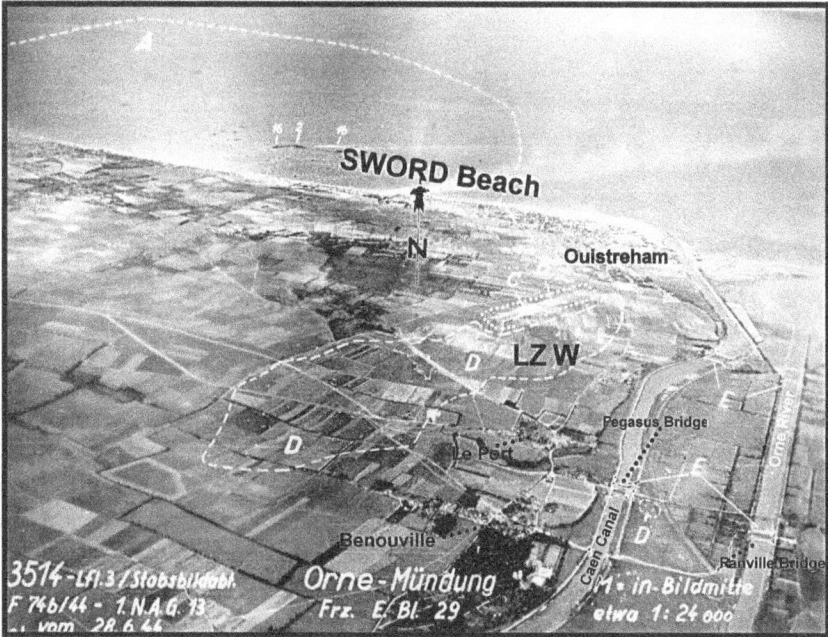

Figure 27.1. German reconnaissance photo of the eastern invasion area
AIR FORCE HISTORICAL RESEARCH AGENCY KARLSRUHE COLLECTION

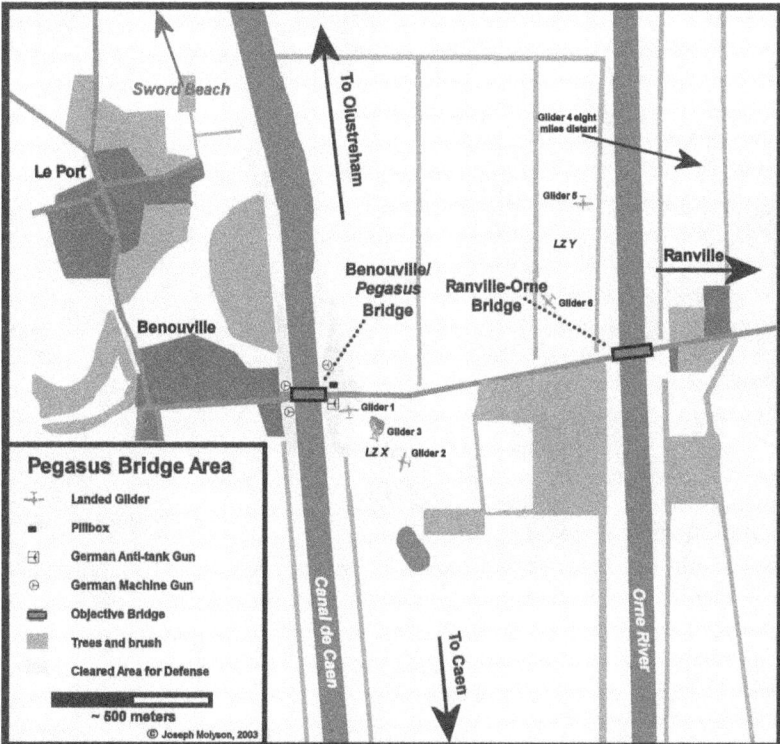

Map 27.1. The Pegasus Bridge Coup de Main MOLYSON AFTER AMBROSE[5]

southwest. As a diversion, the Halifax tow aircraft went on to drop light bombs on the cement factory at Caen.[6]

In Glider 1, flown by glider pilots Sergeant Jim Wallwork and Sergeant John Ainsworth, was D Company commander Major John Howard and a platoon of D Company men commanded by Lieutenant Den Brotheridge. Sergeant Wallwork later remembered that just about every structure in Caen was leveled during the Normandy fighting. The only untouched building was the cement factory! "Thank God they were better at towing gliders than they were at bombing!"[7]

The last intelligence reports indicated that defending the Caen Canal bridge at Bénouville were fifty German troops. They had at least six light machine guns, one heavy machine gun in a pillbox, one heavy machine gun mounted for antiaircraft defense, and an anti-tank gun. There were clear lanes of fire all around the bridge. Howard briefed glider pilot Wallwork on how important it was to get right next to the bridge so that it could be overrun before the Germans manned all this weaponry.

Wallwork promised Major Howard that he would put the nose of the glider into the barbed-wire entanglements around the defended area. Now Wallwork and Ainsworth worked their way toward the target using a stopwatch and dead reckoning. About halfway there, Wallwork saw the twin waterways and the bridges and turned to a direct heading for the LZ. Wallwork was worried about the new arresting

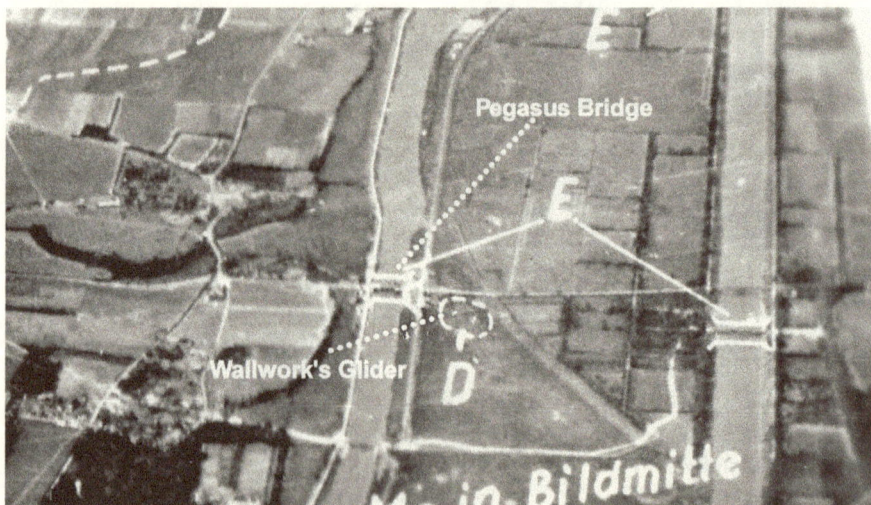

Figure 27.2. German reconnaissance photo of the Bénouville to Ranville Bridge area. The bridges were later nicknamed Pegasus and Horsa, respectively. AIR FORCE HISTORICAL RESEARCH AGENCY KARLSRUHE COLLECTION

parachute that had been recently added to supplement the Horsa's notoriously poor braking system. He deployed it close to the ground at 95 mph, let it slow the Horsa for a few seconds, and then released it.

The glider landed right on the mark as Wallwork had promised, with the nose on the embankment of the bridge. The crash landing was so violent that the men in the glider were dazed for at least thirty seconds. The two pilots were thrown through the glazing of the cockpit.[8] Both men were injured and still strapped in their seats, which had separated from the fuselage. Wallwork would later brag that they were among the first Allied soldiers to touch French soil on D-Day! Inside the glider, Major Howard thought he was blind. He suddenly realized his seatbelt had failed and his head had hit the ceiling during the crash. His helmet was jammed down over his eyes. Pushing it up, he regained his vision and quickly led the men from the glider.[9]

Gliders 2 and 3 landed right behind, giving Howard the three-platoon assault force he had planned on. Glider 3 hit a bank of earth, rebounded into the air, flew over Glider 2, and was demolished on landing. The Germans must have heard the noisy landings, but with flak very active near the coast, they likely thought it was yet another bomber plummeting to earth.[10] Such events were not uncommon in the area.

Now, out of the noisy darkness the invaders came, spraying the defenders and seizing the bridge. A single bullet to the neck fatally injured Lieutenant Brotheridge, the platoon commander in Howard's glider, as he led his men across the bridge. Howard soon received word that the Ranville bridge over the Orne River had also been captured, but Priday's glider was missing.

Not all six DEADSTICK gliders reached their designated assault areas. Glider 4, carrying Priday, landed some 8 miles from its intended LZ Y next to the Ranville bridge. After separation from its Halifax, the glider pilot had become disoriented and landed Priday and his platoon of troops at the Robehomme bridge on the Dives! Landing silently, they surprised a German sentry, who left his helmet on the bridge parapet as he fled in panic. Priday sent Lieutenant Hooper westward to (incorrectly) inform Howard that the Ranville bridge had been taken.

Instead of Howard's men at Bénouville, Hooper encountered another German soldier, who captured him and marched him back toward Robehomme. (See map 26.2.) A firefight ensued; Hooper was rescued and the German soldier killed. One of Priday's men was wounded.[11] Priday held the bridge until the next morning, when a local Frenchman informed him that he was in Robehomme on the Dives, not Ranville on the Orne. With further adventures, Priday's men eventually rejoined Company D. Howard had assumed Priday's men were lost until they rejoined Company D late on June 7.

Other Paras landing in DZ V later destroyed the Robehomme bridge as well as the Varaville bridge to the north. Red Devils who landed in Drop Zone K destroyed the rail and road bridges at Bures and the road bridge at Troarn. Dropping these five bridges over the Dives River, as planned, effectively isolated the 6th Airborne Division from German forces to the east.

## COUNTERATTACK

Howard's radioman sent out the code "Ham and Jam," meaning both bridges had been captured. German counterattacks were not long in coming. German infantry continued to snipe at the Red Devils on the bridge. At 01:30 two German tanks approached the Caen Canal bridge from the west. The Paras' Gammon anti-tank grenades had been lost in the crash landings. To defend against armor, the Brits had only a PIAT (projector infantry anti-tank), a kind of bazooka that launched a shaped anti-armor charge using a strong spring rather than a rocket.

It was not a popular weapon; its range was only 50 yards. The round had a bad tendency to fall out the front if the PIAT was tilted down before firing. This could be most embarrassing if attempting to ambush a tank from an upstairs window. In this case, the PIAT was used effectively to destroy the first tank. The resulting spectacular explosion was enough to cause the second tank to withdraw and the German unit to delay any more attacks until daylight. The first German armored counterattack against the invasion had failed.

At 03:00 the first Paras who had landed in DZ W took up position to the west of the Caen Canal bridge. Other Paras would land to the northeast of Ranville on DZ N.[12] The bridges seized by Howard's Company D were now defended in depth. Around Troarn, east of Caen, veteran German tank commander Lieutenant Colonel Hans von Luck was rousing his 125th Panzer Grenadier Regiment and preparing to counterattack the bridges.[13] Von Luck had served as a panzer officer in Poland, at Dunkirk, in North Africa, and in Russia. He was one of the several capable tank officers who helped forge Erwin Rommel's brilliant career.

Von Luck's unit was a major striking force of the *21st Panzer* Division, located south of the 6th Airborne Division area and concentrated between Caen and Troarn. He hoped to retake the threatened bridges and clear a route north to Sword Beach. Von Luck knew that his unit had no chance in daylight; he had experienced RAF attacks in North Africa and had no desire to repeat the experience.

He also worried about the Royal Navy; he assumed their spotting planes would be overhead at dawn to direct naval gunfire. The spotting aircraft would locate targets, radio their location to the waiting ships offshore, and judge the accuracy of the ships' fire. If the fire was off-target, they would "adjust" the impact point by radio until the Allied shells hit the desired German target. In both assumptions he was correct; the right time to attack was before dawn. He was unable to secure permission to counterattack, however, and endured a long night of angry phone calls with higher headquarters.

In the end, Von Luck's early opportunity to defeat the lightly-armed 6th Airborne Division had been lost, a victim of Hitler's personal control of the armored formations. I could sense his frustration forty-one years later when I interviewed him for this project.[14]

CHAPTER TWENTY-EIGHT

# Merville Battery

Less than 5 miles northeast of the Caen Canal and Ranville bridges was Merville Battery. Due to a chronic shortage of fire control equipment, *Generalfeldmarschall* Rommel ordered a heavy battery to be sited only every 14 miles or so along the coast.[1] So each set of guns was a valuable defense asset against invasion and received appropriate protection from air and commando attack. Merville Battery was one of these protected installations. Allied intelligence estimated that four 150mm heavy guns were emplaced there, each in its own concrete casement.

Such guns could fire a 96-pound shell over 8 miles, endangering the entire length of Sword Beach. American Rangers landed by sea targeted similar guns at Pointe du Hoc between Utah and Omaha Beaches. Glider troops and parachutists of the 9th Para Battalion, 3rd Para Brigade, would attack Merville Battery. This part of NEP-TUNE received no formal designation; it was simply called "the Battery Mission."[2]

The battery was a formidable target. The guns inside their concrete casements were oriented to fire over or on Ouistreham. Circling the battery were two belts of barbed wire, separated by a minefield. While the outer belt of wire was to prevent inadvertent entry into the minefield, the inner belt was 6 feet high and 10 feet in depth. Other mines were placed in marked fields along likely approaches to the battery.

A 15-foot-wide, 10-foot-deep anti-tank ditch some 1,200 feet long protected the Merville Battery on its northeast side, toward the Orne Estuary. This represented the most likely direction of approach for enemy tanks. Inside this formidable cocoon were the four gun casements, protected by weapons positions, each with machine guns. There were also three 20mm flak guns. The garrison, elements of the 1716th Artillery Regiment, 716th Infantry Division, totaled some 160 men.[3]

The plan called for the 9th Para to land in Drop Zone V, then move to the vicinity of the battery in several groups. During this time, a force of one hundred RAF bombers would soften up the battery. It was hoped the bombing would damage the defenses and perhaps provide craters for fighting positions. Once the initial troops arrived, the outer wire would be cut and lanes through the mines marked.

When the parachutists were in position, three Horsa gliders would make the coup de main attack by landing inside the perimeter. Captain Robert Gordon-Brown

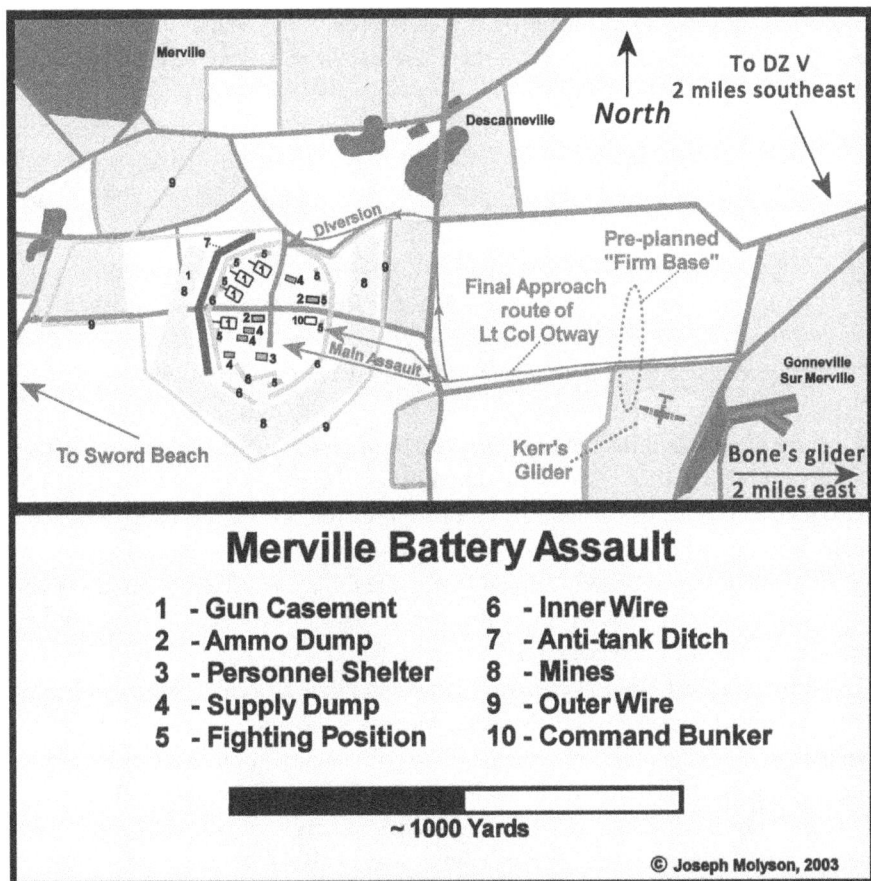

Map 28.1. Merville Battery and Drop Zone V Area MOLYSON AFTER BARBER

led the troops in the three gliders. His troops were known as the "G-B force." Illumination for the landing would be provided by parachute flares fired from a mortar carried by the parachutists. Once the gliders had landed, the troops inside would engage and subdue the garrison with support of the parachutists, who would complete the breaching of the perimeter. Once the garrison was under control, explosives carried in the gliders would be used to destroy the guns. The force would then move on to other objectives with their prisoners.[4]

Beginning at 00:20, the pathfinders arrived on time at DZ V and began their tasks. Unfortunately, several Eureka beacons were damaged in the drop and only two were serviceable. At 00:30 the bombers arrived and mistakenly dropped their bombs on DZ V and the village of Gonneville-sur-Mer rather than the battery itself.[5] Fortunately, there were no casualties on the DZ. When the Dakotas arrived at 00:45 with the 540-man main contingent, they were met with a cloud of dust and debris from the unexpected bombing.

The drop was scattered. Lieutenant Colonel Terance Otway, the 9th Para Battalion commander, landed in chest-high floodwater. As he made his way to the rendezvous, he slowly collected his men. Otway witnessed how treacherous and lethal the flooded marshes were:

> We saw two men come down by parachute and land in the marshes. We tried to pull them out by their parachute harness but it was useless. With their sixty-pound kitbags they sank out of sight at once and were drowned in the mud and slush.[6]

As he approached the rendezvous point, he also encountered two stout German soldiers on bikes. "They were Home Guard types," Otway said, "old enough to be my father. Recognizing the British uniforms, they told Otway that they were "sick of the SS dressing up as Paras and please let them get back to barracks."[7] Otway soon convinced the surprised Germans that he and his men were the real thing and disarmed them. Their rifles went into the marsh, and they were allowed to go on their way. Otway did not reach the rendezvous until 01:30.

During the next hour, he gathered as many troops as he could. Not only were the troops scattered, but many had also fallen victim to the intentional flooding. Some, like the heavily laden men Otway had tried to save, fell into deep water and drowned. Drainage ditches, the bottoms of which were now 8 feet underwater, blocked others. By 02:50 only about 150 men were assembled, and hardly any of the special equipment required to breach the battery defenses was available.

Otway now had to determine whether to go with what he had or cancel the operation.

Otway decided, "It was a question of move off or give up. In the Parachute Regiment, giving up is not an option."[8] Otway started the ninety-minute forced march from DZ V to the battery. Preceding him, advance troops were performing the preparatory tasks at the battery perimeter. The sappers, whose mine detectors and marking tape had not arrived, detected the mines by hand and marked the paths with the toes of their boots.

Although short of men and equipment, Otway prepared for the arrival of the gliders and the beginning of the attack. Pausing at the village of Gonneville-sur-Mer to regroup, he realized that there would be no way to illuminate the battery area for the gliders. The illumination mortar had not been recovered. Assigning the men he had to their final tasks, he led his men through the intended final battalion assembly area, referred to as the "firm base," and to the battery perimeter. There he waited for the gliders to arrive.

## THE BATTERY MISSION GLIDERS

The gliders themselves were having problems. The Horsa flown by Sergeant Arnold Baldwin suffered a broken towrope, fortunately while still over England. The glider safely landed at RAF Odinham, out of the fight. The troops were trucked back to Brize Norton and were flown in on a subsequent glider lift, too late for the night assault. Clouds down to 1,000 feet greeted the second glider, flown by Staff Sergeant Stanley Bone and its Albemarle tow aircraft as they arrived over the coast of France.

The Albemarle tow pilot, Flying Officer Garnett, decided he would bring the glider all the way to the battery. The original plan was for the Albemarle to release the Horsa at 5,000 feet over the coast for a silent approach. The cloud forming near the coast prevented such an early release. Glider pilot Bone saw none of the anticipated navigation aids en route to the battery.

The battery and adjacent LZ were not illuminated as planned, since Otway had no mortar. Only the muzzle blast from 20mm flak guns provided any light on the ground. The rapid-fire guns pummeled both the Albemarle and the glider. In spite of this, Flying Officer Garnett bravely circled the battery four times with his charge in tow, his aircraft and the glider receiving major damage. Near disaster struck when a bullet hit a flamethrower on the back of one of the men, fortunately striking the air cylinder rather than the fuel tank of the apparatus. Otherwise, the glider would have simply become a torch in the night sky.

Finally, tow pilot Garnett gave Bone a choice—return in tow with him to England or cast off. Bone cast off, soon sighting what he thought was Merville Battery. The RAF bombing had so changed the landscape that what was thought to be the objective was in fact the village of Gonneville-sur-Mer. The men at the perimeter watched as Bone's glider flew south under fire. One said with the black humor of combat, "It will be alright chaps; it will come back. The world is round!"

Instead, Bone's glider crashed-landed 2 miles southeast of the battery in a flooded field. Captain Gordon-Brown and his remaining G-B force troops disembarked in waist-high water and moved toward the battery. They watched as Sergeant Dickie Kerr's glider cast off and went down between them and the battery and got their bearing.[9] They moved off in that direction but were engaged by a German patrol. After a short firefight that scattered the Germans, they saw Otway's yellow "success" flares. They eventually rejoined 9th Para for the next phase of operations.[10]

Kerr's glider, the one seen by Gordon-Brown, also encountered flak over the coast, and four men aboard were wounded. Like Sergeant Bone, Kerr had circled the general area for many minutes trying to get a fix on the target. Without an illuminated LZ, the glider was hit by flak again and again as it sought the objective. He passed over the battery itself from west to east and skimmed over Otway's men at the main assault site. Still more hits pounded the glider. This was probably from one or more of the 20mm guns at the battery itself.[11]

Crashing into an orchard, Kerr deployed his arrester parachute, which immediately caught in a tree, slowing the glider sufficiently to save the men inside. Lieutenant Hugh Pond, in the cockpit with the pilots trying to determine exactly where they were, looked back into the cabin and with horror saw one of his men burst into flame from a flak round. On his back was a cheese-shaped explosive charge designed to burn through a steel casement door; instead it immolated the soldier while the others looked on helplessly.[12] Just before landing, Kerr noticed a sign with a skull and crossbones, indicating a minefield. He pulled up the Horsa one last time, skimming the heads of Otway's men and coming to rest in an orchard some 600 yards from the Merville Battery perimeter.

Seeing Kerr's glider crash-land, Otway decided to begin his attack. His men had cleared two lanes to the inner wire, which was breached by Bangalore torpedoes, explosive charges in long pipes. A small party was also sent around the perimeter to the front gate to act as a diversion. Otway shouted, *"Get in!"*

The men from Kerr's glider escaped the aircraft and could tell the assault had begun. The glider itself began burning; smoke grenades in the fuselage had also been hit by flak. They heard Germans approaching, probably hurrying to reinforce the garrison. Instead, they were ambushed by Kerr's men and pinned down. This was fortuitous, for the German's would have caught Otway's assault from the rear.[13] Kerr's fight would continue well after the battery assault itself had been completed.

As the Paras rushed the battery, many could not tell where the cleared lanes in the minefields were—there was no luminous tape to mark them properly. Casualties inevitably resulted, but some of the intrepid force made it through to grapple with the surprised defenders. After that, what the Paras lacked in firepower and equipment they made up for with determination. Soon the surviving Germans surrendered.[14]

Inside the casemates were Czech-made 100mm guns, not the heavier 150mm guns that had been reported. When Neville Chamberlain handed over Czechoslovakia to Adolf Hitler in 1938, he also provided the German Army with a trove of infantry weapons, tanks, and artillery equal to any of the contemporary weapons in the German arsenal. Hitler's army had used many of them to kill British troops in the ensuing war. So much for "peace in our time."

The Czech guns were supposed to be rendered inoperative using spiking charges, which had not arrived. Improvised charges were used instead, although some guns were later repaired by the Germans. One final detail needed to be accomplished. A signal had to be sent to HMS *Arethusa*, a cruiser lying off the Normandy coast. The ship was scheduled to bombard the battery at 05:15 if the Paras did not report it as overrun.[15]

The navy signalers and their radios had not made it to the battery, so the backup system was prepared to cancel the *Arethusa*'s fire. This was a carrier pigeon carried under Lieutenant James Loring's jump smock. Writing the appropriate signal, he released the pigeon. Some say the treacherous bird promptly flew off toward German lines! About this time, having been telephoned that his battery was under attack, the German commander had other coastal defense guns further east shell Merville Battery.

The third backup signal, yellow smoke pots, were lit, but Otway decided that the battery and its imperfectly spiked guns would have to be abandoned. Half of Otway's men were either dead or too seriously wounded to walk. Many of the prisoners were also wounded. There was no reason to remain under threat of bombardment by a British cruiser as well as the other German guns.[16] Otway led his men away from Merville Battery and on to further combat on D-Day.

Merville Battery had been removed as a serious threat to Sword Beach. The Germans eventually retook the battery, but it is unknown if they were able to immediately repair the guns. On June 7 shellfire landed on Sword Beach. It was suspected that one or more of the Merville guns might be the source of the fire. British commandos took the battery a second time but were swiftly driven off by a fierce German counterattack supported by self-propelled guns. When the Germans withdrew from the area in August, they took the original 100mm guns with them.

## Chapter Twenty-Nine

# Red Devil Tenacity

Arriving soon after the DEADSTICK and Merville Battery assaults were more battalions of parachutists in Operation TONGA. These troops connected the DEADSTICK and Merville Battery forces and secured the eastern flank of the whole invasion. After the initial objectives were accomplished, the first support gliders arrived. Sixty-four Horsas and four of the larger Hamilcars delivered a bull-dozer, forty-four jeeps, fifty-five motorcycles, and seventeen anti-tank guns into the 6th Airborne Division bridgehead. The Gee radionavigation sets in the glider tow aircraft had served them well. Most of the surviving gliders arrived on their LZ or within 1 mile of it.[1] All of this happened before the dawn of D-Day.

The Horsas took quite a beating in the predawn operation. Flak and weather accounted for sixteen, a loss rate of over 20 percent. Many more gliders would be damaged beyond repair on landing. Some were wrecked by Rommel's anti-glider poles, others by stone walls or rough landings. Jammed release bolts made it difficult to break the fuselage in two as planned, but the innovative crews were able to recover their valuable cargos.[2]

In most cases the cargo was in serviceable condition. The arrival of anti-tank guns and other equipment later allowed the lightly armed Paras to defeat German counterattacks supported by tanks. By dawn on D-Day, the British 6th Airborne Division had achieved all its objectives, even though in some cases this required improvising new tactics to offset missing equipment and dispersed troops.[3]

At 06:30 the Allied naval bombardment started, cheering the Paras with the knowledge that the seaborne invaders would soon be joining them. Soon after dawn, two Italians who approached the Caen Canal bridge position were taken prisoner. The former German allies were part of the forced labor organization putting up the anti-glider poles. Major Howard had them released. Although their duties were now superfluous, they continued to install poles around the crashed gliders![4] They feared the return of the Germans more than the ridicule of the Red Devils.

Around 09:00, two German patrol boats packed with infantry approached from Ouistreham on the Caen Canal. These were probably units of the *10.R-bootsflotille* based at Ouistreham.[5] The lead boat began raking the bridge with 20mm fire from

Figure 29.1. Two Horsa gliders landed in Normandy. Horsa on right has fuselage opened for unloading NATIONAL ARCHIVES

its deck gun. The Paras responded with a PIAT round that struck and disabled the boat's deckhouse. The patrol craft drifted to the east bank and the crew was captured. D Company swarmed aboard, looking for weapons that could be useful and liberating a bottle of brandy.

The other boat prudently decided to withdraw north toward Ouistreham, the port facility for the city of Caen.[6] During the morning, French commandos landed at Sword Beach and assaulted Ouistreham, opening the east exit from Sword. Clearing this area allowed British commandos to move through Ouistreham, eventually relieving Major Howard's men holding the Bénouville and Ranville bridges.

An Fw 190 fighter-bomber appeared and dropped a bomb on the Caen Canal bridge, one of the few *Luftwaffe* aircraft to penetrate the Allied air armada. The German was a good shot; the top of the superstructure was hit, but fortunately the bomb was a dud. Other than a large dent, the bridge suffered no damage. Two German frogmen were also sighted approaching the bridge from the north and were killed by Para snipers.

The *21st Panzer* Division conducted the only large German armored counterattack on D-Day. At noon, von Luck finally received permission to begin his attack against the Ranville and Caen Canal bridges. His regiment attacked up the east side of the Orne River. Almost immediately, his vehicles were spotted and came under air and naval bombardment.[7]

It would be 13:00 before a seaborne force of commandos and armor under Lord Lovat reinforced the Paras on the bridges. By this time, Von Luck's men were already bringing pressure on the bridge defenders. Other Paras were arriving from the east side of the 6th Airborne Division area, their mission to fell the Dives River bridges completed. They rallied to defend the eastern approaches to the Bénouville-Ranville area, which they held successfully. Von Luck's men never reached either bridge.

At 15:00 another gunboat attacked the Caen Canal bridge, this time coming up from Caen to the south. Like the earlier boat, it was loaded with infantry. The captured German anti-tank gun positioned near the bridge drove it off.[8] By dusk on D-Day, Howard and his men had earned a special place in Red Devil history. The Caen Canal bridge was later formally renamed "Pegasus Bridge" by the French. The critical but less famous Ranville bridge over the Orne River was renamed "Horsa Bridge." Air Chief Marshal Leigh-Mallory would later say that Sergeant Wallwork's pinpoint landing at the bridge was the "finest feat of flying" in World War II. Wallwork was later decorated at Buckingham Palace for his accomplishment.

About the time von Luck began his attack on the Bénouville-Ranville bridges, the rest of *Generalmajor* Edgar Feuchtinger's *21st Panzer* Division attacked north from Caen directly toward Sword Beach. The British 3rd Infantry Division had penetrated to within 2 miles of Caen, where it was engaged by advancing armored units of the *21st Panzer*. Stubborn British resistance, including infantry, armor, and artillery units that had landed at Sword Beach, slowed the determined counterattack.

Naval gunfire support and Typhoon fighter-bombers contributed to the German losses. A few German tanks are thought to have penetrated all the way to the beach. What is sure is that by the end of D-Day, the British had thrown the *21st Panzer* Division back from the beach and inflicted major tank losses.

## MALLARD

The remaining elements of the 6th Air Landing Brigade was the last to arrive in the combat area in Operation MALLARD, landing by glider at 21:00 on D-Day. Two additional gliders had been shot down en route. The surviving gliders landed in LZs W and N. MALLARD included 216 Horsas and 30 Hamilcars, the Hamilcars carrying small airborne Tetrarch tanks and 3,000 troops. These would be valuable in the days ahead.

Seeing the mass of gliders and aircraft flying over his badly battered *21st Panzer* Division, *Generalmajor* Feuchtinger ordered a general withdrawal back to Caen. He was worried this was an attempt to cut off his overly extended unit. Sword Beach was safe for now. Unfortunately, Feuchtinger's retreat into the town ended the British attempt to capture Caen.

## ROB ROY

At midnight of D-Day, 46 Group dispatched fifty Dakotas to perform a resupply drop in Operation ROB ROY. Allied naval gunners managed to shoot down six Dakotas and the men inside despite the recognition stripes, invisible in the dark.[9]

On June 10, six Halifaxes of 38 Group dropped six jeeps and towed antiaircraft guns by parachute. The equipment had been carried in the modified bomb bays of the bombers. Each gun and jeep had twelve 32-foot parachutes attached to a supporting frame. Only one jeep was unserviceable after the drop. This was the first combat delivery of such heavy equipment by parachute. In the aftermath of World War II, the cargo parachute and the helicopter would displace the combat glider from the battlefield.

Without the timely and successful execution of the 6th Airborne Division's objectives, it is likely that the eastern flank of the entire OVERLORD area would have been overrun by German forces. In all, British airborne forces would suffer some 650 casualties on D-Day.[10] Caen itself did not fall to the seaborne invasion troops as planned. There would be many weeks of heavy combat before the remnants of Caen would fall.

By the end of D-Day, the Germans defending Normandy had been pummeled from the air, sea, and by the troops landed on the assault beaches. According to a *Luftwaffe* adjutant on Hitler's staff, the most punishing blow "was the parachute drop by three divisions into the *7th Armée* sector."[11]

# CHAPTER THIRTY

# The Sky Above

*Of all the terrors we faced, however, none seemed more menacing than the threat of German air. For our army, huddled on a narrow beachhead, could be severely mauled should the* Luftwaffe *breakthrough in strength. And a naval force concentrated offshore would offer Goering a tempting target for all-out air attack.*[1]

—LIEUTENANT GENERAL OMAR BRADLEY,
COMMENTS ON THE 1943 INVASION OF SICILY

When the Allied Expeditionary Air Force (AEAF) was established, the critical nature of air supremacy over the beach indicated that an officer with fighter experience should be its commander. This was Air Marshal Trafford Leigh-Mallory, who moved to this job from his position as AOC (air officer commanding) Fighter Command.[2] The *Luftwaffe* had proved to be a formidable threat to the Allied invasion fleets off Sicily, Salerno, and Anzio in Italy. This threat had to be reduced or eliminated for the critical landing in Normandy.

The limited range of the primary RAF air superiority aircraft, the Spitfire, was a serious issue. In 1942, when the disastrous Operation JUBILEE at Dieppe was conducted, the Spitfires could not prevent *Luftwaffe* attacks on the Canadian troops or their vessels offshore. Yet Leigh-Mallory's Fighter Command had bragged that it had won an air victory "over 70 miles" from the English coast.

Not only was there no Allied air victory at Dieppe, but it was also obvious to the planners that either longer-ranged fighters were needed or airfields would have to be captured early in the OVERLORD operation.[3] AEAF got both. Large numbers of long-range American fighters arrived in Britain. To allow the shorter-range RAF fighters to base forward in France, enough American and British aviation engineering units were established to build forward airfields in France after suitable ground was liberated.

As leader of the AEAF, Leigh-Mallory theorized that a great air battle over the invasion area would be necessary to complete the destruction of the *Luftwaffe* on D-Day. By June 1944, the great air battle had already been won. Daytime raids by the Eighth Air Force into Germany had cost the *Luftwaffe* some 1,000 fighter pilots they could not replace. Leigh-Mallory's plan for establishing air superiority in France was flawed, but later his expertise in the air defense of Britain was critical in defending against the V-1 missiles approaching London.

## CONTROL

Arrangements for better Allied air support and fighter cover would be inadequate if the aircraft could not be controlled. On D-day, the headquarters ship for each of the five assault beaches—Utah, Omaha, Gold, Juno, and Sword—had an air staff to integrate air operations with those of the naval and ground forces. Radio-equipped forward air coordinators accompanied the British, American, and Canadian assault units once landed. Their job was to determine air support requirements and radio these back to the headquarters ship for their beach.

While the headquarters ships' air staffs coordinated support for the ground and naval forces, an additional control element was necessary to manage the Allied fighters over Normandy. The task of bringing forward the air control elements was solved by establishing teams afloat and others to be landed onshore. There were three fighter direction tenders, or FDTs, to control fighters supporting the invasion. Each FDT was a specially modified, radar-equipped tank landing ship. The ships were American built, British equipped, and RAF operated. They were deployed in a triangle to provide complete radar coverage of the convoy routes, anchorage, and beachhead (see map 30.1).

## Table 30.1. Beach Headquarters Ships on D-Day

| Beach | Ship | Callsign |
|-------|------|----------|
| Juno | HMS *Hillary* | HEROD |
| Sword | HMS *Largs* | BOATMAN |
| Gold | HMS *Bulolo* | BALDWIN |
| Omaha | USS *Ancon* | BULLET |
| Utah | USS *Bayfield* | GIMLET |

*Note*: Each ship had an air staff.

*Source*: Ken Delve, *D-Day The Air Battle* (London: Arms and Armour Press, 1994), 93; John Terraine, *The Right of the Line: the Royal Air Force in the European War, 1939–1945* (London: Hodder and Stoughton, Ltd., 1985), 633–34.

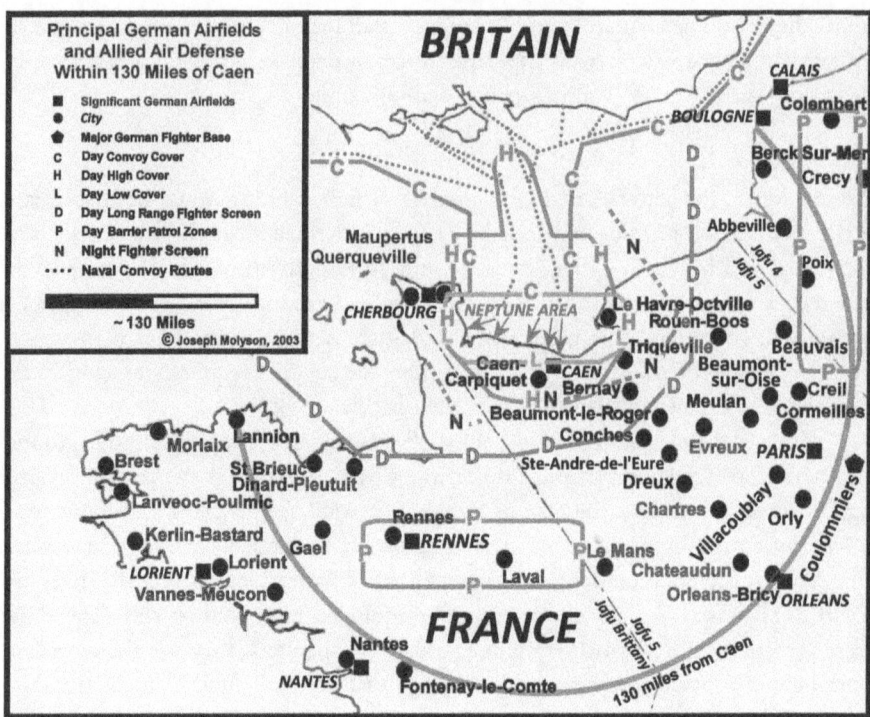

Map 30.1. Principal German Airfields and Allied Air Defense. Air defense was a complex system defending the fleet and troops at all altitudes. MOLYSON[4]

The equipment aboard the FDT was similar or identical to that employed in Britain for supporting air operations, extending the existing RAF air control network to the coast of Normandy and beyond. Among the embarked radars was the Type 11, derived from equipment captured from the Germans to assemble a clone of their air search radar. Even if the Germans were jamming British radar, the Type 11 would still function because it operated on frequencies the Germans would not jam.

The FDTs managed the flow of aircraft arriving over the beach, sometimes a thousand an hour, and provided radar surveillance of nearby airspace. Due to advanced planning and a superb air control system, by D-Day all *Luftwaffe* fields within 130 miles of Caen had been attacked and were periodically monitored for activity. The FDTs ensured that Allied aircraft were patrolling the right airspace and hitting the right targets. Day or night, they detected enemy aircraft and directed their interception.

## Table 30.2. Primary Mission Equipment aboard Fighter Direction Tenders (FDTs) on D-Day

| Equipment | Function | Comments |
| --- | --- | --- |
| Air Operations Room | Location where information was received, processed and employed | Highly classified compartment belowdecks on the FDT |
| Airborne Interception Beacon (AI) | Radar repeater at known location that appeared on the air interception equipment aboard night fighters to allow the aircraft to navigate more accurately | Mounted aboard FDTs to assist Allied night fighters |
| Friendly radio communications equipment | Voice and radiotelegraph for ship-to-ship, ship-to-shore, and ship-to-aircraft communications for coordination of operations | Various communications antennas, signal lights, and flags and semaphore |
| Mark 3 Identification Friend or Foe (IFF) | Equipment fitted to Allied aircraft to identify it as friendly. Used when the Air Movements Liaison Section could not confirm the identity of a particular aircraft. | Standardized Allied system, including the transmitter, receiver, control boxes, and coding units. Located aboard each aircraft and associated with surface-based GCI radar sets. |
| Plan Position Indicator (PPI) | Cathode ray tube radar display | Counteract the effects of Window (chaff) dropped from German aircraft to confuse Allied radar |
| Radio Counter Measures (RCM) | Equipment to counteract German efforts to jam or disrupt Allied communications | Various modules on equipment |

*(continued)*

177

## Table 30.2. *Continued*

| Equipment | Function | Comments |
| --- | --- | --- |
| Type 11 "German" radar | To avoid anticipated German jamming of British frequencies, FDTs also had copied German radar equipment developed from gear captured during a commando raid on Bruneval, France, in 1942. The Germans did not jam their own frequencies. | Rotating antenna gantry at the amidships approximately 30 feet above water |
| Type 15 GCI Radar | Ground control interception radar designed to monitor all air activity in a designated area of the conflict | Rotating antenna gantry at the bow, approximately 30 feet above water |
| Y-Section Signals Intelligence Suite | Interception of German ground-to-air and air-to-air "command and control" communications | Radio intercept antennas |

*Source*: "Fighter Direction Tenders—FTDs 13, 216 & 217," Combined Operations, accessed March 8, 2025, https://www.combinedops.com/FDT.htm; "RADIO IDENTIFICATION SYSTEMS—IDENTIFICATION, FRIEND or FOE, or I.F.F.," *VK2DYM's Radio and Radar Information*, accessed March 8, 2025, https://www.qsl.net/vk2dym/radio/iff.htm.

When sufficient beachhead was captured, the USAAF Control Center and the RAF 83 Composite Group Control Centre were sent ashore and began operating. The USAAF center controlled all aircraft, American or British, operating over the American beaches (Utah and Omaha), while the RAF control center directed aircraft over the British beaches: Gold, Juno, and Sword. The FDTs and the control centers could replace or supplement one another as necessary.[5]

Figure 30.1. B-26s bombing a German airfield AIR FORCE HISTORICAL RESEARCH AGENCY

## FROM PLAN TO REALITY

RAF day and night fighters of the Air Defense of Great Britain (ADGB) protected the ships as they assembled in the harbors prior to D-Day, keeping the Allied fleet hidden from German eyes. The air cordon around the NEPTUNE assault area began at dusk on June 5, when British night fighters crossed the Channel into France. Aircraft from six or more squadrons flew three patrol lines: one east of Le Havre, one south of Caen, and one paralleling the west coast of the Cotentin Peninsula (see map 30.1).

Since there were hundreds of troop carrier and glider tow missions to deliver the three airborne divisions before dawn on D-Day, air superiority was critical. Unfortunately, the new American P-61 Black Widow night fighter was not yet ready for operations. It would not fly combat missions until after D-Day, but the RAF had the pilots and planes to handle the job. The six RAF Mosquito night fighter squadrons were more than adequate to the task.

On the night of June 5–6, the only air-to-air combat was the downing of a German Ju 188 reconnaissance aircraft near the south coast of England, shot down by a Mosquito night fighter. There was too much at stake to allow its survival.[6] The night fighter patrols also enabled the troop carrier units and "bullshit bombers"— aircraft tasked with dropping warning leaflets to the French population—to operate without air opposition. Since the *Kriegsmarine* had canceled its surface vessel patrols because of predicted weather, any chance of *Luftflotte 3* mounting an attack on the invasion fleet during its approach was lost. The *Luftwaffe* was unaware of the tidal wave heading south from England.

The weather, having no allegiance, did not cooperate with either side. The Germans considered it impossible for the Allies to land in such conditions. As the Allies made their move, June 6 dawned with low clouds, gusty winds, and 6-foot waves. The unsettled seas made navigation more difficult and sickened the thousands of troops crossing the Channel. In the air, the bombardiers counted on gravity to bring their carefully aimed bombs down onto their targets. Instead, the westerly winds made them drift east.

The first daylight air cover visible to the seaborne invaders on June 6 arrived at 04:30, when two squadrons of P-38s took station over the invasion fleet at 4,000 feet.[7] The ships had already left their ports and formed convoys and were crossing the Channel and approaching Normandy. This convoy cover mission would occupy all the P-38 units until midday, when the bulk of the ships arrived in the invasion

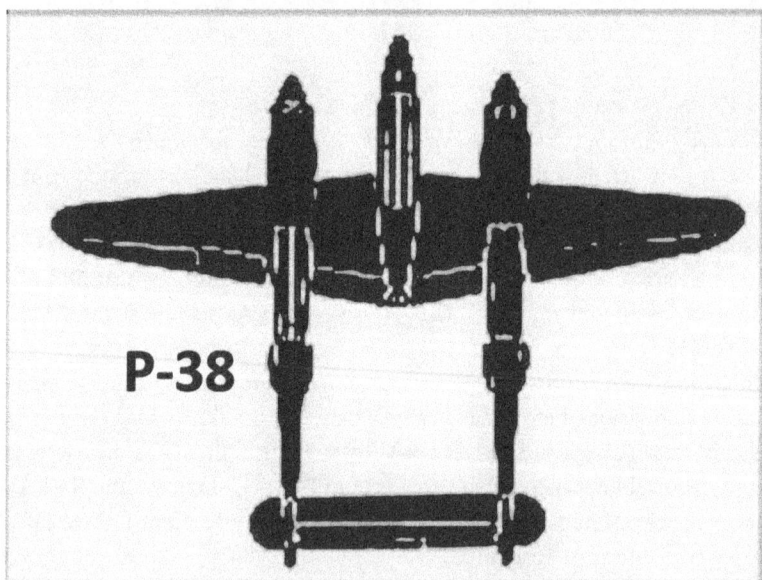

Figure 30.2. The P-38 Lightning planform had a distinctive silhouette unlike any German fighter. AIR FORCE HISTORICAL RESEARCH AGENCY

anchorage in the Baie de la Seine.[8] OVERLORD veteran Edward Giller recalled the unique use for the P-38:

> *The P-38 was used during the invasion as local beach cover because of its recognizable form. Nevertheless, it was discouraging to see the local US gunners shooting at us whenever we flew over their ships. There were so many American airplanes over the beaches that flight collision was the greatest hazard. The controller would give a grid location of a bogie and at least 200 airplanes would converge on that spot.[9]*

Once in the Baie de la Seine, ships came under the protection of additional RAF and American fighters. RAF Spitfires, mainly Spitfire IXs of RAF 2TAF with range-extending "slipper" external fuel tanks, provided low cover from 3,000 to 5,000 feet. Above them, providing high cover were US 9th Air Force P-47s from 8,000 to 15,000 feet. Some 300 Spitfires and P-47s in the low- and high-cover zones greeted the fleet on its approach to France.[10]

The naval antiaircraft capability of the US and Royal Navies, much-feared by airmen on both sides, was bolstered by the deployment of nine "eagle ships." These were so named because the first two of their numbers were the HMS *Royal Eagle* and HMS *Crested Eagle*.[11] Festooned with medium and light antiaircraft guns, they filled gaps in the already formidable surface-to-air defense system. With massive airpower overhead and masses of antiaircraft guns on the warships, the soldiers of the invasion fleet were as safe from direct *Luftwaffe* attack as they had been in England, perhaps more so.

Eighth Air Force P-47 Thunderbolts and P-51 Mustangs formed an outer fighter cordon around NEPTUNE.[12] For the fighter crews who had the earliest defensive orbits, a takeoff as early as 02:00 was necessary. Squadrons had to take off and assemble in the dark. Overcast covered much of England that day, forcing the assembly of units on top of the clouds after hair-raising launches. If a squadron broke up, the various elements were still expected to fly on to the assigned patrol.

Sorties could last seven hours, a long time in a single-seat fighter.[13] Leigh-Mallory's great air battle did not occur, at least not on D-Day. It had been fought and won at great cost by the US Eighth Air Force over Germany back in February and March; now the invasion force was relatively safe from enemy daylight attack. The German planes that had appeared were more of a curiosity than a serious threat to the invasion; many veterans on both sides don't remember seeing any *Luftwaffe* aircraft on D-Day.[14]

On D-Day, the Allied air forces operated over 160 day fighter squadrons, about 3,500 fighters available for multiple sorties from well-protected airfields. Against the invaders, *Luftflotte 3* had eighteen fighter squadrons totaling about 175 Fw 190A-8s and Bf 109G-6s fighters in all of France. It was far from enough.

## HITTING GROUND TARGETS

Since April, Allied fighter pilots had participated in the Transportation Plan and bridge attacks and were well-versed in both air-to-air and air-to-ground combat. German accounts of D-Day allude to the effect of a continuing cloud of Allied fighter-bombers. They called them *Jabos*, short for *Jagdbomber* (hunting bombers). It was the *Jabos*, especially combined with naval bombardment, which overshadowed German attempts to drive the invaders back into the sea. The roads were death traps for German vehicles.

Conversely, there were less than seventy-five German Fw 190F *Jabos* assigned to *Luftflotte 3* in France, too few to seriously impede Allied ground movement in the face of Allied air supremacy. Often, they had to jettison their bombs to defend themselves. The air defense fighters of *Luftflotte Reich* sent from Germany to fight over France as reinforcement had little to no ground-attack training.

By the dawn of D-Day, other Allied airmen were busy too. Gliders continued to deliver heavy equipment to the three airborne divisions guarding the western and eastern flanks of the invasion. C-47s also dropped "door bundles" kicked out the passenger door and paracrates dropped by parachute from shackles mounted on the bottom of the aircraft. Reconnaissance versions of the P-38, P-51, Spitfire, and Mosquito provided situation awareness beyond the immediate beachhead.

Eleven IX Bomber Command groups of American B-26 Marauders and A-20s joined with RAF No. 2 Group Bostons, Mitchells, and Mosquitos to hit German strongpoints and artillery positions. The RAF began landing Air Observation Post (AOP) squadrons of Auster light aircraft to find targets for Royal Artillery batteries accompanying the landing on the British beaches. Their American counterparts soon began operating on Utah and Omaha.

COSSAC Study 2, "Requirements for a Tactical Air Force," clearly defined tasks for the AEAF in support of OVERLORD and its NEPTUNE assault.[15] The top four were gain air superiority over the Channel and assault area; move by air and sea the initial air control element; provide close air support for airborne and amphibious ground forces; and deliver and support the airborne troops. Before noon on D-Day, all four had been almost simultaneously accomplished.[16]

Celebrations in London that night were muted. For both the serving military and naval forces, the merchant mariners, and the civilians, there was a realization that this was the beginning of another phase of the war, not its end. There were more prayer services than parties.[17]

# CHAPTER THIRTY-ONE

# The *Luftwaffe's* Longest Day

*Our job was to provide close support to the ground troops if they needed us, and to sweep the area of any enemy aircraft. The sky was absolutely full of airplanes— ours. I understand that only two krauts showed up, and they strafed the beach once and then beat it for home.*

*Smart guys.*

—P-47 PILOT AND EAGLE SQUADRON VETERAN BILL DUNN[1]

*Luftflotte 3* was much depleted by D-Day, especially in single-engine day fighters. Most of its airfields near the Normandy coast had been severely damaged in weeks of costly Allied air attacks. Once dominant on the battlefield, *Luftflotte 3* was now a furtive presence on the edges of the invasion area outnumbered over 7-to-1 in combat aircraft and an astounding 20-to-1 in fighters. It was able to mount only weak attacks against the Allied fleet and troops ashore.

The RAF spent years developing a fairly accurate picture of how the *Luftwaffe* controlled their fighter forces. German fighter aircraft in each sector were controlled by a senior officer called a *Jagdfliegerführer (Jafü)* located in a control center. Each *Jafü* received information from air surveillance radars and the airbases in his sector via landline with radio backup. The *Jafü* also communicated with his fighters by radio. It was the radio links that were exploited by Allied signals intelligence. Sometimes the links were jammed and sometimes the links were simply monitored for information. Radio chatter was a problem in the *Luftwaffe*, and the men of *Luftflotte 3* were no exception.

In building Fortress Europe, the Germans had liberally deployed various kinds of radar along the coast. In May this was reduced to less than 20 percent of its original strength by heavy air attacks.[2] Not only did the Germans lose tactical warning of the approaching invasion force, but they were also unable to adequately control their fighter forces during and after the invasion. With depleted radar surveillance and compromised communications, German fighter squadrons were most often assigned to "free hunt" missions, essentially sent out to find whatever Allied forces might be

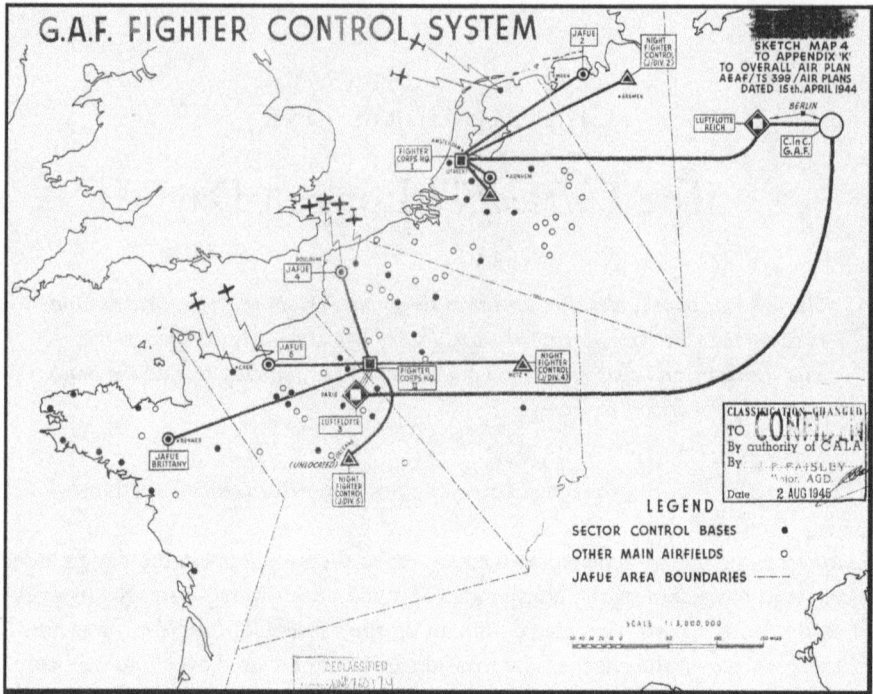

Map 31.1. Estimated German Fighter Control System in Northern France
ORIGINAL AEAF AIR PLAN, APRIL 1944[3]

encountered. So, unlike the RAF in the Battle of Britain, they were often blind to the situation beyond visual range of their cockpits.

On D-Day, *Jadgkorps II* was the air-to-air fighter arm of *Luftflotte 3*, the German air fleet controlling France and Belgium. It included six day fighter and six night fighter groups dispersed across France. Total operational day fighter strength was 173 aircraft, of which 119 were serviceable, ready to fly. Total night fighter strength was 103, with 55 flyable. Months of transportation attacks limited aircraft logistics, while airfield attacks limited aircraft maintenance. It is clear that there were not enough German fighter planes to seriously threaten the landings. It was planned that a number of fighters from *I. Jagdkorps* in Germany would be transferred forward to France, but that would not be enough airplanes to correct the imbalance.

This imbalance also allowed Allied bombers to operate almost unhindered. On D-Day these bombers flew almost 11,000 sorties, dropping more tonnage of bombs than was dropped on the long-suffering city of Hamburg during the entire year of

1943.[4] German historian Paul Carell stated: "It was in the air, and from the air, that the fate of the invasion was decided."[5]

Fighter pilot Bill Dunn (quoted above) knew only part of the story, for the *Luftwaffe* began to launch other small groups of aircraft in response to the invasion alarm. Besides the morning fighter raid by the two Fw 190s, fifteen Ju 88 bombers approached Gold Beach at about 15:15 hours. They were intercepted by RAF 485 (RNZAF) Squadron flying Spitfire IXs. As 485 Squadron veteran Maurice Mayston described: "It was like a feeding frenzy almost, an enemy aircraft would poke its nose out of the cloud, and you'd hear on the radio, 'I've got him. I've got him.' '*No, no, no, I've* got him,' and [it was] the first one there to get another score."

There were so many Spitfires to be seen over the beaches that Mayston's flight leader Johnnie Houlton took his four Spits a bit inland trying to find a victim. Houlton spotted a fast-flying Ju 88 under the overcast. Houlton calmly called to his flight: "Duncan Blue, Bandit, 2 o'clock, Angels 4." "Duncan Blue" was the flight call sign; "Bandit" the code for confirmed enemy aircraft; "2 o'clock" the enemy direction; and "Angels 4" the enemy altitude, 4,000 feet. He then promptly shot it down as wingman Mayston and the rest of Duncan Blue flight covered his tail. The New Zealanders claim this aircraft as the first German bomber shot down by an Allied fighter on D-Day.

Two minutes later, Houlton spotted a second bomber and knocked out an engine. Generously, he took a trailing position and let the other three flight members attack and down the bomber. Other Allied fighters drove off or shot down the rest of the German bomber squadron. No significant damage was reported to vessels or troops.[6]

Later, RAF 164 Squadron Typhoons downed a single Fw 190 behind the beach near Caen. Four more Fw 190s appeared and made an ineffective pass before disengaging. The Typhoons also sighted six Me 109 fighters, but the Germans withdrew without a fight. Although an aluminum wall had been built around the beachhead, it was not all one way. RAF 183 Squadron lost three of twelve Typhoons strafing tanks inland after twelve Me 109s bounced them out of low cloud.[7] Vigilance was the price of survival. Yet losses to German fighters were rare on D-Day. Eisenhower's airmen had established air supremacy over the invasion force.

## COMMAND AND CONTROL

There were three day fighter area control centers under *II.Jagdkorps* in northern France. *Jafü Brittany* was located at Renne and covered Brittany; *Jafü 5* at Bernay covered Lower Normandy and the invasion coast; *Jafü 4* covered Upper Normandy.

When on the ground, German fighter pilots received their orders from the parent unit at the base. Once airborne, they would receive orders from the *Jafü* control center covering their area. Similarly, there were night fighter control centers for *Jagddivision 4* in Metz covering the approaches to Germany and *Jagddivision 5* at Coulommiers controlling night fighters in the west of France.

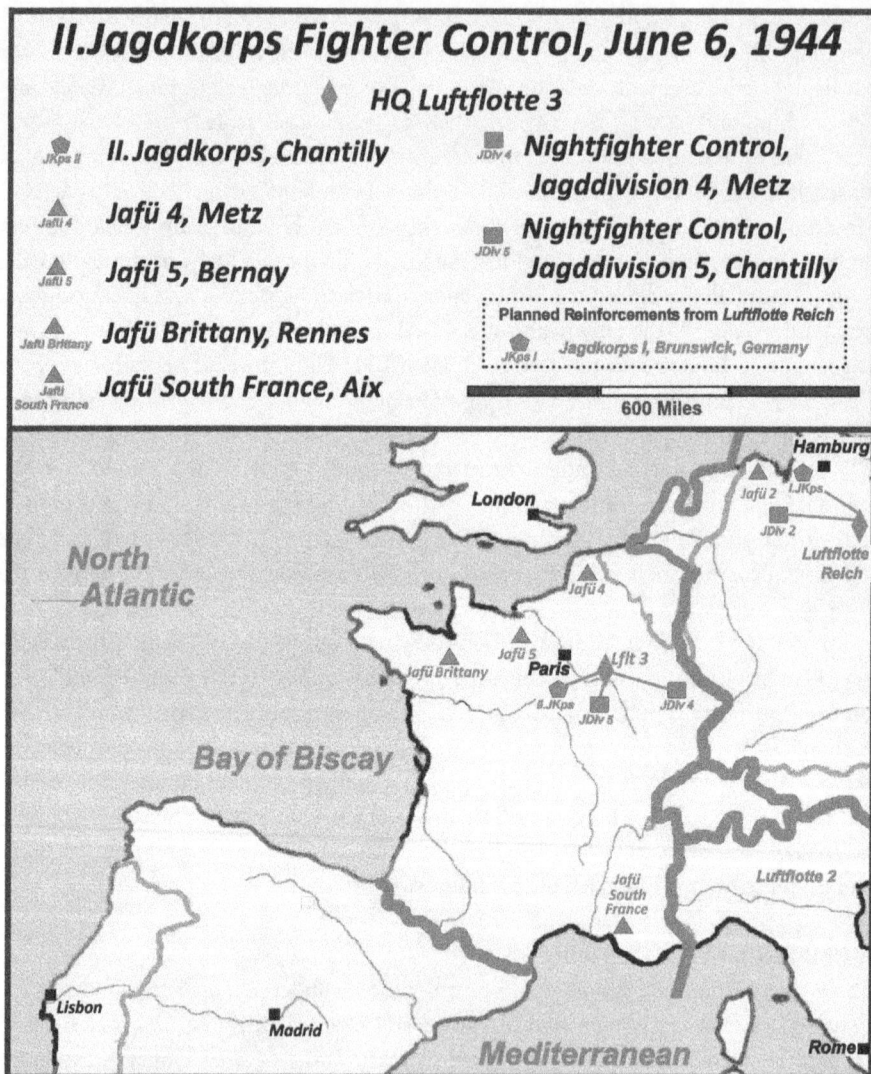

# II.Jagdkorps Fighter Control, June 6, 1944

◆ HQ Luftflotte 3

II.Jagdkorps, Chantilly

Jafü 4, Metz

Jafü 5, Bernay

Jafü Brittany, Rennes

Jafü South France, Aix

Nightfighter Control, Jagddivision 4, Metz

Nightfighter Control, Jagddivision 5, Chantilly

Planned Reinforcements from *Luftflotte Reich*
Jagdkorps I, Brunswick, Germany

600 Miles

Map 31.2. *II.Jagdkorps* Fighter Control, June 6, 1944 MOLYSON[8]

# PIPS

The two fighter wings of *II. Jagdkorps*, *JG 2* and *JG 26*, were widely dispersed across France. *JG 2* was concentrated just north of Paris. Its headquarters and one group were at Chantilly-Creil with two other groups at Cormeilles-en-Vexin. *JG 26* was in eastern France with two groups spread between Lille-Vendeville, Denain, and Nancy-Essey and a group resting far to the south at Mont-de-Marsan.[9]

*Oberst* Josef "Pips" Priller commanded *JG 26* from his headquarters at Lille-Nord airfield and more often from the cockpit of his Fw 190A-8. A Battle of Britain veteran and a man not likely to suffer a fool, he was an *Experte*[10] with a personal score of ninety-six Allied planes downed by D-Day. He was a man not to be trifled with, no matter what uniform you wore.

It was Priller who executed the first successful *Luftwaffe* attack against NEP-TUNE, made famous in Cornelius Ryan's *The Longest Day*. When alerted to the invasion by *Jagddivision 5*, Priller was unable to quickly recall any of the three fighter groups of his wing. All three had significant portions of their ground echelons moving between bases somewhere on the disrupted roads of France.[11] All Priller had immediately available were staff and recently repaired aircraft.

When and if he could get word to the dispersed units, they would be forced to reposition their forces on endangered forward bases at Creil, Cormeilles, Chaumont, Guyancourt, and Villacoublay to be effective.[12] Not one to be deterred by difficulty, Priller and wingman *Unteroffizier* Heinz Wodarczyk took the two serviceable staff Fw 190A-8 aircraft and headed toward Normandy at 08:00. There they slipped in and strafed Sword Beach. It was an insignificant token attack, except for the British soldiers who were killed or wounded.[13]

By the Germans' own account, they would lose seventeen fighters on June 6, mostly Fw 190A-8s that equipped most of the day fighter units. In turn they claimed the downing of twenty-four Allied aircraft of all kinds. By German accounts, the day began with the destruction of four RAF Lancaster bombers at 05:00 in the area between Utah and Omaha Beaches. A fast fighter-bomber unit equipped with Fw 190Fs, *Schnelleskampfgeschwader 10*, claimed the kills. Previously this unit had performed hit-and-run bombing raids against the southern coast of England. Official RAF records note only three Lancasters lost on the predawn bombing raids all along the coast. Perhaps one of the victims was double-claimed, a common problem in all air forces.

During the day, German records indicate *Luftflotte 3* fighters were occasionally able to ambush some of the thousands of Allied planes busy around Normandy, including three P-47s, eight P-51s, and nine Typhoons. Twenty-four Allied planes in exchange for seventeen German aircraft was no bargain for an outnumbered air force over its own ground. It was clear that in the battle of attrition in which they were now engaged, the Germans would quickly run out of planes.

# CHAPTER THIRTY-TWO

# Imminent Danger—West

Toward dusk on D-Day, the American 355th Fighter Group intercepted fifteen antique Ju 87 *Stukas* of *Schlachtgeschwader 103*. Once the terror of the battlefield in 1939–41, the *Stukas* were incredibly obsolete by 1944. Although a school unit, it had some combat capability; the unit was armed and ordered forward into battle. They represented a threat the Americans must repulse. Six were shot down and four damaged, while the rest scattered. It was a desperate move by an overwhelmed *Luftflotte 3*.[1]

## REINFORCEMENTS

There were other desperate actions by the Germans on D-Day. Another fighter corps, *Jagdkorps I*, was available in Germany if and when the invasion alarm *Drohende Gefahr West* (Imminent Danger—West) was declared. By the afternoon of June 6, it was time to act. *Generalfeldmarschall* Rundstedt had promised his troops in France 1,000 *Luftwaffe* aircraft overhead by the third day of the invasion.[2]

The official plan, however, only called for some 400 single-engine fighters to be sent from *Jagdkorps I* in Germany to the depleted *Jagdkorps II* in France. However, only half that number were available on June 7 due to serviceability issues and combat attrition against the American escort fighters enthusiastically searching German airspace for targets.

A total of sixteen understrength day fighter *Gruppe* were dispatched from bases in Germany, Austria, and Hungary. All the groups were more or less understrength due to combat attrition. Of the 336 planes in the tasked units, only 192 aircraft were able to launch on June 7. No specialized all-weather fighters or twin-engine *Zerstörer* were sent; they were too valuable and vulnerable to the expected Allied fighter cover.[3] (See appendix 4.)

It was anticipated that the American heavy bombers would be kept close to the invasion site for tactical work so that the single-engine fighters could be spared for the front. While this was initially true, it left the Reich almost without air defense when General Spaatz increased bombing of the German oil industry.[4] According to the plan, the code words *Doktor Gustav West* from OKL (*Oberkommando der Luftwaffe*/Air Force High Command) would be sent to the affected units to dispatch reinforcements when the Allied invasion began. Supposedly these aircraft would be able to fly to airfields prepared to receive them.

Unfortunately for the German Air Force plan, *Luftflotte 3* had not aggressively prepared to receive their reinforcements, and in those instances where some preparation had been accomplished, Allied air attacks had spoiled the effort.[5] Advanced reception teams were sent to the designated airfields, but the destinations of the flying units then were changed in response to the unanticipated landings in Normandy instead of the Pas-de-Calais. Diversion to alternate landing grounds added to the confusion, which would have been significant in any case.

The reinforcing German pilots were not prepared for anything other than air-to-air combat over their own country; many were newly trained and had questionable navigational skills. Intermediate refueling points were overcrowded. Ground crews had to travel forward by train, a hazardous undertaking in the face of constant Allied air attacks on the German transportation system. Almost half of the reinforcing units were intercepted by Allied fighters and had to dogfight their way forward. Those that survived were diverted to bases not ready to receive them. Essential camouflage and air defense arrangements were not attempted, let alone completed, at many places. "Soon everything was in hopeless chaos."[6]

Another factor that plagued the *Luftwaffe* in these days immediately after the landings was the fact that the bulk of the surviving fighter bases were to the east of the assault beaches. It was there that many of the reinforcements from Germany were sent. Terrain and the pre-invasion bombing made the German plan of deploying the reinforcements to the south or west of the invasion difficult. This simplified the air defense problem for the Allies, although with so many fighters available, all-around air defense was maintained.[7]

One of the reinforcing groups from Germany was *II./JG 1* (Second Group Fighter Wing 1). It moved its Fw 190 day fighters from Störmede in western Germany to Le Mans, an airfield 100 miles south of the landings. On the way, it swept along roads in the *15th Armée* sector, providing temporary top cover. The roads, however, were mostly empty of German troops on the move.

The *15th Armée* was dug in and camouflaged and ordered to remain in place, guarding the coastline in the Pas-de-Calais from an invasion now being executed just next door in the *7th Armée* area. In any case, the fighters arrived in Le Mans unscathed.[8] The orders received there were unusual, they were to load bombs on their aircraft and attack the invasion fleet![9]

On June 8, *II./JG 1* attacked as ordered but hit no ships. This was not surprising, since most of the pilots had never dropped a bomb before in training or combat. They reported "terrific" flak and many of the aircraft were damaged. They repeated the adventure on June 9, with similar results. On June 10, a force of RAF Lancasters and Halifaxes bombed Le Mans, cratering the runway but sparing the German unit's aircraft. The planes were carefully dispersed because the hunters had become the hunted.

It took the Germans six days to repair the runway by hand, and the fighters evacuated to Essay, an airfield in eastern France, some 300 miles from the beaches. For the next four days they flew the long distance into the battle area. Then the unit was returned to the cauldron, deploying forward to an improvised landing ground at Alençon, between Le Mans and Caen. Alençon was some sixty miles southwest of SWORD Beach. Soon after the Germans arrived, Mustangs appeared and ended the short but exciting combat career of *II./JG 1* in the Normandy campaign by strafing and destroying fifteen of the surviving Fw 190s.[10]

German air defense fighters made some Allied air operations costly, but in Normandy they did not stop effective use of Allied airpower. On July 6, D+30, the then current commander of *7th Armée* General Hauser[11] requested reinforcement by *Luftwaffe* flak troops due to "incessant attacks of enemy fighter-bombers."[12] *II. Jagdkorps* fighters were unable to adequately protect the ground troops. Along with Allied artillery, German ground counterattacks against the Lodgement area were crippled by Allied air attack.

## GERMAN BOMBERS

To add to the confusion of D-Day, *Luftflotte 3*'s bombers were also on the move. For attacks against any Allied bridgehead, *Luftflotte 3* was equipped with maritime and conventional bombers and fighter-bombers. All these were already in France, although their bases were dispersed across the country. The bombers were divided among three *Fliegerkorps* (aviation corps) by type.

*II.Fliegerkorps* in Compiègne, recently transferred from Italy, was composed of Fw 190F fighter-bombers and Bf 109G-8 reconnaissance aircraft.[13] These aircraft had some air-to-air capability and could be a useful if limited supplement to the fighters if skillfully employed. In fact, the first German air-to-air kill on D-Day was credited to *3./SKG10* (Third Squadron/Fast Bomber Wing 10) at 05:01, a RAF Lancaster near Isigny.

It had been planned for this air corps to be much larger than it was on D-Day; however, the Eastern Front continually siphoned off German close air support capability. *Fliegerkorps II* also operated the Ju 88C-equipped *Zerstörergeschwader (ZG) 1* based along France's Atlantic coast. The Ju 88Cs, although originally designed as medium bombers, were used as long-range heavy fighters to intercept Allied anti-submarine warfare aircraft in the Bay of Biscay.

## Luftflotte 3 Aviation Corps HQ, June 1944

♦ *HQ Luftflotte 3*

*II.Fliegerkorps, Compienge (Fighter-bombers)*

*IX.Fliegerkorps, Beauvais (Level bombers)*

*X.Fliegerkorps, Angers (Maritime bombers)*

*2.Fliegerdivision, Avignon (Torpedo bombers)*

600 Miles

North Atlantic

London

Hamburg

IX.FKps  II.FKps

Luftflotte Reich

Paris  Lflt 3

X.FKps

Bay of Biscay

Luftflotte 2

2.FDiv

Lisbon

Madrid

Mediterranean

Rome

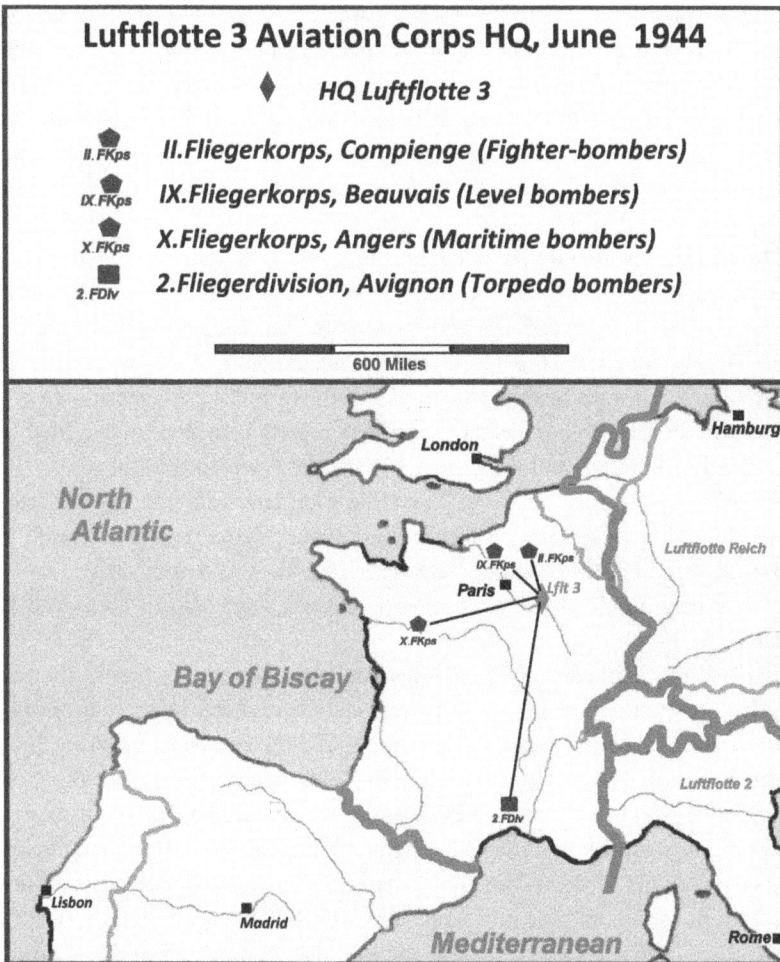

Map 32.1. Location of *Luftflotte 3* Aviation Corps Headquarters, June 6, 1944
MOLYSON

*IX.Fliegerkorps* in Beauvais commanded the conventional German level bombers in France, including Ju 88s, Ju 188s, and Do 217s. This was all that remained of the great level bomber fleets that had attacked Britain in 1940. Medium bomber units under this aviation corps had again suffered heavy losses over Great Britain early in 1944, during the so-called "Little Blitz."

Called Operation *STEINBOCK* (CAPRICORN) by the Germans, the reprisal attacks caused limited destruction in Britain but inflicted unacceptable attrition on the

*Luftwaffe* bomber forces. As well as taking losses, *IX.Fliegerkorps* aircrew had no time to train in the ship attack tactics that might have been useful during the invasion.[14]

*X.Fliegerkorps* in Angers commanded the maritime bombers that had fought the *Luftwaffe* part of the Battle of the Atlantic as well as the missile bombers used so effectively against the Allies in the Mediterranean. This headquarters had replaced the earlier *Fliegerführer Atlantik* in charge of maritime air operations on France's Atlantic coast.[15]

On D-Day, its aircraft included Do 217, He 177, and Fw 200 types. These planes were equipped with radio-controlled Fritz X and Hs 293 anti-ship missiles. Unknown to the *Luftwaffe*, some of these missiles had been captured by the Allied armies overrunning Italy, and electronic countermeasures were available to blunt their attacks. A separate headquarters under *X.Fliegerkorps*, *2.Fliegerdivision* at Avignon flew Ju 88 torpedo bombers and provided maritime defense of the Mediterranean coast. Its aircraft would soon move toward the Normandy battle.

As word of the invasion spread and the Germans suffered and inflicted the first air-to-air kills, *Luftflotte 3* units around France began to move toward Normandy. *III./Sch.G.4* (Third Group Attack Wing 4) moved some fifty Fw-190Fs fighter-bombers from bases in southern and eastern France up to Tours and Laval on June 6.

The lead mechanic for each plane was carried in the rear fuselage of the aircraft behind the pilot. There was no way to provide a parachute. It was dangerous and uncomfortable duty but necessary to ensure the fighter-bombers could be supported between missions. The mechanics were called "black men" because of the color of their overalls, which hid the inevitable stains of grease and oil. In this case, the danger became manifest as some of the fighter-bombers were intercepted. American fighters downed five of them. The pilots refused to bail out and leave their black men behind. Eight of the ten men in the five aircraft did not survive.[16]

*III./Sch.G.4* tried to strike back in the afternoon, launching thirteen aircraft in three groups against the beach. Allied fighters turned two of the three *Schwärme* (flights) back; the third had their attacks disrupted by the immense antiaircraft fire over the beaches. It was also this unit that likely bombed Pegasus Bridge to no effect during the day.[17]

The extensive pre-invasion bombing campaign had pushed the ring of operational German airfields around Normandy back a hundred miles, but the Germans had medium-range bombers capable of reaching the beach. It was defended, of course, and daytime attacks were all but impossible. So the *Luftwaffe* came by night.

On the night of June 6, forty torpedo and missile bombers of *Fliegerkorps X* attacked the invasion fleet to no avail. Allied naval gunners put up a tremendous

Figure 32.1. German bombers attacked the anchorage mainly at night. US ARMY

barrage. German flak gunners nearby—who had been under such continuous Allied bombardment that they were now firing at anything that moved—assisted the Allied fleet in repelling the *Luftwaffe* attack. Four of its He 177 missile carriers fell to the Mosquito XVII night fighters of RAF 456 (RAAF) Squadron.[18]

On the night of June 8, frigate HMS *Lawford* was sunk 12 miles off the Normandy coast. It is uncertain if the ship was hit by an anti-ship missile or encountered a mine. A missile launched by aircraft near Gold Beach sank the headquarters ship *Bulolo* the same night. Destroyer HMS *Boadicea* was sunk in the Channel five days later by Ju 88 torpedo bombers. It was much easier to attack the ships in open water than to risk the defenses on or just off the beach.[19]

In ten days of operations, the crack *III./Kampfgeschwader 100* (Third Group/Bomber Wing 100) lost eight of its fifteen Do 217 missile aircraft attacking the invaders. During the two weeks following the invasion, only two NEPTUNE ships were sunk and seven damaged by bombs and missiles. Smoke screens and electronic jamming made the job of the missile-carrying aircraft much harder.

Three more ships were sunk and two damaged by air-delivered torpedoes.[20] The conventional gravity-bomb-equipped medium bombers of *Fliegerkorps IX* had little luck. Ju 88 medium bombers, for example, attacked at 23:00 on D-Day and lost five aircraft for little gain.[21]

On June 14, a RAF 410 Squadron Mosquito XIII night fighter intercepted and downed a *Mistel* composite aircraft east of Le Havre. A 264 Squadron Mosquito to the north shot down a second *Mistel*. On the night of June 24, the *Luftwaffe* sent four *Mistels* against the invasion fleet. *Kampfgruppe 101* (Bomber Group 101) was deployed forward from Germany to St. Dizier, France, some 240 miles east of Caen. Led by unit commander *Hauptmann* Horst Rudat, the four composite aircraft approached the eastern flank of the invasion fleet near Le Havre. The command aircraft released their Ju 88 flying bombs, but only one caused significant damage. This was to the headquarters frigate HMS *Nith*, which was pelted with bomb splinters. Ten sailors were killed.[22]

A total of ten *Mistels* would be launched during this and subsequent nights. The only other ship damaged was the old decommissioned French battleship *Courbet*, which had been purposely sunk as a breakwater in an artificial harbor.[23] *Courbet* had been interned in Britain since 1940 and was returned to the waters off France to assist in its liberation. Ironically, it was a sister ship to the old French battleship *Ocean*, which had been used to test the *Mistel* warhead at Toulon in March 1944. *Courbet* would also absorb an attack by German midget submarines in August, also without effect, since its intentional role was as a breakwater.

Allied air defense was just too tough for bombing aircraft that needed a relatively benign environment in which to operate. Severe losses for little gain forced the *Luftwaffe* to switch to new tactics. *Oyster* air-delivered pressure mines laid in the shallow waters of the Baie-de-la-Seine and the Thames Estuary were very tough to sweep, and ships had to transit at very low speeds to avoid detonating them. German air-delivered *Oyster* mines sunk twenty-six ships, far more than the five ships sunk by all other air-delivered weapons.[24] Still, this was small percentage of the more than 6,000 vessels in the Allied invasion fleet. Although relatively few ships were lost in the mining campaign, the inconvenience of a low-speed passage somewhat slowed the cargo movement across the Channel to Normandy.[25]

## CHAPTER THIRTY-THREE

# Bombers above the Clouds

*The big bomber, particularly the Command Bombing Force, was not to be misused on targets for which it is not particularly suited.*[1]
—GENERAL EISENHOWER, "MEMORANDUM FOR THE RECORD,"
MARCH 22, 1944

Eisenhower's memorandum of March 22, 1944 quoted above was a self-evaluation of his first three months as Supreme Commander Allied Expeditionary Force. Part of that evaluation was the use of airpower in support of the ground war. He must have contemplated how valuable airpower had been when he was the supreme commander in the Mediterranean. When he brought his colleagues Tedder and Spaatz with him from the Mediterranean to Britain, they were reminders of the contributions Ike's airmen had made to the string of costly victories in North Africa, Sicily, and Italy (see chapter 5).

On March 25, 1944, Eisenhower met with his principal air commanders to sort out air command tasks and relationships for OVERLORD. The officers included Air Chief Marshall Tedder as overall air commander, Air Marshal Leigh-Mallory commanding the AEAF, Air Marshal Harris commanding RAF Bomber Command, and Lieutenant General Spaatz commanding the American heavy bombers of the Eighth and Fifteenth Air Force. Eisenhower made it very clear that all these very senior air officers were subordinate to him, and that their efforts were to be coordinated by Tedder. Harris reluctantly agreed to some RAF Bomber Command daylight bombing of German targets in France.

On the night of March 30–31, 795 RAF heavy bombers were sent against Nürnberg, Germany. This was a continuation of RAF night city bombing, not an attack against German rail transportation supplying German forces in France. Almost 100 bombers were lost and over 700 RAF crewmen killed or taken prisoner. German night fighters and flak had savaged the Brits. This encouraged Harris to take on more OVERLORD tasks.

## PRE-INVASION BOMBING

Eisenhower did not intend for strategic bombers to be used against unsuitable tactical targets, because neither their design nor the training of their crews made this an effective use of resources. It was obvious that with the 1944 level of technology, these bombers were strategic sledgehammers, not tactical rapiers. As the OVERLORD plan evolved, unfortunately, both American and British heavy bombers were called upon to hit unsuitable targets in close proximity to Allied troops and French civilians.

By the beginning of June 1944, more than 1,500 of the 2,000 locomotives in the French railway system had been destroyed or at least badly damaged. Twenty-one of the twenty-four bridges over the Seine were in the river or closed for major repair. Thirty-six major *Luftwaffe* airfields in France and Belgium had various levels of major damage.[2] Safe German use of French roads by day was history except in foggy or bad weather. All this was accomplished by applying the correct aircraft against each kind of target.

## PREDAWN D-DAY BOMBING

The efforts to attack the *Atlantik Wall* coastal fortifications by air were huge, but the results were questionable. For security reasons these attacks could not be concentrated on the invasion coast alone. For each target in Lower Normandy, two outside the area had to be raided. Up to the date of the landing, 23,094 tons of bombs were dropped on the concrete bunkers along the Channel and the Atlantic coast. The bunkers were built to be bombproof and none were permanently disabled, although surrounding unhardened facilities were sometimes destroyed. *Luftwaffe* fighters were not able to significantly interfere with these operations.[3]

As the predawn American and British airborne assaults began to secure the flanks of NEPTUNE, RAF Bomber Command conducted its largest tactical bombing raid of the war yet accomplished, Operation FLASHLAMP.[4] A force of 551 Lancasters, 412 Halifaxes, and 49 Mosquito pathfinders dropped over 5,000 tons of bombs on ten heavy coastal gun batteries on the invasion coast.[5] Early dawn would find these attacks still in progress. Destruction of these batteries was considered by ground and naval commanders essential to the invasion.

The batteries were point, not area, targets. Because the coast was cloudy, the Oboe-equipped Mosquito pathfinder aircraft marked the targets with pyrotechnics. Oboe was an electronic bombing aid that allowed accurate deliveries on known points, even through cloud.[6] Bomb aimer Art Willis, aboard a Halifax bomber, searched for a heavy gun battery defending Sword Beach:

> *(Willis) peered through the nose blister, searching for the target markers they had been told about at briefing. It became apparent that visual identification*

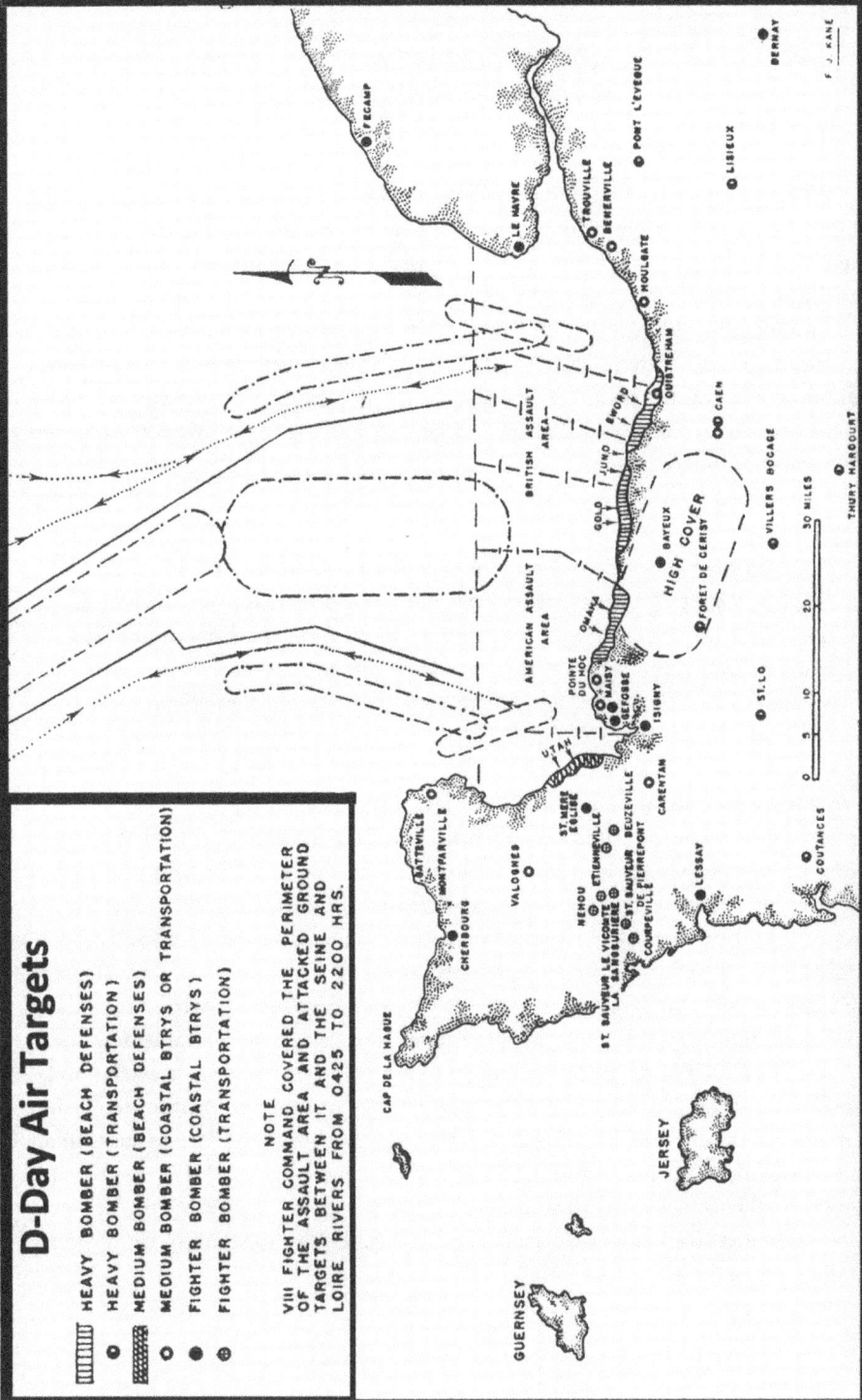

Map 33.1. D-Day Air Targets[7]

*of the target or direct sighting of the markers would be impossible, as there was complete cloud cover. Nevertheless, beneath them on the clouds was the glow of the red markers.*[8]

Willis dropped sixteen 500-pound bombs from 11,000 feet in the area of the illuminated clouds. Significantly, there were no Allied troops near the targets, so there was no concern that the bombs dropped would kill friendly troops. French casualties received no such consideration.

In Operation FLASHLIGHT, about 300 French civilians were killed near the ten targets, but the batteries were not destroyed. At least some were silenced by naval gunfire or overrun by ground troops later in the day. Eight RAF aircraft were lost, three or four to *II.Fliegerkorps* fighter-bombers responding to the invasion alarm and four probably to flak.

The official RAF history states:

*To assess with accuracy the damage done by Bomber Command in this attack— the largest quantity of bombs which had ever been allotted to so small a target—is impossible, despite the very full investigations made during the latter stages of the war and afterwards. Many of the guns were protected by the enormous thickness of their concrete casemates, which with some exceptions could not be penetrated either by shells or bombs.*[9]

## TACTICAL BOMBER AND FIGHTER-BOMBER ATTACKS

Before dawn, a pair of RAF 342 (French) Squadron Bostons laid a smoke screen along the eastern Cotentin coast. This shielded the invasion fleet from the coastal batteries located there. Every ten minutes a new set of aircraft appeared to repeat the process. On the eastern flank, Bostons of RAF 88 Squadron conducted similar operations. This was the smoke screen penetrated by the *Kriegsmarine* torpedo boats from Le Havre to sink the Norwegian destroyer *Svenner*. Two aircraft were lost in these operations, but they saved many lives in the invasion fleet from coastal battery fire.[10]

US Ninth Air Force B-26 medium bombers followed the RAF heavies, bombing German shore batteries and other targets. They operated below the clouds and acquired their targets visually. East of Sword Beach, shore batteries at Ouistreham and Deauville were hit beginning at 05:17 by squadrons of P-47s, B-26s, and A-20s. By 05:50 these aircraft were leaving the target area as 119 Ninth Air Force P-47s attacked German positions on the Cotentin Peninsula south of the airborne landing zones there.

The P-47s departed the target area at 06:20, having effectively attacked some gun batteries, railroad lines, roads, and bridges. Five minutes later, bombing commenced between Utah and Omaha Beaches. A squadron of P-47s bombed targets at Maisy and nearby Géfosse-Fontenay. As they departed at 06:25, a squadron of B-26s bombed targets again at Maisy and Point du Hoc.[11]

## AMERICAN HEAVY BOMBER ATTACKS

The Ninth Air Force attacks were followed by the Eighth Air Force heavy bomber attack on the assault beaches, with the troops approaching the shore in landing craft. During planning for NEPTUNE, there was a controversy as to how many minutes the bombers should attack before the troops were to land. Ground commanders wanted a very short gap to capitalize on the shock effect on the defenders. The air commanders were worried about hitting the troops in the boats and insisted on a much longer interval.

The USAAF estimated that in radar bombing through cloud, only one of seventy bombs would hit within one half mile of the aiming point. Considering that the beaches themselves were to be bombed, anything in the water up to a half mile offshore could be hit. In good weather with a visible aiming point, accuracy was fifty times better.[12] In the end, Ike dictated there would be a five-minute safety gap if there were no clouds, ten minutes if visibility was poor.[13]

Visibility was not good by the time the American heavy bombers arrived on D-Day. Leading the entire Eighth Air Force of 1,100 heavy bombers were the B-24s of the 446th Bombardment Group. In the very early hours of D-Day, the target intelligence briefing was succinct, delivered by the intelligence officer, Major Stahl:

> "You are to strike the beach defenses at Pointe de la Percée, dropping your bombs not later than two minutes before the zero hour (0630). Landing craft and troops will be 400 yards to one mile offshore as we attack, and naval ships may be shelling our targets on shore. Deadline on our primary target is zero hour minus two."[14]

Pointe de la Percée was high ground at the western end of Omaha Beach. If the bombardiers could not bomb the beach before zero hour minus two (06:28), the aircraft were to proceed to the secondary target, the road junction in the Cerisy Forest. The target of last resort was the choke point in the town of Vire. The deadline for bombing, 06:28, reflected the ten-minute safety gap for the troops actually hitting the beach.

The stream of B-17 and B-24 aircraft split before crossing the coast, dropping many tons of bombs through cloud and losing one aircraft to flak.[15] A Gee-equipped pathfinder aircraft led each group of eighteen American heavy bombers. The target was the beach itself and its immediate defenses, but the beach was obscured by cloud and the invading troops were nearing shore.

To mitigate the possibility of cratering the assault beaches to the point of being impassable to the invaders, each plane carried twenty bombs with instantaneous fuses. The bombs were a mix of 100-pound and 500-pound demolition or 120-pound fragmentation bombs. These could detonate landmines, kill exposed defenders, and cut barbed wire. They were known to be ineffective against concrete bunkers,

Figure 33.1. Pre-invasion 1,000- and 2,000-pound bombs craters at Pointe du Hoc. If dropped in this concentration on the beach, they would have made the shoreline impassable to the invaders. Therefore, smaller bombs were employed. USAAF

but destroying concrete was not an objective—the ground commanders wanted to daze and confuse the Germans.

Navigating to the target area was easy. No German radar or navigation jamming was evident.[16] The Gee radionavigation set was very accurate, and the H2X bombing radar could easily discern the coastline. The commander of the 446th, Colonel Brogger later reported:

> We had a good tail wind all the way—we ran into an overcast and as we passed over the Channel I could see through the breaks in the clouds strings of landing barges heading toward France. . . . We were hoping for a break so we could see our bombs hit, but it was a solid overcast ahead of us over the Continent just as far as we could see.[17]

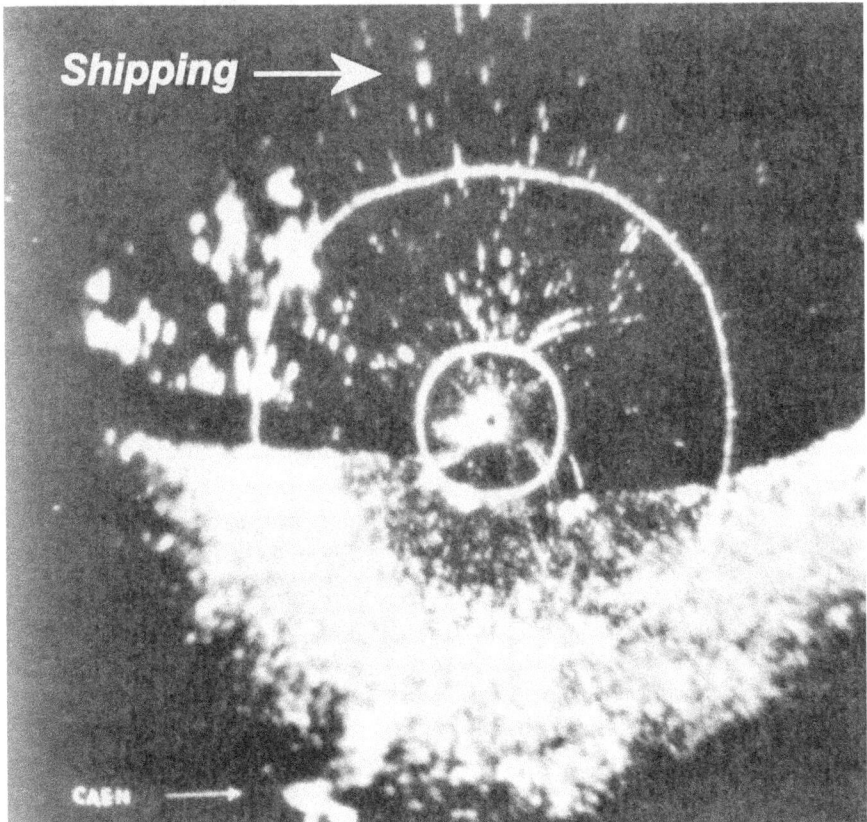

Figure 33.2. Actual H2X bombing radar image of the invasion coast north of Caen. Note the extensive shipping offshore. US ARMY AIR FORCE

## FAILURE

Human nature intervened. Even with the planned Eisenhower safety gap, the planners had added a few seconds to the drop times. Cautious bombardiers with fingers on the bomb release toggle switches added another slight delay before release to avoid hitting the landing craft below. This delay degraded the accuracy of the bombing. Almost nothing would be worse to these airmen than to kill American troops with American bombs.[18]

As a result of these offsets, the tons of bombs intended to daze the defenders and dig shallow foxholes for the invaders actually impacted behind the beach area. It was the most ineffective air attack of the day.[19] Author Paul Carell described how it was to the Germans in a fighting position on the shoreline:

> *"Bombers above the clouds," Sergeant Krone called out. They listened. The air above them was vibrant with the noise. And then began the inferno of bomb bursts. They ducked their heads. But only two bombs fell within the position of the strongpoint. Everything else came down on the open ground behind them. They looked at each other and sighed with relief.*[20]

Heavy bombers were not designed to provide close support to friendly troops. Instead, their job was to hit factory-sized strategic targets deep in enemy territory. A single Norden bombsight could be very accurate in the hands of an experienced bombardier; that is, it could drop a bomb close to the intended target. But to be precise, to land the bombs from an entire formation close to one another, was a separate matter.

Heavy bombers operated in groups, each bombardier normally releasing his ordnance when the lead bombardier in the formation's leading aircraft released his. This produced an impact pattern that was as close together as the bombing formation's aircraft. The looser the formation, the more dispersed the bomb impacts would be. Another factor in the precision of the bombing pattern was how long the trailing bombardiers took to toggle their bombs after seeing the lead aircraft dropping its load.[21]

Winds aloft also help spread the bombs. This was acceptable if your target was a large aircraft factory or oil refinery in Germany. American heavy bombers were trained and equipped to hit such point targets in daylight, but the target beaches were instead area targets. When you were trying to hit an indistinct area target close to your own troops, through clouds, the level of accuracy and precision was inadequate with 1944 technology.

The failure of the heavy bombers to neutralize the beach defenses was only part of the sad picture that day in the heavily contested Omaha Beach area. Naval gunfire support, including a fleet of rocket-equipped landing craft designed to provide "drenching fire" over the German defenses, also failed to silence them.[22] Like the bombers, the safety factor built into this operation placed the impact of the rockets beyond the line of German defenses.

So, despite Eisenhower's memorandum and intent, and over the objection of the air commanders, the big bombers of RAF Bomber Command and the US Eighth Air Force were misused on targets for which they were not suited. The amphibious troops had to directly contend with Rommel's coastal defenses, and the battle to overcome them was costly. Omaha Beach, some 4 miles long and the bloodiest D-day beach, would see over 3,000 casualties by day's end. This meant, sadly, one dead or seriously wounded GI, on average, every 7 feet for the entire length of the beach.

# CHAPTER THIRTY-FOUR

# Under the Clouds

As the day progressed, American P-47 and RAF Typhoon fighter-bombers worked at low altitude, hitting strong points, beach defenses, and headquarters all along the beach. Attacks ranged as far south as Bayeux and Caen. Further inland, RAF and USAAF light and medium bombers continued to interdict German transportation. Strafing and bombing destroyed whole German columns; it was impossible for the Germans to move without attracting the attention of the Allied air forces.

Headquarters and communications services were also of special interest to the Typhoons. At 07:45, eight Typhoons hit a headquarters at Caen and another at Chateau Meauffe an hour later. This was more sand in the eyes of the Germans, who were desperately trying to get a clear picture of what was happening on the coast. The northern part of the *7th Armée* became a black hole; little or no information was getting back to Paris or Berlin.[1]

The level bombers of RAF No. 2 Group and the US IX Bomber Command operated at a much lower altitude than the heavy bombers of their respective air forces. Like the Allied fighter-bombers, this allowed them to hit targets that were below cloud decks, denying sanctuary to German forces. They provided mostly *indirect support*; that is, they hit targets at some distance from the fighting front and friendly troops.

Fifty-four A-20 Havocs of the 416th Bomb Group attacked the critical crossroads at Argentan, devastating it. Twelve RAF Mitchells of 180 Squadron followed the Americans over Argentan, adding their bombs to the devastation below. Twelve other Mitchells of 320 Squadron were unable to find their target, a bridge over the Dives River, due to weather. Eleven Mitchells were tasked to hit a road choke point near Thury-Harcourt, but only five found it because of the low cloud. The rest went to the alternate target, the secondary airfield at Condé-sur-Vire. Typhoons rocketed advancing tanks of the 21st Panzer Division during their abortive drive to Lion-sur-Mer between Juno and Gold Beaches, helping the ground troops throw back the armored attack.[2]

By midafternoon most Allied air units were on their second or third attacks. Just after noon RP Typhoons (aircraft equipped with rocket projectiles) knocked out the

Le Havre radar site, further blinding the defenders. Soon thereafter, Typhoons from 123 Wing spotted a long column of the crack *Panzer Lehr* Division[3] approaching the coast. Just as Rommel had feared, the reinforcements held far from the beaches were too vulnerable to air attack. Five Panzer Mark IV tanks, eighty-four other armored vehicles, forty fuel trucks, and ninety other soft-skinned vehicles (trucks and cars) were destroyed.

*Panzer Lehr* was gutted before ever seeing an Allied soldier. Its members later complained that the air attacks were so intense that the road became a *Jabo Rennstrecke*—a fighter-bomber racecourse.[4] The unguided rocket was not a perfect weapon; it took about 300 shots to kill one tank. Fortunately, destroying its support and infantry vehicles could stop a tank unit just as effectively as killing its tanks, as was proved again and again in Normandy. The rocketeers in their Typhoons and later in P-47s improved their aim as the campaign proceeded. There was lots of target practice available.[5]

It was during the attack on the *Panzer Lehr* that pilots of *Jagdgeschwader 2* (JG 2) downed three Typhoons at low level, killing their pilots. As a result, Typhoon units subsequently would get Spitfire squadrons assigned to provide top cover while they went about their work. Such protection was needed; nine Typhoons were

Figure 34.1. New P-47D Thunderbolts with improved bubble canopies were better able to engage German fighters. USAF

claimed down by the *Luftwaffe* on D-Day as compared to only two P-47s, the American counterpart, in the beachhead area.[6]

Supplementing the direct attacks on reinforcing German units, 508 B-24s of the Second Bomb Division, Eighth Air Force bombed selected towns and villages south of Caen to block key approach roads; inevitably, with liberation at hand, there were French casualties. Some targets were not accurately hit; again low clouds proved to be the greatest challenge to high-altitude bombardment. Results were assessed as "fair."

Forty-five A-20s attacked Carentan at 14:30, followed by twenty-four B-26s hitting Falaise at 0320 and Caen at 0420. Only one aircraft was lost in these attacks. One hundred thirty-nine P-47 fighter-bomber missions were flown later in the afternoon, dropping 60 tons of bombs on enemy positions along and behind the beach, with two Jugs downed by flak.[7]

Working further south, forty-eight Typhoons and fifteen P-38s destroyed twenty-three armored vehicles, railway facilities, and a number of trucks. Bridge-busting P-47s were also active, eighteen Thunderbolts damaging a road bridge at

Figure 34.2. B-24s over Normandy beaches NATIONAL ARCHIVES

Vire and thirty-six more dropping the rail bridge at Oissel, near Rouen. Further afield, US Eighth and Ninth Air Force bombers began dropping any bridges left standing on the Seine north of Paris and every bridge on the Loire from Nantes to Orleans. It was the culmination of the bridge campaign begun in conjunction with the Transportation Plan.[8]

In waning daylight, forty-eight Thunderbolts pounded defenses at Cherbourg and over one hundred B-26s pounded Caen and Trouville. A few minutes later, ninety-nine more Thunderbolts attacked Cherbourg yet again. The daylight attacks ended with seventy-two B-26s and A-20s attacking more transportation targets south of the beachhead. Total losses in these attacks were four A-20s.[9]

Figure 34.3. RAF airman rearming a Typhoon. Maintainers were a critical part of airpower. AIR FORCE HISTORICAL RESEARCH AGENCY

Throughout the day and as the last of the missions were completed, more than 11,000 Allied aircraft returned to their bases in Britain. Most damaged aircraft were repaired; others were scrapped or cannibalized for parts. In the darkness, exhausted maintenance personnel labored through the night as the aircrew debriefed with intelligence personnel, ate a late meal, and then got some sleep. Fuel, bombs, rockets, bullets, and shells were brought from storage areas to the aircraft dispersals and replenished the aircraft.

This day was the first, but not the last, day of liberation. In the darkness overhead, the British night fighters flew south to guard the Allied armada and Lodgement area.

# CHAPTER THIRTY-FIVE

# When Seagulls Became Eagles

All during these massive air attacks, the Allied navies offshore were pounding the beach defenses and subsequent German targets inland. The US Navy had only about half an hour to bombard the German defenses at Omaha and Utah Beaches, clearly inadequate for the task at hand. The British allowed themselves two hours for bombarding Gold, Juno, and Sword, which, combined with more vulnerable terrain, yielded superior results.[1] The disparity was partially due to arrival of the correct tidal conditions for landing. The Americans landed shortly after 06:30, while the Canadians and British landed at 07:30. After the troops landed, the big naval guns continued to bombard further inland.

Even as the Allied Air Expeditionary Force developed its game plan for supporting the ground and naval forces on D-Day and beyond, the Allied Naval Expeditionary Force (ANXF) considered how aircraft might contribute to the success of naval support to the army. At a meeting on November 4, 1943, the leaders of the ANXF met and accepted the necessity of air spotting for the large naval gunfire force that would support the troops ashore.

The 14-inch guns common on the battleships of this force could fire a 1,400-pound shell over 15 miles. Each battleship carried six to nine of these monster guns. On the more numerous cruisers, the guns were smaller but still substantial. This was more sheer firepower than anything the artillery would have on land, and it was essential that this valuable resource be accurately directed, especially early on, when the beachhead was held only by a few troops.

It was also decided that single-seat fighters would be used to observe gunfire rather than the gunfire-spotting floatplanes normally carried on the ships for this purpose.[2] The ungainly floatplanes were too vulnerable to German flak and fighters. During the invasion of Sicily, *Luftwaffe* fighters had downed some of the spotting aircraft. It was decided to not only provide fighter aircraft to the naval gunfire spotting aircrew but also operate them in pairs so that one could provide lookout while the other adjusted the fall of shot.[3]

Although the RAF argued that such naval gunfire observation was a navy mission, a compromise was reached that included squadrons from the RAF and both

Figure 35.1. Spitfire Mk VA, aircraft of VOS-7 and the ASP NATIONAL MUSEUM OF NAVAL AVIATION

the American and Royal Navies. This mixed force became part of the 34 (Recce) Wing of 2TAF. The provisional force was commonly called the Air Spotting Pool (ASP). It included four squadrons of Seafires from the 3 Naval Wing, FAA (Fleet Air Arm). The RAF sent several squadrons of regular Spitfire Mk Vs and attached three squadrons of Mustang Is.

The US Navy assigned seventeen naval aviators and some support personnel off the cruisers and battleships that would participate in the invasion. The Yanks came from VCS-7, the cruiser floatplane unit for Cruiser Division Seven of the US Atlantic Fleet. Cruisers *Quincy*, *Tuscaloosa*, and *Augusta*, as well as battleships *Nevada*, *Texas*, and *Arkansas*, provided personnel.

On the beach, with some of the enlisted men, they became for a few weeks Fleet Observation Squadron Seven, VOS-7. These men had the most gunfire spotting time of any of the ASP and the least time in the Spitfire.[4] The RAF contingent trained in naval gunfire spotting, while the Americans were trained on flying the Spitfire. The naval spotters of the ASP would cooperate with other airmen assigned to the three other RAF squadrons flying Mustang Is.

Although VOS-7 learned to function flawlessly as a team, there were the occasional problems of flying old airplanes under combat conditions.[5] Ensign Bruce Carmichael recalled flying his last operational sortie in a Spitfire:

*My last flight in the Spitfire nearly proved to be the ultimate. I went to the flight line as usual and checked the plane; I asked the mechanic if there were any unusual*

Figure 35.2. Curtiss SOC "Seagull" stored during VCS-7's interlude as VOS-7
US NAVY HISTORICAL CENTER

*characteristics about it, and he said no—it was ready. I made a normal takeoff and we set our course across the Channel. As standard procedure I switched to the belly tank. The white cliffs of Dover were still in sight when the engine failed. I realized that fuel was not feeding from the belly tank, so I switched back to the main tanks. The propeller was barely windmilling, and I had only 2,500 feet altitude.*

*We had been told that there was no way to start the engine in flight, which gave me two options: Bail out or ditch the aircraft. There were no nearby ships, since we were far to the east of the shipping lanes. My wingman eased his throttle and watched my descent. Either way, if I ditched or bailed out, my life expectancy in the water at that temperature would be less than two hours. I opted to bail out. I released my safety belt first and put it on the seat, ready to go headfirst.*

*By now I was at less than 1,800 feet and dropping fast. I noticed that the shoelace of my right shoe was untied, and for some reason I hesitated. Many times I relive those few seconds in my memory—an untied shoelace, that slight hesitation before bailing out. As I looked at the shoe my engine coughed, and the main tanks began giving fuel again. I believe now, as I did then, it was divine intervention that saved me. I returned to base and I told the British crew chief that the connection was bad between the belly tank and the engine. "I know," he said, "we have been having difficulty with that aircraft."*[6]

Figure 35.3. Bluejacket and the Spitfire. LT Francis A. Cahill, USNR, is assisted by his plane captain (name unknown) before leaving for the Normandy coast. NATIONAL MUSEUM OF NAVAL AVIATION

Up to six aircraft were required for each mission sector to be covered because of the distance from their base at RNAS (Royal Navy Air Station) Lee-on-Solent to their targets in France. It took about an hour from takeoff to the target area. During naval gunfire missions, two aircraft would be over the target, two would be on the way home, and two would be on the way in. Each two-ship flight, with drop tanks, could provide about forty-five minutes coverage—less if the occasional rogue *Luftwaffe* fighter made an appearance. To supplement the fliers, twenty-seven Naval Gunfire Shore Parties landed with the paratroopers and on the beaches on D-Day. This allowed for all-weather twenty-four-hour coverage.[7]

On D-Day, the ASP aircraft flew 339 sorties in support of the shore bombardment.[8] All the aircraft were pooled, supporting the fire of any ship regardless of the navy to which it belonged. They were all Ike's ships that day. By noon, the Mustangs Is assigned to the ASP by 2TAF were called away for more normal reconnaissance duty, leaving the ninety-five Spitfires and Seafires to continue the relays over the beach.

Missions were tasked at 6,000 feet, although the weather often forced the aircraft down below 2,000. By the end of D-Day, seven Spitfires/Seafires had been lost to flak.[9] This included one flown by Lieutenant Richard M. Barclay, USN, whose wingman, Lieutenant (JG) Charles S. Zinn, returned to base with severe damage.[10]

Sometimes the men of the ASP got a little too wrapped up in their work. Lieutenant Dick Law, flying an ASP Seafire in support of the battleship HMS *Warspite*, recalls:

> *During one of the early salvoes I was a little overenthusiastic in positioning myself to observe the fall of the shells, with the result that some 35 seconds after* Warspite *fired, my Seafire suddenly shivered and I actually saw one of the giant shells, weighing almost a ton, go sizzling close past me on its way to the target. During subsequent salvoes I made good and sure that I was well to the side of the line of fire! From time to time the German batteries returned* Warspite's *fire; when that happened we were treated to the spectacle of a giant sized tennis match. During one of these exchanges a salvo straddled* Warspite, *but she received only slight damage.*[11]

On June 7 some of the very limited German fighter activity involved runs against the ASP aircraft. Three were lost on June 7–8, but in return they downed two German fighters and claimed a third as a "probable."[12] By June 9 the invaders were firmly ashore and the weather began to close in. Continued work by the ASP as well as the naval gunfire parties with the ground troops ensured that the big guns offshore would continue to add to the misery of the German defenders in the hedgerows of Normandy.

New Zealander Lieutenant (A) Hugh "Sam" Lang, RNZNVR, made the following diary entry concerning his busy day on June 8:

> *Off at 0500 hours (in Seafire L.111 NF525). Ran into intense flak over Le Havre and lost Alan Horstead. Orbited over [the battle area] and called him and HMS* Warspite. *Two Fw 190s made a pass at me but I evaded them and gave the second one a longish burst from 400–600 yards, seeing strikes on his wing root. He turned slowly to starboard and then I saw tracer flashing past underneath me, so I pulled violently to port and a cannon shell hit my [propeller's] constant speed unit. The fan [propeller] stopped and I tried to bail out but the canopy would not open, so I decided to crash-land with the aircraft partly under control.*
>
> *I had to land in a wood but got down somehow, crashing into trees and had my face and arms cut about slightly. Hopped out and, after collecting maps, revolver, first aid and escape kits, scrambled northwest to find our troops.*[13]

Figure 35.4. VOS-7 Squadron Operations Room. Interservice coordination was the key to success. Left to right: Wing Cmdr. Robert J. Hardiman, RAF; Ens. Robert J. Adams, USNR; unidentified American naval officer standing behind Adams; Maj. Noel East, British Army intelligence; Lt. Harris Hammersmith, USNR, and Capt. John Ruscoe, Gunnery Liaison Officer, Royal Artillery. PHOTO 80-G-302115 NATIONAL ARCHIVES

## FORTRESS CHERBOURG

The key port of Cherbourg surrendered on June 27 after fierce fighting on the Cotentin Peninsula. After D-Day, VOS-7 assisted in attacking the Cherbourg defenses, including the big coastal defense guns first attacked by the RAF on the first morning of the invasion. By the time of the surrender, German engineers had effectively destroyed the harbor facilities and blocked the waterway. Although it would be some time before Cherbourg would be useful as a major port, within two weeks the Allies were unloading some ships there.[14]

Cherbourg was the last large engagement for VOS-7, which reverted to VCS-7 and its floatplanes within a few days. It had flown 191 sorties, losing a total of some eight aircraft to flak and a ninth to a noncombat accident. Four VOS-7 aircraft were intercepted by German fighters in June but successfully defended themselves—quite a feat, since the Spitfire V was no longer considered a first-line fighter.[15]

# CHAPTER THIRTY-SIX

# Air Landing Grounds

The US Ninth Air Force received its fighter units as part of the BOLERO buildup, and many were based on temporary airfields on the south coast of England. Britain was so crowded with airplanes that construction of new airfields and expansion of the prewar RAF infrastructure could not keep pace with the growth of Allied airpower. Austere temporary airfields were the answer.

The RAF built twenty-three so-called advanced landing grounds (ALGs) in Britain to temporarily house the American and British AEAF units for which no permanent air stations were available. The same design would be used to build ALGs on the continent after the invasion so that most AEAF units could move forward with the armies they were tasked to support.

## THE FOXWOOD AVENUE DISASTER

The ALGs were dangerous, cramped places limited by lack of available real estate and surfacing materials. The 405th Fighter Group was based at ALG No. 416, also known as the Royal Naval Air Station, HMS *Raven*. The 405th was the unit of then First Lieutenant John "Ace" Drummond. ALG No. 416 and the naval air station were sandwiched into the local terrain at Christchurch, just west of Southampton. Houses were located around the perimeter.[1]

The airfield itself was tiny, surfaced with PSP (pierced steel planking). The men lived in tents and in tiny neighboring cottages taken over for the war. The runway was very short for loaded P-47D Thunderbolt fighters carrying two 500-pound bombs plus ammo. On June 29, a few weeks after D-Day, flight activity was heavy from the airfield, as German targets just across the Channel were numerous. On that day, an accident claimed thirteen lives and fourteen other casualties in what came to be known as the "Foxwood Avenue Disaster." The accident was described to me by John Drummond:

> *You know we had some of the rookies come in there. To get off that strip with bombs you had to go down to the end and lock your brakes, kick in the water injection, and turn it loose! This one guy came in and I had just landed from a mission*

*and this young boy (2Lt. Vincent James) tried to get off and he didn't make it. He crashed near a house down at the end of the runway. Actually it didn't kill him. That old P-47 was pretty tough. So they brought him back and they put him back in another plane for the next mission!*

It was war. Engineers were forced to put airfields where they were needed and otherwise shouldn't be. Commanders were forced to make hazardous decisions about their men every day. Drummond continued:

*So I'm standing there with my wingman ol' Williams (Lt. Arthur F. Williams, Jr.). He had just gotten some mail. The little girl he was engaged to had finished high school and he had sent her a ring. The letter had a picture of her showing him that ring. All of a sudden—BOOM! We looked out at the end of the runway and there was a big old smoke cloud where a bomb had gone off. So we ran across to it. The kid (Lt. James) had crashed again, this time into a house that had a lot of children in it. We knew the family made the children go in the basement when we were taking off.*

There was an immediate reaction from the Royal Navy firemen and engineers responding to the wreck. Lieutenant James had crashed a second P-47 in the same way and in the same place. The plane burst into flame as Drummond and his friend Williams ran towards the crash.

*The house was on fire. So we ran across and I went in that house and the woman was coming up out of the basement, and my God—her skin was hanging off her arms. I starting getting her out and my wingman Williams was taking one of the little kids out. As we went by they were hosing the wreck. They knocked loose one of those bombs that they thought had already exploded.*

Drummond paused and said:

*It was white hot and I remember seeing it and I hollered something but—no one's ever been able to explain this to me—it was total slow motion. I know I was picked up—and rolling around in the air—and I saw Williams come up off the ground—and I saw a big hole in him—I saw blood—and I don't know how far I was thrown and I hit on my right shoulder. And I thought, "What is my mother going to think?" I guess I thought I was dead. I was rolling and everything. A piece of shrapnel had gone through here (in front of the left ear) and just barely cut me and through my ear and out the back. This is how lucky I've been.*

Being blown up was not the end of Drummond's problems:

*And Williams, I didn't know what had happened to him, but I walked on up to the end of the runway and there were people coming from everywhere. The captain in charge of the crash crew was sitting on the curb and he had blood all over him. Of course, I had blood all over me. And here comes a little car and I helped this guy get inside. He was holding his neck; the shrapnel had gone through the back of his neck. We were sitting in the back seat.*

*I'll never forget this; he looked down and blood was flowing from the back of his boot. I grabbed his leg and tried to put pressure, as I pulled his leg up his foot was raised and the blood that had coagulated on the floor came loose. He had part of his heel shot off. He was happy as a lark when he saw that, it could have been worse.*

*They got us to the hospital at Bournemouth. I wasn't hurt much and they put me aside. Twenty-seven people were hurt or killed and they were bringing them in. Here was Williams lying on an old stretcher. He was lying there and all his blood was running down into a bucket at the end of the stretcher.*[2]

## FORWARD INTO FRANCE

RAF Airfield Construction Wings built the ALGs in Britain and would move to France to support 2TAF as it relocated flying units there. In the USAAF, engineering units were under generic Service Command organizations. General Brereton, US Ninth Air Force commander, believed a separate aviation engineering command could better serve his airmen based on his experience in North Africa. He activated the US IX Engineer Command (IX EC) in March 1944 to provide an ALG building capability for his flying units.

IX EC trained sixteen mobile engineering battalions that would move with the front lines in France, building new airfields or refurbishing older ones as the front moved closer to Germany. On D-Day these battalions and their RAF counterparts landed as soon as the assault troops moved off the beaches.[3]

The 819th Engineering Aviation Battalion (EAB) landed on Utah Beach on D-Day. The first American emergency landing strip (ELS-1) behind Utah Beach at Pouppeville was completed by 21:15 on D-Day, between beach exits D-3 and E-1. The 834th EAB landed on Omaha on D plus 1, delayed only by the fierce fighting for the beachhead there. It established ELS-2 behind the beach at St. Laurent-sur-Mer.

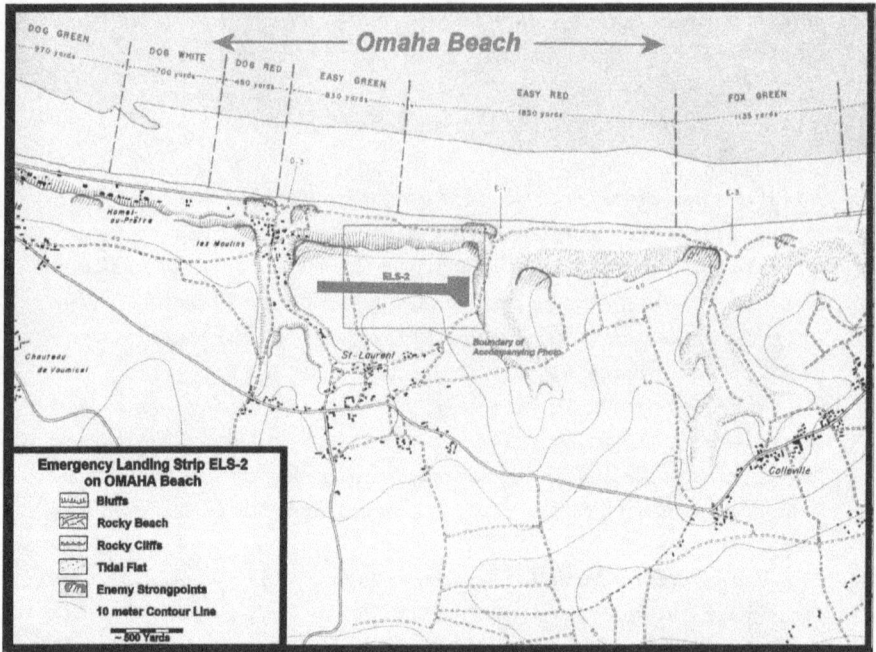

Map 36.1. Emergency Strip ELS-2 on Omaha Beach. The airstrip was cleared by bull-dozers to remove obstacles and level the ground. ELS-2 and other landing grounds in Normandy were noted by both Allied and German pilots as extremely dusty. MOLYSON[4]

ELS-1 and ELS-2 allowed the recovery of damaged aircraft that otherwise might have been abandoned and were also used by C-47s to evacuate the critically wounded to England. A P-38 was the first fighter to land at ELS-2 on June 8 (D+2).[5]

Even as thousands of Allied soldiers crossed the Channel into Normandy, above their heads hundreds of AEAF airmen were moving with them. The emergency strips were only temporary expedients until the larger ALGs were brought into operation. Unlike the emergency strips, the ALGs were austere but fully functional bases from which combat missions could be flown. Major customers of these sites were fighter-bombers, especially the American P-47 Thunderbolt and the British Typhoon. Forward-basing meant they were an hour or more closer to the front lines, extending their ability to loiter over enemy territory. It was as *Jabos* that the Typhoon and Thunderbolt made their mark on German ground operations.

Technically, ALGs were military airfields without all-weather runways. By the end of the war in Europe, nearly 250 airfields had been built or refurbished for Allied use by troops in the IX Engineer Command and their comrades in the five RAF Airfield Construction Wings.[6] It was these units who made the AEAF truly "expeditionary."

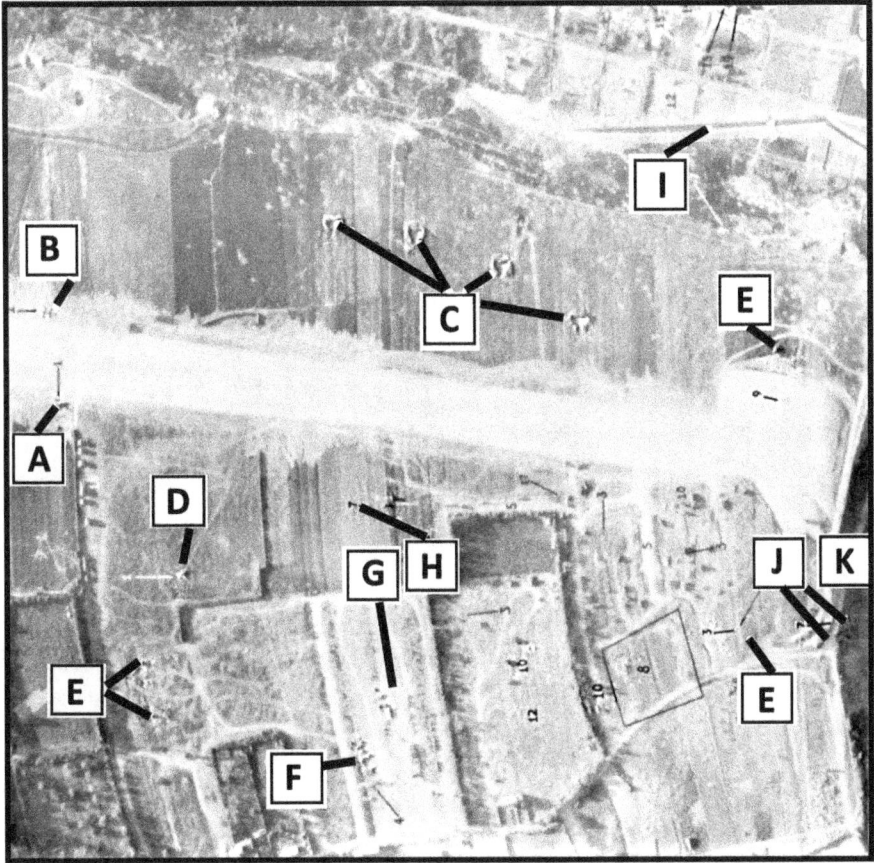

Figure 36.1. Emergency landing strip ELS-2 on Omaha Beach: (A) Damaged Spitfire; (B) Radar; (C) Unoccupied German Gun Emplacements; (D) P-47; (E) American AAA Guns; (F) Crash Crane; (G) Storage Area; (H) Barrage Balloon; (I) German-built Anti-Tank Ditch; (J) Beach Exit E-1; (K) Omaha Beach US ARMY AIR FORCE[7]

Figure 36.2. P-38 on ELS-2. Note the barrage balloons in the distance and the DUKW amphibious supply truck. NATIONAL ARCHIVES

Figure 36.3. ALG-1 built just to the east of Pointe du Hoc. Note that its runway was still dirt at this time. Also note the extensive taxiways along which parking spots for aircraft were later built. USAF

A standard concept in military doctrine is that during river crossings, the troops on the far shore are at risk until significant numbers of their fellows can be put across. The attack across the Channel was in many ways like a river crossing. During the first few hours of assault, the troops on the beach were vulnerable. They counted on heavy and continuous air and naval bombardment to help break through the enemy defenses and to prevent enemy reinforcements based inland from arriving in the battle zone.[8]

The critical question for NEPTUNE was how rapidly Montgomery could seize Caen and then move south to the flat country beyond. Caen was a D-Day objective that was not met; it was weeks before the desired area was overrun. This delayed moving tactical aircraft to France. It also meant that the first ALGs were closely clustered along the recently seized coastline. The airspace was crowded as a result. In July, Normandy was so dry and dusty that aircraft based on the ALGs had to be fitted with dust filters.[9]

The development of each ALG was systematically organized. First, a relatively flat area was selected for the base. It was surveyed for facilities, and residual enemy mines and other obstacles were removed. Flat space was at a premium in Normandy because of the hedgerows and large areas of swampy terrain. Initially, the runway was planned for 3,400 feet, but in most ALGs this was extended to 5,000 feet to accommodate heavily loaded fighter-bombers, perhaps incorporating the lessons of Foxwood Avenue. Temporary surfaces were devised to avoid flying from muddy airfields; concrete runways would take too long to build, and the front was continually moving away from the beachhead.

American ALGs were numbered "A-" and for the British "B-." During peak periods of operations, a new airfield went into service every thirty-six hours.[11] As addi-

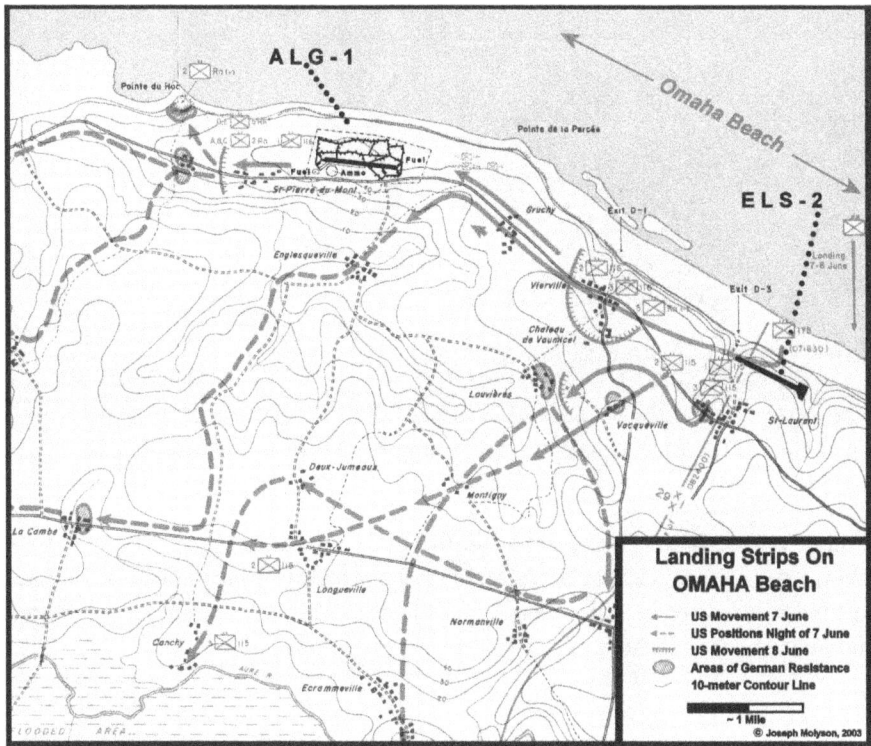

Map 36.2. ALG-1 and ELS-2 on Omaha Beach. Note the proximity to German units holding out nearby. MOLYSON[10]

tional ALGs were built, their locations reflected the course of the battle for France. On June 13 the first full-fledged ALGs were ready for business in the Lodgement area. By June 15, units began to deploy forward to assume residence.[12] By June 21, five fighter-bomber groups were based in Normandy and operating from four new advanced landing grounds. Other Allied *Jabo* units were on the way. (See appendix 5.)

The temporary surfacing materials were referred to in American slang as "chicken wire and tarpaper." The "chicken wire" was a metal grid called an SMT (square mat track) by the Americans and Sommerfeldt wire mesh by the British. It was delivered to the construction site by trucks in large rolls. The "tarpaper" was asphalt-impregnated burlap, also on a roll, known in Britain as "Hessian mat." The Americans called it PHS (prefabricated Hessian surfacing) or PBS (prefabricated burlap surfacing).

SMT and PHS worked best when used together. SMT did nothing to prevent a choking cloud of Norman dust at every takeoff. The PHS was soft and could be split by the heavily loaded fighter-bombers. Used together, the SMT provided

Figure 36.4. An aviation engineer battalion prepares a new ALG runway for use.
NATIONAL ARCHIVES

mechanical protection to the PHS and the PHS reduced the dust associated with SMT. Steel matting, called PSP (pierced steel matting) or Marston mat, sometimes supplemented or replaced these less durable materials as time and supplies permitted and wear and tear dictated.

Figure 36.5. P-51 on recently occupied German airfield AIR FORCE HISTORICAL RESEARCH AGENCY-WB

Figure 36.6. Aerodrome squadrons provided the initial flying unit support at ALGs. Note the soldier transferring aviation gasoline from a jerry can into an aircraft refueling cart. It took approximately 75 jerry cans to fill the internal fuel tanks of each P-47, 15 more cans to fill each 75- gallon drop tank. The cans would then be returned to a depot to be refilled.

The first installations of PSP were in July. Each landing strip required about 2,000 tons of perforated plate.[13] This material could support the weight of medium and light bombers, something the earlier materials failed to do. Derelict *Luftwaffe* airbases were also used on occasion, especially as the war moved out of the immediate area of the beachhead.[14] It was easier to rebuild a devastated airfield than build one from scratch.

For the Yanks, one of the engineering battalions would scrape out the runways, taxiways, and parking areas and lay the designated surfacing material. The unit would then move to its next assignment, giving way to a IX Service Command airdrome squadron. This unit in turn would stock the ALG with its initial supplies, about ten days' worth, and prepare to receive the first air squadron. The airdrome squadrons also provided aircraft maintenance until the air unit's own personnel could assume that function. The RAF used similar procedures for their bases.

The process of relocating an air unit involved moving 2,000 men and 67 tons of equipment.[15] Sometimes units were deployed forward even if the ALG was not fully operational. Through June and early July, some fighter groups used a *roulement system*, rotating each of the group's squadrons forward to an ALG for a limited period of time.[16] When the aircraft maintenance backlog became serious or the squadron resources were exhausted, the unit and its planes were withdrawn to

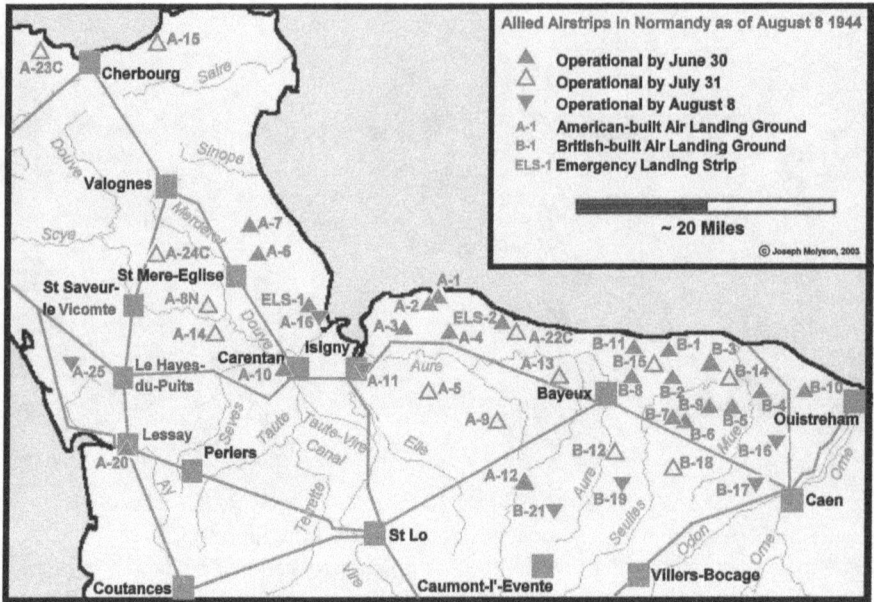

Map 36.3. Allied Airstrips in Normandy as of August 8 (See appendix 5.) MOLYSON

England and a fresh squadron took its place. This system persisted until the parent group, with its aircraft maintenance capability, could be sent from its British base forward into France.[17]

Once the flying unit had arrived and its support personnel set up, the airdrome squadron would follow the engineering battalion to its next assignment. Priority personnel in the air unit would be flown in aboard C-47s; others would be shipped to the beach and then moved by truck to the new base. A squadron's pilots would fly in the combat aircraft while additional unit pilots would travel in C-47s with the priority ground personnel. IX Service Command pilots flew in replacement aircraft as needed from depots at Membury and Chilbolton in the United Kingdom.[18]

ALGs were designed to last 60 or 90 days under "normal" conditions; however, conditions were far from normal in combat. The heavy Typhoons and Thunderbolts made deep ruts in the ends of runways and parking areas. The aircraft were not only heavy but also carried a thousand pounds or more of ordnance. They pushed the SMT into muddy ground when the weather was wet.

In dry weather, clouds of Norman dust were raised whenever they taxied. Even the Hessian mat allowed some dust to escape. PSP was better than SMT/Hessian mat but was not as serviceable as concrete. In any case, the imperfect but functioning ALGs brought Allied airpower closer to their armies than otherwise possible, doom-

Figure 36.7. Busted Jug—many damaged aircraft recovered at ALGs were repairable. This is an older model P-47D "razorback" without the bubble canopy. AIR FORCE HISTORICAL RESEARCH AGENCY

ing many a German vehicle and saving many Allied aircraft from being abandoned by parachute over the battlefield.

German General Galland later observed that the Allies not only maintained their huge margin of air superiority but also quickly built a series of forward airbases for their fighters. The Germans observed twenty-three new Allied airfields by 23 June, mostly in the eastern (English) sector of the bridgehead.[19] Actually there were nineteen occupied; the others were being built. He noted that this immediately and effectively increased the number of Allied fighters over France. It also facilitated the return of Eighth Air Force long-range fighters to the battle over Germany and the Air Defense of Great Britain (ADGB) fighters to their normal missions. By this time, ADGB was heavily involved with intercepting German V-1 flying bombs hitting London.

# CHAPTER THIRTY-SEVEN

# Forward into France

On D-Day, air support requests were sent to the invasion ground force commander at Headquarters 21st Army Group for approval and the invasion air force commander at Advanced Headquarters AEAF for tasking an air unit. This was a cumbersome system and could take up to two hours to get bombs on target. Eleven air requests were submitted in the American sector alone on D-Day, five of which were not accomplished due to weather. The system did not work as well as it should and would be soon improved.[1] (See figure 1.1.)

Eisenhower and Tedder had determined the relationships between various air and ground headquarters, but communications was the key to making air-ground cooperation work. Behind the front, the 2TAF 83 (Composite) Group and the IX Tactical Air Command (IX TAC) headquarters were collocated with the field armies they supported. 83 (Composite) Group and IX TAC supported the Second British Army and First US Army, respectively.[2] Each air headquarters moved with its supported ground headquarters with each advance. This allowed face-to-face conversations to share and exchange identified problems so that mutually feasible solutions could be developed.

As the Allied armies advanced from the beaches, extensive radio networks linked their headquarters behind the lines to forward air controllers at the front. The controllers were mounted in vehicles, eventually tanks, so they could keep pace with fast-moving units. The system allowed pilots over the battlefield to talk with the forward air controllers to identify and attack enemy targets. Sharing the front line with the ground soldiers also meant that casualties among these controllers were high.

## COORDINATION

Medium and light bombers hit targets not in close contact with Allied ground forces, so-called *indirect* support. They normally flew against targets beyond the front line. These aircraft belonged to RAF No. 2 Group and US Ninth Air Force's IX Bomber Command. *Direct support* to the ground forces was provided by the fighters and fighter bombers of 2TAF's 83, 84, and 85 Groups and US Ninth Air Force's IX TCC. The 83 (Composite) Group and the US IX TAC provided *direct support* to the British Second Army and the US First Army, respectively. Their fighters and fighter-bombers flew close to the front line and, when necessary, beyond it. *Direct support* included *close air support* in proximity to friendly troops. Eisenhower had promised that if an aircraft was seen overhead, it would be friendly. That was almost, but not completely, true.

Being assigned to support a particular field army did not preclude aircraft of a particular Composite Group or Tactical Air Command flying in support of other ground forces, as was often the case, regardless of nationality. This was the crucial difference between tactical air support in Normandy as compared with the earlier campaign in North Africa. Airpower could now be massed where needed most, not parceled out to various ground commanders. What is more important is that both air and ground commanders knew of and respected this necessary flexibility.

The first 2TAF units to be based in Normandy were the RAF No. 127, 129, and 144 Wings. No. 127 and 144 Wings flew their Spitfires from B-2 at Bazenville and B-3 at St. Croix-sur-Mer, while the Typhoons of No. 129 Wing flew from B-10 at Plumetot. These were the first of many such deployments as 2TAF attempted to get its short-legged aircraft within easy striking range of their German targets. (See appendix 5 and map 36.3.)

No. 83 and No. 84 Groups had squadrons of Mustang III, Spitfire IX LF, and Typhoon Ib fighter-bombers. The Mustang was a British fighter-bomber version of the American P-51. The Spitfire IX LF was a medium- to low-level variant of the trusty Spit. Both the Mustang III and the Spitfire IX were equipped with shackles for various bombs and had automatic cannon for strafing. The Typhoon Ib was the premier British fighter-bomber of WWII. The engineers at Hawker had designed and built an airplane just as deadly (and ugly) as the P-47. The Jug had a reason for its homely silhouette: Its broad-faced radial engine dictated a bulky fuselage. This provided some frontal protection to the pilot.

The Typhoon, however, had an in-line water-cooled engine like the Mustang and Spitfire, making it somewhat more vulnerable to ground fire. Initial airframe problems with the Typhoon Ia had been largely overcome in the Typhoon Ib by the time of the invasion.[3] In any case, the Typhoon was a hard-hitting plane with 20mm cannon, armor-piercing rockets, and large bomb-carrying capacity. The Typhoons had destroyed some 150 French and Belgian locomotives a month before D-Day. Some twenty-six squadrons were ready to move to France in support of the invasion.[4]

Figure 37.1. John Drummond and his P-47D "Raid Hot Mama" in 1944. Note the bulky forward fuselage with a radial engine inside. COURTESY OF JOHN DRUMMOND

Figure 37.2. RP (rocket-projectile) Typhoon AIR FORCE HISTORICAL RESEARCH AGENCY KARLSRUHE COLLECTION

Another 2TAF unit was RAF 85 Group, which performed day and night air defense. RAF 85 Group included the 141 Wing, consisting of two squadrons of new Spitfire XIVs. The 2TAF traded its wing of new Tempest fighters with ADGB for three squadrons of Spitfire IXs and Typhoons. The Tempests were needed in England to fight the V-1 flying bombs now being fired at London from the Pas-de-Calais. The Tempest, a descendant of the Hawker Hurricane and the more recent Typhoon, was so fast in a diving attack it could run down the V-1.

The Mosquito XIII NF of No. 142 and No. 149 Wings provided night defense. These aircraft could also fly night intruder missions, hitting German troops on the roads as they scurried from place to place.

## Ninth Air Force

The American buildup in Normandy was similar to the RAF effort. While the US Ninth Air Force twin-engine aircraft of IX Bomber Command remained based in England, Major General Brereton pushed as many of his fighters into the beachhead as possible. These were assigned to the IX Tactical Air Command (IX TAC) under Major General Elwood "Pete" Quesada, a protégé of both General Arnold and Lieutenant General Spaatz. Known earlier for his explosive temper, he had matured as deputy to Air Vice Marshal Arthur Coningham in the Mediterranean.

The Thunderbolt-equipped 368th Fighter Group was the first IX TAC unit based in Normandy, arriving on June 14. Other P-47, P-38 Lightning, and P-51 Mustang groups soon followed. Both the Mustang and Lightning performed well as fighter-bombers in Normandy, but pride of place belonged to the trusty Thunderbolt. It would be well into the campaign, however, before the P-47 would receive the rockets already provided to the Typhoon fleet. The P-38 was reborn as an effective low-level fighter. A former Lightning pilot remembered, "The aircraft was more than a match for the German fighters at this altitude, but they very seldom engaged."[5]

Tedder put all of the Allied Air Expeditionary Force aircraft operating over France under AEAF Forward, commanded by Coningham, including Quesada's IX TAC. Tedder, Coningham, Quesada, and the other air leaders who had observed the inefficient application of tactical support airpower in the Mediterranean were bound and determined to do better in France.

Rommel had soundly beaten the American Army at Kasserine Pass, partially because RAF and American air support was poorly managed. In North Africa, American and RAF aircraft had been apportioned among all the various ground commanders. None had sufficient aircraft to provide the support required. A central pool under a single air commander would have been more efficient. The ground commanders and the air commanders had learned a costly lesson—decentralization of airpower meant disaster.[6]

Air Marshal Tedder, as Eisenhower's deputy supreme commander, was uniquely positioned to ensure that none of airpower's capabilities were wasted in this new campaign. After his own experiences supporting General Montgomery in North Africa, Tedder published his *Principles of Air Warfare*. This was codified in the US Army field manual on air support, published in FM 100-20, 21 July 1943, and in a host of other Allied documents.

Among the salient principles stated in FM 100-20 were the following: "Land power and air power are coequal and interdependent forces; neither is the auxiliary of the other"; "the gaining of air superiority is the first requirement for the success of any land operation"; and "control of available airpower must be centralized and command must be exercised through the air force commander if the inherent flexibility and ability to deliver a decisive blow are to be fully exploited."[7]

## BUZZ BOMBS

On June 16, Churchill's War Cabinet noted the increasing V-1 attacks on London, which were launched from France, and considered the appropriate response. The British leadership decided that London must "take it," maintaining the Normandy fighting as the priority mission for the RAF. Churchill announced that the British population would share the dangers their sons faced on the battlefields of Europe.[8] Hitler and Göring's effort to divert Allied combat power from the Normandy campaign was thus spoiled. Only minor adjustments to the air order of battle were allowed, none of which significantly affected the activity in France.

Some 2TAF units remained based in Britain. The RAF Mitchell medium and Boston light bombers of Number 2 Group were too heavy to operate from the soft

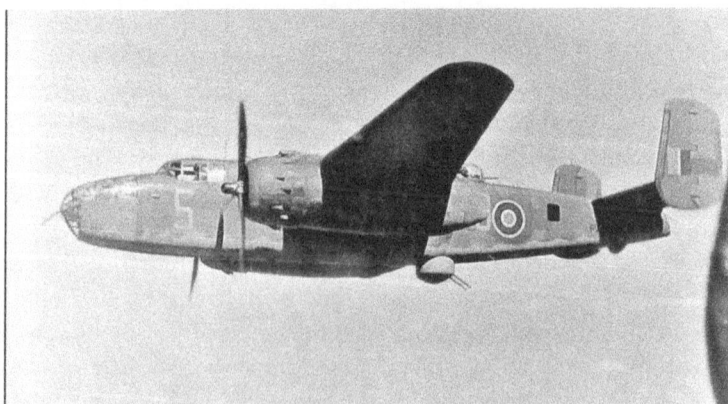

Figure 37.3. RAF Mitchell, standard medium bomber for 2TAF
AIR FORCE HISTORICAL RESEARCH AGENCY KARLSRUHE COLLECTION

runways of the advanced landing grounds, and in any case their range based in Britain was sufficient to reach their targets in France fully "bombed up." In addition to these factors, these bombers consumed prodigious amounts of fuel and bombs, both of which were easier to provide on British than French bases. For similar reasons, the American B-26 medium and A-20 light bombers of Ninth Air Force's IX Bomber Command also remained on British bases until August. Favorite targets for these aircraft were German troop assembly areas and various rail and road targets on the lines of communication in Normandy.

Two squadrons of Mosquito XIII night fighter-bombers of Number 85 Group also stayed, because in Britain their patrol areas were as close to their English bases as the temporary airfields in France. The American P-61 Black Widow joined them in July. Three squadrons of Mustang IIIs of Number 84 Group remained in England because they were assigned to provide long-range escort for the day raids that RAF Bomber Command continued after D-Day.

Allied airmen maintained the defense of Britain and projected airpower across the Channel in Occupied Europe. Once sufficient air landing grounds were established, the full weight of the AEAF could be brought against the *Luftwaffe* and German Army.

# CHAPTER THIRTY-EIGHT

# Death by *Jabo*

During the 1940 invasion of Holland, Belgium, and France by the Germans, the cry of "*Stuka!*" became common as the *Luftwaffe* divebombers battered the Allied armies. Now in Normandy, *Luftwaffe* close support was all but gone and it was German troops who cried "*Jabo!*" as squadron after squadron of Allied fighter-bombers strafed, rocketed, and bombed them. *Jabo* is German slang for *Jagdbomber*, or fighter-bomber, and the name stuck. It started before D-Day and continued as German troops began to move on the morning of June 6.

The interdiction campaign against German rail movement also meant that the beach defenses were not as prepared as they might have been. Even the most impressive of defenses had their shortcomings. The battery at Saint-Marcouf, near Utah Beach, for example, had no fire control equipment; it had not arrived from the depot. The armored loophole plates that protected the firing embrasures of another battery also had not arrived; they were stuck somewhere between the supply depot at Bad Segeberg, Germany, and the Cotentin. They would never be installed. At least one 14-inch round from the battleship *Nevada* penetrated a gun pillbox through its unprotected embrasure, destroying the enemy gun and its crew. The fact that this battery remained a major impediment to securing the Cotentin Peninsula had more to do with German valor than German logistics.[1]

Hitler's delay in responding to the NEPTUNE assault would have a great impact on the German Army. It meant that the German units moving forward after dawn on D-Day faced the brunt of Allied fighter-bomber attacks. Close to the beach the Air Spotting Pool flying Spitfires and Mustang Is directed naval bombardment on advancing Germans within range.

Allied medium and light bombers had crippled many of the railroads intended to bring reinforcements and supplies into Lower Normandy and continued this campaign after the landings. Allied *Jabos* dropped bridges, adding to the Germans' transportation woes. Airpower forced the German Army off the trains onto the roads. The *Jabos* then forced them off the roads and into the ditches and hedgerows,

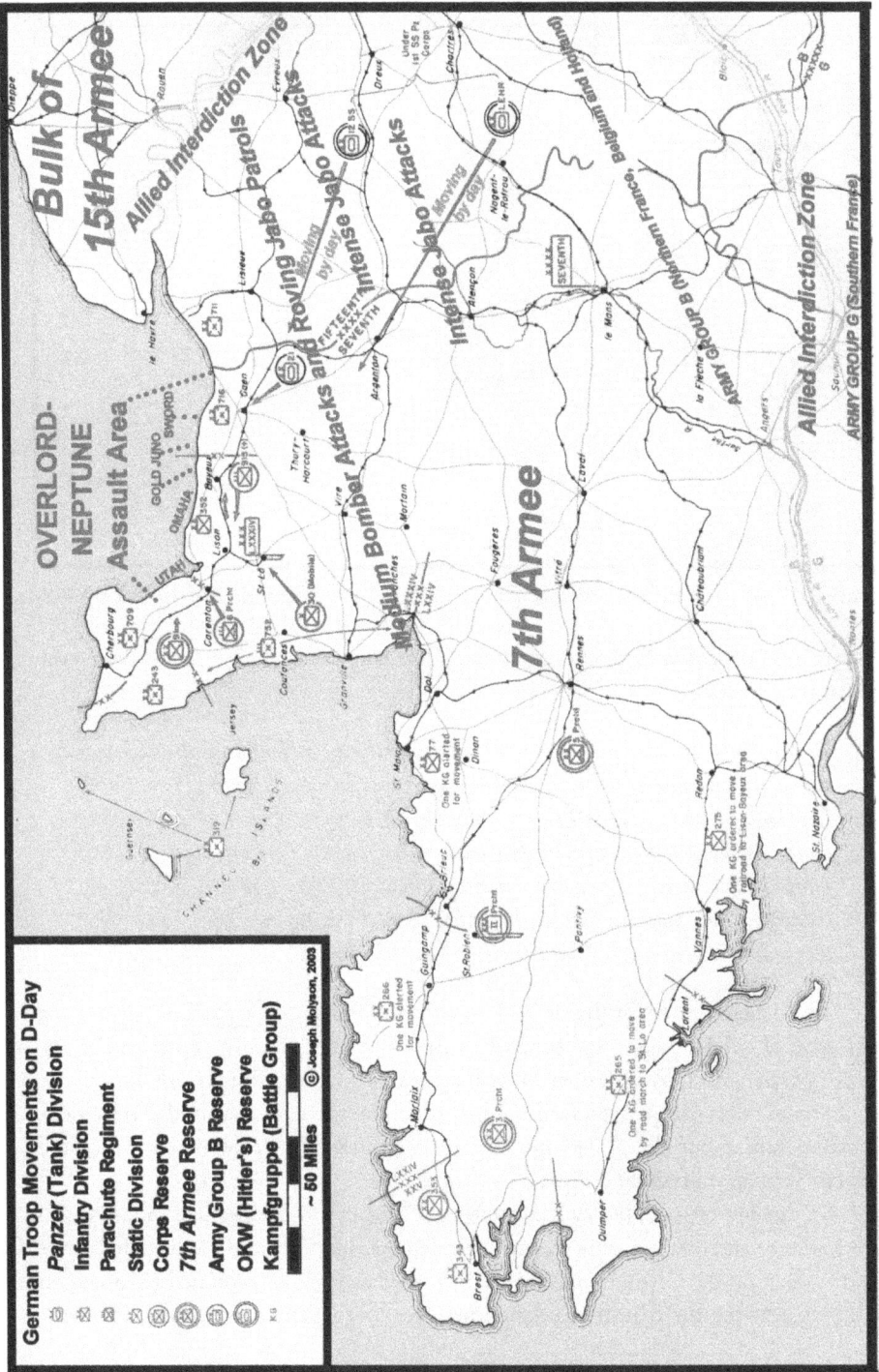

Map 38.1. German Troop Movements on D-Day. Some of these were contrary to Hitler's orders. MOLYSON[2]

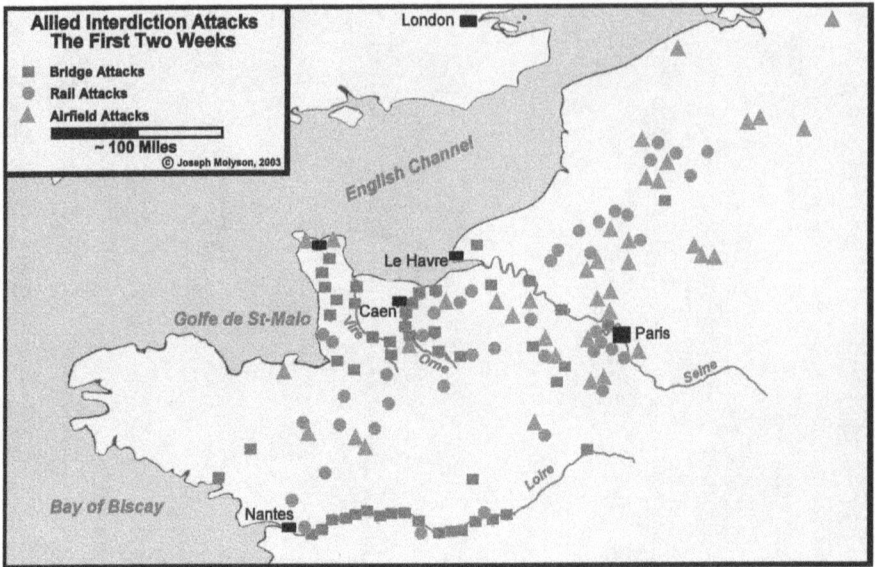

Map 38.2. Allied Interdiction Attacks, First Two Weeks of NEPTUNE–OVERLORD MOLYSON

a dirty business down close to the ground. Pilots like Chuck Yeager found them even when they took cover:

> *Coming in so low, my eyes once met with the driver of a German staff car. I was coming straight at him; one quick burst and that car disintegrated, four bodies tossed out on the . . . road like rag dolls. Another time, I spotted a five- or six-truck German troop convoy; by the time I swooped down on them, the troops had jumped out and were hunkered down in a roadside ditch. I opened up with my six fifty-caliber machine guns and watched those sparkling butterflies dance right up the line in that ditch. Before leaving, I hit their trucks.*[3]

The delays caused by trains had other unintended consequences beyond the objective of delaying logistical support to the front line. Allied prisoners had to be kept in German POW (prisoner of war) camps close to the front, from which they could more easily escape than from camps far behind the lines.[4] Wounded personnel, mostly German but also Allied and civilian, could not be evacuated and were cared for by German military and French civilian doctors.

By the end of June, Hitler had come to believe that the Allies had in fact seized the initiative and that his army was on the defensive. The *Führer* still anticipated a second landing on the Channel coast at the Pas-de-Calais. He now pinned his hopes on a breach between the British and American allies over further prosecution of the war.

Figure 38.1. Allied airpower forced the German Army off the trains . . .
AIR FORCE HISTORICAL RESEARCH AGENCY

Figure 38.2. . . . and then off the roads. AIR FORCE HISTORICAL RESEARCH AGENCY

## DEATH OF THE GENERALS

The Germans lost many of their senior leaders in air attacks. These included *Generalleutnant* Wilhelm Falley, commander of the 91st Air Landing Division in the Cotentin (June 6); *General der Artillerie* Erich Marcks, commander of the LXXIV Corps defending Normandy (June 12); *SS Brigadeführer*[5] Fritz Witt of the 12th SS Panzer Division *Hitlerjugend* (June 14); *Generalleutnant* Heinz Hellmich, commander of the 243rd Division (June 17); *Generalleutnant* Rudolf Stegmann, commander of the 77th division (June 18); and others.

Falley was killed by US paratroopers on D-Day while returning by car from the ill-timed wargames at Rennes. While traveling to inspect the German defensive line northwest of Saint-Lô, General Marcks was killed in a strafing attack. He was hit by a *Jabo* 20mm cannon shell after abandoning his car. *SS Brigadeführer* Witt was killed when British naval gunfire destroyed his headquarters at Venoix after it had been spotted by Allied aircraft.

General Heinz Hellmich was killed by 20mm *Jabo* fire south of Cherbourg, as was *Generalleutnant* Stegmann. Hundreds if not thousands of German soldiers were killed by Thunderbolts, Typhoons, and other Allied fighters. A new German slang term was invented: *Jagd-Tod*, or "Death by *Jabo*."[6] Movement at night offered some relief from Allied aircraft but denied German soldiers the rest they might otherwise have gotten under more normal conditions. The cycle of fight-move-fight could only be repeated so many times before the morale and effectiveness of the combat troops suffered.

As the battle progressed through June, the Germans began to lose the numerical advantage they had enjoyed in Normandy. By mid-June, over 350,000 Allied troops and perhaps 60,000 vehicles had been landed. By the end of July, there were probably no more than 490,000 German troops in Normandy. By this time, the Allies had landed over 1,400,000.[7]

By early June, the thawing ground on the Eastern Front began to dry. This permitted large-scale Soviet tank attacks to proceed uninhibited.[8] Operation BAGRATION, beginning June 22, pushed the German Army back into Poland and further prevented adequate reinforcement of France.[9] The attack was another disaster for the Germans and would put them permanently on the defensive in the east as well as the west. On July 1, Hitler relieved *Generalfeldmarschall* Rundstedt of his post at *OB West*, appointing *Generalfeldmarschall* Günter von Kluge to replace him. Meanwhile, the Allied armies continued to slowly push outward from the Lodgement area.[10]

On July 17, *Generalfeldmarschall* Rommel, no armchair general, was badly injured by strafing *Jabos* while traveling south from Lisieux on one of his endless inspection trips. The attack did not kill him, but he was thrown from the car and suffered head injuries. He was evacuated to a field hospital and then returned to convalesce in Germany.

On July 20, German General Staff conspirators attempted to assassinate Adolf Hitler and failed. Rommel was at least peripherally involved in the plot. He was offered either public disgrace or a hero's death. He chose to take cyanide on October 14, 1944, and received a hero's funeral with full military honors. Only after the war was the truth revealed to the German public.

## FROM ESCORT TO *JABO*

Developing new tactics for attacking German ground targets was important, especially for the P-47D Thunderbolt as it went from long-range fighter escort to ground attack duties. Pilot "Ace" Drummond remembers that Major Ralph C. Jenkins, his flight leader, developed a unique style of dive-bombing. While other units performed a shallow dive-bombing along the line of flight, Jenkins unit of four to eight P-47s did a "split S," descending and reversing course and dropping on their target from a near vertical dive. Drummond's P-47, "Raid Hot Mama," carried out the maneuver dozens of times. This allowed a very accurate delivery of its 500-pound bombs on target.

The Germans evolved tactics to defend themselves in the absence of any effective *Luftwaffe* air cover. This included expert camouflage and becoming expert in the combat procedures of the Allied air armada. This turned into a battle of wills between the Germans and the Allied pilots who pummeled them. Arlie J. Blood, "Ol' Blood," was described by Drummond as the "finest fighter pilot that ever lived!" Blood was aggressive and was shot down six times. Drummond remembers:

> *They would tell us, "We want you to bomb those marshalling yards here with 500-pound bombs." So we went back to the target and Ol' Blood says, "Hell, they're hiding these trains and everything in the tunnels!" They wouldn't move the things while we were there because we'd shoot the hell out of them.*
>
> *"I'll tell you what let's do. Next time when everybody else goes back, let's stay down on the deck way back here and wait till they deliver the clear sign. Then they'll be moving stuff and we'll shoot the hell out of 'em!" And sure enough the first mission, we did it, we got what we thought was a troop train but it had a lot of (French) prisoners on it. And we went in and shot the hell out of it and the prisoners escaped.*[11]

As he passed over the train at 50 feet, flak hit Blood's plane. It turned into a ball of flame, and Drummond thought he was gone. Blood meanwhile pulled hard on the stick. The rugged Jug held together long enough to save its pilot. The plane climbed and he jettisoned the canopy. Blood unbuckled and kicked the stick hard as he left the plane. He continued upward, pulling his ripcord while the Jug fell away. After one swing he hit the ground, literally running.[12]

Blood joined the escaping prisoners from the train, who were rescued by the French Resistance. He fought with the Resistance, was captured once, but escaped to fight on. After four months, US forces recovered him. Blood also fought in the Korean War before retiring to a civilian career with Northrop Grumman. He has since related his story in his book, *Only Angels Have Wings*.

## SIEGE MENTALITY

The interdiction effort against the German Army was matched by attacks on German Air Force installations. Like the army, the GAF was highly dependent on rail service to supply forward air bases. Allied air patrols also intercepted German air reinforcement and supply flights destined for *Luftflotte 3*. All this had a debilitating effect on the morale of the surviving GAF airmen in France, even as it instilled the kind of siege mentality the RAF had suffered during the Battle of Britain. The German flyers were besieged both by the Allies and by their own government. *Luftwaffe* personnel developed a siege mentality, brought closer together by the impending doom of their service and country. German General Galland remembered:

> *Until the fall of Paris I spent several days with the units in the west. My impressions were shattering. In addition to the appalling conditions, there was a far-reaching spiritual decline. This feeling of irrevocable inferiority, the heavy losses, the hopelessness of the fighting, which had never before been so clearly demonstrated to us, the reproaches from above, the disrepute into which the* Luftwaffe *had fallen among the other arms of the forces from no fault of the individual, together with the other burdens the war at this stage had brought to every German, gave the greatest sense of solidarity ever experienced by the* Luftwaffe.[13]

# CHAPTER THIRTY-NINE

# Expansion

With the immediate area of the assault beaches under Allied control and their forces beginning to chafe against the perimeter, the Americans in the west and the British in the east pushed against the battered but stubborn Germans. The *7th Armée* formed a desperately thin but determined ring around the beachhead. The Germans made good use of the bocage in the defense. The hedgerow had replaced the World War I trench as a place to die. Elements of the *Panzer Lehr* and other German tank units were moved alternately between the American and British portions of the front, mainly by night. The stalemate was sustained for weeks after D-Day. Repeated British attempts to take Caen and the flat area to the south failed due to dogged German resistance.

The need for information was critical if the Allied advance was to continue. This was especially true in the bocage, with its myriad small farmers' fields and sunken roads. Good observation points on the ground were rare and invariably involved exposing the observer to enemy fire. Allied soldiers performed risky ground reconnaissance into German-held areas; sometimes whole units were decimated just to find out who owned the next hedgerow. It was a close, vicious infantry fight.

## GRASSHOPPERS

Allied airmen flying reconnaissance aircraft were overhead every day the weather permitted, shooting thousands of photographs that were rushed back for analysis and dissemination. It was these efforts that reported the loading of trains as German units attempted to reach the battle, allowing for their subsequent destruction.[1] While photoreconnaissance allowed for near-term planning, it did little to support the immediate targeting of fleeting targets by Allied army artillery or naval gunfire from offshore.

Initially this was the job of the Air Spotting Pool pilots, but these men would be gone by the end of June as the front moved inland out of range of naval gunfire and the fleet moved on to other duties. As more and more artillery was landed at the five beaches and the first advanced landing grounds were established, other airmen took up the spotting and observation mission.

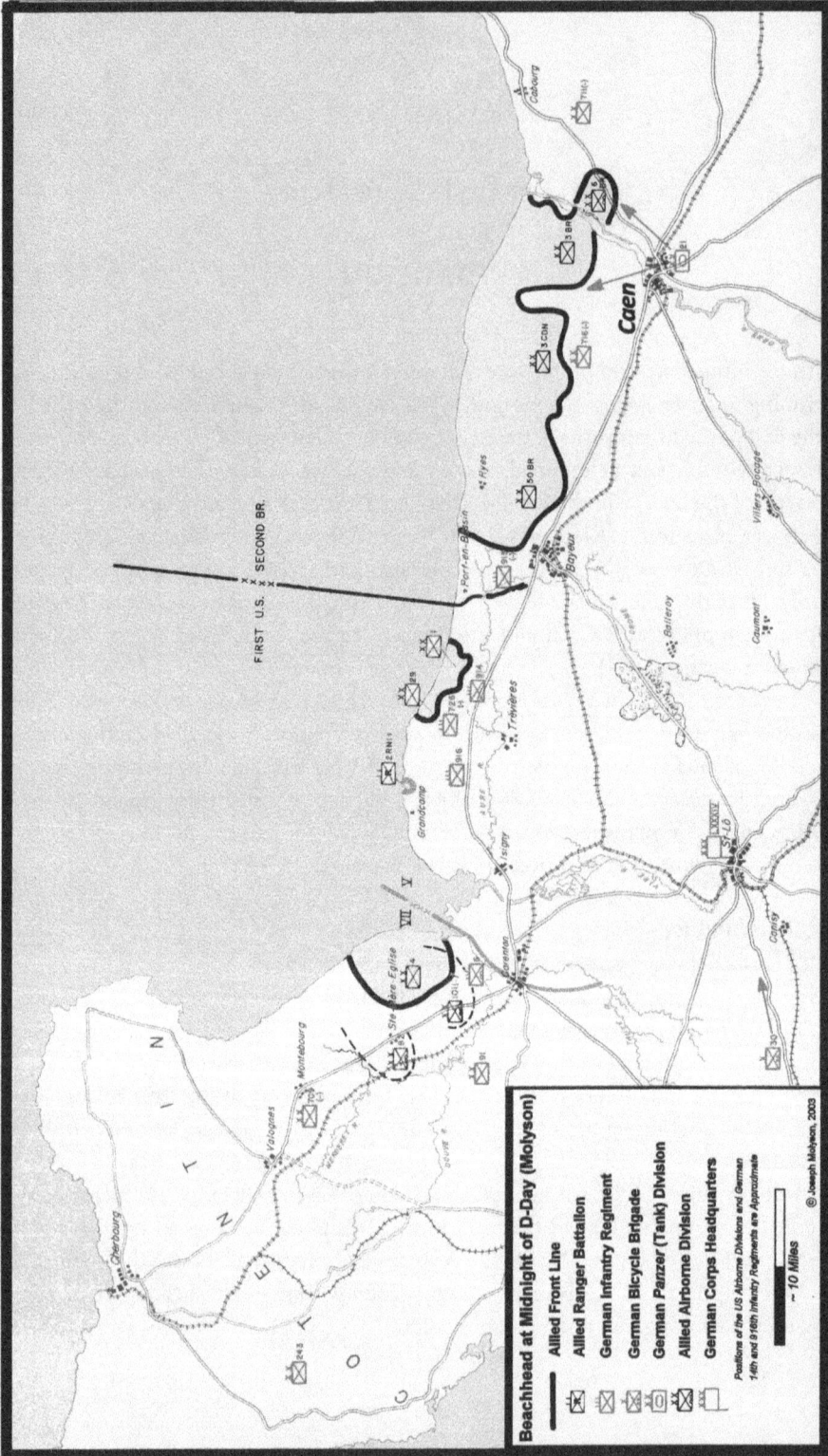

Map 39.1. Beachhead at Midnight of D-Day US ARMY[2]

Figure 39.1. Allied reconnaissance photo of German tanks on flatcars AIR FORCE HISTOR-ICAL RESEARCH AGENCY

Figure 39.2. Artillery spotters in light planes sometimes did almost reckless reconnaissance. US ARMY MILITARY HISTORY INSTITUTE

Artillery-spotting aircraft brought the full weight of Allied artillery firepower into the fight. The aircraft were very lightweight, similar or identical to civilian general aviation aircraft. Courage was their armor. The most commonly employed were the American Piper L-4 and British Taylorcraft Austere IV, nicknamed "grasshoppers" by Allied soldiers. In daylight and sometimes at night, they were constantly lurking overhead. German soldiers called them *Krähen* (crows), always looking for prey. If a German unit broke cover in daylight, the crows summoned the fist of Allied artillery. Even the Panzers were vulnerable to artillery fire.

Grasshoppers had outstanding short-field landing and takeoff capability. Their pilots were assigned to the Field Artillery branch or carried field artillery observers. Their mission was to direct artillery shells onto German targets. The grasshoppers not only located targets but also notified their parent units when the fire was off-target. The fire would then be "adjusted" for accurate impact. The spotter pilots and their aircraft were assigned to live and move with the particular artillery unit they supported in combat.

The larger US Stinson L-5s and British Westland Lysanders were used as courier aircraft, carried VIPs, and could be outfitted to carry stretchers for the critically wounded. They were considered too large to operate from the tiny airstrips from which the L-4 and Auster aircraft operated. They were, however, faster and longer-ranged, which made them ideal to support army headquarters staffs.

The Allied armies were lavishly provided with artillery and used massed firepower in lieu of masses of infantry. It was preferable to spend ammunition rather than lives. The only restriction on ammunition was the ability to deliver it over open beaches, In July 1944, the US First Army alone (excluding the British Second Army and the naval guns offshore) fired 1,500 tons of ammunition, while the German *7th Armée* was sent only 480 tons and fired even less.[3] The Americans had plenty of ammunition, while the Germans lost much of it along the savaged railroad system.

Like naval gunfire, most often artillery firepower was inflicted on targets out of sight of the gun crew. This kind of fire support was termed *indirect fire* and required the services of an observer to correct the aim. Between spotting for current artillery fire, the pilots constantly scouted for new victims. The spotters also supported the naval gunners offshore, especially after the ASP was suspended. German accounts of the Normandy campaign (and thereafter) often mention the presence of these humble aircraft as a prelude to disaster:

*When Lieutenant Bolunbach at last jumped into the five-foot dugout that served as his regimental commander's battle headquarters near Brouay, the last thing he saw in the sky was once more an aircraft. This time it was an artillery spotter. A minute later its purpose became plain: Heavy naval guns began to bombard the area of Brouay where the* 902nd Panzer Grenadier Regiment *not only had its headquarters but where its advance units were standing by ready for action. For a whole hour death and destruction rained down upon the regiment before it had fired a single shot.*[4]

## ATTEMPTED COUNTERATTACK

On June 8, Rommel assigned General Leo Geyr von Schweppenburg's *Panzergruppe West* to control the German defensive line from the Dives River to Tilly. Von Schweppenburg's headquarters was now located at the Chateau-la-Caine, 4 miles northeast of Thury-Harcourt. Von Schweppenburg controlled the German Panzer divisions in the *7th Armée* area, only now entering the battle in force. Under Rommel's original plan, *Panzergruppe West* would have been under his Army Group B and would have counterattacked the Allied landings on June 6.

With its belated release from the *Führer's* grasp, it would now finally be used as Rommel had hoped. *Panzergruppe West* prepared for a massive counterattack on the British beaches within a few days. Von Schweppenburg had assembled the *21st Panzer, 12th SS Panzer, Panzer* Lehr, and the *17th Panzer Grenadier* Divisions for the mission. It was not to be—Allied airpower struck first. The headquarters radio equipment was set up too close to the chateau. It was soon pinpointed by Allied radio direction-finding equipment, and ULTRA confirmed the *Panzergruppe West* move from its peacetime headquarters to the chateau.[5]

On June 10, forty Typhoons of RAF 181, 182, 245, and 247 Squadrons attacked. Unopposed in the air and braving the flak, the fighter-bombers strafed and rocketed Chateau-la-Caine. Then 71 No. 2 Group Mitchells dropped many tons of 500-pound bombs, saturating the area. Von Schweppenburg was wounded. His chief of staff, General von Dawans, and eighteen other senior officers were killed. More importantly, the attack was canceled until another staff could be formed. Decapitation had succeeded, and the Germans were never able to mass such a powerful armored force west of the Seine again. By the time the headquarters was reconstituted, attrition had seriously weakened all four tank units.[6]

## DOGFIGHTS

On the same day as *Panzergruppe West* headquarters was attacked, four dogfights pitted American airmen against the chaotically reinforced fighter forces of *Luftflotte 3*. Twenty-five P-47s of the 366th Fighter Group engaged forty Bf 109s of II and III *Gruppe, Jagdgeschwader 3* (II and III Groups, Fighter Wing 3) near Caen. This was one of the *Drohende Gefahr West* fighter wings sent from *Luftflotte Reich* to France. Around 10:30 a melee began at 9,000 feet that descended to ground level.

The Jugs shot down five 109s, and American antiaircraft fire dragged down two more. The 366th lost four Thunderbolts. Just after 14:00, further east near Lisieux, more than eighty Fw 190s and Bf 109s of JG 27 (another reinforcement unit) had the misfortune to encounter the Thunderbolts of the 78th Fighter Group. Nine German aircraft were downed at a cost of two Jugs.

Less than four hours later, a third big battle began between P-47s of the 365th Fighter Group and *Luftflotte 3* veterans of JG 26. The battle ended in a draw, each side losing three planes. At dusk near Evreux there was another dogfight, the fourth for the day. Two squadrons each of P-51s (359th FG) and P-47s (353rd FG) tangled with fighters from JG 3, the same German wing that had been bested south of Caen that morning. Four Bf 109s were shot down for one P-51. It was another loss for the German aviators, but unfortunately the fight again dragged down to low level. This time it was the German flak that got lucky. Five American planes, four P-47s and one P-51, were downed.[7]

## STOPPING GERMAN TANKS

That night, one of the few German airdrop missions in Normandy was conducted. A small group of Ju 52 transports dropped small arms and mortar ammunition to the beleaguered troops of the 6th *Fallschirm* (Parachute) Regiment. The 6th was defending Carentan against incessant American paratrooper attacks. Carentan, at the eastern base of the Cotentin Peninsula, was a vital objective of the 101st Airborne Division as part of the drive to link Utah and Omaha Beaches.

The 6th's *Fallschirmjäger* (parachutists) under *Oberstleutnant* von der Heydte defended Carentan skillfully; it was their last hope in containing the Americans in the Cotentin. The airdrop enabled the 6th to resist a little longer, but ultimately the Yanks prevailed. Ironically, many of the German *Fallschirmjäger* were drowned during their fighting withdrawal into the same swamps that had claimed American paratroopers on D-Day. By the night of June 11, Carentan and another section of National Route 13 was in American hands. An abortive German attempt to recapture it on June 12 failed.[8]

On the same day, German Tiger tanks slaughtered the advance elements of a Canadian force attempting to take Villers Bocage, a town south of Gold Beach and west of Caen. This was Montgomery's second attempt to take Caen, the first having failed by June 8.

In the bocage, the tank became the nucleus of combat teams on both sides. Many tanks were lost when opposing infantry snuck up on a tank or ambushed it as

## The June Battles

1. Attempt to Seize Caen (June 6-8)
2. Attack on Panzergruppe West (June 10)
3. Linkup at Isigny (June 10)
4. Villers Bocage (June 13)

5. Aborted Panzer Attack (June 13)
6. US VII Corps Reaches Barneville (June 18)
7. Siege of Cherbourg (Begins June 22)
8. Operation EPSOM (Begins June 25)

~ 50 Miles

© Joseph Molyson, 2003

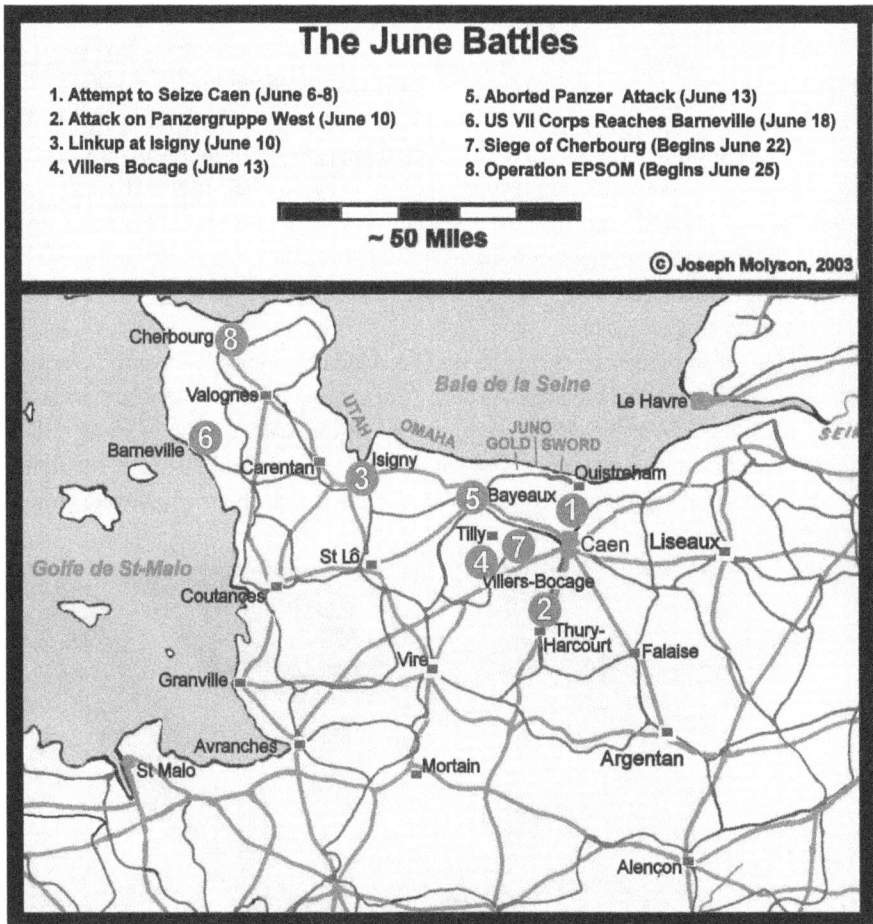

Map 39.2. The June Battles in Normandy MOLYSON

it moved. It was a battle in which Gammon grenades, bazookas, and the *Panzerfaust* (an improved German copy of the bazooka) were at least as successful at killing enemy tanks as *Jabos*, anti-tank guns, and other tanks.

The vaunted German armor, with its low silhouette, was at a distinct disadvantage as an observation platform because of visibility problems in the close terrain. A low-slung Tiger or Panther dominated areas in open country outside the bocage. Conversely, the outclassed but numerous Allied Sherman tanks provided better visibility in close because of their taller profiles. A single Sherman was no match for a Panther or Tiger, but destroying German tanks was not a major part of the Sherman's job. It had been designed to support infantry; the American Army had special anti-tank vehicles to deal with the enemy tanks. Also, the American Army had come to depend on the kind of air support that owning the skies allows.

For the Germans, being spotted in a tank meant your position would soon be hit by *Jabos*, naval gunfire, or Allied artillery. All airplanes were automatically the enemy, and German tank crews became expert in camouflaging their metal chariots. This meant, among other things, that the German tanks had to stay in one place until spotted, robbing them of their mobility in the daytime. The bocage also limited fields of observation, further hobbling the Panzers.[9] The troops began to talk of "death by *Jabo*" as a natural occurrence.[10]

The loss of so many fuel trucks to strafing Allied fighters added to the German tankers' woes. During the big advances, the Allies found a number of German tanks simply abandoned by their crews. By some estimates, based on the work of Allied Operational Research Groups (ORGs) surveying the battlefield just after the fighting, about half the 1,500 German armored vehicles lost in Normandy were simply

Figure 39.3. "Death by *Jabo*," as seen through the gun camera film of a banking Allied fighter NATIONAL ARCHIVES

abandoned by their crew.[11] Airpower's contribution to killing tanks in the Normandy Campaign seems to have been as much by logistical strangulation as by direct attack on armor in the field.

The summer nights of June were short, giving little cover to German units as they attempted to reposition along the line or move toward the beachhead from inland bases. With the sun came the *Jabos* and *Krähen* grasshoppers, relentlessly on the hunt. If airpower had no other effect, it enervated the men who operated without air cover. They marched by night and fought a static defense by day, and for many sleep became just a dim memory. It sapped the energy and dimmed the senses, making the German troops less effective than they might otherwise have been. This kind of psychological attrition was far more damaging than the physical losses inflicted by the aircraft overhead, affecting both leaders and troops. *Generalleutnant* Fritz Bayerlein, commander of the crack *Panzer Lehr Division*, remembers:

> *Unless a man has been through these fighter-bomber attacks he cannot know what the invasion meant. You lie there, helpless, in a roadside ditch, in a furrow on a field, or under a hedge, pressed into the ground, your face in the dirt and there it comes towards you, roaring. There it is, diving at you. Now you hear the whine of the bullets. Now you are for it. You feel like crawling under the ground. Then the bird has gone. But it comes back. Twice. Three times. Not till they think they've wiped out everything do they leave. Until then you are helpless. Like a man facing a firing squad. Even if you survive it's no more than a temporary reprieve. Ten such attacks in succession are a real foretaste of hell.*[12]

# Chapter Forty

# COBRA

*The English and American tactical air forces successfully extended their attempts to interrupt the bringing up of German reserves deep into France. They had made any move by daylight almost impossible. In June alone they destroyed 551 locomotives. . . . The feeling of being powerless against the enemy's aircraft . . . has a paralyzing effect.*

—Adolf Galland, General of the Fighter Arm[1]

The 21st Army Group, consisting of the US First Army and the British Second Army, suffered 62,000 casualties between June 6 and July 1. Even though the Americans had captured Cherbourg, a feeling of stalemate had begun to form in the Allied camp. There was frustration with the bocage; in a way it had replaced the trenches of WWI. Many of the senior men on both sides knew what that meant—a battle of attrition that would bleed both Germany and the Allies white. It must be avoided.

The vital town of Caen was a D-Day objective of the British Second Army. The ground south of Caen was flat and ideal for air landing grounds. The town was not taken on D-Day; instead it was still the center of a bloody stalemate weeks later. The stubborn German defense kept many squadrons of Allied planes operating from British rather than French airfields. German-held Caen crowded the Lodgement area, limiting the ability to maneuver and respond to German attacks. It also made a compressed target area for the remnants of the German Air Force in France.

In early July, Montgomery summoned what would be his strong right hook to expand the Lodgement area. Monty ordered Patton's new Third Army to be landed across Utah Beach. To maintain the FORTITUDE deception, Lieutenant General Leslie J. McNair, actually the administrative commander of all US Army ground forces, was appointed to take over the fictitious First US Army Group (FUSAG). The FORTITUDE ruse was still working and needed to be maintained as long as possible.[2] Monty could not wait for Patton's army to form, however, and ordered Dempsey's British Second Army to continue offensive operations to tie down German armor as much as possible around Caen. Caen was the shield; Patton was the sword.

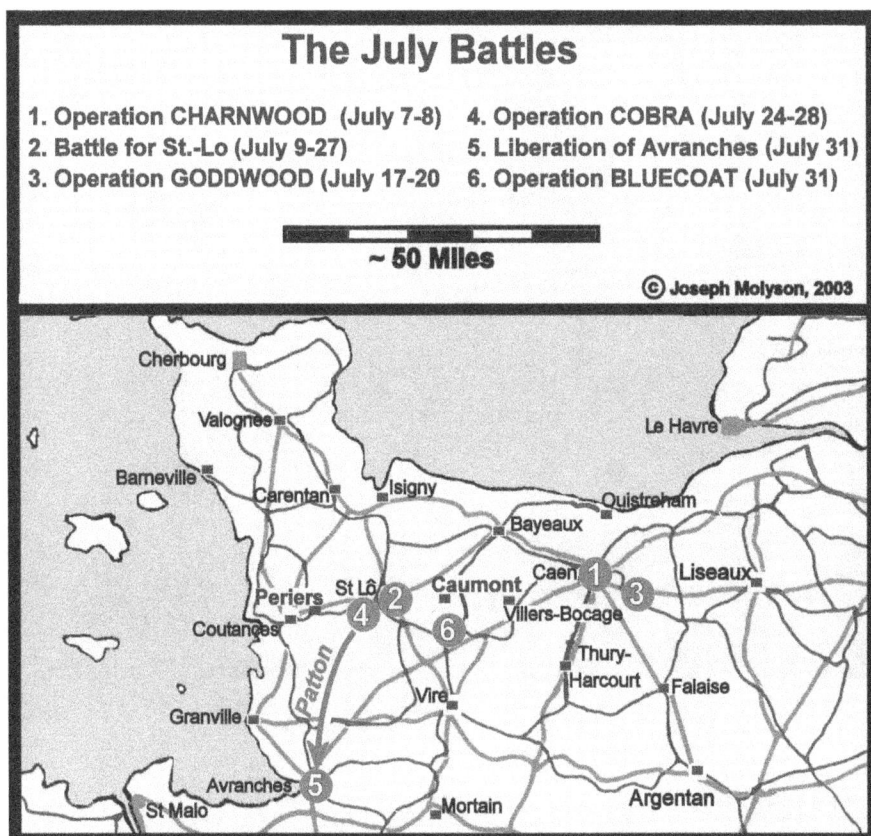

## The July Battles

1. Operation CHARNWOOD (July 7-8)
2. Battle for St.-Lo (July 9-27)
3. Operation GODDWOOD (July 17-20)
4. Operation COBRA (July 24-28)
5. Liberation of Avranches (July 31)
6. Operation BLUECOAT (July 31)

~ 50 Miles

© Joseph Molyson, 2003

Map 40.1. The July Battles in Normandy MOLYSON

On July 2, *Generaloberst* Dollman, commander in chief of the failing *7th Armée*, died of a stroke. A letter relieving him of command was on its way from Hitler, but Dollman did not live to see it. His replacement was *SS Obergruppenführer* Hausser, who promised to repel the invaders. On the same day, General Leo Geyr von Schweppenburg, already wounded by the June 10 air attack on his headquarters, was sacked as commander of *Panzergruppe West*. He had yet to produce the crushing counterattack to drive the Allies into the sea. *Generalfeldmarschall* Günther von Kluge, called "clever Hans" by his troops, replaced von Rundstedt at *OB West* headquarters in Paris. Von Rundstedt had been fired after suggesting that surrender was both honorable and necessary. Von Kluge came from the Eastern Front, where he had maintained a solid reputation as a soldier and leader.[3]

Figure 40.1. Supporting the soldier in ground combat was the main reason for close air support.

## CHARNWOOD AND GOODWOOD

No amount of German leadership shuffling or troop valor could delay the inevitable. On July 7, 1944, 450 RAF heavy bombers saturated Caen with explosives at dusk, heralding the beginning of Operation CHARNWOOD.[4] The burial place of William the Conqueror was all but obliterated. The airmen complained that the ground troops were slow in exploiting the bombing, allowing time for the Germans to recover and regroup. Conversely, the ground troops complained that the desolation greatly slowed their advance.

Perhaps both viewpoints were accurate, perhaps neither. In fact, the bombing was 6,000 yards ahead of the attacking troops as ordered and delivered six hours before the ground advance. Again, the combined effects of misusing heavy bombers and excessive caution resulted in mission failure. In any case, the town was wrecked and the untouched German forward defenses had to be defeated by the ground force. On July 8, British and Canadian troops pushed into the northern end of Caen with heavy losses. They began the slow process of taking the city one wrecked structure at a time. Ironically, the destruction of French towns often turned them into German fortresses and made it harder for advancing troops to clear out the defenders. Caen was rubble; even its limited capability as a port was destroyed. It was still valuable, however; for through it came the roads of eastern Normandy.[5]

After Rommel was badly injured in the July 17 *Jabo* attack, von Kluge assumed command of Army Group B as an additional duty.[6] The next day, carpet-bombing preceded yet another major British attempt to break out of the bridgehead area near Caen. The RAF knew that night bombing was likely to catch some German units on the move. The bombing began after dark, with more than 1,000 Lancasters and Halifaxes of RAF Bomber Command hitting five target areas marked pyrotechnically by pathfinder Mosquito aircraft. This produced a zone of complete destruction across the *21st Panzer* and *16th Luftwaffe* Field Divisions east of Caen.

At dawn, almost 600 B-24s of the Second Bomb Division, Eighth Air Force bombed five more target areas. Then the US Ninth Air Force bombed German troop concentrations with hundreds of A-20s and B-26s. When the last airplane departed, 7,700 tons of bombs had been dropped.[7] One German company of the *21st Panzer* Division at Guillerville was heavily bombed; fifteen tanks were destroyed, with the

Figure 40.2. Effects of bombing on the town of Argentan to interrupt German ground movement. This was a favorite tactic of Montgomery. For the troops, however, the destruction of French towns often turned them into German fortresses. US ARMY MILITARY HISTORY INSTITUTE

rest so immobilized by craters that they could not move.[8] Fifty tanks of the *22nd Panzer* Regiment were destroyed or marooned in another moonscape of craters. Colonel Hans von Luck, whose regiment had failed to retake Pegasus Bridge on June 6 because of intense air and naval bombardment, remembered forty years later the horror of seeing an entire Tiger tank battalion literally overturned by bomb blasts.[9]

The massive bombing was followed by a general advance of the British Second Army in Operation GOODWOOD. British armored units pushed east across the Orne using the bridgehead captured by the Paras on D-Day and then turned south. Canadian troops moved directly south from Caen to protect the western flank of the British attack. Two corps passed through the hole torn in the German defenses by bombing and headed south toward Paris.

The numerous craters slowed the Allied tank brigades that should have rushed deep into German-held territory. The infantry units went ahead slowly without armored support, allowing the dazed Germans time to regroup and dig out of their collapsed positions. Rommel had previously moved many of the dual-purpose flak guns from Caen into ground-defense positions south of the city. These 88mm guns and the surviving Tiger and Panther tanks available at the edge of the carpet-bombing area stopped GOODWOOD.[10] By July 20, the British had lost 400 tanks, and the offensive ground to a halt after advancing only 7 miles. One air marshal at SHAEF complained that "seven thousand tons of bombs for seven miles" was not much of a victory.[11] One might think that at this point, Allied ground commanders would stop asking for heavy bombers providing direct support. Unfortunately, this was not the case.

## SAINT-LÔ

To the west, Bradley was worried about the slow pace of his First Army through the bocage. On July 9, the *2nd SS Panzer* Division attacked and stopped the American forces closing in on the vital road junction at Saint-Lô. On the 11th, the *Panzer Lehr* Division renewed the attack with an attempt to encircle the Americans who had crossed the Vire River. At first the German counterattack went well under low clouds, but by early afternoon the weather cleared and the inevitable Allied *Jabos* appeared. Twenty of the thirty-two tanks in the attack were either hit or abandoned. German infantry went to ground, holding what had been seized, but further advance was impossible.[12] On this occasion the correct type aircraft was used to perform the mission for which it had been designed.

When the NEPTUNE assault phase of OVERLORD ended on July 10, the Allied focus shifted off beaches and onto breaking out of the beachhead into open country. The battle to liberate France west of the Seine began in earnest. On July 15,

Hitler left his German mountain retreat at Obersalzberg for the last time, headed for the *Wolfschanze* (Wolf's Lair), his Eastern Front headquarters. Just prior to departure, he decided to stop building more bombers and make fighter production the top priority. He ignored the chronic pilot shortage and the increasing Allied attack on aviation fuel production and perhaps also ignored the dire situation on the ground in Normandy. It seemed likely to his military adjutant that from this point on, Hitler contemplated the possibility of eventual defeat.[13]

On July 19, despite masterful German defense and attacks by German tanks, American troops fought their way into Saint-Lô after weeks of close combat and 11,000 casualties. This gave them control of the key intersection of all highways serving western Normandy. The stage was now set for a second attempt to break out of the beachhead. The *Panzer Lehr* Division was pushed south.

July 20 was a bad-weather day in Normandy; severe thunderstorms pummeled the men on both sides of the line. At an Army Group B headquarters conference with Field Marshal Kluge, the *7th Armée* commander requested that the *Luftwaffe* fight off the "particularly obnoxious artillery observation planes, and the heavy bombers and fighter-bombers, at least once in a while" as a much-needed boost for troop morale.[14] It was a worse day for Hitler, who narrowly escaped an assassination attempt at his Eastern Front headquarters. *Panzer Lehr* commander Bayerlein summarized the thoughts of many German soldiers that day: "Our eyes were more on the fighter-bombers than on the *Führer*'s headquarters."[15]

## THE COBRA STRIKES

A week after the failed GOODWOOD operation and the successful capture of Saint-Lô, Montgomery and Bradley were ready for the US First Army to break out of the Lodgement area in the west. The American breakout, Operation COBRA, was scheduled for July 24. It would be preceded by the saturation bombing of Germans positions just to the south of and along the Perrier–Saint-Lô road, the general demarcation between the American and German front lines. The bombing would saturate a target box 6,000 by 2,200 yards with almost 3,000 aircraft in four waves. The idea of putting that many aircraft over that small a target box without bombs falling outside was fatally optimistic. Again, heavy bombers were to be used for an inappropriate mission.

Within that box, just south of the Perrier–Saint-Lô road, lay the German main defensive line held by the crack *Panzer Lehr* Division, one of the best-equipped and best-led German divisions in Normandy. Bradley proposed an 800-yard safety withdrawal of his troops. The air commanders recommended 3,000 yards. The senior airmen were worried about using so many heavy bombers so close to friendlies but

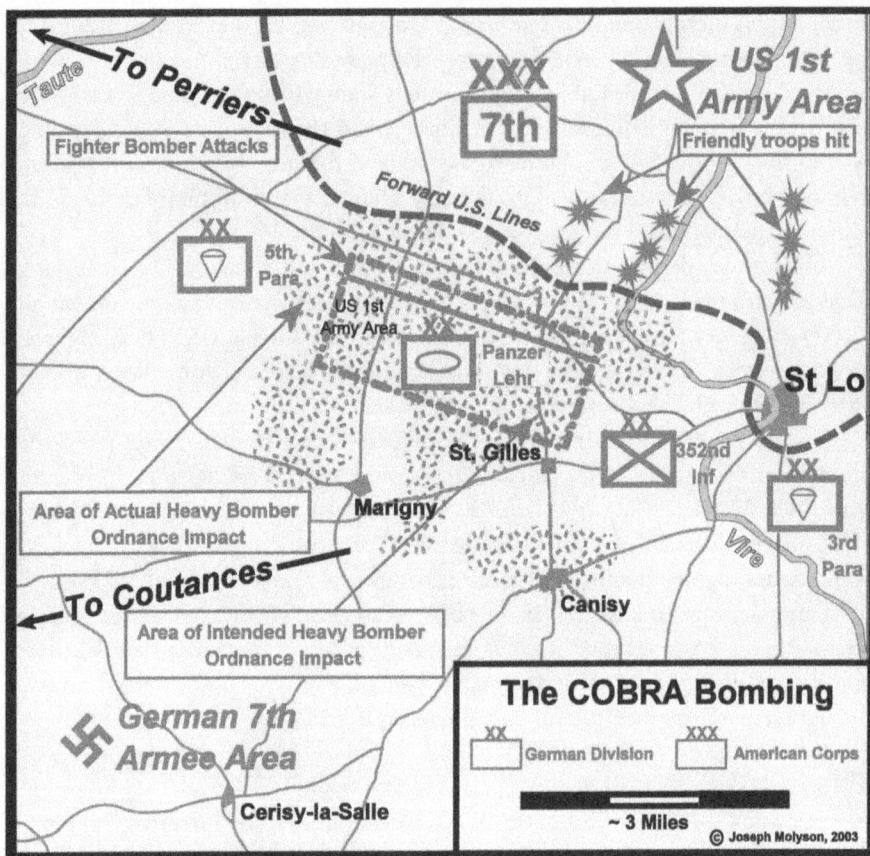

**To Perriers**

Taute

**Fighter Bomber Attacks**

XXX
**7th**

☆ **US 1st Army Area**

**Friendly troops hit**

Forward U.S. Lines

XX
5th Para

US 1st Army Area

XX
Panzer Lehr

**St Lo**

St. Gilles

XX
352nd Inf

**Marigny**

**Area of Actual Heavy Bomber Ordnance Impact**

XX
3rd Para

Vire

**To Coutances**

**Area of Intended Heavy Bomber Ordnance Impact**

**Canisy**

**The COBRA Bombing**

**German 7th Armee Area**

XX
German Division

XXX
American Corps

**Cerisy-la-Salle**

~ 3 Miles

© Joseph Molyson, 2003

Map 40.2. The COBRA Bombing MOLYSON AFTER HALLION AND BLUMENSON[16]

were again overruled by Eisenhower. After negotiation, the leaders settled on 1,200 yards. Again, this was fatally optimistic.

Bradley wanted the aircraft to attack from east to west out of the sun to blind German flak gunners. For the airmen, the east–west side of the target box, almost three times wider than the north–south dimension, fit better with the predicted dispersion of bombs. They failed, however, to adequately explain the intended north–south bombing direction to Bradley. Had they done so, he might have withdrawn his troops further north. The road seemed to be a good target marker for the bombardiers, and no "fudge factor" was built into the plan.

It began with a massive carpet-bombing attack patterned after the one that preceded GOODWOOD. At the last minute, Bradley canceled the attack because of bad weather. Some heavy bomber units did not get the word, and although most of the bombs fell on German positions, a few hit American troops.

The next day, the weather cleared somewhat and the attack was on. The north portion of the target box was hit by 350 low-level fighter-bombers for twenty minutes. The aircraft were the most precise and accurate bombers of the Allied air armada, therefore the most trustworthy to attack near friendly troops. The fighter-bombers concentrated on hitting forward German defenses within a 250-yard belt immediately south of the road. Eighteen hundred heavy bombers followed, dropping bombs from 15,000 to 16,000 feet for sixty minutes, relying on the road and red marking smoke to aim their bombs.

Unlike the D-Day bombing, when caution caused the bombs to be dropped too far from the beach to be effective, this time the bomb pattern hit the Germans hard and then crept back toward and engulfed the forward edge of the waiting American troops. Spaatz's "heavies" bombed to a depth of 2,500 yards behind the German front, accompanied by the artillery fire of 1,000 guns. The heavy bombers would be followed by another 400 fighter-bombers at low level looking for any movement in the moonscape for twenty minutes. The 400 medium bombers then hit targets from 12,000 feet on the roads to the south for another forty-five minutes. Up above the fray, 500 fighters flew top cover, hoping the *Luftwaffe* would try to intervene.[17]

On D-Day, Doolittle's heavy bombers had bombed the invasion beaches from above an overcast using radar. A fudge factor to ensure the safety of the landing craft and troops resulted in a poor showing for the bombardment; most of the ordnance fell harmlessly far beyond the beach.[18] Weather was again a factor as winds blew the dust and smoke from the first explosions north toward the American lines. This obscured both the red marking smoke used to designate the German lines and any view of the narrow Perrier–Saint-Lô road, which was the troop demarcation line. Per normal procedure, with the road obscured the bombardiers bombed the northward-drifting smoke.

The failure of some American troops to pull back the required 1,200 yards may have exacerbated the casualties. This time, many more Americans were hit than in the abortive bombing of the previous day. Lieutenant General Leslie McNair, commander of US Army ground forces, was killed along with 600 other casualties. Fortunately, the bulk of the massive bomber attack fell upon the intended German victims with catastrophic effect.[19]

German *San Uffz* (medical sergeant) Walter Klein was assigned to *Kampfgruppe Heinz*, a unit from Brittany that was attached to the *Panzer Lehr Division*. After the war, Klein described the effects of the air attack:

*The effect was devastating; all our antiaircraft guns and artillery were destroyed. Tanks, which had tried to get away, were destroyed by the pursuit planes (single engine fighters). When a wave of planes had passed, one could hear the crying of the wounded and shouting for help of medical personnel. I had just the time to carry one of my comrades, who had been wounded badly in the thigh, into the dugout, when a second wave started bombing. It was impossible to give any help as long as the air raid lasted. Several companies of the 5th Para Division that had tried to withdraw to the north in the direction of MARIGNY were entirely destroyed by Lightnings, pursuit planes and bombers. On that day my company lost 1 officer, 34 non-commissioned officers and enlisted men. The attack lasted approximately 3 hours.*

A corridor for the advancing American troops was torn in the German lines some 4 miles long and 2 miles wide. The swath of death covered the long-suffering *Panzer Lehr Division* and greatly reduced its combat capability. The *13th* and *15th Fallschirm Regiments* were also hit. Trenches, bunkers, vehicle parks, tanks, and other assets were pummeled. Many troops were buried alive. The force of the explosions dazed the rest.

Then came the infantry and tanks of the US VII Corps, making slow progress because of the torn-up landscape. A German second lieutenant returning from a reconnaissance he had conducted in the zone of destruction reported to *Panzer Lehr* commander General Bayerlein, "I did not find a single strongpoint intact. The main fighting line has vanished. Where it used to be is now a zone of death."[20]

On July 26, German troops near Marigny had begun to recover from COBRA. The response was to hit the area with another carpet, this time dropped by 400 medium bombers. Bayerlein reported to von Kluge at *OB West* that *Panzer Lehr* had been "annihilated." In fact, the remnants would fight on for a while in Normandy. On July 27, American tanks overran Bayerlein's division headquarters. He and his staff were forced to flee on foot.

When dusk fell, he was seen walking down the road to Percy, all alone. This was the commander of the famous *Panzer Lehr Division*, to which Guderian (Inspector General of Tank Troops) had said only three months before, "With this division alone you will throw the Anglo-Americans back into the sea." And now he was footslogging down a French road. At the *Führer*'s headquarters, a little flag was taken off the big situation-map.[21]

Figure 40.3. Building on the success of the RAF Typhoons, rockets were fitted on American P-47s during July 1944. NATIONAL ARCHIVES

## A Portal to Brittany

COBRA created a portal in the German lines that could not be closed. It was the doorway through which Lieutenant General George S. Patton would shortly pass his new Third Army for the drive into Brittany and subsequently across France.[22] On July 31, Patton's troops reached Avranches on the southwest coast of the Cotentin. They were now beyond German lines. The British began a supporting attack, Operation BLUECOAT, from Caumont towards Vire. COBRA and BLUECOAT signaled the beginning of the end for the *7th Armée*.

There was much despair among American heavy bomber airmen who had participated in the COBRA bombing, including Lieutenant General Doolittle, who commanded the heavy bombers of the US Eighth Air Force. On August 2, Doolittle received a letter from General Eisenhower. Eisenhower had made the decision to use the heavy bombers for COBRA, and integrity demanded that he acknowledge what had happened:

> *I know how badly you and your command have felt because of the accidental bombing of some of our own troops. Naturally, all of us have shared your acute*

*distress that this should have happened. Nevertheless, it is quite important that you do not give the incident an exaggerated place either in your mind or in your future planning.*

*All the reports show that the great mass of the bombs from your tremendous force fell squarely on the assigned target, and I want you and your command to know that the advantages resulting from the bombardment were of inestimable value. I am perfectly certain, also, that when the ground forces again have to call on you for help you will not only be as ready as ever to cooperate but will in the meantime have worked out some method so as to eliminate unfortunate results from the occasional gross error on the part of a single pilot or a single group.*[23]

# CHAPTER FORTY-ONE

# Mortain

Among the German forces destroyed in the COBRA bombardment was a battery of *Typhoon B* multiple rocket launchers.[1] The rocket warheads were thermobaric bombs. These rockets were launched in two waves. In the first wave, the rockets dispersed an aerosol of kerosene, which formed a cloud around the target. The second wave of rockets had high-explosive warheads that detonated the fuel-air mix around the target area. The results were devastating.

German Army weapons specialist Konrad Bergmann, who observed a test firing, described the detonation as "the largest explosion that any of us present had ever seen."[2] It was the kind of ordnance that Hitler described as a "wonder weapon." The weapons had to be fired with relatively light or no winds and warm temperatures. Northern France in summer seemed like the perfect environment. Bergmann's platoon of three multiple launchers mounted on half-tracks were deployed to St. Omer in the Pas-de-Calais under the *15th Armée*. It was thought that the Allied bridgehead or a port seized by the Allied invasion force would be an ideal target for a *Typhoon B* barrage.

By July the battery was moved west to the *7th Armée* and opposite the slowly advancing US First Army. The unit was situated well forward in the German lines because its range was only 3 miles. Since the American armored units parked their vehicles in camps near the front line, it was thought a *Typhoon B* attack could wipe out a large tank unit and kill all of its personnel. The estimated kill radius against vehicles from the center of the cloud was estimated to be two-thirds of a mile, even more for personnel. The psychological impact of such an assault might be as valuable as the physical damage and casualties it caused.

On July 24, a massive American tank attack was anticipated for dawn. The battery moved forward and prepared to fire at 01:00. Instead, a well-aimed American artillery barrage suddenly hit the rocket launchers and wrecked them.[3] The kerosene fuel ignited and added to the destruction. It is likely that American signal intercepts had the location of the unit, if not its nature. Not only was this unit destroyed, but German Army interest in the new weapon ended.

## REORGANIZATION

On August 1, Eisenhower reorganized the Allied land forces in Normandy. With the Lodgement area secure and Patton's breakout into open country in progress, it was time to reorganize for the drive to the Seine and beyond to liberate the rest of northern France. Montgomery's 21st Army Group was split into two when Ike created a new US 12th Army Group. Lieutenant General Bradley was promoted from US First Army to command this new group. The First Army passed to Lieutenant General Courtney Hodges. Ike had earlier established the new US Third Army under Patton.

Ike assigned Hodges's veteran First Army and Patton's Third Army to Bradley's 12th Army Group. Free French units used American equipment and also joined Bradley's 12th Army Group. IX TAC remained with First Army, and a new XIX TAC was established for the US Third Army. (See figure 41.1.)

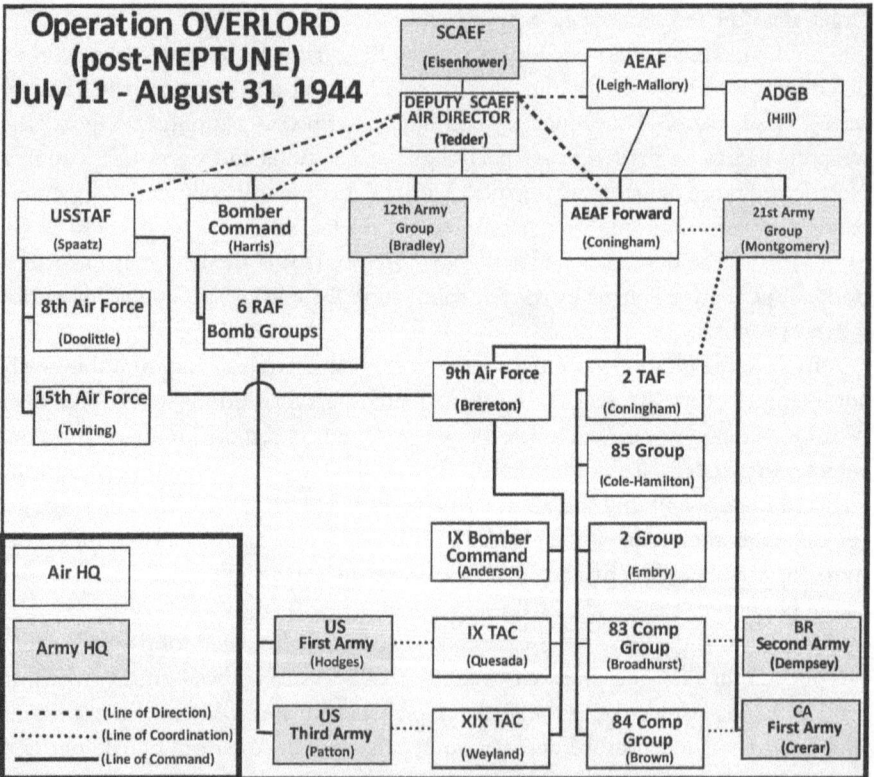

Figure 41.1. Air-ground command relationships for OVERLORD, July 11–August 31, 1944

MOLYSON

A new Canadian First Army was also formed under Lieutenant General H. D. G. Crerar. Crerar's army primarily used British Commonwealth equipment and joined Montgomery's 21st Army Group. The veteran British Second Army remained in 21st Army Group, as did the Commonwealth-equipped Free Polish units. RAF 83 (Composite) Group remained with the British 2nd Army, and RAF 84 (Composite) Group was assigned to support the Canadian First Army. Ike now had two Army Groups in Normandy, one American and one Commonwealth, each with two field armies supported by tactical air forces.

It was Third Army commander Patton and XIX TAC commander Brigadier General Otto Weyland who took the concepts and procedures painfully developed by First Army commander Bradley and IX TAC commander Quesada to create the hardest hitting air-armored team of the latter portion of World War II, the US Third Army. There was little ceremony for the reorganization; Patton's Third Army was already pouring through the hole torn by COBRA. Medals and publicity photos would come later. Patton's first request to XIX TAC was simple: "Don't blow up any more bridges." Third Army would need them to advance.[4]

Figure 41.2. Patton (left center) at XIX TAC air briefing with Weyland (right), the culmination of air-ground coordination at the headquarters level AIR FORCE HISTORICAL RESEARCH AGENCY

## The Jets Arrive

In early August, nine Me 262 "Blitz bombers" of KG 51 began operating from Châteaudun southwest of Paris. The pilots were ordered not to fly below 13,000 feet over enemy territory, making their bombing even less effective than it would otherwise have been. At Hitler's insistence, Messerschmitt had built the planes as fast bombers rather than fighters. The 262's bombsight was ineffective, and although the pilots were able to bomb France from high altitude, they could not hit a smaller target. Scattering a few bombs around the countryside had little effect on the liberators, whose steamroller would soon push the Messerschmitt jets off their airfield.

More effective in their role were the Ar 234C *Blitz* reconnaissance aircraft, which operated with impunity (and generally unnoticed) far above the battlefield. They were based at Juvincourt, near Paris. *Leutnant* Erich Sommer flew the first mission on August 2. He made three passes over Normandy at 34,000 feet and 460 miles per hour. It would take twelve *Luftwaffe* photo interpreters two days to analyze the images. Captured on film were 1.5 million Americans, Brits, Canadians, Free French, and Poles and 300,000 vehicles. For the first time in over a year, the German Army commanders had good photoreconnaissance of the battlefield, if only to document their unfolding disaster in France.[5]

The Arado reconnaissance planes helplessly monitored Patton's breakout. The third Army moved south along the coast to the town of Avranches, the gateway to

Figure 41.3. Me 262A in a grass parking area AIR FORCE HISTORICAL RESEARCH AGENCY
KARLSRUHE COLLECTION

Figure 41.4. Ar 234B *Hecht* (Pike) reconnaissance bomber AIR FORCE HISTORICAL RESEARCH AGENCY KARLSRUHE COLLECTION

Brittany from the Cotentin. While the US VIIIth Corps turned west to seize the Brittany ports, the remainder of the Third Army turned east toward Germany. The key bridge on Patton's route south was the Pontaubault bridge. Through this tiny conduit passed the ground might of Patton's army, protected above and to the flanks by the airmen of Weyland's XIX TAC. Suddenly, the Americans were approaching the Loire, and it looked like nothing stood between them and Paris. (See map 41.1.)

From August 3 to August 7, the *Luftwaffe* tried desperately to destroy the Pontaubault bridges over the Sélune River, knowing they were the only passages available to the Americans out of Normandy and into Brittany. Only the one bridge was hit, and then with only one bomb, causing minor damage. Patton continued to put an unending stream of vehicles across that narrow bridge. The Third Army had broken out of the Normandy Lodgement area. Seven divisions, 15,000 vehicles, and 100,000 men crossed into Brittany. The bocage was behind them.[6] German aircraft occasionally attacked Patton's lengthening supply lines. On the night of August 6, German bombers hit both Third Army headquarters and Ammunition Dump 1, located on the coast at Granville. At the ammo dump, 600 tons of ammunition was destroyed—not enough to stop the advance.[7]

Weyland ordered his fighters to patrol the extended supply lines after completing each armed reconnaissance mission, getting two tasks done for each sortie.[8] This was similar to Major General Bill Kepner's earlier order for the Eighth Air Force escorts to hit German airfields on the way home from strategic bombing targets. Just

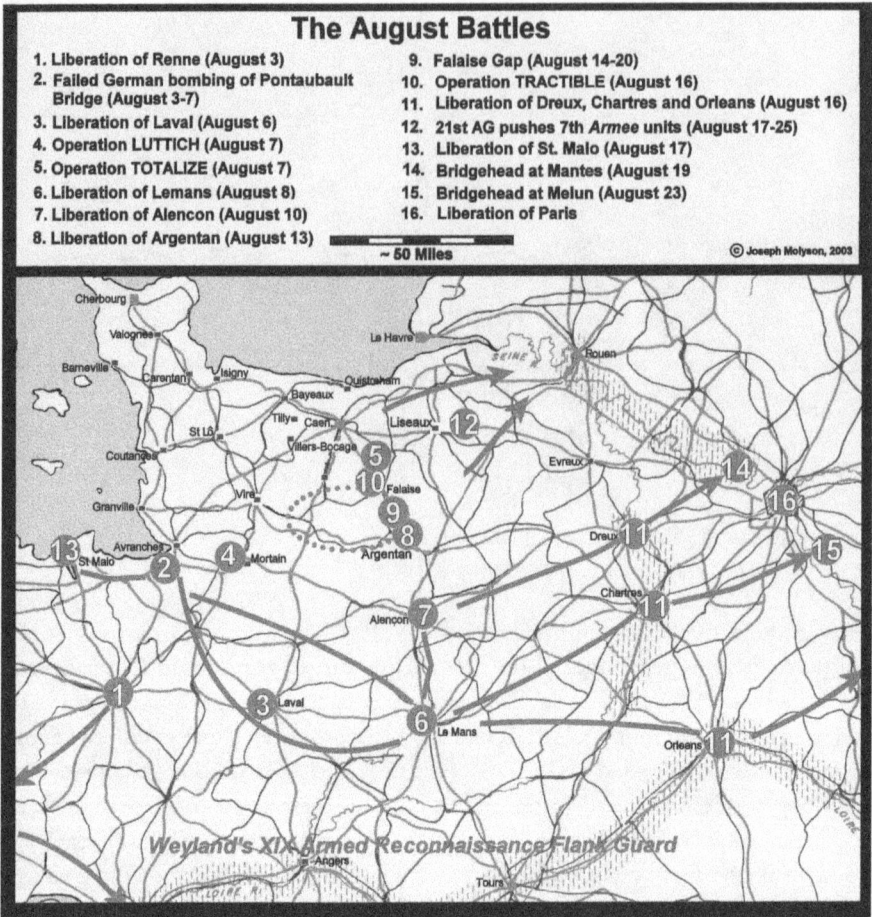

**The August Battles**

1. Liberation of Renne (August 3)
2. Failed German bombing of Pontaubault Bridge (August 3-7)
3. Liberation of Laval (August 6)
4. Operation LUTTICH (August 7)
5. Operation TOTALIZE (August 7)
6. Liberation of Lemans (August 8)
7. Liberation of Alencon (August 10)
8. Liberation of Argentan (August 13)

9. Falaise Gap (August 14-20)
10. Operation TRACTIBLE (August 16)
11. Liberation of Dreux, Chartres and Orleans (August 16)
12. 21st AG pushes 7th *Armee* units (August 17-25)
13. Liberation of St. Malo (August 17)
14. Bridgehead at Mantes (August 19
15. Bridgehead at Melun (August 23)
16. Liberation of Paris

~ 50 Miles

© Joseph Molyson, 2003

Map 41.1. The August Battles MOLYSON

south of Avranches, German aircraft mistakenly bombed a brightly lit POW camp at Marcey, killing twenty-one captured Germans and wounding sixty-two. Patton directed that such camps be lit in the future only in emergencies.[9]

# LÜTTICH

On August 2, about the time that *Leutnant* Sommer flew his Arado over Normandy, Von Kluge's *OB West* headquarters received orders from Hitler for Operation LÜT-TICH, a counterattack against the Americans' Avranches corridor. This coastal corridor was occupied by the rapidly moving Third Army supply columns, but the US

First Army defended it from German attacks approaching from the east. Originating just east of Mortain, it would hopefully cut across the American-held territory and reach the coast at Avranches. The objective was to cut off and maroon the leading American divisions. Hitler even considered the possibility of then rolling up the rest of the invasion from the west.

Such a capability no longer existed, especially since the bulk of *15th Armée* still sat waiting for the fictitious FUSAG to invade the Pas-de-Calais.[10] The August 7 attack was conducted by elements and remnants of five divisions: the *2nd Panzer, 1st SS Panzer, 2nd SS Panzer, Panzer Lehr,* and the *17th Panzer Grenadier Divisions.*[11]

The Mortain attack began soon after midnight on August 7, and by dawn the Germans were almost halfway to Avranches and victory. A ground fog cloaked the battlefield, extending the cover the Germans had enjoyed by night. Determined American resistance slowed the German advance, and a tank battle began to develop between the American 3rd Armored Division and the Germans. The tough GI defense ensnared the Germans, and the going became very slow.

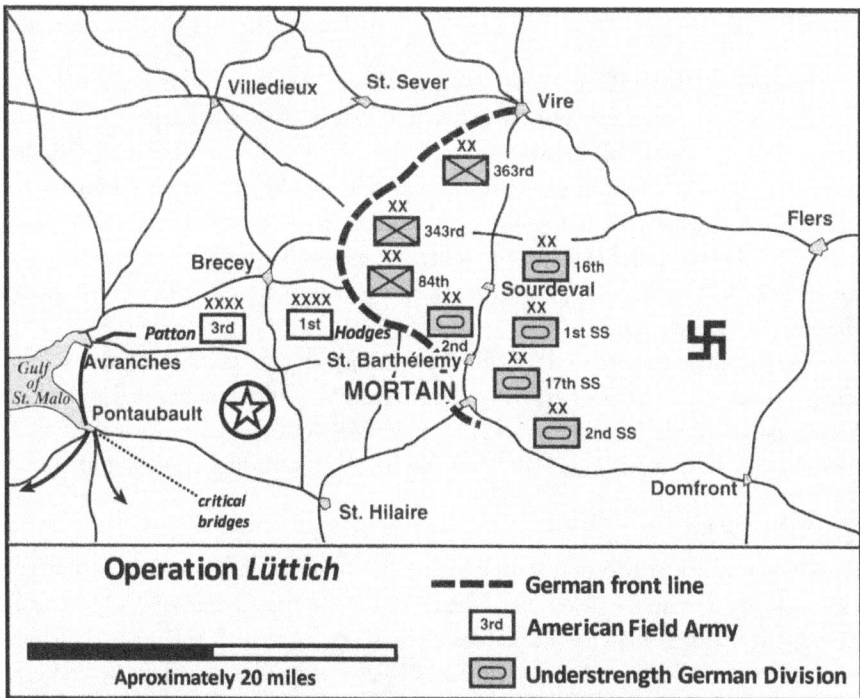

Map 41.2. Operation LÜTTICH, the Failed Attack on Avranches and the Pontaubault Bridges via Mortain[12]

Then the fog lifted. Nineteen squadrons of rocket-firing Typhoons mauled the German tank columns while their brethren in Spitfires, P-51s, P-47s, and P-38s isolated the battle area and destroyed many vehicles by strafing. Formations of *Luftwaffe* support aircraft took off from their airfields near Paris to join the attack. Allied fighters on air defense patrol fell upon the German aircraft. The *Luftwaffe* had promised 300 fighters, but few reached Mortain.[13]

The ever-present American and RAF *Jabos* continued to hit the advancing *Panzers* and supporting German infantry, and by nightfall LÜTTICH had failed.[14] General Walter Warlimont, assistant chief of operations at Hitler's headquarters, had just returned from France and noted in his diary:

> When I got back to the headquarters I found that people already knew that, after making some initial progress, the attack had been smothered by mass Allied air attack. Only then did I find out that there had been considerable disagreement between Hitler and Commander in Chief West the evening before the attack regarding its timing and that Kluge had stuck to his point of view and his intention.[15]

Operation LÜTTICH was yet another disaster for the Germans, especially for von Kluge, who had not wanted it to occur. It was always convenient for Hitler to have a field marshal to blame for his errors. The attack had drawn German divisions northwest toward Mortain at a time when they should have been performing a fighting withdrawal east toward the Seine and potential escape. Much of the German Army's remaining fuel and ammunition in Lower Normandy was wasted in the futile attempt. Mortain also drew German strength away from the Caen area, giving the British an opportunity.

The July 20 attempt on Hitler's life brought suspicion on *Generalfeldmarschall* von Kluge, whose tenure at *OB West* was to be short-lived. Hitler now blamed von Kluge for the failure of the Mortain attack. General Warlimont quoted Hitler's reaction in his memoirs: "The attack failed because Field Marshal von Kluge wanted it to fail."[16]

# TOTALIZE

Even as the attack at Mortain was failing on the evening of August 7, Montgomery mounted his own attack near Caen. The new advance was Operation TOTALIZE; its objective was to match Patton's breakout in the west with a British-Canadian advance in the east. The main objective was Falaise, a small town where several secondary roads came together. A few miles further south was Argentan, a major road center like Saint-Lô and Caen.

Another bomb carpet was laid across two German infantry divisions, one of which had just arrived from Norway. By the morning of August 8, the Canadians broke through and were advancing south. Allied heavy bombers blasted lines of craters on their flanks to impede any German counterattack.

Hundreds of Allied *Jabos* covered the Canadians as they advanced 3 miles into German-held territory. Massive Tiger tanks slowed the Canadian attack, but eventually the Germans were forced to withdraw. The battle moved on, with some Canadians seizing high ground. Unfortunately, they seized the wrong hill and were subjected to an Allied air attack. Confronted by advancing German tanks, the Canadians were forced to surrender. By nightfall TOTALIZE had stopped short of Falaise, just as LÜTTICH had been stopped short of Mortain.

## COLUMN COVER

By August 10, the Americans had recovered the ground they had lost at Mortain. The roads over which the Third Army's supplies traveled were safe again. LÜTTICH had not slowed the Third Army's drive. Patton had total faith in Bradley's ability to hold open the corridor between Mortain and Avranches, and Patton's troops moved at unprecedented speed. American armor and infantry had support trucks, gasoline, and the initiative. They could keep pace with the tanks and other armored vehicles. Patton's breakout was facilitated by new thinking about how air support would be provided to these fast-moving American columns.

One development was *column cover*.[17] Quesada at IX TAC and Weyland at XIX TAC ensured that advancing American units included tanks carrying pilots acting as forward air controllers. They were provided with the same radios and communications frequencies as American fighter-bombers. Now ground unit commanders were in immediate contact with the airmen that supported them. Aircraft assigned to column cover scouted ahead of the supported unit, identifying enemy roadblocks and other defenses.

Column cover became a fine art supporting Patton's fast moving Third Army. It would have been impossible to track the forward line of American troops at an airbase far behind the lines. Instead, the column cover pilots kept track of the ground troops and helped avoid friendly-fire incidents. The support went two ways: American artillery could be called upon to hit nests of enemy flak if things got too hot for the column cover aircraft ahead of the column. Patton used his column cover fighters to maximum effect, often visiting XIX TAC to keep track of problems and other developments at Weyland's headquarters.

Weyland's XIX TAC also borrowed another IX TAC innovation: *armed reconnaissance*. He sent his fighter-bombers many miles in front of the ground units

Figure 41.5. P-47 on column cover duty over Allied tanks—the culmination of air-ground coordination on the front line NATIONAL ARCHIVES

he supported. Their job was to find and attack ground targets. Instead of keeping German units from reaching the battlefield, the mission now was to keep them from escaping. It was Weyland and XIX TAC that allowed Patton to virtually ignore his flanks as he swept ahead toward the Seine and Germany beyond.[18]

Figure 41.6. 20mm flakwagon AIR FORCE HISTORICAL RESEARCH AGENCY KARLSRUHE COLLECTION

# DRAGOON

On August 15, General Alexander Patch's US Seventh Army landed in southern France between Cannes and Toulon in the long-delayed Operation ANVIL, now renamed DRAGOON. German Army Group G south of the Loire suddenly faced Patton's threat from the north and Patch's from the south. The Germans had about ninety serviceable bombers, including sixty-five Ju 88 torpedo planes and twenty-five Do 217 anti-ship missile aircraft, to oppose the landing. A single *Gruppe* of Bf 109s was rushed in from Italy to provide some kind of fighter cover. The Allied ships were protected by land-based as well as carrier-based fighters. It was during this operation that a US Navy Hellcat fighter engaged and destroyed a Bf 109. The Hellcat was the scourge of the Japanese flyers in the Pacific but rarely engaged in such combat in Europe.[19]

Even as the Allied armies advanced from north, west, and south, the Germans continued to bring down numbers of *Jabos* with light antiaircraft guns. These guns were mounted on trucks and sometimes armored vehicles. The airmen collectively called them "flakwagons." Fire from the 20mm guns was a fact of life, ending the careers and lives of many Allied fighter pilots. Operations below 3,500 feet were expensive in terms of aircraft lost but were necessary for victory.[20]

CHAPTER FORTY-TWO

# The Road to Falaise

Third Army expanded west toward Brest and east toward the Seine, while the First Army continued to defend Patton's corridor through Avranches and Pontaubault. (See map 41.1.) With XIX TAC fighters covering his flank on the Loire, Patton sent his US XV Corps north to overrun Alençon and capture the vital town of Argentan.[1] General Bradley ordered them to stop just south of Argentan on August 13, worried that the Americans and the approaching Canadians a few miles north of Falaise would accidentally fire on one another. Also, the ground between them was heavily sown with twelve-hour delay bombs courtesy of Allied airmen dropped in the area to harass the retreating Germans.[2]

On August 13, a 366th Fighter Group P-47 on an armed reconnaissance sortie discovered thirty critical German Army fuel trucks and six tanks near Carrouges, southwest of Argentan. The Jug pilot called in his friends, who left a line of blazing vehicles on the road a mile long. Thunderbolts also discovered another column of several hundred German vehicles moving near Argentan and destroyed large numbers of them.

A sack was forming around the *7th Armée*. By August 16, the Canadian First Army advanced to Falaise in Operation TRACTIBLE. Now only 14 or so miles by air separated Crerar's Canadians from Patton's Americans. This territory, a hole in the ground perimeter surrounding the Germans, became known as the *Falaise Gap*. Elements of sixteen German divisions (100,000 men) were to the west of the Canadian-American pincer and short on gas.

The bulk of *7th Armée* was now encircled in a giant pocket, or *Kessel* (cauldron), just as the *6th Armée* had been eighteen months before at Stalingrad. To escape, the Germans had to pass through the Falaise Gap and a gauntlet of air attacks. Other air attacks and Allied artillery hit the Germans remaining in the pocket. Only about half of them made it out. The Germans who escaped generally got through on foot and without their equipment.[3]

Hitler's response to the burgeoning Falaise crisis was not to withdraw his threatened forces but to order yet another attack at Mortain. Mortain was almost 40 miles from Falaise and on the western perimeter of the *Kessel*. His order doomed the *7th*

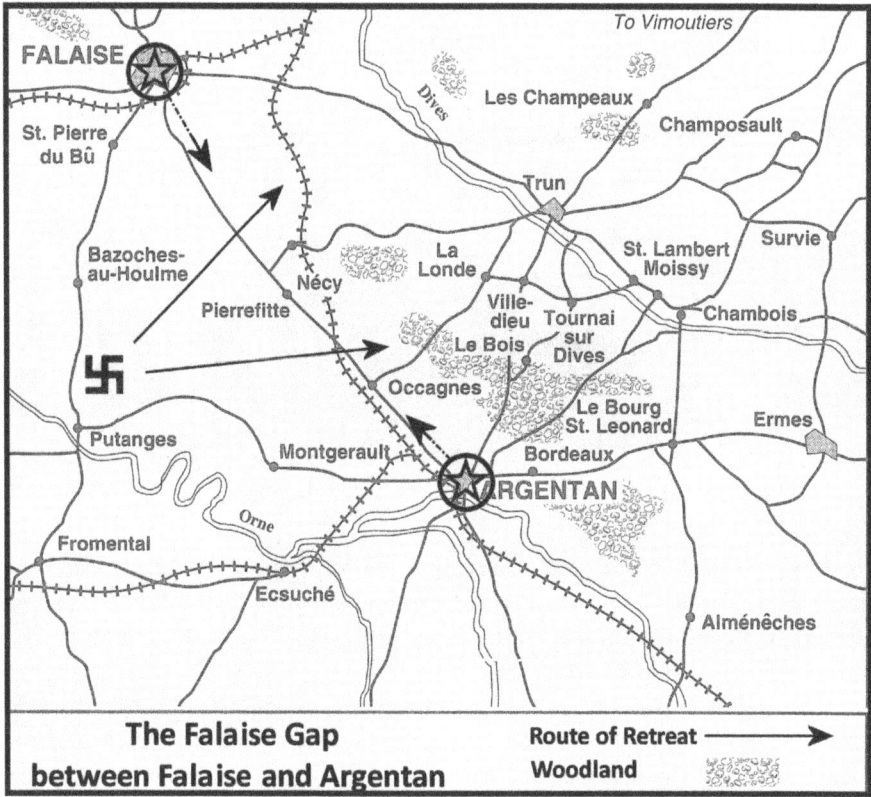

Map 42.1. The Falaise Gap Area from Falaise to Argentan[4]

*Armée* in France, just as he had the *6th Armée* in Russia. The German troops had little remaining ammunition or fuel, and no second Mortain attack could be mounted. Instead, under orders or on their own, the horse-drawn divisions retreated, covered by the motorized ones, toward the Falaise Gap. The German troops in the cauldron were not fighting for Hitler, but for each other.

Time was the Germans' greatest enemy. German commanders waited too long to retreat from the *Kessel*, and abandoned vehicles began to litter the path of their withdrawal. *Jabos* also took their toll. The fearsome but mechanically unreliable Tigers and Panthers were showing the lack of field maintenance over an extended period. Many captured were broken down but intact; others were just out of gas.

The *7th Armée* was finished as a fighting force.[5] The US Third Army surged east along the north bank of the Loire. The way to Paris was open, and Patton did not waste the opportunity. General Alexander Patch, advancing from the Mediterranean

Figure 42.1. Damaged and abandoned Panther tank in Normandy NATIONAL ARCHIVES

coast, not General Patton, would administer the coup de grâce to Army Group G in the south. Patton's target was Berlin; he had no intention of crossing the Loire in strength and continued to use Weyland's airmen to hold his flank as he rushed on toward the Seine. (See map 41.1.)

On August 15, von Kluge was absent from his headquarters, out in the field talking to his commanders. Hitler attempted to contact him but failed, and the *Führer* suspected the field marshal had crossed the lines to negotiate a surrender. Instead, he had been caught in yet another *Jabo* attack and lost his own staff car and two radio cars that accompanied him. Von Kluge reached another command post about midnight and reestablished contact with Hitler's headquarters.

By then it was too late. On August 17, he was relieved of his command and ordered back to Germany. On August 19, von Kluge committed suicide, apparently fearing he had been implicated in the July 20 plot and also that he would become the scapegoat for German failure in France. He was quickly replaced by yet another Eastern Front hero, *Generalfeldmarschall* Walter Model.

By August 20, up to 40,000 Germans had fled the *Kessel*, mainly on foot. They were no longer the *7th Armée*, simply its remnants. In the *Kessel* they left behind 50,000 comrades who would become prisoners and the last 10,000 Germans to die in the Normandy campaign.[6] The Germans who escaped headed for the Seine and then home; they would not really regroup until they reached eastern France.

The Falaise Gap closed on August 21. The toll was staggering. In the northern part of the pocket alone, 344 tanks and self-propelled guns, 2,500 trucks, and more

Figure 42.2. Some of the German troops captured in the Falaise Pocket AIR FORCE HISTORICAL RESEARCH AGENCY

than 250 artillery pieces were destroyed or abandoned. As it disintegrated, the *7th Armée* and its belated reinforcements brought into Normandy since June 6 had lost some 1,500 tanks, 500 self-propelled guns, and 20,000 other vehicles. Fifteen hundred towed artillery pieces and countless anti-tank and antiaircraft guns were also lost.

These were just pieces of hardware and theoretically could be replaced. What Germany could not recover were the 200,000 German POWs and perhaps 200,000 other men killed or seriously wounded. They were irreplaceable human beings.[7]

# CHAPTER FORTY-THREE

# Paris

As the German survivors of the Normandy campaign streamed east across the Seine on improvised bridges and ferries, they continued to be harried by Allied aircraft. The wide, deep Seine had proved an impediment to reinforcement of *7th Armée*; it now also proved an obstacle to its escape. Many Germans were killed either in the attacks themselves or by drowning in the river.[1] At Mantes-Gassicourt, north of Paris, the Third Army's 79th Infantry Division seized their first crossing for Patton on August 19.

The Third Army secured a second crossing south of Paris at Melun on August 25. Bridge repairs were begun immediately. German aircraft began daylight attack against the American bridgeheads with bombs, strafing, and air-to-ground rockets. Many *Luftwaffe* aircraft were downed by Allied air cover and US Army antiaircraft fire.[2] Also on August 25, the British and Canadians of the 21st Army Group crossed the Seine north of Mantes.

It was not originally intended that Paris would be captured, simply bypassed. Eisenhower knew to feed Paris would require enough fuel to move an army corps 25 miles a day.[3] With liberation so close, however, Resistance elements within Paris rose up and began to fight the garrison. General Dietrich von Choltitz, the commander of German forces, did not want Paris destroyed. Hitler ordered him to defend Paris and at costs and finally released units of the *15th Armée* to help.[4]

Even as von Choltitz made his heroic decision to save Paris, the German Army was completing the destruction of Warsaw after a similar uprising while the Russians stood by and let it happen. Eisenhower would not allow that to happen to Paris. A truce was arranged on August 23, and Eisenhower sent in the 2nd French Armored Division and 4th Infantry Division to liberate the city. The last German resistance ended by August 25. Paris and France west of the Seine were free except for a few German garrisons trapped in the fortress ports and along the Seine around Rouen.[5] The Normandy Campaign was over.

By late August, *Luftwaffe* activity south of the Loire had ceased entirely, and the final collapse of *Luftflotte 3* in France was at hand. Four more German fighter groups were flown into France to stave off the inevitable. One unit, *II Gruppe Jagdgeschwader 6*

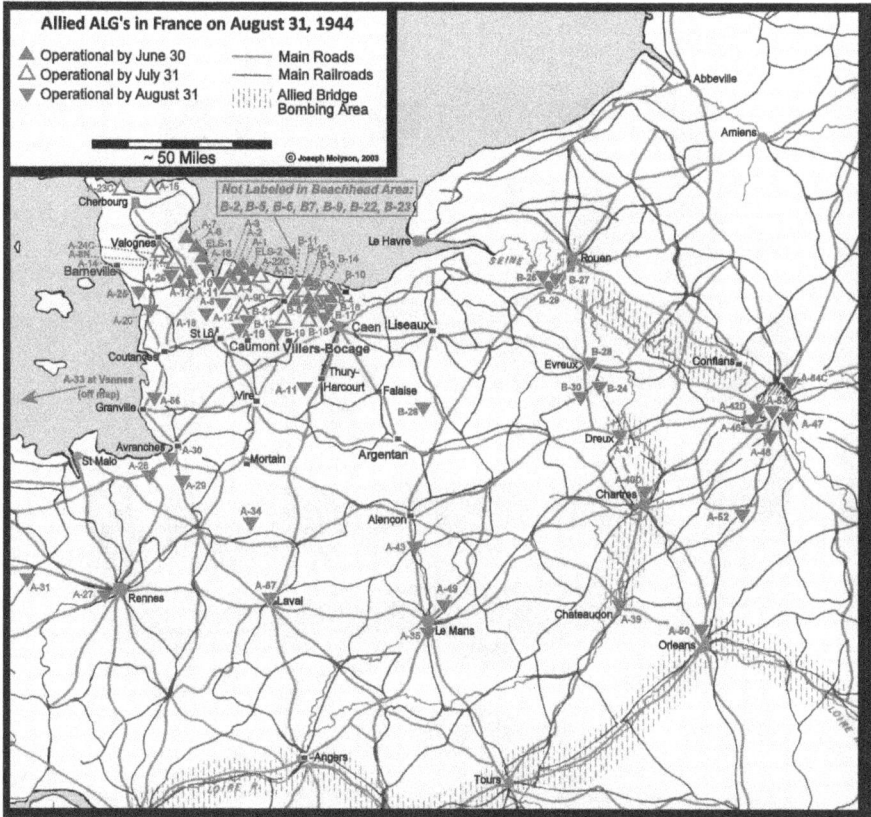

Map 43.1. Allied Airstrips in Normandy as of August 31, 1944 MOLYSON

(II./JG6, Second Group Fighter Wing 6), was moved from home defense duties to an improvised airfield at Herpy near Rheims. Allied troops would soon overrun the airfield. Pilot *Feldwebel* Fritz Buchholz recalled:

*The Allied fighter-bombers seemed to be everywhere and our survival depended on the strictest attention to camouflage . . . we even had a herd of cows which we moved on to the airfield when no flying was in progress; as well as giving the place a rustic look, these performed the valuable task of obliterating the tracks made on the grass by the aircraft.*[6]

On its first offensive sortie on August 25, II./JG6 sent forty Fw 190s to the St. Quentin area southeast of Amiens. They surprised twelve P-38s of the 367th Fighter

Figure 43.1. Paris was both prize and problem as the Allies advanced.
US ARMY MILITARY HISTORY INSTITUTE

Group strafing an airfield at Castres. In the first onslaught, six of the twelve Lightnings were downed, but the surviving Americans called in the other two squadrons of the group. This evened the odds, with *II./JG 6* losing sixteen of its planes while the Americans would lose only one more P-38. Buchholz survived this ordeal, only to be shot down by a P-51 the next day. For the Germans, too, it was "tough in the ETO."[7]

The *Luftwaffe* withdrawal into Germany preceded the German Army by several weeks, except for the *III.Flakkorps*. The flak units continued to be the most dangerous opposition to the advancing Allied air units supporting the ground advance. At the end of August, *Luftflotte 3* Commander in Chief *Generalfeldmarschall* Hugo Sperrle was retired from active service. After its withdrawal from France, it was redesignated *Luftwaffenkommando West*, Air Force Command West. The air battle for France was over.

German units in Army Group G south of the Loire began to disintegrate, although German forces in Bordeaux evacuated and took up defensive positions outside the city. On August 27, the RAF conducted its first major daylight raid into Germany since 1939. On August 28, Free French troops entered Marseilles. Far to the east, Red Army troops occupied the Ploesti oilfields in Romania on August 30, cutting off more than half of Germany's oil supplies. This compounded the German fuel crisis already in progress due to Spaatz's Oil Plan. Bucharest fell on August 31.

August 31 also marked the end of Operation OVERLORD. Eisenhower sent a message to General Arnold in Washington. No one could better summarize the overall contribution of Allied airmen to victory on D-Day and in Normandy:[8]

*The basic conception underlying this campaign was that possession of an overpowering Air Force made feasible an invasion that would otherwise be completely impossible. The Air Force has done everything we asked. It has practically destroyed the German Air Force. It disrupted communications, neutralized beach defenses and it has been vitally helpful in accomplishing certain breakthroughs by ground forces. While all this was being done the Strategic Forces have been committed to the greatest extent possible on strategic targets and have succeeded in preventing substantial rehabilitation of German industry and production.*

*—Eisenhower[9]*

Figure 43.2. The Soviet Summer Offensive whittled away Germany's eastern possessions.
NATIONAL ARCHIVES

# CHAPTER FORTY-FOUR

# Aftermath

Operation NEPTUNE began on May 27, 1944, when the first troop transports left their ports on the west coast of Britain. On the evening of June 6, with the contested landing in progress, celebrations in London were muted. Both civilians and the military realized that the invasion was a path to both liberation and new forms of desperate combat.[1] It ended on July 10, 1944, with the Lodgement area secure.

Then came the breakout operations and the encirclement of the *7th Armée*. After Falaise, no significant ground formations impeded the Allied ground attack for long. Paris fell on August 25, and Patton's Third Army crossed the Meuse River in northeastern France on August 31. On the same day, Operation OVERLORD formally ended. The D-Day planners had hoped to reach the Seine River by D+90; instead, Allied armies had reached the Belgian border and the Meuse River. They passed over much if not most of the World War I trench battlefields in France and were set to liberate Belgium and drive to the Rhine. August 1944 was indeed a remarkable month. (See map 5.4.)

With OVERLORD completed, on 1 September, Eisenhower assumed direct control of the Allied armies in the field. Montgomery, who sought to avoid this

Figure 44.1. Downed Ju 88, symbolic of the fate of *Luftflotte 3* AIR FORCE HISTORICAL RESEARCH AGENCY

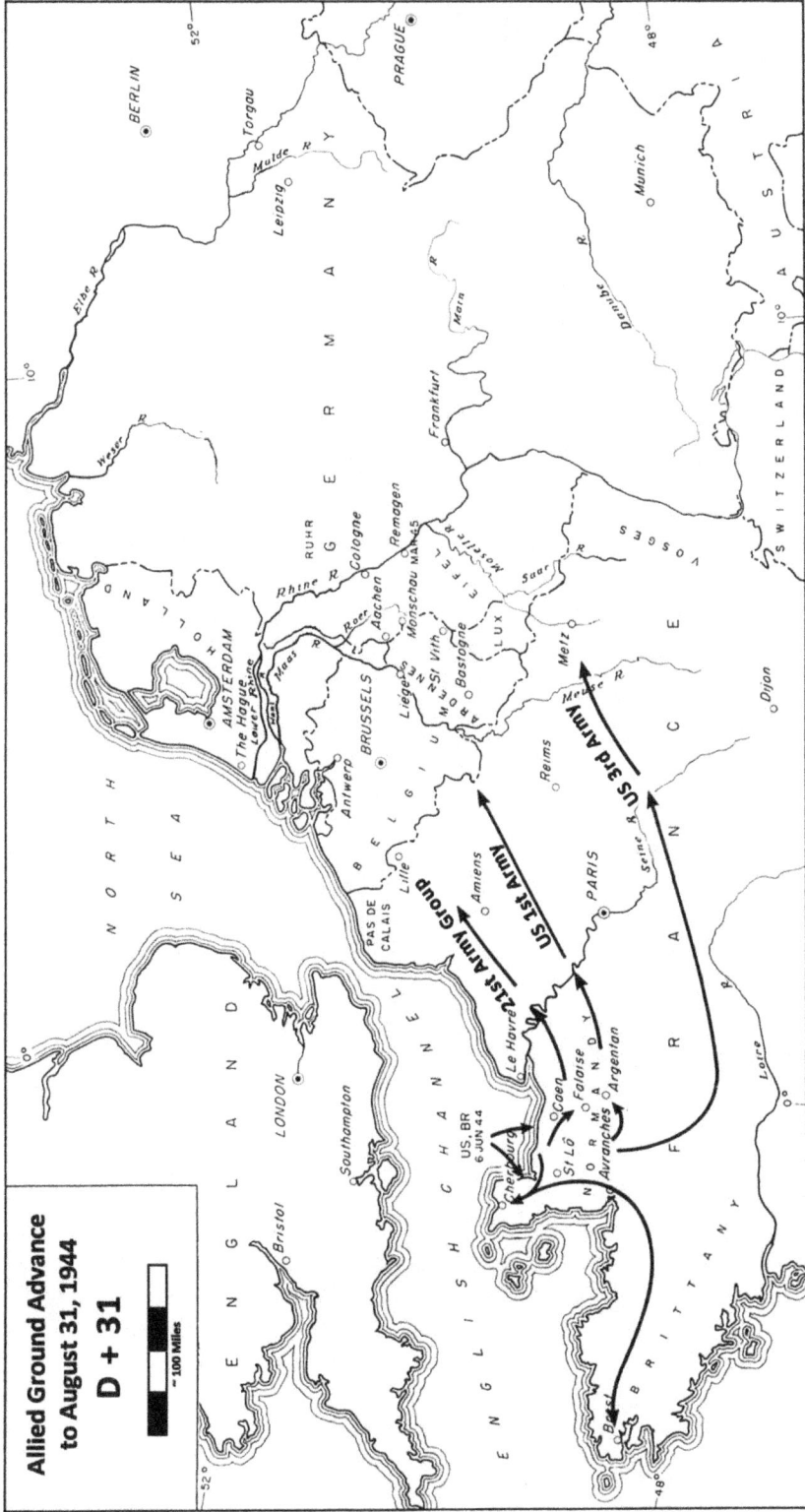

Map 44.1. Allied Advance Beyond Normandy. The Allied armies were approaching the Belgian border, and the critical Meuse River was crossed before the end of August. US ARMY VIA PERRY-CASTANADA MAP LIBRARY, UNIVERSITY OF TEXAS[2]

action, openly displayed frustration and disappointment. The Americans had by far the most troops landed, and the ground forces must now come directly under Eisenhower. Monty's chief of staff, General Freddie de Guingand, tried to explain to Montgomery that Ike was going to take over the ground war "even if the Americans thought you were the greatest (general) in the world—which they do not."[3]

In late August and September, the Allied armies continued their sweep beyond Paris into eastern France and Belgium, operating under Allied air supremacy. Soon the old airfields of the Abbeville Boys, the once-elite German fighter pilots based on the Pas-de-Calais, were British ALGs. There was optimistic talk about getting home for Christmas. No one knew there were nine more months of bitter combat to come before Hitler ended his life and the European war. Supplies were a problem. Cherbourg was still hobbled by German demolitions. There wasn't enough fuel or ammunition to maintain a broad advance.

The V-1 launch sites in the Pas-de-Calais were overrun as the *15th Armée* pulled back from French territory. Monty's 21st Army Group pushed into Belgium. The day after it was announced that the flying bombs had stopped falling on London, the first V-2 rocket hit the city. Another *Blitz* was underway. Ike had a choice: Allow Bradley's 12th Army Group to cross the Rhine in the south, or give priority to Montgomery's 21st Army Group in the north. There wasn't enough bombs or gasoline to do both.

In Germany, scientists worked on air-to-air and surface-to-air missiles and other inventions to stop the Allied bombers. German jet and rocket fighters were operationally deployed as bomber interceptors. British jet fighters were also flying and killing V-1 missiles. American jets were not far behind but would not see this war. The first all-jet combat would be delayed until the Korean War, five years hence. It was just as well; the *Experten* flying the Me 262s had enough problems with the P-51s.

The bag of Allied airmen in German POW camps continued to grow, but thousands more arrived from the training schools and took their places. Spaatz and Doolittle continued their successful campaign to rob Germany of fuel. The Germans and their slave workers built thousands of aircraft that would never fly. The Russians whittled away Germany's eastern possessions.

Montgomery, with his temporary priority on gas and bullets, theorized a campaign through Holland into northern Germany, seizing the Ruhr industrial region. The new 1st Airborne Army, consisting of three airborne divisions, would be dropped in a corridor of paratroopers from Belgium to the gates of the Ruhr. Through this corridor, British Lieutenant General Brian Horrocks's veteran armor-heavy XXX Corps would pass, relieving the airborne and punching through to the German frontier.

The plan—like all plans—was flawed. But that is another story.

# Appendix 1. Senior Allied Air Commanders and Their Forces

| Commander | Headquarters | Operational Control of |
|---|---|---|
| Eisenhower | Supreme Commander Allied Expeditionary Force (SCAEF) | All OVERLORD air, ground, and naval forces |
| Tedder | Deputy Supreme Commander Allied Expeditionary Force (director of OVERLORD air operations) | All OVERLORD air forces; all OVERLORD forces in the absence of Eisenhower |
| Coningham | Forward Headquarters Allied Expeditionary Air Force (AEAF Forward) (under Tedder) | AEAF operations in France |
| Leigh-Mallory | Allied Expeditionary Air Force (AEAF) | ADBG, troop carrier units and limited control of 2TAF |
| Spaatz | United States Strategic Air Forces in Europe (USSTAF)(under Tedder for OVERLORD tasks) | 8th and 15th Air Force heavy bombers, Ninth Air Force tactical aircraft |
| Doolittle | Eighth Air Force (8th AF) (under USSTAF) | 8th Air Force heavy bombers and strategic reconnaissance aircraft based in Britain |
| Twining | Fifteenth Air Force (15th AF) (under USSTAF) | 15th Air Force heavy bombers and strategic reconnaissance aircraft based in Italy |
| Harris | RAF Bomber Command (under Tedder for OVERLORD tasks) | RAF Bomber Command heavy bombers based in Britain |

| Commander | Headquarters | Operational Control of |
|---|---|---|
| Hill | Air Defense of Great Britain (ADGB)(under AEAF) | Once and future RAF Fighter Command defending Allied airspace over Britain and the Channel |
| Coningham | 2TAF (under AEAF Forward) | Support to 21st Army Group |
| Embry | No. 2 Group RAF (under 2TAF) | RAF light and medium bombers supporting OVERLORD |
| Broadhurst | No. 83 (Composite) Group (under 2TAF) | Support to British Second Army |
| Brown | No. 84 (Composite) Group (under 2TAF) | Support to Canadian First Army |
| Cole-Hamilton | No. 85 Group RAF (under 2TAF) | Defense of beachhead and air bases in France |
| Brereton | Ninth Air Force (under AEAF Forward and USSTAF) | Support to 21st Army Group; later, 12th Army Group when established in August |
| Anderson | IX Bomber Command (under 9th AF and AEAF Forward) | USAAF light and medium bombers supporting OVERLORD |
| Quesada | IX Tactical Air Command (IX TAC) (under 9th AF) | Support to US First Army |
| Weyland | XIX Tactical Air Command (XIX TAC) (under 9th AF) | Support to US Third Army |

# Appendix 2. Deceptions and Actual Operations Plans in Support of Operation OVERLORD

| Plan | Active | Intended Operation or Deception |
|------|--------|--------------------------------|
| BAGRATION | June 22–August 19, 1944 | Major Soviet offensive on the Eastern Front that resulted in perhaps 450,000 German casualties in support of FORTITUDE NORTH |
| BODYGUARD | December 1943–August 1944 | Overall Allied deception plan to force German mistakes in defending Western Europe; included FORTITUDE NORTH and SOUTH |
| DIADEM | May 11–Summer 1944 | Actual allied offensive operations in Italy to tie down *10th Armée* |
| FORTITUDE NORTH | Fall 1943–August 1944 | A false invasion threat against Norway, Demark, and Finland by Russian forces supported by the SKYE deception |
| FORTITUDE SOUTH | Fall 1943–August 1944 | A false invasion threat against the Pas-de-Calais supported by the QUICKSILVER deception |
| IRONSIDE | May 23–June 22, 1944 | A false invasion threat against Bordeaux and the German *1st Armée* defending the Biscay coast. |
| QUICKSILVER | Fall 1943–August 1944 | Imaginary First US Army Group (FUSAG) commanded by the very real and much-feared LtGen Patton in southeastern Britain in support of FORTITUDE SOUTH |

| Plan | Active | Intended Operation or Deception |
|------|--------|--------------------------------|
| SKYE | Fall 1943– August 1944 | Imaginary British Fourth Army in Scotland in support of FORTITUDE NORTH |
| VENDETTA | April 30– June 30, 1944 | A false invasion threat against Marseilles and the German *19th Armée* defending the south of France in support of FORTITUDE SOUTH |
| ZEPPELIN | February– July 1944 | A false invasion threat against the Balkans and the German *Heeresgruppe F* defending Greece and the Balkans in support of ZEPPELIN |

*Source*: After Stephen C. Kepher, *COSSAC Lt. Gen. Sir Frederick Morgan and the Genesis of Operation Overlord* (Annapolis, MD: Naval Institute Press, 2020), 245–46; Brown, *Bodyguard of Lies*.

# Appendix 3. German Radar Installations in the Invasion Area, May 1944 (See map 13.1.)

| Map No. | Location | Code Name (Note 1) | Function |
|---|---|---|---|
| 1 | Cap Fréhel | Mammut / Giant Würzburg | Long-range coastal surveillance |
| 2 | Saint-Malo | — | Coastal surveillance |
| 3 | Vire | Giant Würzburg | Long-range coastal surveillance |
| 4 | Rouge Nez (Jersey) | — | Coastal surveillance |
| 5 | Cap de Carteret | — | Coastal surveillance |
| 6 | Nez de Jobourg | Mammut / Giant Würzburg | Long-range coastal surveillance |
| 7 | Cap de la Hague | Giant Würzburg | Long-range coastal surveillance |
| 8 | Omonville | Mammut | Coastal surveillance |
| 9 | Cherbourg | Freya / Giant Würzburg / Wassermann | Long-range coastal surveillance |
| 10 | Cap Lévi | Giant Würzburg | Coastal surveillance |
| 11 | Barfleur | Giant Würzburg | Long-range coastal surveillance |
| 12 | Pointe et Rez de la Percée | Giant Würzburg | Long-range coastal surveillance |
| 13 | Bayeux | — | Coastal surveillance |
| 14 | Arromanches | Giant Würzburg | Coastal surveillance |
| 15 | Caen | Giant Würzburg / Wassermann | Long-range coastal surveillance |
| 16 | Houlgate | Giant Würzburg | Long-range coastal surveillance |

| Map No. | Location | Code Name (Note 1) | Function |
|---|---|---|---|
| 17 | Le Havre | Giant Würzburg | Coastal surveillance |
| 18 | Épinay-sur-Duclair | Giant Würzburg | Long-range coastal surveillance |
| 19 | Neufchâtel-en-Bray | Giant Würzburg | Long-range coastal surveillance |
| 20 | Amiens | Giant Würzburg | Long-range coastal surveillance |
| 21 | Abbeville | Wassermann / Giant Würzburg | Long-range coastal surveillance |
| 22 | Cap d'Antifer | Freya / Giant Würzburg / Wassermann | Long-range coastal surveillance |
| 23 | Fécamp | Mammut / Giant Würzburg | Long-range coastal surveillance |
| 24 | Saint-Léger | Giant Würzburg | Long-range coastal surveillance |
| 25 | Saint-Valéry-en-Caux | Giant Würzburg | Long-range coastal surveillance |
| 26 | Sainte-Marguerite-sur-Mer | Giant Würzburg | Coastal surveillance |
| 27 | Dieppe | Mammut / Giant Würzburg | Long-range coastal surveillance |
| 28 | Le Tréport | Giant Würzburg | Long-range coastal surveillance |
| 29 | Cayeux-sur-Mer | Giant Würzburg | Long-range coastal surveillance |
| 30 | Berck-sur-Mer | – | Coastal surveillance |
| 31 | Fruges | Mammut / Giant Würzburg | Long-range coastal surveillance |
| 32 | Mont Violette | – | Long-range coastal surveillance |
| 33 | Mont Lambert | – | Coastal surveillance |
| 34 | Watermill Saint Georges | Giant Würzburg | Long-range coastal surveillance |
| 35 | Le Touquet | – | Long-range coastal surveillance |

| Map No. | Location | Code Name (Note 1) | Function |
|---------|----------|--------------------|----------|
| 36 | Neufchâtel-Hardelot | Giant Würzburg | Long-range coastal surveillance |
| 37 | Cap d'Alprech | Giant Würzburg | Long-range coastal surveillance |
| 38 | Pointe aux Oies | Mammut / Giant Würzburg | Long-range coastal surveillance |
| 39 | Boulogne | Wassermann | Long-range coastal surveillance |
| 40 | Cap Gris-Nez | Giant Würzburg | Long-range coastal surveillance |
| 41 | Cap Blanc-Nez | Giant Würzburg | Long-range coastal surveillance |
| 42 | Calais | Giant Würzburg | Long-range coastal surveillance |

**Note 1:**

| | |
|---|---|
| Giant Würzburg | Fighter control |
| Freya | Medium-range air surveillance |
| Wassermann | Height-finder (called "Chimney" by RAF) |
| Mammut | Long-range air surveillance (called "Hoarding" by RAF) |

*Source*: John Man, *D-Day Atlas* (New York: New York, NY: Facts on File, 1994), 20.

# Appendix 4. *Jagdkorps I* Reinforcements from Germany to France, June 7, 1944

| Gruppe | Dispatched From | Intended Destination | Available (Note 1) | Serviceable (Note 2) | Predominant Aircraft Type |
|---|---|---|---|---|---|
| Stab./JG 1 | Lippspringe, GE | Beauvais–Tillé, FR | 0 | 0 | Fw 190A-8 |
| I./JG 1 | Lippspringe, GE | Le Mans, FR | 25 | 12 | Fw 190A-8 |
| II./JG 1 | Störmede, GE | Le Flers, FR | 25 | 13 | Fw 190A-7 |
| III./JG 1 | Paderborn, GE | Beauvais–Tillé, FR | 8 | 5 | Bf 109G-6/AS (Note 3) |
| Stab./JG 3 | Salzwedel, GE | Évreux-Fauville | 0 | 0 | Bf 109G-6/AS (Note 3) |
| I./JG 3 | Burg, GE | Unknown | 30 | 13 | Bf 109G-6/AS (Note 3) |
| II./JG 3 | Sachau, GE | Évreux-Fauville | 0 | 0 | Bf 109G-6 |
| III./JG 3 | Nonoperational | St. André-de-l'Eure, FR | 64 | 17 | Bf 109G-6 |
| IV (Sturm)./JG 3 | Burg, GE | Dreux | 22 | 21 | Bf 109G-6 |
| I./JG5 | Herzogenaurach, GE | Montdidier, FR | 16 | 15 | Bf 109G-6/AS (Note 3) |
| Stab./JG 11 | Rotenburg, GE | Rennes, FR | 1 | 0 | Fw 190A-8 |
| I./JG 11 | Rotenburg, GE | Rennes, FR | 14 | 4 | Fw 190A-8 |
| II./JG 11 | Hustedt, GE | Beauvais–Tillé, FR | 17 | 12 | Bf 109G-6/AS (Note 3) |
| Stab./JG 27 | Wien-Seyring, AU | Romilly-sur-Seine, FR | 4 | 4 | Bf 109G-6 |
| I./JG 27 | Fels am Wagram, AU | Reims, FR | 16 | 13 | Bf 109G-6 |
| II./JG 27 | Götzendorf, AU | Eisenstein, AU | 23 | 19 | Bf 109G-6 |
| III./JG 27 | Szombathely, HU | Romilly-sur-Seine, FR | 21 | 17 | Bf 109G-6 |

| Gruppe | Dispatched From | Intended Destination | Available (Note 1) | Serviceable (Note 2) | Predominant Aircraft Type |
|---|---|---|---|---|---|
| 10./JG 27 | Nonoperational | Champfleury, FR | 19 | 12 | Bf 109G-6 |
| II./JG 53 | Öttingen, GE | Nantes, FR | 0 | 0 | Bf 109G-6 |
| III./JG 54 | Unterschlauersbach, GE | Chartres, FR | 19 | 12 | Bf 109G-6 |
| Total | | | 336 | 192 | — |

**Note 1:** *Total aircraft available, including aircraft that could be flown and those not flyable*
**Note 2:** *Aircraft that could be flown during one combat day*
**Note 3:** *The Bf 109G-6/AS was a high-altitude version of this aircraft. Units with this aircraft were termed* Höhengruppe, *high-altitude groups.*

*Source*: Wood, W. J. A. (ed.), Defence of the Reich (*Reichsverteidigung*), 3 June 1944, translation of Enemy Documents, RAF Air Historical Branch (AHB) 6, copied May 1963.

# Appendix 5. Air Landing Grounds Support for OVERLORD Air Operations

| Date Operational | Airfield Number | Location | Aircraft Type | Associated Unit |
|---|---|---|---|---|
| June 6 | ELS-1 | Pouppeville (Utah) | C-47 | Transport and emergency use only |
| June 8 | ELS-2 (later A-21, C-1, and T-1) | St. Laurent-sur-Mer (Omaha) | C-47 | C-47s and emergency use only |
| June 10 | B-1 | Asnelles | C-47 | C-47s and emergency use only |
| June 10 | B-2 | Bazenville | Spitfire IX LF | 127 Wing (RAF) |
| June 10 | B-3 | St. Croix-sur-Mer | Spitfire IX LF | 144 Wing (RAF) |
| | | | Mustang IA/ | 35 (Recce) Wing (RAF) |
| | | | Spitfire PR XI | 35 (Recce) Wing (RAF) |
| | | | Typhoon Ib | 136 Wing (RAF)/263 Sq (June 17?) |
| | | | Typhoon Ib | 146 Wing (RAF)/ 197 Sq (July 20) |
| June 10 | B-10 | Plumetot | Typhoon Ib | 129 Wing (RAF) |
| | | | Spitfire IX LF | 134 Wing (RAF) |
| | | | Spitfire IX LF | 131 Wing (RAF) |
| | | | Mustang IA/ Spitfire PR XI | 35 (Recce) Wing (RAF) |
| June 14 | A-1 | St. Pierre-du-Mont | P-47 | 366th Fighter Group (June 17) |
| | | | P-38 | 401st Fighter Sq (July 31) |
| June 14 | A-3 | Cardonville | P-47 | 368th Fighter Group (June 14) |
| | | | P-38 | 370th Fighter Group (July 24) |

| Date Operational | Airfield Number | Location | Aircraft Type | Associated Unit |
|---|---|---|---|---|
| June 15 | A-6 | Beuzeville-au-Plain | P-47<br>P-38 | 371 Fighter Group<br>(June 17)<br>367th Fighter Group<br>(July 22) |
| June 15 | B-4 | Bény-sur-Mer | Spitfire IX LF<br>Mustang IA/<br>Spitfire PR XI | 126 Wing (RAF)<br>35 (Recce) Wing (RAF)<br>35 (Recce) Wing (RAF) |
| June 15 | B-5 | Le Fresne-Camilly | Typhoon Ib<br>Typhoon Ib<br>Spitfire IX LF | 129 Wing (RAF)<br>121 Wing (RAF)<br>222 Sq (ADGB) |
| June 15 | B-6 | Coulombs | Typhoon Ib<br>Mosquito XIII NF (Intruder) | 124 Wing (RAF)<br>142 Wing (RAF)/ 264 Sq |
| June 17? | B-7 | Rucqueville | Mustang III<br>Typhoon Ib<br>Typhoon Ib | 122 Wing (RAF)<br>123 Wing (RAF)<br>136 Wing (RAF) |
| June 19 | A-2 | Cricqueville-en-Bessin | P-51<br>P-38 | 354th Fighter Group<br>(June 23)<br>367th Fighter Group<br>(Aug 14) |
| June 19 | A-10 | Carentan | P-38<br>P-38 | 50th Fighter Group<br>(June 25)<br>392nd Fighter Sq<br>(31 July) |
| June 21 | B-11 | Longues-sur-Mer | Spitfire IX LF | 125 Wing (RAF) |
| June 22 | B-8 | Sommervieu | Spitfire IX LF<br>Spitfire IX LF<br>Spitfire PR XI<br>Mustang IA<br>Typhoon Ib | 145 Wing (RAF)<br>74 Sq (ADGB)<br>39 (Recce) Wing (RAF)<br>35 (Recce) Wing (RAF)<br>146 Wing (RAF)/266 Sq<br>(July 20) |
| June 22 | B-9 | Lantheuil | Typhoon Ib | 143 Wing (RAF) |
| June 24 | A-7 | Azeville | P-47<br>P-51 | 365th Fighter Group<br>(June 22)<br>363rd Fighter Group<br>(Aug 16) |

| Date Operational | Airfield Number | Location | Aircraft Type | Associated Unit |
|---|---|---|---|---|
| June 26 | A-8N | Picauville | P-47<br>Mosquito XIII NF | 405th Fighter Group (June 29)<br>604 Sq/ 142 Wing (RAF) |
| June 30 | A-4 | Deux-Jumeaux | P-47<br>P-51B/F-6 | 48th Fighter Group (June 30)<br>107th TR Sq (June 28) |
| June 30 | A-9D | Le Molay-Littry | F-5B<br>P-51B/F-6<br>P-51B/F-6<br>F-5B | 30th PR/67th TR Group (July 2)<br>109th TR Sq/ 67th TRG (July 5) 12th TR Sq/ 67th TRG (July 5)<br>31st PR Sq/ 67th TRG (15 Aug)<br>33rd PR Sq/ 67th TRG (15 August) |
| July 4 | A-14 | Cretteville | P-47<br>P-38<br>P-47 | 358th Fighter Group (July 4)<br>393rd Fighter Sq (July 27)<br>406th Fighter Group (August 17) |
| July 4 | A-15 | Maupertus-sur-Mer | P-51<br>P-61<br>Mosquito XIII NF<br>B-26 | 363rd Fighter Group (July 1)<br>422nd Night Fighter Sq (July 25)<br>604Sqn/142 Wing (RAF)<br>387th Bomb Group (August 22) |
| July 5 | A-5 | Chippelle | P-47 | 404th Fighter Group (July 9) |
| July 5 | B-15 | Ryes | Typhoon Ib | 146 Wing (RAF)/ 257 Sq (Aug 7) |
| July 6 | A-23C/ T3 | Querqueville | C-47 | 27th Air Transport Group (det) |
| July 7 | B-14 | Amblie | – | Rearm and refuel only |

| Date Operational | Airfield Number | Location | Aircraft Type | Associated Unit |
|---|---|---|---|---|
| July 13 | A-22C/ T-2 | Colleville-sur-Mer | C-47 | Transport strip |
| July 17 | A-16 | Brucheville | P-47 | 36th Fighter Group (July 17) |
| July 18 | A-12 | Lignerolles | P-47 | 362nd Fighter Group |
| | | | P-47 | (July 7) |
| | | | Spitfire PR XI | 365th Fighter Group (August 15) |
| | | | | 16 Sq /34 (Recce) Wing (RAF) |
| July 18 | B-12 | Ellon | Mustang III | 122 Wing (RAF) |
| July 20 | A-24C/ T-4 | Biniville | L-5 | 125th Liaison Sq |
| July 25 | B-18 | Cristot | – | – |
| July 28 | A-13 | Tour-en-Bessin | P-47 | 373rd Fighter Group |
| | | | P-47 | (July 19) |
| | | | B-26 | 406th Fighter Group (July 17) |
| | | | | 394th Bomb Group (August 20) |
| August 3 | A-20 | Lessay | B-26 | 323rd Bomb Group (August 26) |
| August 5 | A-11 | St. Lambert / Neuilly-Isigny | P-47 | 474th Fighter Group (August 5) |
| August 6 | B-19 | Lingèvres | Spitfire IX LF | 125 Wing (RAF) |
| August 7 | A-25 | Bolleville | C-47 | Transport strip |
| August 7 | B-16 | Villons-les-Buissons | Mustang III | 132 Wing (RAF) |
| August 8 | B-17 | Carpiquet | Spitfire IX LF | 135 Wing (RAF) |
| | | | Spitfire XIV | 148 Wing (RAF) |
| August 8 | B-21 | Sainte-Honorine-de Ducy | Spitfire PR XI | 39 (Recce) Wing (RAF) |
| | | | Mustang I | 39 (Recce) Wing (RAF) |
| August 8 | B-22 | Authie | — | — |
| August 9 | B-23 | Morainville | Typhoon Ib/ Spitfire IX LF | 146 Wing (RAF)/ 193 Sq |

| Date Operational | Airfield Number | Location | Aircraft Type | Associated Unit |
|---|---|---|---|---|
| August 10 | A-27 | Rennes-Saint-Jacques | P-47<br>F-5B<br>F-5B<br>P-51B/F-6<br>P-51B/F-6<br>L-5 | 362nd Fighter Group (August 12)<br>31st PR Sq/ 10th PRG (Aug 18)<br>34th PR Sq/ 10th PRG (Aug 11)<br>15th TR Sq/ 67th TRG (Aug 10)<br>12th TR Sq/ 67th TRG (Aug 11)<br>125th Liaison Sq |
| August 10 | A-28 | Pontorson | P-47 | 358th Fighter Group (August 14) |
| August 11 | A-30 | Courtils | C-47 | Transport Strip |
| August 11 | A-31 | Gael | P-51 | 354th Fighter Group (August 11) |
| August 14 | A-19 | La Vielle (Note 1) | P-38 | 370th Fighter Group (August 14) |
| August 14 | A-29 | St. James | P-47 | 373rd Fighter Group (August 20) |
| August 15 | A-49 | Beille | C-47 | Transport strip |
| August 16 | A-17 | Méautis | P-47 | 50th Fighter Group (August 16) |
| August 16 | A-26 | Gorges | B-26 | 397th Bomb Group (30 August) |
| August 21 | A-57 | Laval Entrammes | L-5 | 47th Liaison Sq |
| August 24 | A-50 | Orléans-Bricy | – | – |
| August 26 | A-39 | Châteaudun | F-5B<br>F-5B<br>F-5B<br>P-51B/F-6<br>P-61 | 31st PR Sq /10th PRG (27 August)<br>12th TR Sq /67th TRG (August 24)<br>34th PR Sq /10th PRG (August 25)<br>15th TR Sq /67th TRG (August 26)<br>422nd Night Fighter Sq (August 28) |

| Date Operational | Airfield Number | Location | Aircraft Type | Associated Unit |
|---|---|---|---|---|
| August 26 | A-40 | Chartres-Champhol | P-47 | 368th Fighter Group (August 26) |
| August 26 | A-41 | Dreux-Vernouillet | P-47 | 366th Fighter Group (August 24) |
| August 27 | A-56 | Le Hamil or Crécy (Note 1) | L-5 | Liaison strip |
| By August 27 | B-25 | Le Theil-Nolent | Various | 2TAF |
| By August 27 | B-26 | Lillers | Various | 2TAF |
| By August 27 | B-27 | Boisney | Various | 2TAF |
| By August 27 | B-29 | Bernay-Valailles | Various | 2TAF |
| August 29 | A-18 | Saint-Jean-de-Daye | – | Refueling and rearming strip |
| August 29 | A-33 | Vannes-Meucon (near Lorient) | P-61 | 425th Night Fighter Sq |
| August 29 | A-34 | Gorron | – | Refuel and rearm strip |
| August 29 | A-48 | Brétigny | P-47 | 404th Fighter Group (August 29) |
| August 29 | A-53 | Issy-les-Moulineaux | L-5 | Liaison strip |
| August 29 | A-54 | Le Bourget | L-5 | Transport strip |
| August 30 | A-42 | Vélizy-Villacoublay | P-47 | 48th Fighter Group (August 29) |
| August 30 | A-46 | Toussus-le-Noble | F-5B<br>P-51B/F-6<br>F-5B | 33rd PR Sq / TRG (August 30)<br>109th TR Sq /67th TRG (August 30)<br>30th PR / 67th TR Group (August 31) |
| August 30 | A-47 | Orly | L-5 | 12th Liaison Squadron |
| August 30 | A-52 | Étampes-Mondésir | C-47 | Transport strip |
| August 31 | A-43 | Saint-Marceau | P-38 | 474th Fighter Group (2 September) |
| By August 31 | B-24 | Saint-André-de-l'Eure | Various | 2TAF |
| By August 31 | B-28 | Évreux-Fauville | Various | 2TAF |
| By August 31 | B-30 | Créton | Various | 2TAF |

| Date Operational | Airfield Number | Location | Aircraft Type | Associated Unit |
|---|---|---|---|---|
| (Recce) Wing | Reconnaissance wing | | | |
| ALG A-series | American-built air landing ground (ALG) | | | |
| ALG B-series | British-built air landing ground (ALG) | | | |
| ALG T-series | Transport strip | | | |
| C suffix | Cargo/transport strip | | | |
| D suffix | Depot airfield | | | |
| ELS | Emergency landing strip | | | |
| Fighter Group | Fighter group | | | |
| N suffix | Designed as night fighter strip | | | |
| PRG | Photo reconnaissance group | | | |
| Sq | RAF squadron of 8–16 planes | | | |
| TR Group | Tactical reconnaissance group | | | |
| Wing | RAF organization with several squadrons, USAAF organization of several groups | | | |
| Group | RAF organization with several wings, USAAF organization of several squadrons | | | |

**Note 1:** Exact location in question.

*Source*: "Location of Allied Airfields (Advanced Landing Grounds) in Normandy," *Skylighters—The Story of the 225th AAA Battalion from Omaha Beach to V-E Day*, n.d., n.p., online, July 15, 2003, available from http:/www.skylighters.org/history/airfields/normandyfields.html; Rust, *The 9th Air Force in World War II*, 88, 90, 98, 117; Raymond Harwood "Stations Used by the 9th US Air Force," 9th U.S. Air Force, n.d., n.p., online, internet, July 18, 2003, available from http:/www.publicenquiry.co.uk/commands/sc9thbase.html; Hallion, *D-Day 1944: Air Power Over the Normandy Beaches and Beyond*, 4–8; Johnson, *U.S. Army Air Forces Continental Airfields (ETO) D-Day to V-E. Day*, 13–25; Collins, *Military Geography*, 362–63; Maurer Maurer, ed., *World War II Combat Squadrons of the United States Air Force* (Woodbury, NY: Smithmark Publishers, Inc., 1992), numerous entries; *France Tourist and Motoring Atlas*, Plates 14–18, 35–41, 54–62, 72–78; Wynn and Young, *Prelude to Overlord*, 30–33; John Nicholls, "The 'A' Airfields," Allied Airfields and Landing Grounds, January 2003, n.p., online, July 19, 2003, available from http://www.publicenquiry.co.uk/commands/sc9thbase.html; John Nicholls, "The 'B' Airfields," Allied Airfields and Landing Grounds, January 2003, n.p., online, July 19, 2003, available from http://www.publicenquiry.co.uk/commands/sc9thbase.html; David N. Spires, *Air Power for Patton's Army* (Washington, DC: Air Force History and Museums Program, 2002), 72; Maurer Maurer (ed.), *Air Force Combat Units of World War II* (Washington, DC: Office of Air Force History, United States Air Force and U.S. Center of Military History, 1983), 51, 91–92, 106–07, 110–11, 133–34, 203–04, 240–41, 244–47, 249–60, 274, 289–93, 346–47.

# Acknowledgments

The people listed below are only the tip of the iceberg. Mentioning the topic to anyone connected with the military, especially if they're baby boomers, immediately engenders wide eyes and flaring nostrils followed by that person's favorite story about smashing Hitler's *Festung Europa*. So I've have enjoyed working on this project if for no other reason than I've gotten to talk with so many knowledgeable people about it, starting with a conference at the University of New Orleans in 1984.

I have many folks to thank for getting me through this book, most of all my wife, Margaret; daughters, Elizabeth and Katherine; sons-in-law, Justin and David; and grandchildren, Mia and Anna. Like myself, they are the beneficiaries of the better world the Allied airmen, soldiers, and sailors of World War II fought to create. Margaret also photo-processed the photography in this book to get the most out of eighty-year-old pictures taken in difficult conditions. Dr. James Arnold helped greatly by proofing the manuscript, clarifying many issues. The airmen I served with during my thirty-two US Air Force years inspired me to do my best— because they always did theirs.

Historians Stephen Ambrose, Ron Drez, and Kathi Jones first introduced me to the world of professional military history at the Eisenhower Center at the University of New Orleans in the late 1980s. Air Force Reserve Command Historian Charles O'Connell renewed my interest toward the end of my active USAF career.

Research long ago led me to this series of books. At the Air Force Historical Research Agency (AFHRA), archivists Milton Steele and Dennis Case were never too busy to help me during my frequent forays to Maxwell Air Force Base. James Furguson provided many USAF photographs with an eye to both the dramatic and the informative. David A. Giordano introduced me to "Finding Aids" and the wonderful treasure house of materials that is our National Archives. Jeff Duford gave me a backstage tour of the Air Force Museum at Wright-Patterson Air Force Base, including a close look at a Bf 109. Steve Paczolt of the Library of Congress Map Room spent a whole morning showing me every map they have on World War II in Europe.

To all of you who helped, thanks again!

# Notes

## POEM

1. "The Eleanor Roosevelt Wartime Prayer," *The Eleanor Roosevelt Papers Project*, accessed May 25, 2021, https://www2.gwu.edu/~erpapers/teachinger/q-and-a/q21-prayer.cfm. (Public). The prayer is in the public domain.

## INTRODUCTION

1. Paraphrased from Alistair Horne, *To Lose a Battle: France 1940*. Penguin Books Ltd., Kindle edition, 657.

2. Figures provided by the *Mémorial de Caen L'Histoire pour la Paix*, Caen, France.

## CHAPTER 1: AIR PLANS FOR OVERLORD

1. Albert Speer, *Spandau: The Secret Diaries*, trans. Richard and Clara Winston (New York: MacMillan Publishing, 1976), 340.

2. "CONTROL OF STRATEGIC BOMBING FOR 'OVERLORD'." CCS Memorandum 520, 17 March 1944, Record Group 331, Box 11, National Archives at College Park, MD, 1.

## CHAPTER 2: THE OIL PLAN

1. Lt. Gen. Carl Spaatz to Gen. Dwight Eisenhower, memorandum, March 31, 1944, "Use of Strategic Bombers in Support of OVERLORD."

2. Walt W. Rostow, *Pre-Invasion Bombing Strategy: General Eisenhower's Decision of March 25, 1944* (Austin, TX: University of Texas Press, 1981), 88–98. The term *Command Bombing Force* referred collectively to the heavy bombers of the US Eighth Air Force and the RAF Bomber Command.

3. The spelling of this country was either "Rumania" or "Roumania" in World War II but has since become "Romania."

4. Richard G. Davis, *Carl Spaatz and the Air War in Europe* (Washington, DC: Center for Air Force History, US Air Force, 1983), 397.

5. Richard G. Davis, "Carl Spaatz and D-Day," *Airpower Journal* (Winter 1997). Accessed August 21, 2023, https://www.airuniversity.af.edu/Portals/10/ASPJ/journals/Volume-11_Issue-1-4/1997_Vol11_No4.pdf.

6. Earl R. Beck, *Under the Bombs* (Lexington, KY: The University of Kentucky Press, 1986), 129–32.

7. Albert Speer, *Inside the Third Reich*, trans. Richard and Clara Winston (New York: The Macmillan Company, 1970), 346–49.

8. Alfred Price, *The Last Year of the Luftwaffe* (Gaithersburg, MD: Wrens Park Publishing, 2001), 93.

## CHAPTER 3: MISTLETOE IN MARCH

1. Hans-Peter Dabrowski, *Mistel: The Piggy-Back Aircraft of the Luftwaffe* (Atglen, PA: Schiffer Publishing Ltd., 1994), 10.
2. Brian Filley, *Junkers Ju 88 in Action, Part 1* (Carrollton, TX: Squadron/Signal Publications, Inc., 1994), 54.
3. Quoted in Robert Forsyth, *Mistel German Composite Aircraft and Operations 1942–1945* (Norwalk, CT: Airtime Publishing, Inc., 2001), 83.
4. A total of 400mm of armor, or over 15 inches.
5. Forsyth, *Mistel German Composite Aircraft and Operations 1942–1945*, 80–81.
6. Forsyth, *Mistel German Composite Aircraft and Operations 1942-1945*, 81.
7. Fritz-X and Hs 293, used earlier against Allied ships in the Mediterranean.

## CHAPTER 4: ARENA

1. De Koog, Bergan Alkmarr, Valkenburg, and Haamstede airfields, in that order.
2. Stephen C. Kepher, *COSSAC Lt. Gen. Sir Frederick Morgan and the Genesis of Operation Overlord* (Annapolis, MD: Naval Institute Press, 2020), 5.
3. *David Stafford, Ten Days to D-Day* (London: Little, Brown, 2003), 22–23.
4. Stéphane Costa, "The High Normandy Chalk Cliffs: An Inspiring Geomorphosite for Painters and Novelists," *Landscapes and Landforms of France*, ed. Monique Fort and Marie-Françoise André, eds. (New York: Springer Science + Business Media *Dordrecht*, 2014), 29–30.
5. Gordon A. Harrison, *Cross-Channel Attack*, United States Army in World War II, European Theater (Washington, DC: Center of Military History United States Army, 1989), Map III.
6. Tim Marshall, *Prisoners of Geography* (London: Elliot and Thompson, 2015), 5–6.
7. *France* (New York: DK Publishing, 2021), 244.
8. *France*, 244.
9. *France*, 246.
10. Jean-Pierre Peulvast, "Introduction: Landscapes and Landforms of France, A Large Diversity," *Landscapes and Landforms of France*, ed. Monique Fort and Marie-Françoise André (New York: Springer Science + Business Media *Dordrecht*, 2014), 2.
11. William Morris Davis, *A Handbook of Northern France* (Cambridge, MA: Harvard University Press, 1918), 136–37.
12. William Morris Davis, *A Handbook of Northern France* (Cambridge, MA: Harvard University Press, 1918), 3.
13. Tim Marshall, *Prisoners of Geography* (London: Elliot and Thompson, 2015), 78–82, and William Morris Davis, *A Handbook of Northern France* (Cambridge, MA: Harvard University Press, 1918), 13.
14. Transcript of briefing by Colonel Truman Smith, 17 November 1943, in File 142.05-10, Albert F. Simpson Historical Research Center, Air University, Maxwell AFB, AL; Sir Max Hastings, *Overlord: D-Day and the Battle for Normandy* (Simon & Schuster), Kindle, 310.
15. Transcript of briefing by Colonel Truman Smith, 22 December 1943.
16. Molyson after Martin Blumenson, *Breakout and Pursuit*, United States Army in World War II, European Theater (Washington, DC: Center of Military History United States Army, 1989), Map I; Ken Ford, *D-Day 1944 (3) Sword Beach and the Airborne Landings*, Osprey Campaign Series, vol. 105, ed. Lee Johnson (Oxford, UK: Osprey Publishing Ltd., 2002), 26.

17. Sir Max Hastings, *Overlord: D-Day and the Battle for Normandy* (Simon & Schuster), Kindle, 188.

18. Stephen C. Kepher, *COSSAC Lt. Gen. Sir Frederick Morgan and the Genesis of Operation Overlord* (Annapolis, MD: Naval Institute Press, 2020), 111.

19. Hastings, *Overlord: D-Day and the Battle for Normandy*, 48.

20. Omaha Beach was originally on the west end of the Neptune area. Utah, on the Cotentin Peninsula, was added later.

21. Hastings, *Overlord: D-Day and the Battle for Normandy*, 188.

22. *David Stafford, Ten Days to D-Day* (London: Little, Brown, 2003), 7; Hastings, *Overlord: D-Day and the Battle for Normandy*, Kindle, 49.

23. Steven J. Zaloga, *D-Day 1944 (1)*, Osprey Campaign Series, vol. 100 (Oxford, UK: Osprey Publishing Ltd, 2018), 8, 47.

24. Hastings, *Overlord: D-Day and the Battle for Normandy*, 33–34.

25. John Terraine, *The Right of the Line: the Royal Air Force in the European War, 1939–1945* (London: Hodder and Stoughton, Ltd., 1985), 564–65.

26. Richard G. Davis, *Carl Spaatz and the Air War in Europe* (Washington, DC: Center for Air Force History, US Air Force, 1983), 407 (map).

## CHAPTER 5: BEST LAID PLANS

1. In this case, a brigade being one-third of a division.

2. Based on a description in Gordon A. Harrison, *Cross-Channel Attack*, United States Army in World War II, European Theater (Washington, DC: Center of Military History United States Army, 1989), 72–73; Omar Bradley, *A Soldier's Story* (New York: Henry Holt and Company, 1951), 212–14.

3. Bradley, *A Soldier's Story*, 183.

4. Harrison, *Cross-Channel Attack*, Map II (attached); Bradley, *A Soldier's Story*, 232–33.

5. After Samuel Eliot Morison, *The Invasion of France and Germany 1944–1945*, History of the United States Navy in World War II, vol. XI (Boston: Little, Brown and Company, 1984), 85.

6. Harrison, *Cross-Channel Attack*, , Map III (attached).

7. Stephen C. Kepher, *COSSAC Lt. Gen. Sir Frederick Morgan and the Genesis of Operation Overlord* (Annapolis, MD: Naval Institute Press, 2020), 128–29.

## CHAPTER 6: *FESTUNG EUROPA*

1. *Waffen SS (Schutzstaffel)*. The units were sometimes termed the Nazi Party's private army and were considered elite and ruthless fighting units.

2. The reader should note that these statistics vary a bit by source.

3. James F. Dunnigan and Albert A. Nofi, *Dirty Little Secrets of World War II* (New York: William Morrow and Company, Inc., 1994), 212–13.

4. Based on Gordon A. Harrison, *Cross-Channel Attack*, Map V (attached), and Joint Intelligence Sub-Committee of the Joint Planning Staff of the (UK) War Cabinet, "Operations 'Overlord' and 'Anvil'," CCS Report 381, 2 February 1944, in JCS Central Decimal File 1942–1945, Records Group 218, National Records and Archives Administration Archive II, College Park, MD.

## CHAPTER 7: IMPROVING THE ODDS

1. Omar N. Bradley, *A Soldier's Story* (New York: Henry Holt and Company, 1951), 114.

2. John J. Sullivan, *Overlord's Eagles* ( Jefferson, NC: McFarland & Company, Inc., Publishers, 1997), 1.

3. Transcript of briefing by Colonel Truman Smith, 17 November 1943, in File 142.05-10, Albert F. Simpson Historical Research Center, Air University, Maxwell AFB, AL.

4. David Stafford, *Ten Days to D-Day* (London: Little, Brown, 2003), 69, 83.

5. Gordon A. Harrison, *Cross-Channel Attack*, United States Army in World War II, European Theater (Washington, DC: Center of Military History United States Army, 1989), 455.

6. Joint Planning Staff of the (UK) War Cabinet, "Operation OVERLORD," J.P. Report (43) 260, 3 August 1943, in SHAEF SGS Minutes Decimal File May 43–Aug 45, Records Group 331, National Records and Archives Administration Archive II, College Park, MD, 1.

7. Joint Planning Staff of the (UK) War Cabinet, "Operation OVERLORD," 1.

8. Alfred Goldberg, " Air Campaign: Overlord: To D-Day," *D-Day: The Normandy Invasion in Retrospect*, ed. Eisenhower Foundation (Lawrence, KS: The University of Kansas Press, 1971), 64.

9. Harrison, *Cross-Channel Attack*, Map IV (attached).

10. Goldberg, "Air Campaign: Overlord: To D-Day," 71.

11. Robin Higham, "Technology and D-Day," in *D-Day: The Normandy Invasion in Retrospect*, Eisenhower Foundation (Lawrence, KS: The University of Kansas Press, 1971), 222–23.

## CHAPTER 8: THE OUTER RAMPART

1. Paul Carell, *Invasion—They're Coming*, trans. Ewald Osers (New York: E. P. Dutton & Co, 1963), 9–10.

2. For the German defenders, the *Atlantik Wall* continued along the North Sea coasts of Germany, Denmark, and Norway up to 61 degrees north. It extended tenuously even further north, along the Norwegian coast to North Cape. North of Holland, air defense was a more important function than defense against an amphibious landing.

3. Francis Russell and the editors of Time-Life Books, *The Secret War* (Alexandria, VA: Time-Life Books, 1981), 11.

## CHAPTER 9: POSTCARDS

1. John Man, *D-Day Atlas* (New York: Facts on File, 1994), 13–14.

2. "RAF Destroys German Secret Archives with New U.S. Bomb," *Impact Book 4, July 1944, May–August 1944*, ed. James Parton (Harrisburg, PA: National Historical Society, 1980), 64.

## CHAPTER 10: FORTITUDE

1. The Combined Chiefs of Staff (CCS) was the supreme military council of the Western Allies, the United States and the United Kingdom. It consisted of the US Joint Chiefs and their British counterparts. When meeting in Washington, the British chiefs were represented by senior British officers.

2. Combined Chiefs of Staff, "Plan Bodyguard," CCS 459/2, 20 January 1944, in File 119.04-8, Albert F. Simpson Historical Research Center, Air University, Maxwell AFB, AL.

3. Joint Intelligence Sub-Committee of the Joint Planning Staff of the (UK) War Cabinet, "Operations "Overlord' and 'Anvil'," JIC Memorandum for Information Number 31,

1 February 1944, in JCS Central Decimal File 1942–1945, Records Group 218, National Records and Archives Administration Archive II, College Park, MD.

4. John Chomeau, "All Is Fair in Love and War," *After D-Day*, n.d., n.p., online, September 15, 2000, available from http://militaryhistory.archives.webjump.com.

5. Adapted from Anthony Cave Brown, *Bodyguard of Lies* (New York: HarperCollins, 1975).

6. Brown, *Bodyguard of Lies*, 385.

7. F. H. Hinsley, "Deception," *The D-Day Encyclopedia*, ed. David G. Chandler and James Lawton Collins (New York: Simon & Schuster, 1994), 174.

8. Alfred Goldberg, "Air Campaign: Overlord: To D-Day," *D-Day: The Normandy Invasion in Retrospect*, ed. Eisenhower Foundation (Lawrence, KS: The University of Kansas Press, 1971), 68–69.

9. Goldberg, " Air Campaign: Overlord: To D-Day,", 69.

10. Roy M. Stanley II, *To Fool a Glass Eye* (Washington, DC: Smithsonian Institution Press, 1998), 47.

11. Alfred Price, "Electronic Warfare," *The D-Day Encyclopedia*, ed. David G. Chandler and James Lawton Collins (New York: Simon & Schuster, 1994), 212.

12. Quoted in Cornelius Ryan, *The Longest Day* (New York: Simon & Schuster, 1959), 79.

13. *Übersichtskarte Frankreich* (Overview Map France), German Army Intelligence Map dated 3 July 1944.

14. Ibid., 437.

## CHAPTER 11: THE INFORMATION WAR

1. "Control of The SOE," British Forces in World War II, n.d., n.p., online, July 24 2000, available from http://british-forces.com/world_war2/index1.html.

2. "Leaflets Are Weapons of Attack," *Impact Book 3, March 1944, January–April 443-46, [AU: Please fix date.] 1944*, ed. James Parton (Harrisburg, PA: National Historical Society, 1980), 22–23.

3. Phillip M. Taylor, "Allied Propaganda," *The D-Day Encyclopedia*, ed. David G. Chandler and James Lawton Collins (New York: Simon & Schuster, 1994), 439–41.

4. Ibid., 440.

5. "Psychological Bombing by the AAF," *Impact Book 6, March 1945, January–April 1945*, ed. James Parton (Harrisburg, PA: National Historical Society, 1980), 19.

6. Robin Higham, "Technology and D-Day," *D-Day: The Normandy Invasion in Retrospect*, ed. Eisenhower Foundation (Lawrence, KS: The University of Kansas Press, 1971), 225.

7. M. R. D. Foot, "Enigma," *The Oxford Companion to WWII*, ed. I. C. B. Dear and M. R. D. Foot (New York: Oxford University Press, 1995), 340.

8. Chief of Staff to the Supreme Allied Commander, "Support of Military Operations by Resistance Groups in France," Appendix P to COSSAC (43) 28, undated 1943, in File 505.14-3, Albert F. Simpson Historical Research Center, Air University, Maxwell AFB, AL.

9. Ernest F. Fisher, "German Signal," *The D-Day Encyclopedia*, ed. David G. Chandler and James Lawton Collins (New York: Simon & Schuster, 1994), 518.

10. F. H. Hinsley, "Intelligence," *The D-Day Encyclopedia*, ed. David G. Chandler and James Lawton Collins (New York: Simon & Schuster, 1994), 317.

11. Higham, "Technology and D-Day," 225.

12. Alfred Goldberg, "Air Campaign OVERLORD: To D-Day." *D-Day: The Normandy Invasion in Retrospect*, ed. the Eisenhower Foundation (Lawrence, KS: The University of Kansas Press, 1971), 62.

## CHAPTER 12: WOUNDED HEARTS
1. The original message can be heard at 1:40 on the YouTube file: https://www.youtube .com/watch?v=VqXsgujDjOY).
2. "Were the BBC messages really announcing the Normandy Landings?" D-Day Overlord, accessed February 7, 2025, https://www.dday-overlord.com/en/D-Day/german-forces/kriegsmarine.
3. Quoted in Cornelius Ryan, *The Longest Day* (New York: Simon & Schuster, 1959), 33.
4. Gen. Walter Warlimont, *Inside Hitler's Headquarters 1939–45*, trans. R. H. Barry (Novato, CA: Presidio, 1999), 422–23.
5. Ryan, *The Longest Day*, 85, 96–97.

## CHAPTER 13: BLINDED
1. A "sortie" is one flight by one aircraft.
2. Robin Higham, "Technology and D-Day," *D-Day: The Normandy Invasion in Retrospect*, 226; V. E. Tarrant, *The Last Year of the Kriegsmarine* (London: Arms & Armour Press, 1996), 56; Alfred Price, "Electronic Warfare," *The Oxford Companion to WWII*, 333; Alfred Price, "Electronic Warfare," *The D-Day Encyclopedia*, 211.
3. David Stafford, *Ten Days to D-Day* (London: Little, Brown, 2003), 94.
4. Alfred Goldberg, "Air Campaign: Overlord: To D-Day," *D-Day: The Normandy Invasion in Retrospect*, 70.
5. John Man, *D-Day Atlas* (New York: Facts on File, 1994), 20.
6. Ibid., 32.
7. Price, "Electronic Warfare," *The D-Day Encyclopedia*, 211.
8. Price, "Electronic Navigation Systems," 328.
9. "D-Day Deception Operation 'Glimmer'," Bomber Command, n.d., n.p., online, July 28, 2000, available from http://www.hellzapoppin.demon.co.uk/glimmer.htm.

## CHAPTER 14: STORMS
1. Quoted in Cornelius Ryan, *The Longest Day* (New York: Pocket Books, 1984), 62.
2. Ryan, *The Longest Day*, 30.

## CHAPTER 15: UNFINISHED BUSINESS
1. Directive 51, quoted in Friedrich Ruge, "Notes on German Naval Ops on D-Day," *Retrospect* (Lawrence, KS: The University of Kansas Press, 1971), 150.
2. Richard Townshend Bickers, *Air War Normandy* ( London: Leo Cooper, 1994), 7.
3. Winston S. Churchill, *Closing the Ring*, The Second World War, Volume V (Boston, MA: Mariner Books, 1985), 631.
4. V. E. Tarrant, *The Last Year of the Kriegsmarine* (London: Arms & Armour Press, 1996), 52–53.
5. Alfred Price, "The Air Battle," *D-Day Operation Overlord*, ed. Bernard Nalty (New York: Salamander Books, 1999), 134.

6. Alfred Goldberg, "Air Campaign OVERLORD: To D-Day," *D-Day: The Normandy Invasion in Retrospect*, ed. the Eisenhower Foundation (Lawrence, KS: The University of Kansas Press, 1971), 60–61; Price, "The Air Battle," 138.

7. Ibid., 130.

8. Gordon Smith, "Campaign Summaries of World War 2—Normandy Landings, North West France Operation "Overlord"—June 1944," Military and Naval Campaign Summaries of World War 2, n.d., n.p., online, August 5, 2002, available from http://www.naval-history .net/WW2CampaignsNormandy.htm.

9. Friedrich Rüge, *Sea Warfare 1939–1945*. trans. Commander M. G. Saunders, RN (London: Cassell & Company Ltd., 1957), 222–23; Tarrant, 126–28.

## CHAPTER 16: THE SLAPTON SANDS DISASTER

1. Robert Heege, "Exercise Tiger: Deadly D-Day Rehearsal," Warfare History Network, November 2015, accessed February 16, 2025, https://warfarehistorynetwork.com/article /exercise-tiger-deadly-D-Day-rehearsal/.

2. Gordon A. Harrison, *Cross-Channel Attack*, United States Army in World War II, European Theater (Washington, DC: Center of Military History United States Army, 1989), 269–70; Samuel Eliot Morison, *The Invasion of France and Germany, 1944–1945*, History of the United States Navy in World War II, vol. XI, 65–66.

3. Morison, *The Invasion of France and Germany, 1944–1945*, 66.

4. Charles B. MacDonald, "Slapton Sands: The Cover-up That Never Was," Naval History and Heritage Command, accessed February 15, 2025, https://www.history.navy.mil/content /history/nhhc/research/library/online-reading-room/title-list-alphabetically/s/slapton-sands -the-cover-up-that-never-was.html; "TIGER—The E-boat Attack," extracted from Lieutenant Clifford L. Jones, *The Administrative and Logistical History of the ETO, Part VI, Neptune: Training, Mounting, The Artificial Ports*, Historical Division, United States Army Forces, European Theater, March 1946; "Exercise TIGER: Disaster at Slapton Sands 28 April 1944," Naval History and Heritage Command, accessed February 15, 2025, https://www.history.navy.mil /browse-by-topic/wars-conflicts-and-operations/world-war-ii/1944/exercise-tiger.html

5. James Foster Tent, *E-Boat Alert* (Annapolis, MD: Naval Institute Press, 1996), 21.

## CHAPTER 17: DEFENDING THE COAST

1. Lawrence Paterson, *Hitler's Forgotten Flotillas* (Barnsley, South Yorkshire, UK: Seaforth Books, 2017), 111.

2. Adapted from V. E. Tarrant, *The Last Year of the Kriegsmarine* (London: Arms & Armour Press, 1996), 42.

3. Paterson, *Hitler's Forgotten Flotillas*, 151.

4. Joseph T. Molyson Jr., *Air Battles Before D-Day* (Mechanicsburg, PA: Stackpole Books, 2025), 175.

5. Friedrich Rüge, *Sea Warfare 1939–1945*, trans. Commander M. G. Saunders, RN (London: Cassell & Company Ltd., 1957), 208; Tarrant, *The Last Year of the Kriegsmarine*, 40.

6. Rüge, *Sea Warfare 1939–1945*, 200.

7. Friedrich Rüge, "Notes on German Naval Ops on D-Day," *D-Day: The Normandy Invasion in Retrospect* (Lawrence, KS: The University of Kansas Press, 1971), 160.

8. Ibid., 159.

9. Ibid., 161.

## CHAPTER 18: WATER'S EDGE

1. Vincent P. O'Hara, *The German Fleet at War 1939–1945* (Annapolis, MD: Naval Institute Press, 2020), 208; "History of the Kriegsmarine—German Navy—in Normandy in 1944," D-Day Overlord, accessed February 7, 2025, https://www.dday-overlord.com/en/D-Day/german-forces/kriegsmarine.

2. V. E. Tarrant, *The Last Year of the Kriegsmarine* (London: Arms & Armour Press, 1996), 57.

3. "History of the Kriegsmarine—German Navy—in Normandy in 1944"; L. F. Ellis, G. R. G. Allen, A. E. Warhurst, and Sir J. Robb, *Victory in the West: The Battle of Normandy*, History of the Second World War United Kingdom Military Series, vol. I (London: Naval & Military Press 2004), Kindle edition.

4. O'Hara, *The German Fleet at War 1939–1945*, 2209–210.

5. 15.Vp-Flotille Report, 6 June 1944, quoted in Lawrence Paterson, *Hitler's Forgotten Flotillas* (Barnsley, South Yorkshire, UK: Seaforth Books, 2017), 289–90.

6. William C. Ray, "The German Navy during D-Day Landings," *Warship International* 1, no. 1/12 (1964): 60–62, http://www.jstor.org/stable/44887277.

7. Stephen E. Ambrose, *The Supreme Commander* (Jackson, MS: The University of Mississippi Press, 1999), 420.

8. Paterson, *Hitler's Forgotten Flotillas*, 291; Tarrant, *The Last Year of the Kriegsmarine*, 60–64.

9. Jean-Philippe Dalles-Labourdette, *S-boote: German E-boats in Action 1939–1945*, trans. Janice Lert (Paris: Histoire and Collections, 2006), 106.

10. Some sources misidentify LCT 715 as "LST 715," which was not present in Normandy.

11. "Oyster mines" were a new type of pressure-activated mine that could be delivered by both aircraft and surface vessels. The Allies developed countermeasures to these weapons.

12. Tarrant, *The Last Year of the Kriegsmarine*, 156.

13. "SS *Dungrange*, SS *Brackenfield*, and HMS *Halsted*" wreck site, accessed February 8, 2025, https://wrecksite.eu/Wrecksite.aspx; Benjamin S. Yates, "David vs. Goliath: Small Boat Challenges to Naval Operations in Coastal Warfare," master's thesis (Marine Corps University, March 30, 1998), Appendix C; Tarrant, *The Last Year of the Kriegsmarine*, 68–69.

14. John Terraine, *The Right of the Line: the Royal Air Force in the European War, 1939–1945* (London: Hodder and Stoughton, Ltd., 1985), 624.

15. James Foster Tent, *E-Boat Alert* (Annapolis, MD: Naval Institute Press, 1996), 148–82.

16. Samuel Eliot Morison, *The Two-Ocean War* (New York: Galahad Books, 1997), 405.

17. "Incidents and losses of Allied naval forces from D-Day to the end of September 1944," D-Day Overlord, accessed February 7, 2025, https://www.dday-overlord.com/en/D-Day/armada/losses.

18. Benjamin S. Yates, "David vs. Goliath: Small Boat Challenges to Naval Operations in Coastal Warfare," Appendix C; "Allied Warships," uboat.net, accessed February 13, 2025, boat.net/allies/warships/ship/4628.html.

19. Quoted in David Clark, *Angels Eight Normandy Air War Diary* (Bloomington, IN: 1stBooks, 2003), 138. Comments in parentheses are the author's.

20. Paterson, *Hitler's Forgotten Flotillas*, 293–294.

21. Charles M. Sternhell and Alan M. Thorndike, *OEG Report 51. Antisubmarine Warfare in World War* II (Washington, DC: Operations Evaluation Group, Office of the Chief of Naval Operations, Navy Dept, 1946), 65, accessed February 19, 2025, www.ibiblio.org/hyperwar /USN/rep/ASW-51/index.html#contents.

22. Paterson, *Hitler's Forgotten Flotillas*, 291.

## CHAPTER 19: AIRBORNE

1. Charles H. Young, *Into the Valley*, ed. Charles D. Young (Dallas: PrintComm, Inc., 1995), 108.

2. Roger Cirillo and Stephen Badsey, "D-Day," *D-Day Operation Overlord*, ed. Bernard Nalty (New York: Salamander Books, 1999), 80–81.

3. Field Marshal Erwin Rommel, *The Rommel Papers*, trans. and ed. Sir B. H. Liddell Hart (New York: Da Capo Press, 1953), 460.

4. Cornelius Ryan, *The Longest Day* (New York: Pocket Books, 1984), 28–29.

5. Cirillo and Badsey, "D-Day," 80–81; Michael E. Haskew, "Operation OVERLORD, The 101st's Baptism of Fire," *World War II Band of Brothers Special Collectors' Edition*, n.d. (Fall 2001), 45.

6. Cornelius Ryan, *The Longest Day* (New York: Pocket Books, 1984), 57–58.

7. John M. Collins, *Military Geography* (Washington, DC: Brassey's, 1998), 354.

8. IX Troop Carrier Command, USAAF, "Analysis, Enemy Order of Battle—Air," Appendix "B" to Annex No 1 to IX Troop Carrier Command Field Order No 1 for Operation "Neptune," 22 March–13 June 1944, in File 533.451-12, Albert F. Simpson Historical Research Center, Air University, Maxwell AFB, AL.

9. *Oberstleutnant* Freidrich Freiherr von der Heydte, with comments by *Generalleutnant* Max Pemsel, Historical Division, Headquarters, United States Army Europe, "A German Parachute Regiment in Normandy," MS #B-839, 1954, in Box 11 of the James M. Gavin Papers, US Army Heritage and Education Center, Carlisle Barracks, PA.

## CHAPTER 20: GETTING THERE

1. The C-53 was derived from the C-47 and was specifically a paratroop delivery aircraft with a single passenger door in the left rear fuselage. The C-47 was derived from the DC-3 airliner. The C-47 had a double cargo door in the left rear fuselage, allowing it to load and carry bulky loads as well as paratroopers.

2. Charles H. Young, *Into the Valley*, ed. Charles D. Young (Dallas: PrintComm, Inc., 1995), 106.

3. Wesley Frank Craven and James Lea Cate, *The Army Air Forces in World War II, Volume 6, Men and Planes* (1955; new imprint, Washington, DC: Office of Air Force History, US Air Force, 1983), 621–24.

4. The 13th meridian was, and is, further west than the 12th.

5. Gerald C. Berry, transcript of oral history interview by Col. Joseph T. Molyson, USAFR (Ret.), April 28, 2003.

6. Maj. Michael C. Chester, to Lt. Gen. James M. Gavin, letter, March 30, 1959, in Box 11 of the James M. Gavin Papers, US Army Heritage and Education Center, Carlisle Barracks, PA. Author's comments are in parentheses.

7. Robin Higham, "Technology and D-Day," *D-Day: The Normandy Invasion in Retrospect*, 226–27; "AN/TPN-1 and *AN/PPN-1 Light Weight Long Wave 'Eureka' Racons," *U.S. Radar Operational Characteristics of Radar Classified by Tactical Application*, FTP 217, (Washington, DC: Joint Chiefs of Staff, August 1, 1943), 85, accessed February 24, 2025, https://www.history.navy.mil/research/library/online-reading-room/title-list-alphabetically/u/operational-characteristics-of-radar-classified-by-tactical-application.html.

8. "AN/TPN-1 and *AN/PPN-1 Light Weight Long Wave 'Eureka' Racons,", 85.

9. *Condensed Analysis of the Ninth Air Force in the European Theater of Operations*, ed. Richard H. Kohn and Joseph P. Harahan (Washington, DC: Office of Air Force History, US Air Force, 1984), 75.

10. Maj. Michael C. Chester to Lt. Gen. James M. Gavin, letter, March 30, 1959.

11. Michael N. Ingrisano Jr., *Valor Without Arms* (Bennington, VT: Mirriam Press, 2001), 48.

12. *Luftlande*, or air-landed, troops were transported in troop carrier aircraft or gliders that landed at their destinations.

13. ULTRA Intelligence, quoted in Young, *Into the Valley*, 108.

14. Bradley, *A Soldier's Story*, 235.

## CHAPTER 21: THE EVE OF BATTLE

1. Cornelius Ryan, *The Longest Day* (New York: Pocket Books, 1984), 98.

2. Christopher J. Anderson Jr., "Screaming Eagles at Pointe-du-Hoc," *WWII History*, July 2001, 35.

3. Roger Airgood, transcript of oral history, October 24, 1992, courtesy of Randolph Hils, 440th Troop Carrier Group Association.

4. Otis L. Sampson, "June 6 1944," in Box 11 of the James M. Gavin Papers, US Army Heritage and Education Center, Carlisle Barracks, PA.

5. Captain Bob Piper, quoted in Charles H. Young, *Into the Valley*, ed. Charles D. Young (Dallas: PrintComm, Inc., 1995), 129.

6. Minutes of the 82nd Airborne Division on the topic of Debriefing Conference—Operation Neptune, August 13, 1944, in Box 11 of the James M. Gavin Papers, US Army Heritage and Education Center, Carlisle Barracks, PA.

7. Gerald C. Berry, transcript of oral history interview by Col. Joseph T. Molyson, USAFR (Ret.), April 28, 2003.

8. Quoted in Stephen E. Ambrose, *Band of Brothers* (New York: Simon & Schuster, Inc., 1992), 65.

## CHAPTER 22: THE APPROACH

1. The term "C-47" will include both the double-door C-47 and the single-door C-53. The C-53 was a close match for the C-47 other than the door arrangement.

2. David R. Berry to Joseph Molyson, subject: chapter 11 feedback, June 13, 2003.

3. *Utah Beach to Cherbourg*, American Forces in Action Series (Washington, DC: Center of Military History United States Army, 1990), 14; Charles Young to Joseph Molyson, subject: chapter 11 feedback, June 9, 2003.

4. Map prepared from 50th Field Order Number 1 NEPTUNE (Bigot), June 2, 1944, in the Michael N. Ingrisano Jr. Collection; Wesley Frank Craven and James Lea Cate, *Europe:*

*Argument to V-E Day, January 1944 to May 1945,* The Army Air Forces in World War II, vol. 3 (1949; new imprint, Washington, DC: Office of Air Force History, United States Air Force, 1983), 187; *The Battle of Normandy (Michelin Map 102)* (1947; new imprint, Paris: Michelin, 1993); Bill Brinson quoted in Lew Johnston, "The Troop Carrier D-Day Flights," 2002, in 61st Troop Carrier Squadron Collection, 8; Philippe Esvelin, *D-Day Gliders* (Bayeaux, France: Heimdal, 2001), 80, 135; "Fulbeck," RAF History, n.d., n.p., online, May 15, 2003, available from http://www.raf.mod.uk/bombercommand/stations/s72.html.

5. William L. Brinson, *Airborne Troop Carrier Three-One-Five Group* (New Orleans: Walka, 2003), i.

6. Wesley Frank Craven and James Lea Cate, *Europe: Argument to V-E Day, January 1944 to May 1945,* The Army Air Forces in World War II, vol. 3, 186–88; Randolph Hils to Lt. Gen. E. M. Flanagan, USA (Ret.), subject: An Open Letter to the Airborne Community on the History of Operation NEPTUNE, June 6, 1944 (January 17, 2003).

7. "1944," RAF History, n.d., n.p., online, November 13, 2001, available from http://www.raf.mod.uk/history/line1944.html.

8. Ibid.

9. 50th TCW Field Order Number 1 NEPTUNE (Bigot), June 2 1944.

10. Roger Airgood, transcript of oral history, October 24, 1992, courtesy of Randolph Hils, 440th Troop Carrier Group Association.

11. Leonard Luck to Joseph Molyson, "chapter 11 feedback," June 13, 2003.

## CHAPTER 23: OVER THE COTENTIN

1. Martin Wolfe, *Green Light* (Washington, DC: Center for Air Force History, US Air Force, 1992), 83.

2. Colonel Vito Pedone, "The Truth About D-Day," presentation to the Troop Carrier Reunion 2003, Sheraton Hotel and Conference Center, Dover, Delaware, April 29, 2003.

3. David R. Berry to Randolph Hils, subject: Pathfinders/DZ D, June 11, 2003.

4. John C. Warren, *Airborne Operations in World War II, European Theater*. USAF Historical Study 97 (Maxwell AFB, AL: Research Studies Institute, 1956), 32–33.

5. Ibid.

6. Maj. Michael C. Chester to Lt. Gen. James M. Gavin, letter, March 30, 1959, in Box 11 of the James M. Gavin Papers, US Army Heritage and Education Center, Carlisle Barracks, PA.

7. Minutes of the 82nd Airborne Division on the topic of Debriefing Conference—Operation Neptune, August 13, 1944, in Box 11 of the James M. Gavin Papers, US Army Heritage and Education Center, Carlisle Barracks, PA.

8. James M. Gavin, *On To Berlin, Battles of an Airborne Commander 1943–1946* (New York: Viking, 1978), 104.

9. Minutes of the 82nd Airborne Division on the topic of Debriefing Conference—Operation Neptune, August 13 1944.

10. "Invasion of France," *Impact Book 4, July 1944, May–August 1944*, ed. James Parton (Harrisburg, PA: National Historical Society, 1980), 7.

11. Adapted from *Utah Beach to Cherbourg,* American Forces in Action Series (Washington, DC: Center of Military History United States Army, 1990), Maps No. II, IV, and V.

12. Gerald C. Berry, transcript of oral history interview by Col. Joseph T. Molyson, USAFR (Ret.), April 28, 2003.

13. Ibid.

14. Gerald C. Berry, April 28, 2003.

15. David R. Berry, June 11, 2003.

16. Navigator Captain Robert Stubblefield, quoted in Brinson, *Airborne Troop Carrier Three-One-Five Group*, 110.

17. Ibid.; Stephen E. Ambrose, *Band of Brothers* (New York: Simon & Schuster, 2001).

18. "EUREKA," *The Oxford Companion to WWII*, ed. I. C. B. Dear and M. R. D. Foot (New York: Oxford University Press, 2001), 267.

19. Ben Kendig, pilot leading the 44th Troop Carrier Squadron, 316th Troop Carrier Group, unpublished comments, April 28, 2003.

20. Minutes of the 82nd Airborne Division on the topic of Debriefing Conference—Operation Neptune, August 13, 1944.

21. Hugo B. Olson to Lt. Gen. James M. Gavin, March 30 1959, in Box 11 of the James M. Gavin Papers, US Army Heritage and Education Center, Carlisle Barracks, PA.

22. Minutes of the 82nd Airborne Division on the topic of Debriefing Conference—Operation Neptune, August 13 1944.

23. Lt. Col. S. L. A. Marshall, History Branch G-2 War Department, "Reports on Operation NEPTUNE," n.d., in Box 11 of the James M. Gavin Papers, US Army Heritage and Education Center, Carlisle Barracks, PA.

24. Pilot Lt. Col. Robert Gibbons, quoted in Brinson, *Airborne Troop Carrier Three-One-Five Group*, 100.

25. Pilot Capt. Julius H. Peterson, quoted in Brinson, *Airborne Troop Carrier Three-One-Five Group*, 106.

## CHAPTER 24: SHOT UP AND SHOT DOWN

1. Charles Young to Joseph Molyson, subject: chapter 11 feedback, June 9, 2003.

2. Roger Airgood, transcript of oral history, October 24, 1992, courtesy of Randolph Hils, 440th Troop Carrier Group Association.

3. Annotations from Gordon A. Harrison, *Cross-Channel Attack*, United States Army in World War II, European Theater (Washington, DC: Center of Military History United States Army, 1989), Map VII (attached); *Utah Beach to Cherbourg*, American Forces in Action Series (Washington, DC: Center of Military History United States Army, 1990), Map VII (attached).

4. Capt. Harrison Boesch, 62nd Troop Carrier Squadron, "314th Troop Carrier Group Mission Report," June 6, 1944, in Box 11 of the James M. Gavin Papers, US Army Heritage and Education Center, Carlisle Barracks, PA.

5. Christopher J. Anderson Jr., "Screaming Eagles at Pointe-du-Hoc," *WWII History*, July 2001, 34–40.

6. Charles Bortzfield to Joseph Molyson, letter, undated, n.d., June 2003.

7. Charles Bortzfield, transcript of oral history interview by Col. Joseph T. Molyson, USAFR (Ret.), April 28, 2003.

8. Roger Airgood in Lew Johnston, "The Troop Carrier D-Day Flights," 2002, in 61st Troop Carrier Squadron Collection, n.p.

9. Charles H. Young, *Into the Valley*, ed. Charles D. Young (Dallas: PrintComm, Inc., 1995), 110.

## CHAPTER 25: GLIDERS

1. Charles H. Young, *Into the Valley*, ed. Charles D. Young (Dallas: PrintComm, Inc., 1995), 111.

2. Philippe Esvelin, *D-Day Gliders* (Bayeaux, France: Heimdal, 2001), 89.

3. 1Lt. Neal Beaver, quoted in Lew Johnston, "The Troop Carrier D-Day Flights," 2002, in 61st Troop Carrier Squadron Collection, 48.

4. *Utah Beach to Cherbourg*, American Forces in Action Series (Washington, DC: Center of Military History United States Army, 1990), 14–15.

5. Kenn C. Rust, *The 9th Air Force in World War II* (Fallbrook, CA: Aero Publishers, 1970), 76–77.

6. *DZ Europe 440th Troop Carrier Group, 1945*, 43–44.

7. *Utah Beach to Cherbourg*, 15–16.

8. Department of Defense, "D-Day Facts," June 6, 1984, in Box 11 of the James M. Gavin Papers, US Army Heritage and Education Center, Carlisle Barracks, PA.

9. Kenn C. Rust, *The 9th Air Force in World War II* (Fallbrook, CA: Aero Publishers, 1970), 78.

10. Maj. Gen. M. B. Ridgway, "82nd Airborne Division—Operation NEPTUNE," 82nd Airborne Division, July 26, 1944. Box 11 of the James M. Gavin Papers. US Army Heritage and Education Center, Carlisle Barracks, PA.

## CHAPTER 26: THE PARAS

1. Neil Barber, *The Day the Devils Dropped In* (Barnsley, South Yorkshire, UK: Leo Cooper, 2002), 9.

2. John C. Warren, *Airborne Operations in World War II, European Theater*, USAF Historical Study 97 (Maxwell AFB, AL: Research Studies Institute, 1956), 13.

3. Alexander Morrison, *Silent Invader* (London: Airlife Publishing, 2002), 22.

4. Quoted in Kevin Shannon and Stephen Wright, *One Night in June* (London: Airlife Publishing, Ltd., 2002), 12.

5. Quoted in Morrison, *Silent Invader*, 15.

6. Quoted in Shannon and Wright, *One Night in June*, 31.

7. Richard Townshend Bickers, *Air War Normandy* (London: Leo Cooper, 1994), xiv.

8. Shannon and Wright, *One Night in June*, 18.

9. Barber, *The Day the Devils Dropped In*, 24.

10. Gregor Ferguson and Kevin Lyles, *The Paras 1940–1944*, Osprey Elite Series vol. 21, ed. Martin Windrow (London: Osprey Books, 1984), 15–16.

11. Warren, *Airborne Operations in World War II, European Theater*, 79.

12. Quoted in Shannon and Wright, *One Night in June*, 57.

13. Barber, *The Day the Devils Dropped In*, 44.

14. Stephen E. Ambrose, *D-Day June 6, 1944: The Climactic Battle of WWII* (London: Simon & Schuster UK Ltd., 1994), 28.

15. Morrison, *Silent Invader*, 31.

16. R. W. Thompson, *D-Day Spearhead of Invasion* (New York: Ballantine Books, Inc., 1968), 122–23.

# CHAPTER 27: DEADSTICK

1. Ronald J. Drez, "Forgotten Fate of Glider Four," *World War II*, July 2003, 46

2. Stephen E. Ambrose, *D-Day, June 6, 1944: The Climactic Battle of WWII* (London: Simon & Schuster UK Ltd., 1994), 78.

3. Ibid., 19.

4. Stephen E. Ambrose, *Pegasus Bridge, June 6, 1944* (New York: Simon & Schuster, 1985), 91; Milton Dank, *The Glider Gang* (Bennington VT: Merriam Press, 2003), 77–78, 91; Roger Cirillo and Stephen Badsey, "D-Day," *D-Day Operation Overlord*, ed. Bernard Nalty (New York: Salamander Books, 1999), 99–100.

5. Ken Ford, *D-Day 1944 (3) Sword Beach and the Airborne Landings*, Osprey Campaign Series, vol. 105, ed. Lee Johnson (Oxford, UK: Osprey Publishing, Ltd., 2002), 32

6. Julian Thompson, *The Imperial War Museum Book of Victory in Europe* (London: Sidgwick & Jackson, Ltd., 1994), 35.

7. Sgt. James Wallwork, in a conversation with Maj. Joseph T. Molyson, USAFR, May 7, 1985.

8. Carl Shilleto, *Pegasus Bridge & Merville Battery* (Conshohocken, PA: Combined Publishing, 1999), 47–48.

9. Maj. John Howard, in a conversation with Maj. Joseph T. Molyson, USAFR, May 7, 1985.

10. Ambrose, *D-Day, June 6, 1944: The Climactic Battle of WWII*, 89–90.

11. Drez, "Forgotten Fate of Glider Four," 51, 88.

12. Stephen Chicken, *Overlord Coastline* (New York: Hippocrene Books, Inc., 1993), 86.

13. Col. Hans Von Luck, *Panzer Commander* (New York: Dell Publishing, 1989), 174.

14. Col. Hans Von Luck, in an interview by Maj. Joseph T. Molyson, USAFR, May 7, 1985.

# CHAPTER 28: MERVILLE BATTERY

1. Robin Higham, "Technology and D-Day," *D-Day The Normandy Invasion in Retrospect*, Eisenhower Foundation (Lawrence, KS: The University of Kansas Press, 1971), 228.

2. Col. Terance Otway, quoted in Neil Barber, *The Day the Devils Dropped In* (Barnsley, South Yorkshire, UK: Leo Cooper, 2002), 25; Kevin Shannon and Stephen Wright, *One Night in June* (London: Airlife Publishing, Ltd., 2002), 28.

3. Stephen Chicken, *Overlord Coastline* (New York: Hippocrene Books, Inc., 1993), 90–91.

4. Carl Shilleto, *Pegasus Bridge & Merville Battery* (Conshohocken, PA: Combined Publishing, 1999), 77–85.

5. Ibid., 88.

6. Lt. Col. Terance Otway, quoted in Neil Barber, *The Day the Devils Dropped In* (Barnsley, South Yorkshire, UK: Leo Cooper, 2002), 64.

7. Barber, *The Day the Devils Dropped In*, 66.

8. Quoted in Shilleto, *Pegasus Bridge & Merville Battery*, 93.

9. Barber, *The Day the Devils Dropped In*, 80.

10. Kevin Shannon and Stephen Wright, *One Night in June* (London: Airlife Publishing, Ltd., 2002), 88–89; Shilleto, *Pegasus Bridge & Merville Battery*, 96–97.

11. Chicken, *Overlord Coastline*, 93.

12. Shannon and Wright, *One Night in June*, 90.

13. Ibid., 91.

14. Shilleto, *Pegasus Bridge & Merville Battery*, 94–103.
15. Chicken, *Overlord Coastline*, 92.
16. Shilleto, *Pegasus Bridge & Merville Battery*, 102–04.

## CHAPTER 29: RED DEVIL TENACITY

1. John C. Warren, *Airborne Operations in World War II, European Theater*, USAF Historical Study 97 (Maxwell AFB, AL: Research Studies Institute, 1956), 79.

2. Kevin Shannon and Stephen Wright, *One Night in June* (London: Airlife Publishing, Ltd., 2002), 32.

3. Ibid., 32.

4. Carl Shilleto, *Pegasus Bridge & Merville Battery* (Conshohocken, PA: Combined Publishing, 1999), 69.

5. Friedrich Rüge, "Notes on German Naval Ops on D-Day," *D-Day: The Normandy Invasion in Retrospect* (Lawrence, KS: The University of Kansas Press, 1971), 165.

6. Stephen E. Ambrose, *D-Day June 6, 1944: The Climactic Battle of WWII* (London: Simon & Schuster UK Ltd., 1994), 136.

7. Ibid., 143–144.

8. Ibid., 147.

9. Charles D. Young, "From Sebkra d'Oran to the Rhine River Crossing," *Into the Valley*, n.d., n.p., on-line, March 4, 2003, available from http://www.usaaftroopcarrier.com/Historical per cent20Overview.htm.

10. Department of Defense, "D-Day Facts," June 6 1984, in Box 11 of the James M. Gavin Papers, US Army Heritage and Education Center, Carlisle Barracks, PA.

11. Nicolaus Von Below, *At Hitler's Side*, trans. Geoffrey Brooks (London: Greenhill Books, 2001), 202.

## CHAPTER 30: THE SKY ABOVE

1. Omar N. Bradley, *A Soldier's Story* (New York: Henry Holt and Company, 1951), 114.

2. John Terraine, *The Right of the Line: the Royal Air Force in the European War, 1939–1945* (London: Hodder and Stoughton, Ltd., 1985), 565–66.

3. Ibid., 564–65.

4. Alfred Goldberg, "Air Campaign OVERLORD: To D-Day," *D-Day: The Normandy Invasion in Retrospect*, 60–61; Allied Expeditionary Air Force, "Annex K Sketch Map 4 GAF: Fighter Control System" to "Operation Neptune Overall Air Plan," AEAF/TS399/Air Plans, 15 April 1944; *Air Interdiction World War II, Korea, and Vietnam*, ed. Richard H. Kohn and Joseph P. Harahan (Washington, DC: Office of Air Force History, US Air Force, 1986), 25; Allied Expeditionary Air Force, "Annex K Sketch Map 2 Principal Airfields within 100 & 130 Miles of Caen" to "Operation Neptune Overall Air Plan," AEAF/TS399/Air Plans, 15 April 1944, in WWII Combat Operations REPORTS 1942–1946, Records Group 18, National Records and Archives Administration Archive II, College Park, MD.

5. Richard Townshend Bickers, *Air War Normandy* (London: Leo Cooper, 1994), 71–72.

6. Alfred Price, "The Air Battle," *D-Day Operation Overlord*, 131.

7. Michael Armitage, "Convoy Cover," *The D-Day Encyclopedia*, ed. David G. Chandler and James Lawton Collins (New York: Simon & Schuster, 1994), 169.

8. A "roadstead" or "anchorage" is a sheltered area for ships in which the vessels can ride at anchor.

9. BG Edward B. Giller, USAF, quoted in Martin Caidin, *Forked-Tailed Devil: The P-38* (New York: ibooks, inc., 2001), 151.

10. Armitage, "Convoy Cover," *The D-Day Encyclopedia*, 1994, 169.

11. Eric J. Grove, "Air Defense Ships," *The D-Day Encyclopedia*, ed. David G. Chandler and James Lawton Collins (New York: Simon & Schuster, 1994), 23.

12. "Air's Tasks on D-Day in the Normandy Invasion Formed a Pattern of Enormous Complexity," *Impact Book 7, May 1945, May–July 1945*, ed. James Parton (Harrisburg, PA: National Historical Society, 1980), 23.

13. Fighter pilot Bill O'Brien, quoted in Lew Johnston, "The Troop Carrier D-Day Flights," 2002, in 61st Troop Carrier Squadron Collection, 72.

14. Alfred Price, "The Air Battle," *D-Day Operation Overlord*, 134.

15. "COSSAC" is the acronym for Chief of Staff, Supreme Allied Commander. This was the Title of Major General Morgan, in charge of planning for OVERLORD-NEPTUNE.

16. Chief of Staff to the Supreme Allied Commander, "Requirements for a Tactical Air Force," COSSAC Study No. 2, undated 1943, in File 505.13-3, Albert F. Simpson Historical Research Center, Air University, Maxwell AFB, AL.

17. David Stafford, *Ten Days to D-Day* (London: Little, Brown, 2003), 303–04.

## CHAPTER 31: THE *LUFTWAFFE*'S LONGEST DAY

1. Lt. Col. William R. Dunn, transcript of US Air Force oral history interview by Maj. Gilmartin and Captains Porter and High, 2 November 73, in File K239.0512-922, Albert F. Simpson Historical Research Center, Air University, Maxwell AFB, AL.

2. Alfred Goldberg, "Air Campaign OVERLORD: To D-Day," *D-Day: The Normandy Invasion in Retrospect*, ed. the Eisenhower Foundation (Lawrence, KS: The University of Kansas Press, 1971), 70.

3. Allied Expeditionary Air Force, "Annex K: Sketch Map 4 GAF: Fighter Control System" to "Operation Neptune Overall Air Plan," AEAF/TS399/Air Plans, 15 April 1944, in WWII Combat Operations Reports 1942–1946, Records Group 18, National Records and Archives Administration Archive II, College Park, MD.

4. Paul Carell, *Invasion—They're Coming*, trans. Ewald Osers (New York: E. P. Dutton & Co, 1963), 55.

5. Carell, *Invasion—They're Coming*, 75.

6. Maurice Mayston, "Sound: 485 Squadron in action on D-Day" (oral history transcript), *New Zealand History*, accessed January 27, 2025, https://nzhistory.govt.nz/media/sound/485-squadron-in-action-on-D-Day (Manatū Taonga—Ministry for Culture and Heritage), updated 1 May 2020; Richard Townshend Bickers, *Air War Normandy* (London: Leo Cooper, 1994), 49.

7. Bickers, *Air War Normandy*, 49.

8. Allied Expeditionary Air Force, "Annex K: Sketch Map 4 GAF: Fighter Control System" to "Operation Neptune Overall Air Plan," AEAF/TS399/Air Plans, 15 April 1944, in WWII Combat Operations Reports 1942–1946, Records Group 18, National Records and Archives Administration Archive II, College Park, MD; Humphrey Wynn and Susan Young,

*Prelude to Overlord* (Novato, CA: Presidio Press, 1983), 47; Alfred Price, "The Air Battle," *D-Day: Operation Overlord*, ed. Bernard Nalty (New York: Salamander Books, 1999), 140.

9. Tony Wood and Bill Gunston, *Hitler's Luftwaffe* (London: Salamander Books, 1997), 108.

10. German term for fighter ace.

11. Donald L. Caldwell, *Top Guns of the Luftwaffe* (New York: Ivy Books, 1991), 230.

12. James H. Kitchens III, PhD, "The *Luftwaffe* and D-Day," Lecture to the Ninth AF Conference "D-Day Remembered," University of New Orleans, New Orleans, LA, April 30, 1994.

13. Alfred Price, "The Air Battle," *D-Day Operation Overlord*, 139.

## CHAPTER 32: IMMINENT DANGER—WEST

1. Alfred Price, "The Air Battle," *D-Day: Operation Overlord*, ed. Bernard Nalty (New York: Salamander Books, 1999), 134.

2. Paul Carell, *Invasion—They're Coming*, trans. Ewald Osers (New York: E.P. Dutton & Co, 1963), 22.

3. Wood, W. J. A. (ed.), Defence of the Reich (*Reichsverteidigung*), 3 June 1944. Translation of Enemy Documents. RAF Air Historical Branch (AHB) 6, copied May 1963.

4. Alfred Price, "Third Air Force," *The D-Day Encyclopedia*, ed. David G. Chandler and James Lawton Collins (New York: Simon & Schuster, 1994), 549.

5. James H. Kitchens III, PhD, "The *Luftwaffe* and D-Day," Lecture to the Ninth AF Conference "D-Day Remembered," University of New Orleans, New Orleans, LA, April 30, 1994; General der Flieger Adolph Galland, *The First and the Last* (Cutchogue, NY: Buccaneer Books, 1997), 211.

6. General der Flieger Adolph Galland, *The First and the Last* (Cutchogue, NY: Buccaneer Books, 1997), 214–15.

7. Galland, *The First and the Last*, 215; Lt. Col. Maris McCrabb, "Drohende Gefahr West—The Pre-Normandy Air Campaign," *Airpower Journal* (Summer 1994), n.p., online, April 11 2000, available from http://www.airpower.maxwell.af.mil/airchronicles/apj/apj94/mccrabb2.html.

8. Originally scheduled for Le Flers airfield, 60 miles closer to the landing beaches.

9. Alfred Price, "The Air Battle," 134, 140.

10. Ibid., 141.

11. *Waffen SS Generaloberst* Paul Hausser, who Hitler ordered to replace *Generaloberst* Friedrich Dollmann on June 28, 1944, as commander of *7th Armée*. Various sources attribute Dollmann's death to a heart attack or suicide.

12. Paul Hausser, *Normandy—Seventh Army 29 Jun–24 Jul 44*, MS #A-974, trans. A. Rosenwald, Historical Division, HQ US Army Europe, Feb. 25, 1946, 14–16, Foreign Military Studies Branch, RG 338, NARA, College Park, MD.

13. Price, "Third Air Force," 548.

14. Alfred Price, "IX Air Corps," *The D-Day Encyclopedia*, ed. David G. Chandler and James Lawton Collins (New York: Simon & Schuster, 1994), 391.

15. Dr. John Pimlott, *Luftwaffe* (Osceola, WI: Motorbooks International Publishers & Wholesalers, 1998), 148.

16. Price, "The Air Battle," 136.
17. Ibid.
18. Janusz Piekalkiewicz, *The Air War: 1939–1945*, trans. Jan van Huerck (Harrisburg, PA: Historical Times, Inc., 1985), 352.
19. Gordon Smith, "Campaign Summaries of World War 2—Amphibious Operations, Part 2 of 2 1944–45," Military and Naval Campaign Summaries of World War 2, n.d., n.p., online, August 5, 2002, available from http://www.naval-history.net/WW2Campaigns Amphibious2.htm.
20. Alfred Price, "X Air Corps," *The D-Day Encyclopedia*, ed. David G. Chandler and James Lawton Collins (New York: Simon & Schuster, 1994), 546.
21. Kitchens, "The *Luftwaffe* and D-Day," April 30, 1994.
22. Robert Forsyth, *Mistel German Composite Aircraft and Operations 1942–1945* (Norwalk, CT: Airtime Publishing, Inc., 2001), 102–05.
23. Price, "The Air Battle," 144.
24. Richard R. Muller, "German Aircraft," *The D-Day Encyclopedia*, ed. David G. Chandler and James Lawton Collins (New York: Simon & Schuster, 1994), 21.
25. Samuel Eliot Morison, *The Two-Ocean War*, 408; Price, "The Air Battle," *D-Day Operation Overlord*, 143.

## CHAPTER 33: BOMBERS ABOVE THE CLOUDS

1. Quoted in Walt W. Rostow, *Pre-Invasion Bombing Strategy: General Eisenhower's Decision of March 25, 1944* (Austin, TX: University of Texas Press, 1981), 48–49. The term "Command Bombing Force" referred to the heavy bombers of the US Eighth Air Force and the RAF Bomber Command.
2. Price, "The Air Battle," *D-Day Operation Overlord*, 130.
3. Galland, *The First and the Last*, 210–211.
4. Stephen A. Bourque, *D-Day 1944: The deadly failure of Allied heavy bombing on June 6*, Osprey Air Campaign Series, vol. 28 (Oxford, UK: Osprey Publishing Ltd., 2022), 35.
5. "Invasion of France," *Impact Book 4, July 1944, May–August 1944*, ed. James Parton (Harrisburg, PA: National Historical Society, 1980), 2.
6. Price, "The Air Battle," *D-Day Operation Overlord*, 131.
7. Wesley Frank Craven and James Lea Cate, *Europe: Argument to V-E Day, January 1944 to May 1945*, The Army Air Forces in World War II, vol. 3 (Washington, DC: Office of Air Force History, US Air Force, 1983), map page 191.
8. Stephen Darlow, *D-Day Bombers: The Veterans' Story* (London: Grub Street, 2004), 148.
9. Denis Richards and Hilary St. George Saunders, *Royal Air Force 1939–1945—Volume III: The Fight Is Won.* (London: HMSO, 1993), 110.
10. Price, "The Air Battle," *D-Day Operation Overlord*, 133.
11. "Air's Tasks on D-Day in the Normandy Invasion Formed a Pattern of Enormous Complexity," *Impact Book 7, May 1945, May–July 1945*, ed. James Parton (Harrisburg, PA: National Historical Society, 1980), 23.
12. Davis, "Carl Spaatz and D-Day," *Airpower Journal* (Winter 1997).
13. McCrabb, "*Drohende Gefahr West*—The Pre-Normandy Air Campaign," *Airpower Journal* (Summer 1994).

14. Quoted in Edward H. Castens, *The Story of the 446th Bomb Group*, unpaginated, accessed August 23, 2023, digicom.bpl.lib.me.us/ww_reg_his/110/, digitized by Bangor Community Digital Commons, Bangor Public Library.

15. Price, "The Air Battle," *D-Day Operation Overlord*, 134.

16. John W. Holland, *D-Day Attack by the 8th Air Force* (Carthage, TX: Complete Printing & Publishing, 2000), 5–6.

17. Castens, *The Story of the 446th Bomb Group*.

18. Gen. James H. Doolittle, *I Could Never Be So Lucky Again* (New York: Bantam Books, 1992), 373.

19. Richard G. Davis, "Eighth Air Force," *The D-Day Encyclopedia*, ed. David G. Chandler and James Lawton Collins (New York: Simon & Schuster, 1994), 197; Bradley, *A Soldier's Story*, 268.

20. Carell, *Invasion—They're Coming*, 79.

21. Darlow, *D-Day Bombers: The Veterans' Story*, 125–26.

22. John C. Reilly Jr., "Close Gunfire Support," *The D-Day Encyclopedia*, ed. David G. Chandler and James Lawton Collins (New York: Simon & Schuster, 1994), 156–57.

## CHAPTER 34: UNDER THE CLOUDS

1. Delve, *D-Day: The Air Battle*, 99–95.

2. "To the Shore: The Ride of the 21st Panzer Division," The Reception: The Germans on D-Day, the National WWII Museum, accessed October 23, 2024, https://www.nationalww2 museum.org/war/articles/reception-Germans-D-Day.

3. *Lehr* means "training" in German, and originally the *Panzer Lehr* Division had that function. While in France, it had been upgraded with both troops and equipment and in June 1944 was one of the most power tank divisions in the regular German Army.

4. Thomas Alexander Hughes, *Overlord General Pete Quesada and the Triumph of Tactical Air Power in World War II* (New York: The Free Press, 1995), 12.

5. Delve, *D-Day: The Air Battle*, 98–99.

6. Jean-Bernard Frappé, *Luftwaffe Face au Debarquement Allie 6 juin au 31 août 1944* (The Luftwaffe-Opposing the Allied Landings June 6th to August 31, 1944) (Bayeaux, France: Editions Heimdal, 1999), 302.

7. Delve, *D-Day: The Air Battle*, 101–02.

8. McCrabb, "Drohende Gefahr West—The Pre-Normandy Air Campaign," *Airpower Journal* (Summer 1994); Strategic Intelligence Branch, G-2 European Theater of Operations (US Army), "An Evaluation of the Effects of the Bomber Offensive on 'Overlord' and 'Dragoon'," 1944, in 519.553-2, Albert F. Simpson Historical Research Center, Air University, Maxwell AFB, AL.

9. Delve, *D-Day: The Air Battle*, 102.

## CHAPTER 35: WHEN SEAGULLS BECAME EAGLES

1. Morison, *The Two-Ocean War*, 405–06.

2. Chief of Staff to Naval Commander Expeditionary Force, "Provision of Spotting Aircraft—Progress Report," X/0927/8b, 4 November 1943, in COS File 373.14/1, Records Group 331, National Records and Archives Administration Archive II, College Park, MD.

3. Cdr. Elmo L. Moss, USN (Ret.), "Brown Shoes and Wild Horses," *Naval Aviation News* 76, no. 6 (September–October 1994): 26.

4. Steven D. Hill, "Invasion! Fortress Europe," *Naval Aviation News* 76, no. 4 (May–June 1994): 31–35.

5. The ex-RAF Spitfires had been in service for several years.

6. Paul A. Ludwig and Lt. Bruce Carmichael, USNR (Ret.), "The U.S. Navy Spitfires of VCS-7," *Foundation* (Fall 1999): 80–93.

7. Morison, *The Invasion of France and Germany 1944–1945*, 104–05.

8. David Brown, "Air Spotting Pools," *The D-Day Encyclopedia*, ed. David G. Chandler and James Lawton Collins (New York: Simon & Schuster, 1994), 31.

9. Commander Peter Mersky, "Naval Aviators in Spitfires," *Proceedings* (December 1996), 106.

10. Hill, "Invasion! Fortress Europe," *Naval Aviation News* 76, 33.

11. Price, "The Air Battle," *D-Day Operation Overlord*, 134.

12. Brown, "Air Spotting Pools," *The D-Day Encyclopedia*, 31.

13. Quoted in Malcolm Laird, *D-Day to Victory! Fighters in Europe 1944–45* (Wellington, New Zealand: Ventura Publishing, ca. 2000), 6.

14. Carell, *Invasion—They're Coming*, 199–221; and Morison, *The Two-Ocean War*, 409–11.

15. Mersky, "Naval Aviators in Spitfires," *Proceedings*, 105–06.

## CHAPTER 36: AIR LANDING GROUNDS

1. "Service marks 65th anniversary of Christchurch air disaster," *Daily Echo*, June 21,2009, accessed November 4, 2024, https://www.bournemouthecho.co.uk/news/4449798 .service-marks-65th-anniversary-of-christchurch-air-disaster/; Aviation Safety Network, Flight Safety Foundation, undated, accessed November 4, 2024, https://asn.flightsafety.org /wikibase/116502.

2. 1Lt. John Drummond, oral history, January 22, 2003.

3. Wesley Frank Craven and James Lea Cate, *Europe: Argument to V-E Day, January 1944 to May 1945*, The Army Air Forces in World War II, vol. 3, 117–18; Bickers, *Air War Normandy*, 61–63.

4. Michael Swift and Michael Sharpe, Historical Maps of World War II Europe (London: PRC Publishing Ltd, 2000), 94–95; "USAAF Advance Landing Ground A-1 St.-Pierre-du-Mont/St.-Laurent-sur-Mer, France," *Skylighters—The Story of the 225th AAA Battalion from Omaha Beach to V-E Day*, n.d., n.p., online, July 11 2003, available from http://www.skylight ers.org/history/airfields/alga1.html; John M. Collins, *Military Geography* (Washington, DC: Brassey's, 1998), 362–63; *France Tourist and Motoring Atlas*, Scale 1:200,000 (Greenville, SC: Michelin Travel Publications, 1999), Plates 14–15; *Omaha Beachhead* (6 June–13 June 1944), American Forces in Action Series (Washington, DC: Center of Military History United States Army, 1990), Map II (attached).

5. "The Days after D-Day," *Impact Book 5, July 1944, May–August 1944*, ed. James Parton (Harrisburg, PA: National Historical Society, 1980), 22–23; "The Invasion and the Days that Followed," *Impact Book 7, May 1945, May–July 1945*, ed. James Parton (Harrisburg, PA: National Historical Society, 1980), 25.

6. "New Strip in Normandy viewed from air," *Impact Book 4, August 1944, May–August 1944*, ed. James Parton (Harrisburg, PA: National Historical Society, 1980), 40.

7. "Airfield Construction Branch History," Royal Air Force Airfield Construction Officers' Association, n.d., n.p., online, July 15 2003, available from http://www.rafacoa.freeserve.co.uk/branch.htm.

8. Carell, *Invasion—They're Coming*, 98.

9. Swift and Sharpe, Historical Maps of World War II Europe, 94–95; "USAAF Advance Landing Ground A-1 St.-Pierre-du-Mont/St.-Laurent-sur-Mer, France," Skylighters—The Story of the 225th AAA Battalion from Omaha Beach to V-E Day; Collins, *Military Geography*, 362–63; *France Tourist and Motoring Atlas*, Plates 14–15. Based on Historical Division War Department American Forces in Action Series, Omaha Beachhead (6 June–13 June 1944), Map XII (attached).

10. Richard P. Hallion, *D–Day 1944: Air Power Over the Normandy Beaches and Beyond*, The U.S. Army Air Forces in World War II (Washington, DC: Air Force History and Museums Program, 1994), 6.

11. Dr. Ronald B. Hartzer, "Foundation for the Future: A History of Air Force Civil Engineers," Air Force Civil Engineering Support Agency, n.d., n.p., online, July 11, 2003, available from http://www.afcesa.af.mil/Directorate/ES/History/cehist.html.

12. Price, "The Air Battle," *D–Day Operation Overlord*, 130.

13. Ambrose, *The Supreme Commander*, 151.

14. David C. Johnson, *U.S. Army Air Forces Continental Airfields (ETO) D–Day to V-E Day* (Maxwell AFB, AL: Research Studies Institute, 1988), 5–6.

15. Hughes, *Overlord: General Pete Quesada and the Triumph of Tactical Air Power in World War II*, 248.

16. Craven and Cate, *Europe: Argument to V-E Day, January 1944 to May 1945*, 132.

17. Ibid., 132.

18. Ibid., 132.

19. Galland, *The First and the Last*, 216–17.

## CHAPTER 37: FORWARD INTO FRANCE

1. Wesley Frank Craven and James Lea Cate, *Europe: Argument to V-E Day, January 1944 to May 1945*, The Army Air Forces in World War II, vol. 3 (1949; new imprint, Washington, DC: Office of Air Force History, US Air Force, 1983), 194; Delve, *D–Day: The Air Battle*, 93–94.

2. After the First Canadian Army was established in July, the existing RAF 84 Group was assigned as its air support organization. 84 Group units were already operating over France under 83 Group control. After the US Third Army was established in August, the XIX TAC was assigned as its air support organization. Its units were already operating under IX TAC control.

3. Chris Thomas, *Typhoon and Tempest Aces of World War 2*, Osprey Aircraft of the Aces, vol. 27, ed. Tony Holmes (Oxford, UK: Osprey Books, 1999), 7–30.

4. John Terraine, *The Right of the Line: the Royal Air Force in the European War, 1939–1945* (London: Hodder and Stoughton, Ltd., 1985), 606.

5. Giller, quoted in Caidin, *Forked-Tailed Devil: The P-38*, 153.

6. Gen. Dwight D. Eisenhower, *Crusade in Europe* (Baltimore, MD: The Johns Hopkins University Press, 1997), 140–43

7. Walter J. Boyne, *Clash of Wings World War II in the Air* (New York: Touchstone, 1997), 187–88.

8. Winston S. Churchill, *Triumph and Tragedy*, The Second World War, vol. VI. (Boston: Mariner Books, 1985), 40.

## CHAPTER 38: DEATH BY *JABO*

1. Carell, *Invasion—They're Coming*, 128–29.

2. Based on Gordon A. Harrison, *Cross-Channel Attack*, United States Army in World War II, European Theater (Washington, DC: Center of Military History United States Army, 1989), Map XIII (attached).

3. General Chuck Yeager and Leo Janos, *Yeager* (New York: Bantam Books, 1985), 62.

4. Arlie J. Blood, *Only Angels Have Wings* (self-published, Victoria Graphics, 1997), 75.

5. Equivalent to a Brigadier General.

6. Robert Citino, "Danger Zone," WWII The National WWII Museum, September 18, 2018, accessed November 5, 2024, https://www.nationalww2museum.org/war/articles /danger-zone.

7. Niklas Zetterling, *Normandy 1944* (Winnipeg, Manitoba, Canada: J. J. Fedorowicz Publishing, Inc., 2000), 30–34.

8. Bradley, *A Soldier's Story*, 221.

9. Chris McNab, *Hitler's Armies* (Oxford, UK: Osprey Publishing Ltd., 2011), 338–42.

10. Von Below, *At Hitler's Side*, 204–07.

11. 1Lt. (now Senator) John Drummond, transcript of oral history interview by Col. Joseph T. Molyson, USAFR (Ret.), January 22, 2003.

12. "Arlie Blood Hanging from a Tree," 510th Fighter Squadron, n.d., n.p., online, accessed July 27, 2003, available from http://www.510fs.org/history/WWII/Caricatures_Medium /Caricatures02.html.

13. Galland, *The First and the Last*, 218–19.

## CHAPTER 39: EXPANSION

1. Capt. C. P. Kindleberger, quoted in Walt W. Rostow, *Pre-Invasion Bombing Strategy: General Eisenhower's Decision of March 25, 1944* (Austin, TX: University of Texas Press, 1981), 123.

2. Based on *Omaha Beachhead (6 June–13 June 1944)*, Historical Division War Department American Forces in Action Series (Washington, DC: Center of Military History United States Army, 1989, undated new imprint), Map X (attached).

3. Zetterling, *Normandy 1944*, 33.

4. Carell, *Invasion—They're Coming*, 118.

5. David Clark, *Angels Eight Normandy Air War Diary* (Bloomington, IN: 1stBooks, 2003), 65–66; Carell, *Invasion—They're Coming*, 161.

6. Carell, *Invasion—They're Coming*, 161.

7. Clark, *Angels Eight Normandy Air War Diary*, 66–67.

8. Carell, *Invasion—They're Coming*, 144–45.

9. Ibid., 154–55.

10. Ibid., 186.

11. Zetterling, *Normandy 1944*, 83.

12. Quoted in Carell, *Invasion—They're Coming*, 115–16.

## CHAPTER 40: COBRA

1. Galland, *The First and the Last*, 218.

2. Forrest C. Pogue, *The Supreme Command*, United States Army in World War II, European Theater (Washington, DC: Center of Military History United States Army, 1989), 183.

3. Carell, *Invasion—They're Coming*, 234–35.

4. John Terraine, *The Right of the Line. the Royal Air Force in the European War, 1939–1945* (London: Hodder and Stoughton, 1985), 650–51.

5. Group Captain Peter W. Gray, "Caen: The Martyred City," *Royal Air Force Airpower Review* V, no. 2 (Summer 2002): 99–101.

6. Ibid., 255.

7. Ambrose, *The Supreme Commander*, 437–41.

8. Price, "The Air Battle," *D-Day Operation Overlord*, 144.

9. Col. Hans Von Luck, in an interview by Maj. Joseph T. Molyson, USAFR, May 7, 1985.

10. Carell, *Invasion—They're Coming*, 249–54.

11. Pogue, *The Supreme Command*, 189.

12. Carell, *Invasion—They're Coming*, 241–42.

13. Von Below, *At Hitler's Side*, 207–09.

14. Quoted in Historical Division War Department American Forces in Action Series, *St-Lo (7 July–19 July 1944)* (undated, new imprint; Washington, DC: Center of Military History United States Army, 1984), 128.

15. Quoted in Carell, *Invasion—They're Coming*, 256.

16. Hallion, *D-Day 1944: Air Power Over the Normandy Beaches and Beyond*, 28–30; Martin Blumenson, *Breakout and Pursuit*, United States Army in World War II, European Theater (Washington, DC: Center of Military History United States Army, 1989), Map IV (attached).

17. Michael E. Haskew, "Deadly Cobra Strike," *Warfare History Network* (Winter 2014), accessed March 16, 2025, https://warfarehistorynetwork.com/article/deadly-cobra-strike/.

18. Doolittle, *I Could Never Be So Lucky Again*, 373.

19. Richard P. Hallion, *Strike from the Sky: The History of Battlefield Air Attack, 1911–1945* (Washington, DC: Smithsonian Institution Press, 1989), 208–12; Thomas E. Griess, ed., *The Second World War Europe and the Mediterranean* (New York: Square One Publishers, 2002), 331–33.

20. Quoted in Carell, *Invasion—They're Coming*, 261.

21. Carell, *Invasion—They're Coming*, 263.

22. "St. Lo Breakthrough; France is Sewed Up," *Impact Book 7, May 1945, May–July 1945*, ed. James Parton (Harrisburg, PA: National Historical Society, 1980), 27–32.

23. Doolittle, *I Could Never Be So Lucky Again*, 377.

## CHAPTER 41: MORTAIN

1. The reader should not confuse the nickname of these rockets with the RAF Typhoon fighter-bomber.

2. Quoted in Allyn Vannoy, "Nazi Germany's Thermobaric Weapon, Typhoon B," *Strategic & Tactics*, no. 351 (March–April 2025): 71.

3. Nicknamed by American infantry "the Queen of Battle."

4. Ibid., 5.

5. Price, "The Air Battle," *D-Day Operation Overlord*, 145–46.

6. Ibid., 271.

7. Charles M. Province, *Patton's Third Army* (New York: Hippocrene Books, Inc., 1992), 20.

8. *Air-Ground Teamwork on the Western Front*, Wings at War Series, vol. 5, 12.

9. Province, *Patton's Third Army*, 21.

10. General Walter Warlimont, *Inside Hitler's Headquarters 1939–45*, trans. R. H. Barry (Novato, CA: Presidio Press, 1964), 447–48.

11. Carell, *Invasion—They're Coming*, 275.

12. Adapted from Richard P. Hallion, *D-Day 1944: Air Power Over the Normandy Beaches and Beyond*, 31.

13. Carell, *Invasion—They're Coming*, 279.

14. Ibid., 148–49.

15. Warlimont, *Inside Hitler's Headquarters 1939–45*, 449.

16. Ibid., 449.

17. Bradley, *A Soldier's Story*, 337.

18. *Air-Ground Teamwork on the Western Front*, Wings at War Series, vol. 5, 5–7.

19. Ambrose, *The Supreme Commander*, 442–58; Price, "The Air Battle," *D-Day: Operation Overlord*, 149.

20. Price, "The Air Battle," in *D-Day Operation Overlord*, 149.

## CHAPTER 42: THE ROAD TO FALAISE

1. Price, "The Air Battle," *D-Day Operation Overlord*, 148–49.

2. Blumenson, *Breakout and Pursuit*, 506–07.

3. Adapted from Hallion, *D-Day 1944: Air Power Over the Normandy Beaches and Beyond*, 37.

4. Carell, *Invasion—They're Coming*, 284–85.

5. Price, "The Air Battle," *D-Day Operation Overlord*, 149.

6. Griess, *The Second World War Europe and the Mediterranean*, 338.

7. Carell, *Invasion—They're Coming*, 306.

## CHAPTER 43: PARIS

1. *Air-Ground Teamwork on the Western Front*, Wings at War Series, vol. 5, 21.

2. Province, *Patton's Third Army*, 28.

3. Larry Collins and Dominique Lapierre, *Is Paris Burning?* (New York: Pocket Books, 1965), 50.

4. Ibid., 9–28.

5. Griess, *The Second World War Europe and the Mediterranean*, 343.

6. Price, "The Air Battle," *D-Day Operation Overlord*, 149.

7. Ibid.

8. Mike Spick, *Luftwaffe Fighter Aces* (New York: Ivy Books, 1996), 176–77.

9. Message, no date/time group, General Eisenhower to General Arnold, September 3, 1944, in File 519.553-2, "An Evaluation of the Effects of the Bomber Offensive on 'Overlord' and 'Dragon,'" Albert F. Simpson Historical Research Center, Air University, Maxwell AFB, AL.

## CHAPTER 44: AFTERMATH

1. Stafford, *Ten Days to D-Day*, 303–04.

2. "Northern Europe," US Army map, World War II Maps, Perry-Castanada Library Map Collection (University of Texas at Austin), accessed March 18, 2025, https://maps.lib.utexas.edu/maps/historical/history_ww2.html.

3. Hastings, *Overlord: D-Day and the Battle for Normandy*, Kindle, 482–83.

# Bibliography

50th TCW Field Order Number 1 NEPTUNE (Bigot) June 2, 1944. In the Michael N. Ingrisano Jr. Collection.

*AAF: The Official World War II Guide to the Army Air Forces.* New York: Bonanza Books, 1988.

Airgood, Roger. 440th Troop Carrier Group History Project oral history, courtesy of Randolph Hils, October 24, 1992.

*Air-Ground Teamwork on the Western Front.* Wings at War Series, vol. 5. Washington, DC: Center for Air Force History, US Air Force, 1992.

Allied Expeditionary Air Force (AEAF). *Principal Airfields Within 100 & 130 Miles of Caen.* Annex K to Operation Neptune Overall Air Plan Sketch Map 2. AEAF/TS399/Air Plans AEAF, 15 April 1944. In WWII Combat Operations Reports 1942–1946 Records Group 18. National Records and Archives Administration Archive II, College Park, MD.

Allward, Maurice. *An Illustrated History of Seaplanes and Flying Boats.* New York: Dorset Press, 1981.

Ambrose, Stephen E. *D-Day June 6, 1944: The Climactic Battle of WWII.* London: Simon & Schuster UK Ltd., 1994.

———. *Pegasus Bridge.* New York: Simon & Schuster, Inc., 1985.

———. *The Supreme Commander.* Jackson, MS: The University of Mississippi Press, 1999.

"AN/TPN-1 and AN/PPN-1 Light Weight Long Wave 'Eureka' Racons." *U.S. Radar.*

Arnold, H. H. *Global Mission.* New York: Harper Brothers, 1949.

Assistant Chief of Air Staff for Intelligence, US Army Air Force. Interview of Capt. Lewis F. Powell, 28 August 1943. File 142.052 Powell. Albert F. Simpson Historical Research Center, Air University, Maxwell AFB, AL.

———. Interview of Col. Craw T. Demas, 6 July 1942. File 142.05-3. Albert F. Simpson Historical Research Center, Air University, Maxwell AFB, AL.

———. Interview of Col. Elliot Roosevelt by Lt. Col. Palmer Dixon, 30 July 1943. File 152.052 Roosevelt. Albert F. Simpson Historical Research Center, Air University, Maxwell AFB, AL.

———. Interview of Col. Homer Case. Undated 1942. File 142.05-3. Albert F. Simpson Historical Research Center, Air University, Maxwell AFB, AL.

———. Interview of Col. J. E. Smart, 26 August 1943. File 142.052 Smart. Albert F. Simpson Historical Research Center, Air University, Maxwell AFB, AL.

———. Interview of Col. L. C. Craigle, Col. M. S. Roth and Col. J. F. Philips, 12 January 1943. File 142.052-Craigle. Albert F. Simpson Historical Research Center, Air University, Maxwell AFB, AL.

———. Interview of Col. William B. Hohenthal, 24 June 1942. File 142.05-3. Albert F. Simpson Historical Research Center, Air University, Maxwell AFB, AL.

———. Interview of Frederick C. Oechsner, 10 June 1942. File 142.05-3. Albert F. Simpson Historical Research Center, Air University, Maxwell AFB, AL.

———. Interview of Maj. Kingman Douglas, 23 October 1942. File 142.05-3. Albert F. Simpson Historical Research Center, Air University, Maxwell AFB, AL.

———. Interview of Col. P.W. Tibbets, 20 February 1943. File 142.052 Tibbets. Albert F. Simpson Historical Research Center, Air University, Maxwell AFB, AL.

———. Interview of Col. William Shipp, 29 August 1942. File 142.05-3. Albert F. Simpson Historical Research Center, Air University, Maxwell AFB, AL.

Bagby, Col. R. B. G-2 SHAEF. Memorandum. To General Nevins. Subject: Troop Carrier—Airborne Operations, March 7, 1944. In Box 11 of the James M. Gavin Papers. US Army Heritage and Education Center, Carlisle Barracks, PA.

Baldwin, Hanson W. " Teamwork on Land at Sea and in the Air." *Impact 5, May–July 1944*, Harrisburg, PA: National Historical Society, 1989), viii.

Barber, Neil. *The Day the Devils Dropped In*. Barnsley, South Yorkshire, UK: Leo Cooper, 2002.

Barr, Niall. *Eisenhower's Armies*. New York: Pegasus Press, 2015.

Bekker, Cajus. *The Luftwaffe War Diaries*. Translated by Frank Ziegler. New York: Da Capo Press, 1994.

Bernard, H. "Radar." *The Historical Encyclopedia of World War II*. Edited by Marcel Baudot et al., trans. Jesse Dilson. New York: Facts on File, 1997.

Berry, Gerald C. Interview by Col. Joseph T. Molyson, USAF, April 28, 2003.

Bickers, Richard Townshend. *Air War Normandy*. London: Leo Cooper, 1994.

Bishop, Jim. *FDR's Last Year April 1944–April 1945*. New York: William & Company, 1974.

Blood, Arlie J. *Only Angels Have Wings*. Self-published, Victoria Graphics, 1997.

Blumenson, Martin. *Breakout and Pursuit*. United States Army in World War II, European Theater. Washington, DC: Center of Military History United States Army, 1989.

Boesch, Captain Harrison. "314th Troop Carrier Group Mission Report." 62nd Troop Carrier Squadron, June 6, 1944. Box 11 of the James M. Gavin Papers. US Army Heritage and Education Center, Carlisle Barracks, PA.

Bortzfield. Charles. Interview by Col. Joseph T. Molyson, USAF, April 28, 2003.

Bourque, Stephen A. *D-Day 1944: The deadly failure of Allied heavy bombing on June 6*. Osprey Air Campaign Series. Oxford, UK: Osprey Publishing Ltd., 2022.

Bowman, Martin W. *The USAAF Handbook 1939–1945*. Mechanicsburg, PA: Stackpole Books, 1996.

Boyne, Walter J. *Clash of Wings: World War II in the Air*. New York: Touchstone, 1997.

*BR 1736 (26) Royal Navy Staff History—Raid on Dieppe*. Battle Summary No. 33, Historical Section, Admiralty. Accessed August 20, 2023. https://www.navy.gov.au/sites/default/files/documents/Battle_Summary_33.pdf.

Bradley, General of the Army Omar N. *A Soldier's Story*. New York: Henry Holt and Company, 1951.

Breuer, William B. *Secret Weapons of World War II*. New York: John Wiley & Sons, Inc., 2000.

Brinson, William L. *Airborne Troop Carrier Three-One-Five Group*. New Orleans: Walka, 2003.

Brown, Anthony Cave. *Bodyguard of Lies*. New York: HarperCollins, 1975.

Brown, David. "Air Spotting Pools." *The D-Day Encyclopedia*. Edited by David G. Chandler and James Lawton Collins. New York: Simon & Schuster, 1994.

Buffetaut, Yves. *The Falaise Pocket Normandy August 1944*. Havertown, PA: Casemate Publishers, 2019.

Caidin, Martin. *Forked-Tailed Devil: The P-38*. New York: ibooks, inc., 2001.

Caldwell, Donald, and Richard Muller. *The Luftwaffe Over Germany Defense of the Reich.*

Carell, Paul. *Invasion—They're Coming.* Translated by Ewald Osers. New York: E. P. Dutton & Co., 1963.

Carter, Kit C., and Robert Mueller, compilers. *U.S. Army Air Forces in World War II: Combat Chronology 1941–1945.* Washington, DC: Center for Air Force History, US Air Force, 1991.

Chester, Major Michael C., to Lt. Gen. James M. Gavin. Letter, March 30, 1959. Box 11 of the James M. Gavin Papers., US Army Heritage and Education Center, Carlisle Barracks, PA.

Chicken, Stephen. *Overlord Coastline.* New York: Hippocrene Books, Inc., 1993.

Chief of Staff to Naval Commander Expeditionary Force. Provision of Spotting Aircraft—Progress Report X/0927/8b, November 4, 1943. In COS File 374.14/1 Records Group 331. National Records and Archives Administration Archive II, College Park, MD.

Chief of Staff to the Supreme Allied Commander (COSSAC). *Attainment of the Necessary Air Situation.* Appendix K to COSSAC (43) 28 Plan, 1943. In File 505.14-3. Albert F. Simpson Historical Research Center, Air University, Maxwell AFB, AL.

———. *Operation OVERLORD Beaches and Ports France and the Low Countries Beaches and Theoretical Beach Capacities and Major Port Capacities.* COSSAC (43) 28 Map MA. Undated 1943. In Box 11 of the James M. Gavin Papers. US Army Heritage and Education Center, Carlisle Barracks, PA.

———. *Requirements for a Tactical Air Force.* COSSAC Study No. 2, undated 1943. In File 505.13-3. Albert F. Simpson Historical Research Center, Air University, Maxwell AFB, AL.

———. *Support of Military Operations by Resistance Groups in France.* Appendix P to COSSAC (43) 28. Chief of Staff to the Supreme Allied Commander. Undated 1943. In File 505.14-3. Albert F. Simpson Historical Research Center, Air University, Maxwell AFB, AL.

Chiefs of Staff (COS) Committee of the Joint Planning Staff of the (UK) War Cabinet. *Bombing Policy in Connection with Overlord.* COS Report (44) 125 t, 17 April 1944. In SHAEF SGS Minutes Decimal File May 43–Aug 45 Records Group 331. National Records and Archives Administration Archive II, College Park, MD.

Churchill, Winston S. *Closing the Ring.* The Second World War, vol. V. Boston, MA: Mariner Books, 1985.

———. *Triumph and Tragedy.* The Second World War, vol. VI. Boston, MA: Mariner Books, 1985.

Clark, David. *Angels Eight.* Bloomington, VT: 1st Books, June 2003.

Collins, Larry, and Dominique Lapierre. *Is Paris Burning?* New York: Pocket Books, 1965.

"Control of Strategic bombing for 'OVERLORD'." CCS Memorandum 520, 17 March 1944. Record Group 331, Box 11. National Archives at College Park, Maryland.

Craven, Wesley Frank, and James Lea Cate. *Argument to V-E Day, January 1944 to May 1945.* The Army Air Forces in World War II, vol. III, Europe. Washington, DC: Office of Air Force History, US Air Force, 1983.

Craven, Wesley Frank, and James Lea Cate, eds. *Men and Planes.* The Army Air Forces in World War II, vol. VI. Washington, DC: Office of Air Force History, US Air Force, 1983.

———. *Services Around the World*. The Army Air Forces in World War II, vol. VII. Washington, DC: Office of Air Force History, US Air Force, 1983.

Crosby, Harry H. A. *Wing and A Prayer*. New York: Open Road Media, 2001.

D'Este, Carlo. *Decision in Normandy*. New York: Diversion Books, 2020.

Dabrowski, Hans-Peter. *Mistel: The Piggy-Back Aircraft of the Luftwaffe*. Atglen, PA: Schiffer Publishing Ltd., 1994.

Dalles-Labourdette, Jean-Philippe. *S-boote: German E-boats in Action 1939–1945*. Translated by Janice Lert. Paris: Histoire and Collections, 2006.

Dank, Milton. *The Glider Gang*. Bennington, VT: Merriam Press, 2003.

Darby, H. C. *The Relations of History and Geography*. Exeter, UK: University of Exeter Press, 2002.

Darlow, Stephen. *D-Day Bombers: The Veterans' Story*. London: Grub Street, 2004.

Davis, Richard G. "Carl Spaatz and D-Day." *Airpower Journal* (Winter 1997). Accessed August 21, 2023. https://www.airuniversity.af.edu/Portals/10/ASPJ/journals/Volume-11_Issue -1-4/1997_Vol11_No4.pdf.

———. "IX Troop Carrier Command." *The D-Day Encyclopedia*. Edited by David G. Chandler and James Lawton Collins. New York: Simon & Schuster, 1994.

———. "Pointblank versus Overlord: strategic bombing and the Normandy invasion." *Air Power History* 41 no. 2 (Summer 1994): 4–13.

———. *Carl Spaatz and the Air War in Europe*. Washington, DC: Center for Air Force History, US Air Force, 1983.

Davis, William Morris. *A Handbook of Northern France*. Cambridge, MA: Harvard University Press, 1918.

De Planhol, Xavier, and Paul Claval. *An Historical Geography of France*. Translated by Janet Lloyd. Cambridge University Press, 1994.

Deichmann, General der Flieger Paul. *German Air Operations in Support of the Army*. Maxwell AFB, AL: Air University Press, June 1962.

Deighton, Len. *Blood, Tears and Folly*. Edison, NJ: Castle Books, 1999.

Delve, Ken. *D-Day: The Air Battle*. Revised edition. Ramsbury, Wiltshire, UK: Crowood Press, 2004.

———. *The Source Book of the RAF*. Shrewsbury, UK: Airlife Publishing, Ltd., 1994.

Devlin, Gerard M. *On Silent Wings*. New York: St. Martin's Press, 1985.

deZeng IV, Henry L. *Luftwaffe Airfields 1935–45 France*. June 2014 ed. Accessed August 27, 2023. www.ww2.dk/Airfields%20-%20France.pdf.

———. *Luftwaffe Airfields 1935–45 General Information*. June 2014 ed. Accessed August 27, 2023. www.ww2.dk/Airfields%20-%20General%20Introduction.pdf.

deZeng IV, Henry L., and Douglas G. Stankey with Eddie J. Creek. *Bomber Units of the Luftwaffe*, vol. 1. Hinkley, UK: Ian Allan Publishing—Midland, 2007.

———. *Bomber Units of the Luftwaffe*, vol. 2. Hersham, Surrey UK: Ian Allan Publishing—Classic, 2008.

Doolittle, Gen. James H. *I Could Never Be So Lucky Again*. New York: Bantam Books, 1992.

Doolittle, Lt. Gen. James H. Oral history by Prof. Ronald Schaffer, California State University, 24 August 79. File K239.0512-1206. Albert F. Simpson Historical Research Center, Air University, Maxwell AFB, AL.

————. Oral history by US Air Force Historical Division, 23 June 65. File K239.0512-623. Albert F. Simpson Historical Research Center, Air University, Maxwell AFB, AL.

————. US Air Force oral history by Brig. Gen. George W. Goddard, 20 July 67. File K239.0512-998. Albert F. Simpson Historical Research Center, Air University, Maxwell AFB, AL.

Doolittle, Lt. Gen. James H., and Col. Beirne Lay Jr. "Daylight Precision Bombing." *Impact 6, January–April 1945.* Harrisburg, PA: National Historical Society, 1980.

Dornberger, Walter. *V-2.* Translated by James Cleugh and Geoffrey Halliday. New York: The Viking Press, 1954.

Dougherty, Martin J. *Military Atlas of Air Warfare.* New York: Chartwell Books, 2014.

Drummond, John "Ace." Oral history interview by Col. Joseph Molyson, USAFR (Ret.), January 22, 2003.

Dugard, Martin. *Taking Paris.* New York: Caliber, 2021.

Dunn, Lt. Col. William R. Oral history by Major Gilmartin et.al., 2 November 73. US Air Force Historical Division, File K239.0512-922. Albert F. Simpson Historical Research Center, Air University, Maxwell AFB, AL.

Dunnigan, James F., and Albert A. Nofi. *Dirty Little Secrets of World War II.* New York: William Morrow and Company, Inc., 1994.

Ehlers, Robert S., Jr. *Targeting the Third Reich: Air Intelligence and the Allied Bombing Campaigns.* Modern War Studies Series. Lawrence, KS: University of Kansas Press, 2009.

Eisenhower, Gen. Dwight D. *Crusade in Europe.* Garden City, NY: Doubleday & Company, 1948.

————. US Air Force oral history by Brig. Gen. George W. Goddard, undated. File K239.0512-999. Albert F. Simpson Historical Research Center, Air University, Maxwell AFB, AL.

Ellis, Maj. L. F., G. R. G. Allen, A. E. Warhurst, and Sir J. Robb. Edited by J. R. M. Butler. *Victory in the West: The Battle of Normandy.* History of the Second World War United Kingdom Military Series, vol. I. London: Naval & Military Press, 2004 (Kindle edition).

Engelmann, Joachim. *V1: The Flying Bomb.* Atglen, PA: Schiffer Publishing Ltd., 1992.

Esvelin, Philippe. *D-Day Gliders.* Bayeux, France: Heimdal, 2001.

Faber, Harold., ed. *Luftwaffe: A History.* New York: Quadrangle/The New York Times Book Company, 1977.

Ferguson, Gregor, and Kevin Lyles. *The Paras 1940–1944.* Osprey Elite Series vol. 21. Edited by Martin Windrow. London: Osprey Books, 1984.

Fisher, Ernest F. "German Signal." *The D-Day Encyclopedia.* Edited by David G. Chandler and James Lawton Collins. New York: Simon & Schuster, 1994.

Ford, Ken. *Caen 1944.* Osprey Campaign Series, vol. 143. Oxford, UK: Osprey Publishing Ltd., 2004.

————. *D-Day 1944 (3) Sword Beach and the Airborne Landings.* Osprey Campaign Series, vol. 105. Oxford, UK: Osprey Publishing Ltd., 2002.

————. *D-Day 1944 (4) Gold and Juno Beaches.* Osprey Campaign Series, vol. 112. Oxford, UK: Osprey Publishing Ltd., 2002.

————. *Falaise 1944: Death of an Army.* Osprey Campaign Series, vol. 149. Oxford, UK: Osprey Publishing Ltd., 2005.

———. *Operation Neptune 1944.* Osprey Campaign Series, vol. 268. Edited by Lee Johnson. Oxford, UK: Osprey Publishing Ltd., 2014.

Forsyth, Robert. *Mistel German Composite Aircraft and Operations 1942–1945.* Norwalk, CT: Airtime Publishing, Inc., 2001.

*France.* New York: DK Publishing, 2021.

Franks, Norman. *Typhoon Attack.* London: Grub Street, 2003.

Frappé, Jean-Bernard. *Luftwaffe Face au Debarquement Allie 6 juin au 31 août 1944* (The Luftwaffe-Opposing the Allied Landings June 6th to August 31, 1944). Bayeaux, France: Editions Heimdal, 1999.

Freeman, Roger A., with Alan Crouchman and Vic Maslen. *Mighty Eighth War Diary.* New York: Jane's, 1981.

Galland, General der Flieger Adolph. *The First and the Last.* Cutchogue, NY: Buccaneer Books, 1997.

Gavin, Lt. Gen. James M. US Army Military History Institute oral history by Lt. Col. Donald G. Andrews, USA, and Lt. Col. Charles H. Ferguson, USA. Undated 1975. Box 1 of the James M. Gavin Papers. US Army Heritage and Education Center, Carlisle Barracks, PA.

*German Aircraft and Armament.* Informational Intelligence Summary No. 44-32. Washington, DC: Office of the Assistant Chief of Air Staff, Intelligence, 1944.

*German Order of Battle: The Directory Prepared by Allied Intelligence of Regiments, Formations, and Units of the German Armed Forces, 1944.* Mechanicsburg, PA: Stackpole Books, 1994.

Goldberg, Alfred. "Air Campaign OVERLORD: To D-Day." *D-Day: The Normandy Invasion in Retrospect.* Edited by the Eisenhower Foundation. Lawrence, KS: The University of Kansas Press, 1971.

Gray, Group Captain Peter W. "Caen: The Martyred City." *Royal Air Force Airpower Review* no. 2 (Summer 2002): 88–102.

Greiss, Thomas E., ed., *West Point Atlas for the Second World War: Europe and the Mediterranean.* Wayne, NJ: Avery Publishing, 1984.

Hallion, Richard P. *D-Day 1944: Air Power Over the Normandy Beaches and Beyond.* The US Army Air Forces in World War II. Washington, DC: Air Force History and Museums Program, 1994.

Harris, Marshal of the RAF Sir Arthur. *Bomber Offensive.* Mechanicsburg, PA: Stackpole Books, 1990.

Harrison, Gordon A. *Cross-Channel Attack.* United States Army in World War II, European Theater. Washington, DC: Center of Military History United States Army, 1989.

Hart, Stephen A. *Operation Totalize 1944.* Osprey Campaign Series, vol. 294. Oxford, UK: Osprey Publishing, Ltd., 2016.

Hastings, Max. *Overlord: D-Day & the Battle for Normandy.* New York: Simon & Schuster, Inc., 1984.

Hausser, Paul. *Normandy—Seventh Army 29 Jun–24 Jul 44*, MS #A-974. Translated by A. Rosenwald. Historical Division, HQ US Army Europe, Feb. 25, 1946, 14–16. Foreign Military Studies Branch, RG 338, NARA, College Park, MD.

Hess, William. *P-47 Thunderbolt at War.* Garden City, NY: Doubleday & Company, 1976.

Higham, Robin. "Technology and D-Day." In *D-Day The Normandy Invasion in Retrospect.* Eisenhower Foundation. Lawrence, KS: The University of Kansas Press, 1971.

Hill, Steven D. "Invasion! Fortress Europe." *Naval Aviation News* 76 no. 4, May–June 1994: 31–35.

Hinsley, F. H. "Deception." *The D-Day Encyclopedia*. Edited by David G. Chandler and James Lawton Collins. New York: Simon & Schuster, 1994.

———. "Intelligence." *The D-Day Encyclopedia*. Edited by David G. Chandler and James Lawton Collins. New York: Simon & Schuster, 1994.

Hogg, I. V. *German Secret Weapons of World War II*. New York: Arco Publishing, Inc., 1970.

Holland, John W. *D-Day Attack by the 8th Air Force*. Carthage, TX: Complete Printing & Publishing, 2000.

Howard, Maj. John. A conversation with Major Joseph T. Molyson, USAFR, May 7, 1985.

Howorth, David. *Dawn of D-Day*. Mechanicsburg, PA: Stackpole Books, 2001.

Hughes, Thomas Alexander. *Overlord: General Pete Quesada and the Triumph of Tactical Air Power in World War II*. New York: The Free Press, 1995.

Ingrisano, Michael N., Jr. *Valor Without Arms*. Bennington, VT: Merriam Press, 2001.

Isby, David C. *Fighting the Breakout The German Army in Normandy from Cobra to the Falaise Gap*. Barnsley, South Yorkshire, UK: Frontline Books, 2014.

Jackson, Robert, ed. *Kriegsmarine*. Osceola, WI: MBI Publishing, 2001.

Jacobs, Peter. *Airfields of the D-Day Invasion Air Force*. Barnsley, South Yorkshire: Pen & Sword Books, Ltd., 2009.

Jacobs, W. A. "British Strategic Air Offensive." In *Case Studies In Strategic Bombardment*, edited by R. Cargill Hall, 91–182. Washington, DC: Center for Air Force History, US Air Force, 1998.

———. "Operation OVERLORD." In *Case Studies in the Achievement of Air Superiority*, edited by Benjamin Franklin Cooling, 297. Washington, DC: Center for Air Force History, US Air Force, 1991.

———. "The Battle for France, 1944." In *Case Studies in the Development of Close Air Support*, edited by Benjamin Franklin Cooling, 237–93. Washington, DC: Center for Air Force History, US Air Force, 1990.

Jakeman, Robert J. "Air Special Operations." *The D-Day Encyclopedia*. Edited by David G. Chandler and James Lawton Collins. New York: Simon & Schuster, 1994.

Jefford, Wing Commander C. G. *RAF Squadrons*. Shrewsbury, UK: Airlife Publishing Ltd., 2001.

Johnsen, Frederick A. "Working on the Railroad." *Airpower*, vol. 32, no. 3, May 2002: 48–49.

Johnson, Mr. Robert S. US Air Force oral history by Lt. Col. John N. Dick, 9 February 77. File K239.0512-1074. Albert F. Simpson Historical Research Center, Air University, Maxwell AFB, AL.

Johnson, Robert S. *Thunderbolt!* Spartanburg, SC: The Honoribus Press, February 1999.

Johnston, Lew. *The Troop Carrier D-Day Flights*. San Francisco: 61st Troop Carrier Squadron Collection, 2002.

Joint Intelligence Sub-Committee (JIC) of the Joint Planning Staff of the (UK) War Cabinet. *Effects of the Allied Bombing Offensive on the German War Effort With Particular Reference to "Overlord."* JIC Report (44) 177, 1 May 1944. In SHAEF SGS Minutes Decimal File May 43–Aug 45 Records Group 331. National Records and Archives Administration Archive II, College Park, MD.

———. "Operations 'Overlord' and 'Anvil.'" JIC Memorandum for Information Number 3, 1 February 1944. In JCS Geographic File 1942–1945 Records Group 218. National Records and Archives Administration Archive II, College Park, MD.

Joint Planning Staff of the (UK) War Cabinet. "Operation OVERLORD," 3 August 1943. In SHAEF SGS Minutes Decimal File May 43–Aug 45 Records Group 331. National Records and Archives Administration Archive II, College Park, MD.

Jones, Jay. *The 370th Fighter Group in World War II*. Atglen, PA: Schiffer, 2003.

Kagan, Niel, and Stephen G. Hyslop. *Atlas of World War II*. Washington DC: National Geographic, 2018.

Kaufmann, J. E., and H. W. Kaufmann. *Fortress Third Reich*. Cambridge, MA: Da Capo Press, 2003.

Kaufmann, J. E., and Robert M. Jurga. *Fortress Europe: European Fortifications of World War II*. Translated by H. W. Kaufmann. Cambridge, MA: Da Capo Press, 2002.

Keil, *Oberstleutnant* Guenther. "Report covering the questions of the Historical Division about operations of Infantry Regiment 1058 and *Kampfgruppe Keil* (Combat Team)." MS #B-844. Historical Division, Headquarters United States Army Europe, June 11, 1946. Box 11 of the James M. Gavin Papers. US Army Heritage and Education Center, Carlisle Barracks, PA.

Keller, Shawn P., Major USAF. "Turning Point: A History of German Petroleum in World War II and Its Lessons for the Role of Oil in Modern Air Warfare." Research Paper, ACSC, Air University, Maxwell AFB, AL, undated.

Kent, George. "The Man Who Saved London." *In Secrets & Spies*. Edited by Reader's Digest Association. Pleasantville, NY: Reader's Digest Association, 1964.

Kepher, Stephen C. *COSSAC Lt. Gen. Sir Frederick Morgan and the Genesis of Operation Overlord*. Annapolis, MD: Naval Institute Press, 2020.

Kershaw, Alex. *The Bedford Boys*. Cambridge, MA: Da Capo Press, 2003.

Kitchens, James H., III, PhD. "The *Luftwaffe* and D-Day." Lecture. Ninth Air Force Conference: "D-Day Remembered," University of New Orleans, New Orleans, April 30, 1994.

Kloeppel, Maj. Kirk M. "The Military Utility of German Rocketry during World War II." Air University Research Report, March 1997, n.p. Online, May 30, 2002. Available from http://research.maxwell.af.mil/papers/student/ay1997/acsc/97-0609O.pdf.

Kluss, Lt. Col. W. L. Interview by the Assistant Chief of Air Staff for Intelligence, 27 May 1942. File 142.05-3. Albert F. Simpson Historical Research Center, Air University, Maxwell AFB, AL.

Knoke, Heinz. *I Flew for the Führer*. Translated by R. H. Barry. Novato, CA: Presidio Press, 1991.

Kohn, Richard H., and Joseph P. Harahan, eds. *Condensed Analysis of the Ninth Air Force in the European Theater of Operations*. Washington, DC: Office of Air Force History, US Air Force, 1984.

———. *Air Interdiction World War II, Korea, and Vietnam*. Washington, DC: Office of Air Force History, US Air Force, 1986.

Kudrycz, Dr. Walter. "A Practical Prophet? Arthur Harris, the Legacy of Lord Trenchard, and the Question of 'Panacea' targeting." *Royal Air Force Airpower Review*, no. 1 (Spring 2002): 30–42.

Kuter, Brig. Gen. L. S., Assistant Chief of Air Staff, Plans Memorandum. To Lt. Gen. Carl Spaatz. Subject: Air Operations in Western Europe, February 4 1944. File 168.04-27. Albert F. Simpson Historical Research Center, Air University, Maxwell AFB, AL.

*Landscapes and Landforms of France.* Edited by Monique Fort and Marie-Françoise André. New York: Springer Science + Business Media *Dordrecht*, 2014.

Love, Terry M. *L-Birds. American Combat Liaison Aircraft of World War II.* New Brighton, MN: Flying Books International, 2001.

Ludwig, Paul A., and Lt. Bruce Carmichael, USNR (Ret.). "The U.S. Navy Spitfires of VCS-7." *Foundation*, Fall 1999: 80–93.

Macintyre, Donald. *The Naval War Against Hitler.* New York: Charles Scribner's Sons, 1971.

Man, John. *D-Day Atlas: The Definitive Account of the Allied Invasion of Normandy.* New York: Facts on File, 1994.

Marrin, Albert. *Overlord: D-Day and the Invasion of Europe.* New York: Atheneum, 1982.

Marshall, Lt. Col. S. L. A. "Reports on Operation NEPTUNE." History Branch G-2 War Department. Undated. Box 11 of the James M. Gavin Papers. US Army Heritage and Education Center, Carlisle Barracks, PA.

Marshall, Tim. *Prisoners of Geography.* London: Elliot and Thompson, 2015.

———. *The Power of Geography.* New York: Scribner, 2021.

Mason, Frank. *Luftwaffe Aircraft.* New York: Crescent Books, 1986.

Maurer, Maurer., ed. *Air Force Combat Units of World War II.* Washington, DC: Office of Air Force History, US Air Force, 1983.

———. *World War II. Combat Squadrons of the U.S. Air Force.* Woodbury, NY: Smithmark Publishers, Inc., 1992.

McCrabb, Lt. Col. Maris. "*Drohende Gefahr West*—The Pre-Normandy Air Campaign." *Airpower Journal* (Summer 1994). Accessed August 21, 2023. https://www.airuniversity.af.edu/Portals/10/ASPJ/journals/Volume-08_Issue-1-Se/1994_Vol8_No2.pdf.

McFarland, Stephen L., and Wesley Phillips Newton. *To Command the Sky.* Washington, DC: Smithsonian Institution Press, 1991.

McGovern, James. *Crossbow and Overcast.* New York: William Morrow and Company, Inc., 1964.

McNab, Chris. *Hitler's Armies.* Oxford, UK: Osprey Publishing Ltd., 2011.

———. *Order of Battle: German Luftwaffe in WWII.* London: Amber Books, 2009.

Mersky, Commander Peter, USNR. "Naval Aviators in Spitfires." *Proceedings*, December 1996, 105–06.

Message 221835B JUNE 1944. Air Ministry Whitehall. To Main HQ AEAF, June 22 1944. SHAEF SGS Minutes Decimal File May 43–Aug 45. Records Group 331. National Records and Archives Administration Archive II, College Park, MD.

Message 241315B May 1944. U.S.S.T.A.F. (Spaatz). To ETOUSA for relay AGWAR, May 24 1944. SHAEF SGS Minutes Decimal File May 43–Aug 45. Records Group 331. National Records and Archives Administration Archive II, College Park, MD.

Message. No Date/Time Group. General Eisenhower. To General Arnold, September 3 1944. File 519.553-2 "An Evaluation of the Effects of the Bomber Offensive on 'Overlord' and 'Dragoon'." Albert F. Simpson Historical Research Center, Air University, Maxwell AFB, AL.

Messenger, Charles. *The D-Day Atlas. Anatomy of the Normandy Campaign.* New York: Thames & Hudson, 2004.

Middlebrook, Martin. *The Schweinfurt-Regensburg Mission.* New York: Charles Scribner's Sons, 1983.

Middlebrook, Martin, and Chris Everitt. *The Bomber Command War Diaries 1939–1945.* Leicester, UK: Midland Publishing, 1996.

Minutes of a meeting on the topic of Alternate Plans for the Employment of Strategic Bomber Forces Meeting Office of the Deputy Supreme Commander SHAEF, May 3 1944. SHAEF SGS Minutes Decimal File May 43–Aug 45. Records 331. National Records and Archives Administration Archive II, College Park, MD.

Minutes of the Debriefing Conference—Operation Neptune 82nd Airborne Division, August 13 1944. Box 11 of the James M. Gavin Papers. US Army Heritage and Education Center, Carlisle Barracks, PA.

Mitcham, Samuel W., Jr. *The Desert Fox in Normandy.* Westport, CT: Praeger, 1997.

Molyson, Joseph T., Jr. *Air Battles Before D-Day.* Mechanicsburg, PA: Stackpole Books, 2025.

———. *Six Air Forces Over the Atlantic.* Mechanicsburg, PA: Stackpole Books, 2024.

Morgan, Hugh, and John Weal. *German Jet Aces of World War 2.* Osprey Aircraft of the Aces, vol. 17. Edited by Tony Holmes. Oxford, UK: Osprey Books, 1998.

Morgan, Lt. Gen. COSSAC. To CINC AEAF. Subject: 'Overlord' Bombing Policy, January 10 1944. SHAEF SGS Minutes Decimal File May 43–Aug 45. Records Group 331, National Records and Archives Administration Archive II, College Park, MD.

Morison, Samuel Eliot. *History of the United States Navy in World War II, Vol. XI: The Invasion of France and Germany 1944–1945.* Little, Brown and Company, 1984.

Morrison, Alexander. *Silent Invader.* London: Airlife Publishing, 2002.

Mosley, Leonard. *On Borrowed Time.* New York: Random House, 1969.

Moss, Cdr. Elmo L., USN (Ret.). "Brown Shoes and Wild Horses." *Naval Aviation News* 76, no. 6, September–October 1994): 26–27.

Munro, Ronald Lyell. *Above the Battle.* Barnsley, UK: Pen and Sword Aviation, 2016.

Murray, Williamson. *Strategy for Defeat: The Luftwaffe 1933–1945.* Osceola, WI: Motorbooks International Publishers & Wholesalers, 1998.

Natkiel, Richard. *Atlas of World War II.* Greenwich, CT: Brompton Books, 1999.

"'NEPTUNE' JOINT FIRE PLAN. NCJ/00/74/38, April 8, 1944. Accessed October 22, 2024. https://rafoverlord.blogspot.com/p/njc007438-dated-8-april-1944-neptune.html.

Neufeld, Michael J. *The Rocket and the Reich.* Cambridge, MA: Harvard University Press, 1996.

"New Strip in Normandy." *Impact 4, August 1944, May–August 1944.* Harrisburg, PA: National Historical Society, 1980.

Nolte, Reginald G. *Thunder Monsters Over Europe.* Manhattan, KS: Sunflower Press, 1989.

O'Hara, Vincent P. *The German Fleet at War 1939–1945.* Annapolis, MD: Naval Institute Press, 2020.

*Omaha Beachhead (6 June–13 June 1944).* American Forces in Action Series. Washington, DC: Center of Military History United States Army, 1989.

*Operational Characteristics of Radar Classified by Tactical Application.* FTP 217, Washington: Joint Chiefs of Staff, August 1, 1943. Accessed February 24, 2025. https://www.history.navy.mil/research/library/online-reading-room/title-list-alphabetically/u/operational-characteristics-of-radar-classified-by-tactical-application.html.

Parr, Wally. Interview by Major Joseph T. Molyson, USAFR, May 7, 1985.

Paterson, Lawrence. *Hitler's Forgotten Flotillas*. Barnsley, South Yorkshire, UK: Seaforth Books, 2017.

Pedone, Col. Vito USAF (Ret). "The Truth About D-Day." Lecture. Troop Carrier Reunion 2003. Sheraton Hotel and Conference Center, Dover, Delaware, April 29, 2003.

Planhol, Xavier, and Paul Claval. *An Historical Geography of France*. Cambridge, UK: Cambridge University Press, 1994.

*Planning and Preparation of the AEAF for the Landings in Normandy*. RAF Narrative, vol. I. London: Air Historical Branch, Air Ministry. Released July 11, 1984. PDF. Accessed September 27, 2023. https:// www.raf.mod.uk/our-organisation/units/air-historical-branch /second-world-war-campaign-narratives/liberation-of-north-west-europe-vol-i/.

Powell, Matthew. *The Development of British Tactical Air Power, 1940–1943*. London: Palgrove MacMillan, 2016.

Price, Alfred. "Electronic navigation systems." *The Oxford Companion to World War II*. Edited by I. C. B. Dear and M. R. D. Foot. New York: Oxford University Press, 2001.

———. "Electronic Warfare." *The D-Day Encyclopedia*. Edited by David G. Chandler and James Lawton Collins. New York: Simon & Schuster, 1994.

———. "Electronic warfare." *The Oxford Companion to World War II*. Edited by I. C. B. Dear and M. R. D. Foot. New York: Oxford University Press, 2001.

———. "II Air Corps." *The D-Day Encyclopedia*. Edited by David G. Chandler and James Lawton Collins. New York: Simon & Schuster, 1994.

———. "IX Air Corps." *The D-Day Encyclopedia*. Edited by David G. Chandler and James Lawton Collins. New York: Simon & Schuster, 1994.

———. "The Air Battle." *D-Day Operation Overlord*. Edited by Bernard Nalty. London: Salamander Books, 1999.

———. "Third Air Force." *The D-Day Encyclopedia*. Edited by David G. Chandler and James Lawton Collins. New York: Simon & Schuster, 1994.

———. "X Air Corps." *The D-Day Encyclopedia*. Edited by David G. Chandler and James Lawton Collins. New York: Simon & Schuster, 1994.

———. *The Last Year of the Luftwaffe*. Gaithersburg, MD: Wrens Park Publishing, 2001.

———. *Luftwaffe Handbook 1939–1945*. New York: Charles Scribner's Sons, 1977.

———. *Sky Battles*. London: Cassell & Company, 1998.

———. *The Luftwaffe Data Book*. Mechanicsburg, PA: Stackpole Books, 1997.

Probert, Henry. "84th Composite Group." *The D-Day Encyclopedia*. Edited by David G. Chandler and James Lawton Collins. New York: Simon & Schuster, 1994.

———. "85th Composite Group." *The D-Day Encyclopedia*. Edited by David G. Chandler and James Lawton Collins. New York: Simon & Schuster, 1994.

Province, Charles M. *Patton's Third Army*. New York: Hippocrene Books, Inc., 1992.

*Recognition Pictorial Manual* FM 30-30. Washington, DC: War Department. Undated, unpaginated.

Reilly, John C., Jr. "Close Gunfire Support." *The D-Day Encyclopedia*. Edited by David G. Chandler and James Lawton Collins. New York: Simon & Schuster, 1994.

Richards, Denis, and Hilary St. George Saunders. *Royal Air Force 1939–1945, Volume II: The Fight Avails*. London: HMSO, 1993.

———. *Royal Air Force 1939–1945, Volume III: The Fight Is Won*. London: HMSO, 1993.

Richey. Robert W. Interview by Col. Joseph T. Molyson, USAF, April 28, 2003.

Ridgway, Maj. Gen. M. B. "82nd Airborne Division—Operation NEPTUNE." 82nd Airborne Division, July 26, 1944. Box 11 of the James M. Gavin Papers. US Army Heritage and Education Center, Carlisle Barracks, PA.

Robb, AVM J. M. *Direction of Operations of Allied Air Forces Against Transportation Targets.* Secretary General Staff SHAEF, April 15, 1944. SHAEF SGS Minutes Decimal File May 43–Aug 45, Records Group 331. National Records and Archives Administration Archive II, College Park, MD.

Rommel, Field Marshall Erwin. *The Rommel Papers.* Translated and edited by Sir B. H. Liddell Hart. New York: Da Capo Press, 1953.

Rostow, Walt W. *Pre-Invasion Bombing Strategy: General Eisenhower's Decision of March 25, 1944.* Austin, TX: University of Texas Press, 1981.

Rüge, Friedrich. *Sea Warfare 1939–1945.* Translated by Commander M. G. Saunders, RN. London: Cassell & Company Ltd., 1957.

Rust, Kenn C. *Eighth Air Force Story in World War II.* Temple City, CA: Historical Aviation Album, 1978.

———. *The 9th Air Force in World War II.* Fallbrook, CA: Aero Publishers, 1970.

Ryan, Cornelius. *The Longest Day.* New York: Simon & Schuster, 1959.

Saward, Group Captain Dudley. "Attacks by Night." *Impact 6, January–April 1945.* Harrisburg, PA: National Historical Society, 1980.

Schuster, Cdr. Carl O. "Weather War." *Command,* no. 13 (November–December 1991): 70–73.

Scott, Peter. *The Battle of the Narrow Seas.* Annapolis, MD: Naval Institute Press, 1945.

Shackelford, 1Lt. Lyne M. Assistant Secretary SHAEF General Staff. To Lt. Gen. W. Bedel Smith, Chief of Staff SHAEF. Subject: Summary of results of attacks on rail transportation targets, May 27, 1944. SHAEF SGS Minutes Decimal File May 43–Aug 45. Records Group 331, National Records and Archives Administration Archive II, College Park, MD.

Shannon, Kevin, and Stephen Wright. *One Night in June.* London: Airlife Publishing, Ltd., 2002.

Shilleto, Carl. *Pegasus Bridge & Merville Battery.* Conshohocken, PA: Combined Publishing, 1999.

Shores, Christopher. *Duel for the Sky.* London: Grub Street, 1999.

Shores, Christopher, and Christ Thomas. *2nd Tactical Air Force Volume 1: Spartan to Normandy, June 1943 to June 1944.* Hersham, Surrey, UK: Classic, 2004.

———. *2nd Tactical Air Force Volume 2: Breakout to Bodenplatte, July 1944 to January 1945.* Hersham, Surrey, UK: Classic, 2005.

———. *2nd Tactical Air Force Volume 3: From the Rhine to Victory January to May 1945.* Hersham, Surrey, UK: Classic, 2005.

———. *2nd Tactical Air Force.* Reading, UK: Oxford, 1970.

Showell, Jak P. Mallmann. *Hitler's Naval Bases.* Stroud, UK: Fonthill Media, 2020.

———. *The German Navy in World War Two.* Annapolis, MD: Naval Institute Press, 1979.

Smith, Lt. Gen. W. Bedel, Chief of Staff SHAEF. To CG U.S.S.T.A.F., AOCINC Bomber Command and Air Commander in Chief AEAF. Subject: Letter. Air Support of "Overlord" during the preparatory period, April 20, 1944. SHAEF SGS Minutes Decimal

File May 43–Aug 45. Records Group 331, National Records and Archives Administration Archive II, College Park, MD.

Smith, Peter. *Naval Warfare in the English Channel 1939–1945*. Barnsley, South Yorkshire, UK: Pen & Sword Books, Ltd., 2007.

———. *The Battle of the Narrow Seas*. Annapolis, MD: Naval Institute Press, 2009.

Speer, Albert. *Inside the Third Reich*. Translated by Richard and Clara Winston. New York: The Macmillan Company, 1970.

———. *Spandau: The Secret Diaries*. Translated by Richard and Clara Winston. New York: MacMillan Publishing, 1976.

*St-Lo (7 July–19 July 1944)*. American Forces in Action Series. Washington, DC: Center of Military History United States Army, 1984.

Stafford, David. *Ten Days to D-Day*. London: Little, Brown and Company, 2003.

Steinhoff, Johannes., Peter Pechel, and Dennis Showalter. *Voices from the Third Reich*. New York: Da Capo Press, 1994.

Strategic Intelligence Branch, G-2, US Army, European Theater of Operations. *An Evaluation of Military Effects of R.A.F. Bombing of Germany*, 1944. In 519.553-3. Albert F. Simpson Historical Research Center, Air University, Maxwell AFB, AL.

Stubbs, David. "A Blind spot? The Royal Air Force and Long-Range Fighters, 1936–1944." *Journal of Military History*, April 1, 2014. Accessed January 29, 2024.

Sturtivant, Ray, and Theo Balance. *The Squadrons of the Fleet Air Arm*. Tonebridge, Kent, UK: Air-Britain (Historians) Ltd., 1994.

Suchenwirth, Professor Richard. *Command Leadership in the German Air Force*. Maxwell AFB, AL: Air University Press, July 1969.

Sullivan, John J. *Overlord's Eagles*. Jefferson, NC: McFarland & Company, Inc., Publishers, 1997.

*Sunday Punch in Normandy*. Wings at War Series, vol. 2. Washington, DC: Center for Air Force History, US Air Force, 1992.

Tarrant, V. E. *The Last Year of the Kriegsmarine*. London: Arms & Armour Press, 1996.

Tent, James Foster. *E-boat Alert Defending the Normandy Invasion Fleet*. Annapolis, MD: Naval Institute Press, 1996

Terraine, John. *The Right of the Line: The Royal Air Force in the European War, 1939–1945*. London: Hodder and Stoughton, Ltd., 1985.

*The Administrative Preparations*. RAF Narrative, vol. II. London: Air Historical Branch, Air Ministry. Released July 11, 1984. PDF. Accessed September 27, 2023. https://www.raf .mod.uk/our-organisation/units/air-historical-branch/second-world-war-campaign-nar ratives/liberation-of-north-west-europe-vol-ii-the administrative preparations/.

*The Breakout and Advance to the Lower Rhine 12 Jun–30 Sep 1944*. RAF Narrative, vol. IV. London: Air Historical Branch, Air Ministry. Released July 11, 1984. PDF. Accessed September 27, 2023. https:// www.raf.mod.uk/our-organisation/units/air-histori cal-branch/second-world-war-campaign-narratives/liberation-of-north-west-europe -vol-iv-the-breakout-and-advance-to-the-lower-rhine-12-jun-30-sep-1944/.

*The Landings in Normandy*. RAF Narrative, vol. III. London: Air Historical Branch, Air Min istry. Released July 11, 1984. PDF. Accessed September 27, 2023. https://www.raf.mod .uk/our-organisation/units/air-historical-branch/second-world-war-campaign-narra tives/liberation-of-north-west-europe-vol-iii-the landings in Normandy/.

*The Oxford Companion to World War II.* Edited by I. C. B. Dear and M. R. D. Foot. New York: Oxford University Press, 2001.

*The Rise and Fall of the German Air Force 1933–1945.* Air Ministry Pamphlet No. 248. A.C.A.S.[I], 1948. (HMSO reprint, 2001).

*The Second World War Airborne Forces.* Air Ministry Publication No. 3231. Air Ministry (A.H.B.), 1951.(The Naval & Military Press reprint, undated).

*The U.S. Army in World War II A Pictorial Record, Vol. I, The War Against Germany: Europe and Adjacent Areas.* Washington, D.C.: Office of the Chief of Military History, U.S. Army, 1951.

*The United States Strategic Bombing Surveys. European War. September 30, 1945.* New imprint. Maxwell AFB, AL: Air University Press, 1987.

Thomas, Chris. *Typhoon and Tempest Aces of World War 2.* Osprey Aircraft of the Aces, vol. 27. Tony Holmes. Oxford, UK: Osprey Books, 1999.

Thompson, Julian. *The Imperial War Museum Book of Victory in Europe.* London: Sidgwick & Jackson, Ltd., 1994.

Thompson, R. W. *D-Day: Spearhead of Invasion.* New York: Ballantine Books, Inc., 1968.

Thomsen, Paul A., and Joshua Spivak. "Through an Interrogator's Eyes." *Military History* (April 2002): 59–64, 74.

Tilley, Col. Reade F. US Air Force oral history by Mr. Frederick D. Claypool, 4TFW/HO, 15 August 85. File K239.0512-1757. Albert F. Simpson Historical Research Center, Air University, Maxwell AFB, AL.

TM-E 30-451. *Handbook on German Military Forces, 15 March 1945* (Washington, DC: War Department, 1945). Figure 15, accessed May 20, 2021. https://www.ibiblio.org/hyper war/Germany/HB/HB-10.

"Transportation." *Impact 7, May 1945, May–July 1945.* Harrisburg, PA: National Historical Society, 1980.

Troop Carrier Command, USAAF. *Analysis, Enemy Order of Battle—Air.* Appendix B to Annex No. 1 to IX Troop Carrier Command Field Order No. 1 for Operation "Neptune, 22 March–13 June 1944. In File 533.451-12. Albert F. Simpson Historical Research Center, Air University, Maxwell AFB, AL.

US Army Air Force. Compilation of interviews by various Air Intelligence Contact Units at AAF Redistribution Centers, 13 April 1945. File 142.05-11. Albert F. Simpson Historical Research Center, Air University, Maxwell AFB, AL.

*Übersichtskarte Frankreich* (Overview Map France). German Army Intelligence Map dated 3 July 1944.

Unwin, Peter. *The Narrow Sea.* London: Headline Book Publishing,

*Utah Beach to Cherbourg.* American Forces in Action Series. Washington, DC: Center of Military History United States Army, 1990.

Van Creveld, Martin. *Fighting Power: German and U.S. Army Performance, 1939–1945.* Westport, CT: Greenwood Press, 1982.

Vimpany, John, and David Boyd. *To Force the Enemy off the Sea.* Warwick, UK: Helion & Company, 2022.

Von Below, Nicolaus. *At Hitler's Side.* Translated by Geoffrey Brooks. London: Greenhill Books, 2001.

von der Heydte, *Oberstleutnant* Freidrich Freiherr, and *Generalleutnant* Max Pemsel. "A German Parachute Regiment in Normandy." MS #B-839. Historical Division, Headquarters United States Army Europe, 1954. Box 11 of the James M. Gavin Papers. US Army Heritage and Education Center, Carlisle Barracks, PA.

Von Luck, Col. Hans. Conversation with Major Joseph T. Molyson, USAFR, May 7, 1985.

———. *Panzer Commander*. New York: Dell Publishing, 1989.

Waddell, Lt. Col. Hugh B. Interview by the Assistant Chief of Air Staff for Intelligence, 25 November 1942. File 142.05-3. Albert F. Simpson Historical Research Center, Air University, Maxwell AFB, AL.

Wakefield, Ken. *Light Planes at War. US Liaison Aircraft in Europe 1942–1947*. Charleston, SC: Tempus Books, 1999.

Wallwork, Sgt. Jim. Conversation with Major Joseph T. Molyson, USAFR, May 7, 1985.

Warlimont, Gen. Walter. *Inside Hitler's Headquarters 1939–45*. Translated by R. H. Barry. Novato, CA: Presidio Press, 1964.

Warren, John C. *Airborne Operations of World War II, European Theater*. USAF Historical Maxwell AFB, AL: Research Studies Institute, Air University, 1956.

Webster, Sir Charles, and Noble Frankland. *The Strategic Air Offensive against Germany, Volume II: Endeavour*. London: HMSO, 1961.

———. *The Strategic Air Offensive against Germany Volume III: Victory*. London: HMSO, 1961.

———. *The Strategic Air Offensive against Germany, Volume IV: Annexes and Appendices*. London: HMSO, 1961.

Werrell, Kenneth P. *The Evolution of the Cruise Missile*. Maxwell AFB, AL: Air University Press, September 1985.

———. *Archie, Flak, AAA, and SAM: A Short Operational History of Ground-Based Air Defense*. Honolulu: University Press of the Pacific, 2002.

Westermann, Edward B. *Flak German Anti-Aircraft Defenses 1914–1945*. Lawrence, KS: University Press of Kansas, 2001.

Whiteford, Maj. Gen. P. G., Assistant Chief of Staff G-2 (AEAF). To Maj. Gen. H. R. Bull, Maj. Gen. C. A. West, and Brig. K. McLean. Subject: Letter. "Overlord" Bombing Policy (untitled), January 25, 1944. In SHAEF SGS Minutes Decimal File May 43–Aug 45. Records Group 331, National Records and Archives Administration Archive II, College Park, MD.

Williamson, Gordon. *E-Boat vs MTB The English Channel 1941–1945*. Duel 34. New York: Osprey, 2011.

———. *Kriegsmarine Coastal Forces*. New Vanguard 151. New York: Osprey, 2009.

Willmott, H. P., Charles Messenger, and Robin Cross. *World War II*. New York: DK Publishing, 2004.

Wolfe, Martin. *Green Light*. Washington, DC: Center for Air Force History, US Air Force, 1993.

Wood, Tony, and Bill Gunston, *Hitler's Luftwaffe*. London: Salamander Books, 1997.

Wood, W. J. A. (ed.). Defence of the Reich (*Reichsverteidigung*), 3 June 1944. Translation of Enemy Documents. RAF Air Historical Branch (AHB) 6. Copied May 1963.

Wragg, David. *RAF Handbook 1939–1945*. Sutton Publishing, 2007.

Wynn, Humphrey, and Susan Young. *Prelude to Overlord*. Novato, CA: Presidio Press, 1983.

Yeager, Chuck, and Leo Janos. *Yeager*. New York: Bantam Books, 1985.

Young, Charles H., and Charles D. Young, ed. *Into the Valley—The Untold Story of USAAF Troop Carrier in World War II.* Dallas: PrintComm, Inc., 1995.

Zaloga, Steven J. *Brittany 1944.* Osprey Campaign Series, vol. 320. Oxford, UK: Osprey Publishing, Ltd., 2018.

———. *Cherbourg 1944.* Osprey Campaign Series, vol. 278. Oxford, UK: Osprey Publishing, Ltd., 2015.

———. *D-Day 1944 (1) Omaha Beach.* Osprey Campaign Series, vol. 100. Oxford, UK: Osprey Publishing, Ltd., 2003.

———. *D-Day 1944 (2) Utah Beach and the US Airborne Landings.* Osprey Campaign Series, vol. 104. Oxford, UK: Osprey Publishing, Ltd., 2004.

———. *D-Day Fortifications in Normandy.* Osprey Fortress Series, vol. 37. New York: Osprey Publishing, Ltd., 2005.

———. *Liberation of Paris 1944.* Osprey Campaign Series, vol. 194. Oxford, UK: Osprey Publishing, Ltd., 2008.

———. *Mortain 1944.* Osprey Campaign Series, vol. 335. Oxford, UK: Osprey Publishing, Ltd., 2019.

———. *Operation Cobra 1944.* Osprey Campaign Series, vol. 88. Oxford, UK: Osprey Publishing, Ltd., 2001.

———. *Operation POINTBLANK 1944.* Osprey Air Series, vol. 236. Oxford, UK: Osprey Publishing, Ltd., 2011.

———. *Ploesti 1943.* Osprey Air Campaign Series, vol. 12. Oxford, UK: Osprey Publishing, Ltd., 2019.

———. *St. Lo The Battle of the Hedgerows.* Osprey Campaign Series, vol. 308. Oxford, UK: Osprey Publishing, Ltd., 2017.

———. *The Atlantic Wall (1) France.* Osprey Fortress Series, vol. 63. Oxford, UK: Osprey Publishing, Ltd., 2007.

———. *The Atlantic Wall 3 (The Südwall).* Osprey Fortress Series, vol. 109. Oxford, UK: Osprey Publishing, Ltd., 2015.

———. *The Oil Campaign 1944–45.* Osprey Air Campaign Series, vol 30. Oxford, UK: Osprey Publishing, Ltd., 2022.

Zetterling, Niklas. *Normandy 1944.* Winnipeg, Manitoba, Canada: J. J. Fedorowicz Publishing, Inc, 2000.

www.ingramcontent.com/pod-product-compliance
Lightning Source LLC
Chambersburg PA
CDHW030632150426
42811CB00049B/197

* 9 7 8 0 8 1 1 7 7 7 7 8 0 *